MORAL MINORITY

POLITICS AND CULTURE
IN MODERN AMERICA

Series Editors
Margot Canaday, Glenda Gilmore,
Michael Kazin, and Thomas J. Sugrue

Volumes in the series narrate and analyze political and
social change in the broadest dimensions from 1865 to
the present, including ideas about the ways people have
sought and wielded power in the public sphere and the
language and institutions of politics at all levels—local,
national, and transnational. The series is motivated by
a desire to reverse the fragmentation of modern U.S.
history and to encourage synthetic perspectives on social
movements and the state, on gender, race, and labor,
and on intellectual history and popular culture.

MORAL
MINORITY

─────

THE EVANGELICAL LEFT
IN AN AGE OF CONSERVATISM

DAVID R. SWARTZ

PENN

UNIVERSITY OF PENNSYLVANIA PRESS

PHILADELPHIA

Published by
University of Pennsylvania Press
Philadelphia, Pennsylvania 19104-4112
www.upenn.edu/pennpress

Printed in the United States of America
on acid-free paper

10 9 8 7 6 5 4 3 2 1

Library of Congress Cataloging-in-Publication Data
Swartz, David R.
    Moral minority : the evangelical left in an age of conservatism /
David R. Swartz. — 1st ed.
        p.   cm. — (Politics and culture in modern America)
    Includes bibliographical references and index.
    ISBN 978-0-8122-4441-0 (hardcover : alk. paper)
        1. Evangelicalism—United States—History—20th century.   2.
Christianity and politics—United States—History—20th century.
3. Christian conservatism—United States—History—20th
century.   4. United States—Politics and government—20th century.
I. Title.   II. Series: Politics and culture in modern America.
    BR1642.U6S93   2012
    261.70973'09045—dc23   2012014396

CONTENTS

Introduction

Evangelical activists, proclaimed the *Washington Post*, sought to "launch a religious movement that could shake both political and religious life in America." This prediction referred not to efforts in 2000 to elect George W. Bush to the White House, nor to the Reagan Revolution of the 1980s during which the president once famously told a gathering of evangelical pastors, "I know you can't endorse me, but I want you to know that I endorse you." Rather, the *Post* was reporting on what has become a mere footnote in the history of evangelical politics: a gathering at a run-down YMCA Hotel on South Wabash Street in downtown Chicago led by a young, unknown evangelical named Ron Sider. The year was 1973, nearly a decade before the height of the Moral Majority, and the assembled activists were strategizing about how to move the nation in a more evangelical direction through political action.[1]

That intended direction, however, was to the left, not the right. In front of a national audience, Sider and his colleagues condemned American militarism, sexism, economic injustice, and President Richard Nixon's "lust for and abuse of power." The YMCA itself was a fitting venue for this new evangelical progressivism. Its spare interior suggested simple living, and its urban location indicated a commitment to the nation's poor. As Calvin College professor and congressional candidate Paul Henry declared that evangelicals "dare no longer remain silent in the face of glaring social evil," the echoes of stray gunfire from outside rang through the hall. After several days of intense discussion, the group emerged from the YMCA with "The Chicago Declaration," a manifesto for a new evangelical left.[2]

The following decades proved the *Washington Post* both right and wrong in its forecast. Anticipating most news outlets by half a decade, the *Post* correctly suggested that evangelical participation in the political sphere was intensifying. In fact, the incipient progressive movement launched in Chicago, along with a rising religious right, itself seeking to mobilize a significant

sector of apolitical pietists in the 1960s and 1970s, helped politicize the nation's 75 million evangelicals. But in the end it was the religious right that
built a viable movement that would come to shake political and religious life
in America. And so the *Post* also got its prediction profoundly wrong, mis-
identifying which evangelicals would ultimately move the nation's electorate, and in what direction.

This miscalculation, however, should not obscure just how plausible the
Post prediction was from the perspective of the early 1970s. The evangelical
left, especially from the 1973 Chicago meeting through the early years of the
Jimmy Carter administration, seemed promising indeed amid the cacoph-
ony of a diverse and fluid evangelicalism that was politically up for grabs.
Competing political interests, institutions, and activities—ranging from the
right, center, and left—rolled across the evangelical spectrum amid the ferment of the Cold War. The *Post*, observing the scene at the Chicago YMCA,
could suggest with a straight face that these "young evangelicals," as they
were dubbed in the 1970s, might be the wave of the future.[3]

A close look at metropolitan Chicago in those years reveals the full
dimensions of politics and piety at work in the nation. Outnumbering both
evangelical progressives at the YMCA and right-wingers in the suburbs,
many evangelicals in the early 1970s nurtured a passive cultural conservatism. Moody Church, for example, located on the northern edge of downtown just a short bus ride away from the YMCA, had long sustained a
single-minded focus on soul-winning. While inclined toward political conservatism and punching their ballots for Republicans if they voted, Moody
members did not mobilize politically. They instead sought to nurture personal holiness as quiet, upstanding citizens. Not surprisingly, its members
had been aghast at the events of the 1968 Democratic presidential convention in Chicago. There, the participatory democracy and peaceful protests of
the New Left had devolved into outrageous displays of anti-Americanism,
free love, violence, and drugs. The disorder of Grant Park, which marked the
disintegration of a long-presumed liberal consensus in American politics
built around poverty relief, civil rights, and economic growth, would go on
to inflame right-wing evangelical mobilization in subsequent years.

Both Moody Church and Grant Park, so geographically proximate to the
coming-out party of the evangelical left, cast long shadows over the YMCA.
Participants at the gathering, however, sought to transcend these stark
polarities of the emerging culture wars by merging progressive politics and
personal piety. Or, put negatively, befitting the meeting's oppositional tone,

they sought to repudiate the passive conservatism of Moody Church and the anarchic profanity of leftist protests. In an era often, but mistakenly, considered the Reagan Revolution-in-waiting, many evangelicals stood for antiwar, civil rights, anti-consumer, communal, New Left, and third-world principles, even as they stressed doctrinal and sexual fidelity.

The rise of the evangelical left raises important questions about the contours of twentieth-century American politics. From where did this progressive evangelical social consciousness and conscience emerge? What motivated these young activists to repudiate the Vietnam War when most of their pastors preached obedience to authority? What motivated some of their leaders to preach simple living and to criticize unfettered capitalism? And last, but hardly least given its initial promise, why did the evangelical left not take substantial shape electorally? Why, in the dawn of the twenty-first century, is evangelicalism now so closely identified with conservative, rather than progressive, politics?

This book seeks to answer those questions by chronicling the rise, decline, and legacy of the evangelical left. Part I describes the emergence of the evangelical left in the years leading up to the 1973 Chicago Declaration. Chapters on the ascent of neo-evangelicalism, civil rights, Vietnam, electoral politics, and intentional community, each organized around biographical sketches of key delegates at the YMCA meeting in Chicago, highlight important sociological, cultural, and ideological changes within evangelicalism following World War II. These changes—and the figures they produced—offered a sharp alternative to the superpatriotism of sectarian fundamentalists and the more typical mid-century posture of passive conservatism among many mainstream evangelicals.

Carl Henry, a journalist and theologian, embodied the growing cultural maturity of evangelicals. Following the Scopes Trial in 1925 and defeats in mainline denominations during the 1920s, many fundamentalist evangelicals largely withdrew from social engagement. Henry, however, repudiated fundamentalism's closed subculture in a 1947 treatise entitled *The Uneasy Conscience of Modern Fundamentalism*. Over the next decades Henry then drove the cultural re-engagement of "neo-evangelical" institutions such as the Billy Graham Evangelistic Association, *Christianity Today*, Wheaton College, and Fuller Theological Seminary. Evangelicals associated with these institutions enjoyed the white, middle-class benefits of Eisenhower prosperity. Their gains in education and wealth left them poised to engage mainstream American politics.

John Alexander, a white fundamentalist Baptist turned civil rights activist, emerged as one of the first visible practitioners of Henry's call for social engagement. In the mid-1960s he founded *Freedom Now*. Alongside African-American evangelicals Tom Skinner, Bill Pannell, and John Perkins, Alexander regularly indicted white evangelicals for not joining the civil rights movement. *Freedom Now* also echoed liberalism's social scientific approach to race and poverty and followed, in a lagged chronology, the broader movement's trajectory from racial integration to Black Power.

Evangelical antipathy toward the Vietnam War followed close on the heels of evangelical civil rights activism. Jim Wallis, a child of suburban Detroit and the youngest delegate at the Thanksgiving Workshop, reflected the alienation felt by some evangelical youth over their tradition's refusal to reject the war. Participation in the Michigan State University chapter of Students for a Democratic Society exposed Wallis to the New Left critique of liberalism. At Trinity Evangelical Divinity School in 1970, he founded the Post-American community, which melded the rhetoric and activist style of New Left politics with evangelical piety and theology.

If Wallis represented the New Leftist, antiliberal impulse of some in the evangelical left, his unlikely friend, Senator Mark Hatfield of Oregon, embodied the revitalized evangelical interest in electoral politics. Hatfield, who enjoyed a meteoric rise from Oregon state legislator to two-term governor to U.S. senator to vice-presidential contender, confounded critics with his progressive politics and evangelical piety. This nationally prominent politician— a fiscal and moral conservative who came out in favor of civil rights, against the Vietnam War, and opposed to capital punishment—illustrated the relative fluidity of party politics and evangelical practices before both hardened in the 1970s.

Sharon Gallagher, an influential member of the Christian World Liberation Front (CWLF) in Berkeley, California, represented the communitarian impulse within the evangelical left. In the wake of increasingly violent New Left tactics in the late 1960s, CWLF emerged as an alternative (and in Berkeley, a rival) to Students for a Democratic Society. Gallagher suggested that the New Left was neglecting the resources of orthodox religion in its efforts to reconstruct a failed liberal society. CWLF merged the evangelical piety of the Jesus People and the communitarian, "small is beautiful," antitechnocratic ethos of the seventies.

Part II follows how the political impulses represented by Gallagher, Hatfield, Wallis, Alexander, and Henry broadened out considerably through the efforts of ethnic evangelicals. Previously on the margins of American evangelicalism, non-Anglo groups—including Dutch Reformed, Swiss-German Anabaptists, Latin American Christians, and other third-world evangelicals—joined a growing chorus of voices on the left. They contributed significantly to the coalition of evangelical progressives that met at Chicago's YMCA.

Samuel Escobar, an evangelical church worker from Peru, reflected the influence of the non-Western world on North American evangelicals. One of a triumvirate of evangelicals instrumental in establishing the Latin American Theological Fraternity, Escobar leveled devastating critiques at laissez-faire capitalism and American imperialism. At the Lausanne Congress of World Evangelization in 1974, Escobar condemned North American conservatives as "well-behaved middle-class people" who were ignoring the "exploitation, intrigue, and dirty political maneuvering done by great multi-national corporations." These critiques, especially prevalent in InterVarsity Christian Fellowship's worldwide networks, mirrored the global dimensions of the New Left and the third-world origins of liberation theology.

Richard Mouw, a professor of philosophy at Calvin College, represented another important ethnic constituency of the evangelical left. The child of recent Dutch Calvinist immigrants, young Mouw joined Students for a Democratic Society in the 1960s. After growing disillusioned with the increasing violence of the New Left, Mouw returned to a more conventional politics rooted in the Reformed theology of Calvin College. Seeking to bring all things under the "Lordship of Christ," Mouw espoused gradualism and pragmatic avenues toward social justice.

Ron Sider promoted a Swiss-German Anabaptist strain of progressive evangelicalism. Author of the best-selling book *Rich Christians in an Age of Hunger*, Sider espoused an ethic of simple living and service to the downtrodden that extended the critique offered by third-world evangelicals. He also followed Senator Mark Hatfield's lead into electoral politics. In 1972 Sider founded Evangelicals for McGovern, a group that campaigned on behalf of Democratic candidate George McGovern. This effort led directly to the first organized gathering of the evangelical left.

Except for Mark Hatfield, who still sent a supportive telegram from his Senate office, all these individuals—and several dozen more—met together in downtown Chicago on November 23, 1973. The Thanksgiving Workshop for Evangelical Social Action attracted urban, educated evangelicals committed to progressive political reform. As they looked to take the lead among their fellow evangelicals, optimism soared. The press—both evangelical and secular—took note of their growing numbers, proliferating literature, and political mobilization. It seemed plausible that this small but dedicated group of evangelical activists, like abolitionists who had successfully protested the slave trade two centuries before, could spark great social change. *Newsweek* magazine's famous "Born Again! The Year of the Evangelicals" cover story noted that "younger believers are re-examining the social teachings of the Bible . . . in the hope of closing the gap between private and public demonstrations of faith." Citing Mark Hatfield, Sojourners, the Chicago Declaration, and Evangelicals for Social Action, the article implied that evangelical politics could take a progressive shape.[4]

The coalition, however, failed to live up to its initial promise. Part III charts the declining fortunes of the evangelical left. Identity politics sabotaged this nascent progressive coalition of evangelicals, despite their remarkably similar theological convictions, religious cultures, and critiques of conservative politics. Following its secular counterpart, the evangelical left fragmented along gender, racial, and ideological lines. Female, African-American, Anabaptist, and Reformed evangelicals created separate institutions when the Thanksgiving Workshop movement failed to construct a common language and political philosophy. This failure deprived the broader movement of momentum and much-needed resources.

Political displacement exacerbated the corrosive effect of identity politics. The postwar political left, suspicious of evangelicals' conservative theology and sexuality, remained unimpressed and indifferent toward the Chicago Declaration. The nation's liberal coalition, in fact, seemed to be trying hard—by exercising a libertine sexuality and giving a more prominent voice to activist secularists—to alienate a potentially powerful constituency. At the same time, the religious right, stirred by the abortion issue and encouraged by the Republican Party, enjoyed greater visibility in the wider evangelical world. President Jimmy Carter and the broader evangelical left were "left behind" by both the political left and the religious right.

The precarious position of the evangelical left continued through the 1980s. Two energetic campaigns—an attempt to promote justice in Nicaragua and an attempt to promote a consistent life ethic—ran aground when progressive evangelicals refused to conform to political orthodoxies on abortion. The movement found itself politically homeless, obscured by a burgeoning religious right and an unfriendly progressive coalition. In stark political terms, the evangelical left had suffered debilitating defeat. Its political heroes—George McGovern, Mark Hatfield, and Jesse Jackson—failed to take the White House. Its anti-heroes—Richard Nixon, Ronald Reagan, and George W. Bush—meanwhile enjoyed political success. To be sure, the evangelical left did not disappear. It occasionally had real political impact, and a significant grassroots movement shaped the culture of millions of moderate evangelicals on issues such as poverty, women's rights, the environment, and inequities in the global economy. But most evangelicals populated the right. Leaders of the evangelical left were never able to inspire its constituents and millions of evangelical Democratic voters into a movement as coherent, organized, and politically powerful as the religious right. Evangelical progressives, whose story speaks powerfully to our understanding of American political culture generally and of evangelical social activism in particular, ended the Reagan years with a whimper, cowed by the conservative movement's decisive claim on a constituency they had hoped to count for themselves.[5]

Decades after the Chicago Declaration, the evangelical left of the 1970s had been largely forgotten. As culture wars raged, scholars understandably rushed to describe the self-immolation of the New Deal coalition in the 1960s and the surge of conservatism in the 1980s that swept Ronald Reagan into power. Many journalists, covering the highly visible Moral Majority of the 1980s, Christian Coalition of the 1990s, and evangelical networks that elected George W. Bush in the 2000s, created a caricature of evangelicalism as a monolithic political bloc energized by only a few conservative political issues. More recently, historians have carefully tracked the rise of the religious right from well before mid-century. Covering activism on the other end of the political spectrum, scholars have also ably charted religious progressivism within mainline Protestant, Catholic, and Quaker circles. But in implicitly suggesting an irrevocable dichotomy between social gospel mainliners and rightist fundamentalists, these discrete historiographies obscure connections between progressive politics and evangelicalism.[6]

Those connections were—and are—startlingly substantial. Even as progressive evangelicals were being upstaged by the religious right during the Reagan Revolution, a significant minority of white evangelicals voted Democratic. Into the twenty-first century, a surprisingly strong faction of non-rightist evangelicals persisted. Forty-five percent of all evangelicals called themselves moderates and 19 percent liberals in a 2000 Princeton University survey. To this day, moderates and progressives—as represented by groups such as Sojourners, Evangelicals for Social Action, InterVarsity Christian

Fellowship, and the Association for Public Justice—comprise roughly a third of American evangelicals and point to the tradition's remarkable political, theological, and cultural diversity. Moreover, new figures, such as Emergent Church pastor Brian McLaren, former National Association of Evangelicals policy director Richard Cizik, activist Shane Claiborne, and megachurch pastor Bill Hybels, suggest the possibilities of revitalized evangelical activism on poverty, the environment, and human trafficking. This legacy of the Chicago Declaration underscores the persistence of a progressive impulse in an evangelical tradition often portrayed as uniformly traditionalist and politically right.[7]

The reality of a politically diverse and fluid evangelicalism is, in fact, embedded in the tradition's very structure. Rooted in the decentralized church structures of the Reformation and in early American democratization, evangelicalism is fundamentally fragmented and nonhierarchical. The National Association of Evangelicals consists of dozens of denominations and thousands of parachurch agencies. The antihierarchical nature of evangelicalism offers helpful context for scholar Gordon Spykman's 1975 observation: "Evangelical Christians look much like a gathering army of recruits without strong leadership or clearly understood marching orders." Thus the concurrent emergence of the evangelical left and surge of the religious right into electoral politics should have come as no surprise.[8]

The evangelical left, in fact, contributed to the broader politicization of evangelicalism. Characterized by a complex mix of fundamentalist right-wing politics, populist agitation, and passive conservatism in the 1950s and 1960s, a new evangelical political culture began to flex its muscles in the 1970s. To be sure, a fundamentalist fringe and some neo-evangelicals— including J. Howard Pew, co-founder of Sunoco; John Conlan, a Republican politician; and Walter Judd, a strong anticommunist Congressman—were politically active during the 1940s, 1950s, and 1960s, especially in southern California. But many did not mobilize self-consciously *as* evangelicals. Nor did most mobilize electorally and nationally across a spectrum of political issues. According to historian Curtis J. Evans, even Billy Graham, the pastor to presidents, maintained a "dour view of social transformation" and urged Christians to "devote themselves to missionary work and not get distracted by undue attention to political and social issues." Out of this pietistic context, the evangelical left helped open the world of politics and the language of social justice to a wider spectrum of non-fundamentalist evangelicals. If the roots of the religious right and their level of partisanship can be attributed to the demographic boom of the suburbs, the legalization of abortion, and battles over school prayer in the South, its methods and mobilization can also be tied to progressive evangelicals. The evangelical left's expansion of its conception of morality from the personal to the social, for example, both reflected and accelerated mainstream evangelical participation in political activism. Now evangelicals of nearly all political and denominational persuasions view social engagement as a fundamental responsibility of the faithful.[9]

The *Washington Post* prediction that the evangelical left might herald a transformation in American political and religious life thus turned out to be remarkably—if ironically—prescient. To many observers, evangelical politics had triumphantly, even inevitably, emerged in conservative form. But the path of postwar evangelical politics also passed through a moral minority. Ron Sider, one of the authors of the Chicago Declaration, recognized this complexity, quipping that "we called for social and political action, [and] we got eight years of Ronald Reagan." The following narrative attempts to explain how.[10]

PART I

An Emerging Evangelical Left

CHAPTER 1

Carl Henry and Neo-Evangelical
Social Engagement

There is no room here for a gospel that is indifferent to
the needs of the total man nor of the global man.
—Carl Henry in *The Uneasy Conscience*
of Modern Fundamentalism

Evangelicals reemerged in the mainstream political consciousness in the year of the nation's bicentennial. With the 1976 election of Jimmy Carter, himself a born-again Christian, evangelicals had captured the White House. At the time, more than 50 million Americans claimed to be born again. Major news magazines ran cover stories on the recent surge in evangelical political and cultural power. *Newsweek* even dubbed 1976 the "year of the evangelical." Evangelist Dave Breese told the national gathering of the National Association of Evangelicals (NAE), "It no longer fits to picture us as redneck preachers pounding the pulpit. Evangelical Christianity has become the greatest show on earth. Twenty to forty years ago it was on the edge of things. Now it has moved to the center." Future presidential candidate John B. Anderson told NAE delegates that "evangelicals had replaced theological liberals as the 'in' group among Washington leaders." Within a few years, the Moral Majority emerged and was instrumental in the election of Ronald Reagan, capping a conservative evangelical ascendancy.[1]

This image of a forceful evangelical politics stood in stark contrast to its public perception half a century earlier. Not even the most optimistic fundamentalist evangelical in the 1920s would have predicted that the movement would again stand as a significant factor in American life. Indeed, for many decades after the disastrous 1920s, when theological modernists took over mainline denominational structures, fundamentalist evangelical politics was profoundly incoherent. On the populist left, plainfolk evangelicals in southern California supported New Deal policies. Pentecostal laborers, joining the interracial Southern Tenant Farmers' Union, harnessed the democratic potential of evangelicalism against commodity agriculture. On the right, many evangelicals opposed the anti-Prohibition, Catholic presidential candidate Al Smith in 1928 and supported Barry Goldwater's run for the White House in 1964. On the far right, a handful of conspiratorialist fundamentalists such as Fred Schwartz, Carl McIntire, and Billy James Hargis mobilized in support of a rabid anti-communist agenda. In the middle of the political spectrum, Billy Graham cautiously promoted racial integration in the South as the civil rights movement gained momentum. Featuring a range of political agendas at mid-century, evangelical politics was characterized by uncertainty.[2]

Evangelical apoliticism, often overshadowed by a much louder (though marginal) far-right fundamentalism, compounded this uncertainty. *The Fundamentals*, a twelve-volume set of articles published from 1910 to 1915 that repudiated the Protestant modernist movement, warned against getting too caught up in politics, and most fundamentalists generally limited their haphazard political interests to votes for Prohibition and nonactivist sentiments against evolution and communism. Political activism during the 1930s "went into eclipse," according to historian Mark Noll. From the 1930s to the 1960s, fundamentalist evangelicals devoted much more time to congregational life, holy living, and missionary work than to partisan politics. Those who came to associate with Billy Graham crusades in the 1950s (usually called "new" or "neo" evangelicals to distinguish them from their fundamentalist evangelical cousins) also largely retreated to a quietist stance. They either eschewed social engagement altogether or manifested social conservatism in ways that precluded overt politics. During this period the overwhelming majority of articles in the magazine of the college ministry InterVarsity Christian Fellowship were devoted to topics such as evangelism, hard work and discipline, devotional and inspirational literature, holiness, prayer, Bible-reading, and sexual purity. With significant exceptions, fundamentalist evangelicals did not mobilize on behalf of political candidates nor tie their faith closely to their politics. As late as the 1960s, according to political scientist Lyman A. Kellstedt, data showed that evangelicals were "less likely to be interested in politics, less likely to vote in presidential elections, and less likely to be involved in campaign activities than other religious groups." Concern for theological orthodoxy and piety subordinated politics, which would emerge finally in the 1970s as a more salient characteristic of evangelicals nationwide.[3]

No figure embodied the vital shift to political engagement more than Carl Henry, a theologian, editor, and architect of neo-evangelicalism. A leader in many key evangelical institutions—Wheaton College, Fuller Theological Seminary, the National Association of Evangelicals, and *Christianity Today*—Henry helped drive evangelicalism from its marginal position in the 1930s to the cover of *Newsweek* magazine in 1976. Significantly, Henry pursued this mission with significant help from the era's best-known public evangelist, revival preacher Billy Graham. By the 1970s a revitalized evangelical movement, carried along by Henry and Graham, took its place as one of the most important interest groups in postwar America. It was out of this newly engaged movement that the evangelical left would emerge.

I

Carl Ferdinand Howard Henry, born in 1913 as the first of eight children, grew up on Long Island, New York. His nonreligious German immigrant parents, who owned no Bibles and said no prayers before meals, nurtured very little of the evangelical piety their son would practice as an adult. Young Carl played outside on Sunday afternoons, went to vaudeville shows, and served as a sentry for the illicit enterprises of his father, who stole apples from a nearby orchard and sold alcohol from the family farm during Prohibition. The son, however, showed considerably more promise. Taking a job as a reporter for the *Islip News*, Henry, at age nineteen, became the youngest weekly newspaper editor in the state of New York. Sporting a healthy ambition, a religious skepticism, and an appetite for women and horse racing, Henry was an authentic creation of the roaring twenties.[4]

An itinerant evangelist dramatically redirected the trajectory of Henry's life. Following his conversion to evangelical Christianity in 1933, Henry sensed God calling him to a vocation of Christian service. He enrolled at Wheaton College, a school in suburban Chicago that stood at the center of organized neo-evangelicalism. Henry was attracted to the school's emphasis on thoughtful faith even as he chuckled at its "no-movie, no-dancing, no-card-playing" regulations. Despite the restrictive cultural codes, Wheaton quickly drew the recent convert into the neo-evangelical orbit, filling Henry's schedule on the energetic and growing campus with study, athletics, chapel, prayer meetings, and theological discussions.[5]

Henry's experiences at Wheaton reflected the economic, cultural, and theological ambitions of neo-evangelicalism. Rising prosperity at mid-century sparked a new willingness on the part of apolitical evangelicals to engage broader social spheres. Unable in the 1930s to rely on "old money" as wealthier mainline denominations could, Wheaton's administrators and its lower-middle-class students like Henry scraped their way through the Great Depression. But in the mid-1940s the college, one of the fastest growing institutions in the nation, embarked on a building binge. It also enjoyed a rapid rise in enrollment as thousands of students and World War II veterans armed with G.I. Bill benefits streamed to the outskirts of Chicago.[6]

Wheaton's use of the federal funds points to the critical—and ironic (given many evangelicals' conservative animus against big government)— role government largesse played in the upward social and economic mobility of neo-evangelicals. Students participated in the Federal Relief Administration work-study program, part of the New Deal legislation of the 1930s. In the 1940s and beyond, G.I. Bill funds paid for tuition, fees, textbooks, and supplies. Others received low-interest loans through the National Defense Education Act. The institution itself received grants from the Atomic Energy Commission and the National Science Foundation. Most important, a favorable tax climate nearly eliminated estate taxes on donations to nonprofit organizations, exempted private colleges from nearly all taxes, and offered lower postal rates.[7]

By the 1960s the boon of government largesse, a growing national economy, and a concomitant rise in its students' socioeconomic status tripled the size of Wheaton's student body to nearly 2,000. Other schools—such as Gordon College near Boston; Calvin College in Grand Rapids; Seattle Pacific University in Seattle; Asbury College in Wilmore, Kentucky; Westmont College in Santa Barbara; and dozens of others—also benefited from growing prosperity. The proportion of evangelicals who had been to college tripled between 1960 and 1972. While the level was still below the national average, it was an impressive leap and an indicator of evangelicalism's rising social status.[8]

Henry's Wheaton also reflected neo-evangelicalism's pursuit of a more ambitious academic program. Under the leadership of James Buswell, Wheaton's president, and Gordon H. Clark, an influential philosophy professor with a doctorate from the University of Pennsylvania, the college in the 1940s earned regional accreditation, sought and realized more impressive faculty and student credentials, and contemplated a bold cultural agenda. Clark beckoned his students to contemplate a vision in which Christians would "save and rebuild the West" by transforming culture. Stirred by this far more ambitious vision than the sectarian faith of their parents, dozens of Wheaton students pursued degrees from prestigious graduate schools at a rate comparable to the most elite liberal arts schools in the nation. Many of these students, including Henry, who earned a Ph.D. from Boston University just two years before Martin Luther King, Jr., became leaders of a rising neo-evangelicalism.[9]

Wheaton during Henry's tenure was translating this growing intellectual rigor into engagement with the wider culture. Henry himself remained connected to the non-evangelical world as a stringer for the *Chicago Tribune*. By the 1950s his Wheaton classmates participated in the National Student Association and the Model United Nations. Sports teams competed in intercollegiate athletics with state schools. Meanwhile, American society increasingly glimpsed evangelicalism's new image. In 1949 Billy Graham, the college's most recognized alumnus, held an eight-week crusade in Los Angeles, during which syndicated newspapers across the nation printed positive coverage. The dynamic young evangelist, the nation soon saw, was not a wild-eyed preacher of dogmatism; he wore a stylish suit and could speak the language of youth culture. Such public attention helped bring evangelicals out of the exile to which they had retreated during the Scopes era. Increasingly, this well-educated, upwardly mobile variety of evangelical aspired to represent all the nation's many varieties of evangelical Protestants, including quietist holiness adherents, big-tent Pentecostals, Anabaptist pacifists, ethnic confessionalists, and strident fundamentalists.[10]

Transformations in neo-evangelical theology mirrored—and shaped—this cultural engagement. Specifically, Henry and others began to reject the dispensational premillennial eschatology of their heritage. The end times theory of dispensationalism, a nineteenth-century innovation of British evangelist John Darby, divided history into discrete time periods and argued that Christians would be "raptured," that is, removed from the earth prior to Jesus Christ's return and millennial reign. Fundamentalist evangelicals considered the rapture to be imminent. Such a framework emphasized getting the world ready for the rapture, for fear that many might be "left behind." While at no time did fundamentalists uniformly hold to dispensationalism,

many did, and the implications for their social and political action were profound. An all-encompassing concern for saving souls eventually subsumed
nineteenth-century evangelical activism on issues such as abolition and
women's suffrage. Dispensationalist eschatology inhibited social action
among many fundamentalists.[11]

But by the 1940s the hold of dispensationalism was beginning to slip
in some quarters. At Fuller Theological Seminary in Pasadena, California,
Henry's next stop on the expanding neo-evangelical circuit, professors were
quietly putting aside premillennial dispensationalism. Henry, for example,
always attached the word "broadly" when speaking of his premillennial
eschatology. Other inaugural Fuller faculty—including celebrity pastor
Harold Ockenga, bibliophile Wilbur Smith, Old Testament scholar Everett
Harrison, New Testament scholar George Eldon Ladd, and all-around facto-
tum Harold Lindsell—showed considerable coolness to dispensationalism
in the pages of Fuller's scholarly journal *Theology News & Notes*. Within
decades, antipathy toward dispensationalism had nearly become a litmus
test for neo-evangelical orthodoxy. Prospective Fuller faculty had to defend
themselves against sympathies *for* dispensationalism. Though the dismissal
of dispensationalism may not have been as unambiguous in other evangelical quarters (in part for fear of offending conservative constituents), there
seemed to be a clear correlation between theological change and neo-
evangelicals with designs on social engagement. Rejecting the "kingdom
later" view of the dispensationalists, some felt compelled to offer whatever
measure of temporal justice and mercy they could in a hurting world. Neo-
evangelicals were refashioning their image from fundamentalist refugees in
a crumbling Babylon to custodial heirs of a Reformation legacy dedicated to
ushering in a new Jerusalem in America.[12]

"Fundamentalism" had become a bad word for many neo-evangelicals.
In *United Evangelical Action*, the magazine of the National Association for
Evangelicals, an organization he had helped launch in the early 1940s, Henry
wrote that "fundamentalism is considered a summary term for theological
pugnaciousness, ecumenic disruptiveness, cultural unprogressiveness, scientific obliviousness, and/or anti-intellectual inexcusableness . . . extreme
dispensationalism, pulpit sensationalism, excessive emotionalism, social
withdrawal and bawdy church music." Students at Henry's alma mater, who
recognized this movement away from fundamentalism, were glad to abandon the cultural idiosyncrasies of their tradition. An editorial in the student
newspaper *Wheaton Record* entitled "Farewell to Fundamentalism" read,

Figure 1. Carl Henry, pictured here in the early 1950s as a faculty member at Fuller Theological Seminary, sought to recover evangelical social engagement. Henry would become the founding editor of the neo-evangelical standard *Christianity Today.* Courtesy of Archives and Special Collections, Wheaton College, Wheaton, Illinois.

"I hereby resign [fundamentalists] to their slow, convulsive death in both peace and isolation." By the 1950s a coterie of neo-evangelical leaders, most of them associated in some way with Wheaton or Fuller, had risen to lead the way from cultural separatism to social engagement. They articulated a more comprehensive evangelical agenda for the twentieth century that proposed increased political, scholarly, and social activity. Henry himself emerged as the preeminent prophet and theologian of the emerging neo-evangelical movement.[13]

II

Still a young scholar at the just-established Fuller Theological Seminary, Henry in 1947 released a movement-defining manifesto that carved out space between the social gospelism of Protestant liberalism and the separatist, socially pessimistic tendencies of fundamentalism. *The Uneasy Conscience of Modern Fundamentalism*, Henry's 88-page tract, sharply indicted the "evaporation of fundamentalist humanitarianism." Its call for social involvement, according to historian Robert Linder, "exploded in the field of evangelical thought . . . like a bombshell." Modernity, Henry began, was replete with social evils, among them "aggressive warfare, racial hatred and intolerance, liquor traffic, and exploitation of labor or management, whichever it may be." But fundamentalism, motivated by an animus against religious modernism, had given up on worthy humanitarian efforts. According to Henry, this lack of social passion was a damnable offense. Instead of acknowledging the world-changing potential of the gospel, fundamentalists had narrowed it to a few world-resisting doctrinal and ascetic concerns such as "intoxicating beverages, movies, dancing, card-playing, and smoking." The redemptive message of Christ, Henry wrote, had implications for all of life, not just the personal.[14]

Henry also targeted religious liberals with a sharp critique. The liberal social gospel, he argued, cultivated a social ethic in its efforts to build "higher civilizations," but it did so to the exclusion of personal salvation. Like fundamentalism, Protestant liberalism served as an important foil for the middle course Henry and neo-evangelicals were trying to chart—a doctrinally pure, socially engaged faith between social gospel advocate Walter Rauschenbusch and fundamentalist Carl McIntire. In Henry's vision the new course would confront important social issues such as racism, labor disputes, and military aggression by communistic and totalitarian regimes, all the while retaining conservative theology and evangelical piety. "There is no room here," he wrote, invoking John the Baptist, Jesus, and the Apostle Paul, "for a gospel that is indifferent to the needs of the total man nor of the global man." *Uneasy Conscience* was a commanding call to a new social mission.[15]

It was a call, however, without a well-defined program. The tract did offer a few clues suggesting a conservative political orientation, such as his suspicion of the efficacy of increasing labor wages and reducing work hours. Yet other passages suggested more progressive reforms, such as his proposal that the United States should work closely with the then-emerging United Nations. As a whole, however, the text of *Uneasy Conscience*—and Henry's subsequent writings—was devoid of any coherent plan for what evangelical social engagement might look like. As late as 1966, after Henry had moved on from Fuller, former colleague Lewis Smedes wished that Henry "would land on some specific points and call his shots. . . . Is he against the War on Poverty? Is he against social security and Medicare? Is he for government legislation on civil rights? . . . Dr. Henry is not specific. . . . The net impression of Dr. Henry's essay is that evangelicals do not yet have a social ethic." Smedes was correct. Henry's imprecision reflected the fluid state of postwar evangelical politics, and it allowed a politically diverse spectrum of evangelicals to claim *Uneasy Conscience* as their inspiration.[16]

In the end, Henry's clearest suggestion for social change had less to do with party politics than with personal transformation. Authentic social transformation could only be sparked by spiritual transformation, he declared. Referring to the universal imperatives of the Ten Commandments, Henry wrote that "no culture can hope to fulfill such high prerequisites, minus a relationship with that God, holy and redemptive, who is the precondition for their very disclosure to man." Consequently, converted believers were needed to fill the ranks of the social and political elite. "To the extent that any society is leavened with Christian conviction," wrote Henry, "it becomes a more hospitable environment for Christian expansion." It was important not to sacrifice "world statesmanship to men of godless convictions." Henry's conception of social engagement thus consisted largely of placing redeemed individuals in positions of social importance rather than specifying particular political policy. Aiming to cultivate such individuals, neo-evangelicals began to build a growing and substantial infrastructure. Charles Fuller's *Old Fashioned Revival Hour*, for example, enjoyed a nationwide audience of 20 million listeners over 456 stations on the Mutual System by the 1940s.

Youth for Christ, a high-school-age parachurch ministry, filled up Madison Square Garden for rallies in the 1950s. Billy Graham drew millions to his evangelistic crusades around the world. Each of these enterprises drew inspiration, in no small measure, from Henry's classic tract.[17]

In retrospect, *Uneasy Conscience* seems both less and more revolutionary than it actually was. Amid the full-throated rise of the religious right in the 1980s, it seemed tame indeed. But understood in context—amid the separatist impulses of 1930s fundamentalism—*Uneasy Conscience* was radical. Henry's rebuke of cultural isolationism so inspired one evangelical student, restive under the constraints of fundamentalism at Westmont College, that he slept with a copy of *Uneasy Conscience* under his pillow during his entire junior year. The student, David Allen Hubbard, would go on to serve as Fuller's president at a time when many at the seminary actively opposed the Vietnam War. For Hubbard, as for many others, Henry's call to engagement catalyzed the politicization of evangelicalism.[18]

III

In 1956 Henry left Fuller to become the editor of *Christianity Today*. Founded nine years after the publication of *Uneasy Conscience*, the magazine was intended by its founder Billy Graham to be a premier periodical that inserted evangelicals into the national conversation. Henry left the growing campus of Fuller for the heart of Washington, D.C. According to Henry, *Christianity Today*'s location on Pennsylvania Avenue, from which staffers could glimpse the White House and "other symbols of national power," reflected "the place of the evangelical witness in the life of a republic." Henry, bankrolled by oilman J. Howard Pew, president of Sun Oil Company (now called Sunoco), mailed the first issues gratis to over 140,000 Protestant church workers. The magazine, which enjoyed 148,900 paid subscribers by 1967, shot ahead of the mainline journal *Christian Century*, which had only 37,500 subscribers. *Christianity Today* emerged immediately as the preeminent neo-evangelical journal and one of the most read religious journals in the nation. If the publication's initial effort, in its ambition and attentiveness to the social implications of the gospel, mirrored its geography, its promoters still kept their distance from the dominant cultural discourses of the Eastern seaboard. *Christianity Today*, even as it sought to repudiate fundamentalist disengagement, sought to challenge rather than join the liberal consensus. Henry re-mained wary of the ecumenical sensibilities of the "triple melting pot" and hostile toward the soulless optimism of political liberalism. Religious intel-lectuals, for their part, often viewed Henry, Graham, and their ilk as hay-seeds.[19]

Evangelicals in fact tended to confirm the fears of political liberals by voting reflexively for conservative politicians. After all, mid-century con-servatism, which stressed states' rights over federal activism and resisted governmental social engineering, resonated with most evangelicals' sense of an individualistic spirituality. Wanting a government that governed less was a political judgment that suited their apolitical sensibilities. One student put it this way: "We tended to be apolitical, but when political instincts did sur-face, they were conservative." Many neo-evangelicals thus voted for Repub-licans: Dwight Eisenhower in 1956, Richard Nixon in 1960 (especially because he was pitted against the Roman Catholic Kennedy), and Barry Goldwater in 1964.[20]

But liberal critics often failed to notice an elemental suspicion of politics. While those reading between the lines could easily discern a conservative bent in the pages of *Christianity Today*, political activism was still only a marginally legitimate activity for the church. Henry's ambivalent posture toward the civil rights movement was telling. "I thought President Johnson's civil rights message to Congress was his high hour, and wrote him so," he explained, "although I thought it was no business of the institutional church to endorse any specific legislative proposal in the name of the Church, and still have some personal reservations about some aspects of civil rights leg-islation." As Henry suggested, Jesus first of all transformed individuals, who would then transform the world as millions of Americans were swept up in a wave of spiritual revival. Believing that the "basic needs of the social order must meet their solution first in the redemption of the individual," Henry regularly warned readers not to drown in a sea of political maneuvering. While participating in governance was good, it was not wise to put too much faith in the state as an instrument of social reform. Nor was it always clear which politics were best. "There is no one direct line from the Bible to the ballot box," Henry declared. Into the 1970s neo-evangelical leaders only rarely mobilized on behalf of—or even endorsed—political candidates.[21]

Given the explicit alliance between evangelicals and the Republican Party that emerged in the 1980s, scholars have not fully appreciated the tenuous roots of this relationship. While many evangelicals sympathized with conservative politics from the 1940s through the 1970s, the mobilization of some into the political juggernaut of the religious right was not at all certain. Even as evangelicals moved toward social engagement at mid-century, their fundamental priority and basis for social change remained personal transformation. They were becoming more likely to bring spiritual values into the political realm, but as yet not ready to immerse themselves in the gritty politicking of American politics.

*   *   *

That reluctance had begun to fade by 1973, when Henry joined representatives of a burgeoning evangelical left in Chicago. The meeting itself was an organizational offshoot of Evangelicals for McGovern. Evangelical Senator Mark Hatfield had just issued sharp denunciations of the Vietnam War. Students at evangelical colleges—including Henry's own son Paul, who would join the U.S. House of Representatives in the 1980s—echoed the rhetoric and policy prescriptions of the political left. "Here we are, most of us well-off offspring of middle-class parents," said one student, disquieted by the growing wealth and prestige of evangelicalism. "Not a whole lot for many of us to worry over, suffer for. Looking at us here, who would guess what victims we are? We are victims of our past. Our Evangelical history with its immersion in the American Way of Death seems almost to drown us."[22]

Henry's response to the angst, flamboyant rhetoric, and specific policy prescriptions of his younger colleagues was understandably ambivalent. After all, he was an elder evangelical statesman presiding over the muted social conservatism of *Christianity Today*, the National Association of Evangelicals, the Evangelical Theological Society, and other institutions he had helped to establish. Henry was no longer an evangelical provocateur. Yet he admired their heightened social consciences, and he knew that he was partly responsible for setting in motion a trajectory away from principled passivism. A postwar wave of economic prosperity, rising social status, a new rhetoric of engagement, and a transformed eschatology—all elements epitomized and driven by movement-builder Carl Henry—had brought evangelicals to the brink of sustained political activism.

Henry's path out of a fundamentalist exile took many directions. It led to Jerry Falwell, to James Dobson, and to a conspicuous politicization on the right. It also led to John Alexander, Jim Wallis, Mark Hatfield, Sharon

Gallagher, and a movement of progressive evangelicals. The story of postwar evangelicalism, a politically contested and fluid movement, does not equal the prehistory of the Christian Right. In the 1970s the future of a newly heightened evangelical politics remained strikingly uncertain. Whether it went left or right was secondary to Henry's more fundamental call for evangelicals to go public with their spiritual commitments.

CHAPTER 2

John Alexander and Racial Justice

I believe segregation is sin, and through this magazine's
pages I hope to do something about it.
—John Alexander in *Freedom Now*

Northern evangelicals' posture toward civil rights reflected Carl Henry's emphatic but vague call for increased social action in *The Uneasy Conscience of Modern Fundamentalism*. Like Henry, many spoke forthrightly against segregation, yet they hesitated to protest demonstratively against Jim Crow. Some preferred slow electoral and legislative solutions. Others took an individualistic approach to social change that emphasized personal holiness over against the systemic change and racial activism advocated by Martin Luther King, Jr. Most had little appetite for the 1955 bus boycott in Montgomery, nor for the freedom rides sponsored by the Student Nonviolent Coordinating Committee (SNCC) in the early 1960s. Bred to avoid confrontation with civil authorities, many mid-century evangelicals did not instinctively challenge social mores, let alone advocate civil disobedience. Most never put it so starkly, but the response of a church elder to one young evangelical's newfound sensitivity to civil rights in the early 1960s—"Christianity has nothing to do with racism. That's political. Our faith is personal"—was typical of many lay evangelicals.[1]

When pressed, northern evangelicals took a gradualist approach toward integration. But most simply wished that the racial tumult would go away. Between 1957 and 1965 *Christianity Today* printed on average less than two articles a year on race relations. Despite inviting Martin Luther King, Jr. to offer the opening prayer at his historic New York City crusade in July 1957 and despite integrating stadiums for his evangelistic crusades in the South, Billy Graham nevertheless called for a "period of quietness in which moderation prevails." He urged King to "put on the brakes a little bit." Mainline theologian and public intellectual Reinhold Niebuhr, while acknowledging that Graham was indeed "rigorous on the race issue," nonetheless scoffed at the evangelist's "pietistic individualism." In *Christian Century*, Niebuhr wrote that an individualistic approach to faith stood in danger of "obscuring the highly complex tasks of justice in community." The conspicuous paucity of evangelicals on freedom rides reflected a weak, individualistic-oriented commitment to civil rights.[2]

Yet this weakness is not the whole story. Small groups of white evangelical students in the North, who are all but absent in the burgeoning scholarship on religion and the civil rights movement, went much further than Billy Graham. "To many of us," wrote Donald Dayton, a Houghton College (New York) student who in 1964 worked with SNCC and the wildcat Mississippi Freedom Democratic Party, "the civil rights movement and its principles of fundamental human equality seemed not only more right, but more biblical and Christian than positions taken by our elders." Members of InterVarsity Christian Fellowship favored federal intervention in southern states by an overwhelming majority. They cheered Ruth Lewis, a black InterVarsity chapter leader, as she attempted to integrate the University of Alabama-Birmingham campus. Stories championing Lewis and other civil rights actions in InterVarsity's magazine reached 26,000 students in over 850 chapters across the nation. At Calvin College in Grand Rapids, Michigan, nearly 300 students marched to protest the 1963 bombings of black churches in Birmingham. The student newspaper regularly editorialized in favor of the Civil Rights Amendment and in opposition to Barry Goldwater's states-rights stance. Two years later over 200 students braved a bitterly cold day in Grand Rapids to protest the death of Boston Unitarian minister James Reeb, who had been beaten to death in Selma, Alabama. A week later dozens of white evangelicals—most unbeknownst to each other—joined the march from Selma to Montgomery. They included Anderson (Indiana) and Wheaton College students, Christian Reformed ministers, and congregants from Church of the Saviour in Washington, D.C., and Elm-LaSalle Church in Chicago.[3]

At Wheaton College, pro-civil rights students picketed a Barry Goldwater rally. The presidential candidate had rented the college's football stadium for a 1964 campaign event that sparked reaction from all sides of the civil rights debate. Goldwater's racial politics were complex. He supported racial integration and called for racist hearts to be transformed. His western libertarianism and fear of communism, on the other hand, directed him away from forced integration by the federal government. Many students interpreted Goldwater's states-rights rhetoric—"Enforcement of the law is a state and local responsibility. There is no room in this country for a federal police force"—as unconscionable. Fifty of them, accompanied by a group of black children from Chicago's South Side dressed in black-and-white dresses and suits, protested Goldwater's denunciation of forced integration and held aloft "LBJ-USA" banners to a chorus of catcalls and boos from Goldwater supporters. Kenneth Landon, one of the protest ringleaders, mourned the opposition he felt while holding his pro-Johnson sign: "I came away from that unbelievable night sorrowing for America, with a fear, not of Goldwater, but of well-dressed, middle-class suburbia, as well as the crowd-following type who kicks from behind—who cry together, "For Goldwater and God!" Many more came to Landon's aid in the following weeks. A week before the election, a half-page "Johnson for President" ad signed by 120 students and faculty appeared in the student newspaper. Anti-segregation sentiment pervaded published discourse at Wheaton and many other evangelical college campuses.[4]

These uncoordinated racial activities intensified through the 1960s. By the end of the decade, white activists had joined black evangelical activists. Together they organized around a pronounced rhetoric of racial integration that stood between Black Power and law-and-order gradualism. John Alexander, son of a white fundamentalist Baptist pastor turned civil rights activist, reflected this position on civil rights. His story carries the narrative of the emerging evangelical left into the early 1970s.

I

Alexander's activist politics began in the early 1960s at Trinity College, an ethnically Scandinavian school in the northern suburbs of Chicago. He chafed under the campus's conservatism, especially after one student leader refused to take up an offering to alleviate global poverty. Souls, explained the student, were more important than bodies. This stance alienated Alexander, nearly leading him to renounce his faith. A long pilgrimage through Scripture, however, led him to fall "in love with the God of the Bible" even as he continued to "utterly reject" the god of his peer. After graduating in 1964, Alexander and his wife Judy moved to Cleveland, Ohio, to work alongside his father Fred, an ordained pastor in the General Association of Regular Baptists (GARB) denomination. Working at Faith Bible Center, a black fundamentalist college, and living in the inner city during the burgeoning civil rights movement fundamentally transformed this white family's views on the racial separatism of their Baptist heritage. The Alexanders, newly awakened to broad conceptions of social concern, trained their sights directly on civil rights issues, joined the NAACP, and renounced their votes for states' rights and Goldwater.[5]

Their stint at Faith lasted only three years. Alexander came to the disquieting realization that his leadership of a black institution was tinged with racial insensitivity. "I came as a white knight to save blacks from their oppressors," he later wrote. "It did not occur to me that I was one of the oppressors." Visiting the congregations of his students showed him that his effort to teach them standard English was an act of racial oppression. "It was sad. . . . I soon realized that these preachers didn't need me to teach them how to express themselves. . . . I concluded that my being there as a white authority did as much harm as good. . . . It reinforced a false image of white superiority and black incompetence." The Alexanders left Faith with a new mission—to transform the racial beliefs of "almost officially segregationist" white fundamentalist Baptists who referred to blacks as "boy" and "nigger in the woodpile." Toward that end, the Alexanders in 1965 founded *Freedom Now*, a 12-page, *Reader's Digest*-size magazine "especially directed to the white fundamentalist." *Freedom Now* would go on to print some of the most forthright religious statements on racial equality within evangelicalism.[6]

Freedom Now's earliest issues were modest. Crudely printed on an antiquated press in the Alexanders' basement, they sold for less than 20 cents and were mailed from a post office in Savannah, Ohio, that served a population of 300 residents. The magazine's rhetoric, however, soared. "I'm all fired up about *Freedom Now*," wrote John in the second issue, "because I believe segregation is sin, and through this magazine's pages I hope to do something about it." Many who read these words were neither amused nor convinced. One reader ran the magazine through a shredder, stuffed the remains into an envelope and mailed it back. A more typical response came from an Ohio pastor who in 1966 forthrightly declared his opposition: "I am not in agreement with your stand for complete integration of the races. I am of the old school of 'equal but separate,' for otherwise it leads to intermarriage,

Figure 2. In 1975 Mark Olson, John Alexander, Pat Osborne, Phil Harnden, and Fred Alexander posed in front of the tiny post office where the first issues of *Freedom Now* had been mailed a decade earlier. Courtesy of Mark Olson.

which I think the Bible is against. Praying that you will be able to lead many of the colored to a saving knowledge of Christ as Lord." Most, however, did not bother to articulate their hostility; they simply didn't read the magazine. *Freedom Now* seemed to teeter on the edge of irrelevance in fundamentalist Baptist circles.[7]

Another group, which Alexander described as "fairly orthodox but less fundamentalist," did respond. Neo-evangelicals associated with Carl Henry began avidly reading *Freedom Now*, which enjoyed a respectable 3,000 subscribers after several years of publication. "So we started reaching out to them," wrote Alexander, for broader evangelicalism better reflected "who I was anyway." Alexander's choice of contributors began to reflect this shift. Black fundamentalists from Moody Bible Institute (Illinois) and Cedarville College (Ohio) gave way to black evangelicals associated with Wheaton College, Fuller Seminary, Westmont College (California), Taylor University (Indiana), InterVarsity, *Christianity Today*, and the National Association of Evangelicals.[8]

In 1966, as *Freedom Now* began to flourish with a new constituency, Alexander moved from Cleveland to Chicago. He continued to edit the magazine, but he also began graduate work in philosophy at Northwestern University and taught at Wheaton College, where he introduced his fiery brand of racial activism to a key center of evangelicalism. A bright, energetic, and edgy young professor, Alexander soon gained a following of students, especially members of progressive clubs such as the Social Action Forum, Americans for Democratic Action, the Young Democrats, and the Jonathan Blanchard Association (named after Wheaton's founding president, who was an abolitionist). His presence helped to jumpstart a new awakening of racial concern in the last half of the 1960s at the college. Others—newly hired black professor Ozzie Edwards, Filipino sociologist Ka Tong Gaw, and J. Edward Hakes, the chair of the department of theology and member of the city's civil rights commission—also emerged as campus leaders on civil rights. By the mid-1960s the use of states' rights rhetoric to slow integration came to be uniformly opposed in public discussions on campus.[9]

In what became one of his most enduring legacies, Alexander introduced Wheaton-style evangelicals to a compelling trio of black evangelical activists. Reading John Perkins of Mississippi, Tom Skinner of Harlem, and Bill Pannell of Detroit in the pages of *Freedom Now* decisively shaped the racial attitudes of many young evangelicals. Perkins, one of the earliest contributors to *Freedom Now*, was born in 1930 on a cotton plantation in rural

New Hebron, Mississippi. After witnessing his brother's shooting death at the hands of a white deputy marshal, Perkins and his wife Vera Mae moved to California, vowing never to return to the South. After a 1957 conversion in a black holiness church and then growing prominence as an evangelist in the mushrooming evangelical subculture of southern California, Perkins felt an irresistible call to evangelize poor blacks in the rural areas surrounding Jackson, Mississippi. His 1960 homecoming came as the civil rights movement was in full swing. Concentrating on building a new congregation, Perkins at first dismissed racial agitation. He had come, after all, to save souls, not stamp out Jim Crow. But as he toured poor black areas like "Baptist Bottom," "Sullivan's Holler," and "Rabbit Road" in a beat-up old Volkswagen wearing ragged blue jeans, faded sports shirt, and dusty black shoes, Perkins noticed the "desperate physical needs of many of our people." He decided that "real evangelism brings a person face to face with all the needs of a person. We had to see people not just as souls but as whole people." Perkins adjusted his approach, and by 1965 he had built a thriving mission called Voice of Calvary that included a day-care center, a gymnasium, a playground, a cooperative farming store, and a church.[10]

As Perkins addressed the spiritual and social needs of his parishioners, he could not escape the unmistakable link between economic degradation and the southern caste system. His assessment of the civil rights movement softened, and he began to allow activists to stay at Voice of Calvary during Freedom Summer in 1964. After he himself suffered a brutal beating by a white policeman, Perkins became a more thoroughgoing activist. Faith *was* politics, he began to argue. "'New birth in Jesus," he said, "meant waging war against segregation just as much as it meant putting the honky-tonks and juke joints out of business." Racism, in fact, "is satanic, and I knew it would take a supernatural force to defeat it." By 1970 Perkins's active pursuit of racial justice had gained him a reputation as "a Bible-believing fundamentalist for black power." The emerging evangelical left chronicled his exploits in community development and evangelism, and he eventually became a minor evangelical celebrity, befriended by luminaries such as Carl Henry, Billy Graham, and Nixon-hatchet-man-turned-prison evangelist Charles Colson. Senator Mark Hatfield of Oregon called Perkins "a modern saint." He spoke at Billy Graham crusades, political prayer breakfasts in Washington, and InterVarsity's Urbana conferences. He wrote for *Freedom Now, Sojourners, Christianity Today, Decision, Campus Life,* and *Moody Monthly.* Perkins's autobiography *Let Justice Roll Down* became a bestseller, ranking fourth in sales of religious paperbacks for a time in the 1970s. All the while, whites in Jackson treated him with hostility and indifference, a reality that stunned white student volunteers who traveled south to work with him.[11]

Several urban voices added to Perkins's southern rural voice. Tom Skinner, a former Harlem Lords gang leader with 27 notches on his knife handle (marking how many bodies he had slashed), launched a vibrant evangelistic career at the age of twenty. At a sensational 1962 crusade at the Apollo Theater, Skinner converted 2,200 people with sermons entitled "The White Man Did It" and "A White Man's Religion." Described by the *New York Times* as "a fervent, square-jawed young evangelist in gray flannel trousers with a Bible in his hands," Skinner catapulted to prominence among white evangelicals with an unusual blend of conversionist piety and sharp racial rhetoric. His weekly half-hour radio program, in which Skinner intoned a gravelly voiced mix of religious and political programming, aired across the nation on 70 stations. In his 1970 book *How Black Is the Gospel?* Skinner urged a return to "that masculine, contemporary, revolutionary Jesus." Skinner's Jesus denounced racists as "You brood of vipers!" As younger white evangelicals warmed to political activism in the late 1960s, the evangelist's contentious language and publicity in *Freedom Now* propelled Skinner as a rising star and an important voice in the evangelical left. An acquaintance of both King and Malcolm X, Skinner also moved in evangelical circles. He was a featured speaker at the 1969 U.S. Congress on Evangelism. He enjoyed "great respect" from Campus Crusade for Christ president Bill Bright. He frequently traveled with Graham as an associate evangelist. Numerous influential evangelical institutions encouraged his racial activism.[12]

Like Skinner, Bill Pannell served as a contributing editor and regular columnist for *Freedom Now*. Brought up by a white Plymouth Brethren family in suburban Detroit, then educated at Fort Wayne Bible College, Pannell learned the warm piety and enjoyed the close friendships of evangelical culture. He also suffered the limitations of being "a colored stranger" in a white church. Pannell, who complained of the "anxiety and agony of being an alien in one's own land," only reluctantly called evangelicalism racist. Yet in his immensely popular 1968 book *My Friend, the Enemy,* he asserted that "this conservative brand of Christianity perpetuates the myth of white supremacy. It tends also to associate Christianity with American patriotism, free enterprise, and the Republican party." The white evangelical was "my friend, the enemy." He worshiped the same God, opposed the KKK, decried violence, supported the Constitution, and encouraged black voting rights.

At the same time, Pannell maintained, a white evangelical might denounce racial agitators and maybe even "agree it is best that I not live in his city's limits." Despite declaring that he was "more grateful to SNCC than to Southern Baptists," Pannell remained within evangelical boundaries, encouraging his tradition to pursue racial justice.[13]

The new activist voices of Pannell, Skinner, Perkins, and Alexander made especially deep inroads within InterVarsity Christian Fellowship. Previously characterized by a singular focus on missions, InterVarsity's triennial Urbana conferences, held on the main campus of the University of Illinois, were becoming more clearly attuned to broader cultural disruptions. At Urbana '67 many of the 9,200 students seemed to resent speakers simply because they were white and male. One resolution read from the floor complained that "there are no black men in leadership positions on the national staff." Others, black and white, complained that InterVarsity was paying too little attention to urban and black concerns. For the first time at an Urbana convention, InterVarsity staffers guarded the stage to prevent students from commandeering the microphone. Following Urbana '67, *HIS* magazine wrote that very little "escaped criticism at the convention. . . . Anything that seemed to show intolerance came under their indictment, with impatience toward racism leading the list." An all-night session of fervent prayer with other black attendees convinced Carl Ellis, a sophomore at the historically black Hampton Institute in Virginia and president of the school's InterVarsity chapter, that he should remain involved in order to urge the racially "inept" organization toward greater racial sensitivity. After being named to the national advisory committee for Urbana '70, Ellis recruited hundreds of black students to attend and enlisted Tom Skinner as a speaker.[14]

The funky strains of Soul Liberation, a band of black musicians sporting Afros, colorful outfits, and African symbols, greeted Urbana '70 attendees. The mostly white audience hesitated at first, unsure of what to make of "Power to the People," a song full of idioms from the Black Power movement. But a throng of students soon rose to its feet to sing and clap along, delighted by the radical departure from the usual hymns. Skinner then delivered the evening sermon, a searing critique of racial prejudice in American society. Cheered on by over 500 black students who had arrived early to secure seats right in front of the podium, Skinner said, "You soon learn that the police in the black communities become nothing more than the occupational force in the black community for the purpose of maintaining the interests of white society. . . . You soon learn that what they mean by law and order is all the order for us and all the law for them." Skinner got laughs when, referring to interracial marriage, he said, "I don't know where white people get the idea that they are so utterly attractive that black people are just dying to marry them." He received thunderous applause when he denounced the injustices of the economic and political system in which the top 5 percent of the wealthiest Americans sat in "smoke-filled rooms at political conventions" to determine our fate. "As a black Christian," he said, "I have to renounce Americanism. I have to renounce any attempt to wed Jesus Christ off to the American system. I disassociate myself from any argument that says a vote for America is a vote for God."

In the speech Skinner also indicted historic white evangelicalism. "In general," Skinner declared, "the evangelical, bible-believing, fundamental, orthodox, conservative church in this country was strangely silent. . . . Christians supported the status quo, supported slavery, supported segregation." Even today, evangelicals "go back to their suburban communities and vote for their law-and-order candidates who will keep the system the way it is." Ending his sermon with a rhetorical flourish—"Go into the world that's enslaved, a world that's filled with hunger and poverty, racism and all those things that are the work of the devil. Proclaim liberation to the captives, preach sight to the blind, set at liberty them that are bruised. Go into the world and tell them who are bound mentally, spiritually, physically. The liberator has come!"—Skinner received a standing ovation. Pannell described the response as deafening and electric, "the most powerful moment that I've ever experienced at the conclusion of a sermon." For many students, Skinner's speech portrayed all that was wrong, and suddenly hopeful, about evangelicalism.[15]

If African American evangelicals associated with *Freedom Now* harshly criticized white evangelicals, they equally faulted certain black voices. Skinner, for instance, made it clear that the black church held little promise for him. A pastor's son, he grew up unimpressed with his father or his church. "Like so many churches across America, in my church there was no real worship. Sunday morning was a time for the people to gather and be stirred by the emotional clichés," explained the evangelist. "So long as the service was liberally sprinkled with those time-worn phrases, the people felt good." Skinner longed for the seriousness and theological rigor, if not the cultural accretions, of white evangelicalism. Skinner and others were even more troubled by the separatist impulse of the emerging Black Power movement, which captured the attention of many students disillusioned by the inability of the

Figure 3. In 1970 nearly 10,000 InterVarsity students gathered in the University of Illinois's Assembly Hall gave black evangelist Tom Skinner a thunderous standing ovation after he concluded his sermon with the words, "The liberator has come!" Courtesy of the Archives of the Billy Graham Center, Wheaton, Illinois.

civil rights movement to sustain racial equality. Skinner likened advocates of Black Power to Barabbas, the character in the Gospel narrative condemned to death for insurrection. In his 1970 book *How Black Is the Gospel?* Skinner wrote, "So Jesus would have said to Barabbas, Barabbas, you're right, the Roman system stinks. It's corrupt to the core. But you are going to tear it down with your own corrupt nature; and in the name of getting rid of corruption, you are being corrupt, and you are going to replace the Roman system with your own messed-up kind of system." The Black Panthers, like Barabbas, had correctly diagnosed the disease, but applied the wrong treatment. "Few black evangelicals in the late sixties," remembers black Wheaton graduate Ron Potter, "were able to take on the charismatic evangelists of the secular

Black Power movement. But Tom was able to help us address the attacks made upon us."[16]

Blacks associated with northern white evangelicals like John Alexander thus resisted growing pressure in the late 1960s to establish separate black institutions. Perkins, Skinner, and Pannell contended that too many separate institutions would deviate from the example of the interracial New Testament church—and from the early civil rights movement, which disavowed black separatism. Skinner urged black and white evangelicals to follow the example of Martin Luther King, Jr., who in 1967 warned that "there is no separate black path to power and fulfillment that does not intersect white paths." Skinner crisscrossed the country as an evangelist and "minister of reconciliation," preaching that Christ "has made the two one and has destroyed the barrier, the dividing wall of hostility . . . to reconcile both of them to God through the cross, by which he put to death their hostility." He urged disgruntled black evangelicals suffering under subtle forms of discrimination at white colleges and InterVarsity chapters to stay the course. When a group of black students at Wheaton complained of racial insensitivity, Skinner came to offer guidance and interpret white evangelicalism for them. Student Ron Potter explained that "Tom was able to articulate for us what we had been feeling. He helped us to differentiate between biblical Christianity and the Christ of the white evangelical culture." Skinner also reconciled racial divides during Urbana '70. After a black caucus voted to exclude whites from a chaotic meeting, Skinner calmed frayed nerves as indignant students told stories of white discrimination. He also smoothed the ruffled feathers of the dismissed whites who bitterly accused the caucus of "practicing reverse discrimination." He sought to convince evangelicals of all colors that the true path to racial justice was the creation of an interracial community that together worshipped God. This notion of "beloved community," language borrowed from the civil rights movement, animated much of Skinner's activism.[17]

Back at Wheaton, Alexander sought in vain to nurture Skinner's ideal of beloved community. Alexander complained that too few Wheaton students, while supporting the ideal of integration, favored demonstrative protests. The college's NAACP chapter lacked extensive support on campus, and the presence of latent racism continued to be felt by minorities. On a campus retrenching under the conservative leadership of ex-Navy commander Hudson Armerding, Alexander had quickly gained notoriety as the most radical professor on campus. In a 1968 chapel service Alexander told students to quit "thinking white" and demanded that blacks compose 20 percent of the student body. Wheaton's administration, fearful of offending conservative constituents, barred sales of *Freedom Now* in the college bookstore, though they kept copies under the counter for patrons who requested it. Alexander soon left, frustrated that more students and faculty were not willing to mobilize.[18]

Comparisons with other religious traditions offer helpful context for Alexander's activism within a politically cautious evangelical sphere. Mainline Protestants and Catholics, for example, offered more substantial dissent to Jim Crow. Students for a Democratic Society's president Paul Potter, who worked with liberal Protestant groups in Cleveland, was beaten during a march near McComb, Mississippi, in 1961. Theologian Reinhold Niebuhr and Martin Luther King, Jr., profoundly shaped by the mainline revival of original sin, faced down segregation as well. But for every marching nun in Selma, there was a New Orleans priest urging civil rights activism to slow down. For every mainline pronouncement from Manhattan's Upper West Side, there was a segregation academy being founded in southern suburbs. Evangelicalism featured a similarly wide spectrum.[19]

II

Alexander's failure to get Wheaton-style evangelicals to view racism as more than willful oppression by a white person against a black person reflected the individualist orientation of mid-century evangelicalism. "My parents," remembered one young activist of the late 1960s, "rebuked the 'colored jokes' we kids brought home from our friends and their parents. . . . But their response to institutional racism was very different. When their country or its system was accused of being racist, they became defensive. They had a personal view of everything, which left them virtually unaware of the social, economic, and political injustices of America." This individualistic conception of racism typified the majority evangelical response to civil rights. The lively debate over race in the pages of *Freedom Now* and new attempts at beloved community, by contrast, revealed a heightening sensitivity to structural racism among the emerging evangelical left. This broader approach to combating the problem defined the movement as Alexander and Wheaton students Mark Olson and Phil Harnden moved to Philadelphia in 1970 to launch *Freedom Now's* successor *The Other Side*. Carrying on as a critical voice for racial justice (the magazine's subscription base rose from 7,300 in 1978 to 13,000 in 1988), it represented an important shift within broader evangelicalism from personal to corporate responsibility.[20]

Significantly, Alexander's early racial activism emphasized evangelicalism's individualized social ethic. He echoed the mid-century evangelical mantra that changing hearts, not laws, could best transform society. He printed exegetical work that sought to convince white readers that black inferiority was biblically unsupportable. He urged his readers to convert white racists, which would lead to better treatment of blacks. Similarly, the conversion of blacks would lead to more disciplined behavior, which would lift them out of the ghetto. The accumulation of millions of "saved" citizens would result in a more humane and just society. Conversely, forcing the hands of lawmakers through protest might hamper the success of evangelistic efforts among racist whites, in turn hurting the black cause. For this reason, though he ultimately welcomed the removal of Jim Crow laws and the passage of the Civil Rights Act, Alexander initially worried that protest might detract from the racial justice brought about by transformed souls. In fact, at first Alexander initially nurtured a robust skepticism of Martin Luther King, Jr. He eyed King's connections to socialists and communists with suspicion, and he worried that King's protests might provoke white backlash. Early articles in *Freedom Now* reflected these concerns. William Banks, an African-American professor at Moody Bible Institute, repeatedly urged readers to practice patience and moderation. Banks wrote, "The social gospeler who thinks that changing the environment and raising the standards of living is the answer is badly mistaken. . . . He must not prostitute his calling by dabbling in politics and stressing the physical aspects of life." The evangelical preoccupation with salvation, repentance, and regeneration—and strategy of treating individual blacks with respect—left little room for structural solutions to social problems.[21]

Yet as the 1960s wore on, Alexander began to doubt the efficacy of personal salvation in sparking social change. Many of the pious evangelicals that *Freedom Now* contributors knew best—Baptists in the South, members of their congregations, even their own parents—remained flagrantly racist. How, asked a disparate but growing group of younger evangelicals, could their parents' generation sing about blacks being precious in God's sight, yet fail to condemn outrages perpetrated by police against southern blacks? How could they decry the March on Washington as a "mob spectacle"? How could they condemn interracial marriage? Alexander wondered if evangelicalism had constructed the equation backward. Perhaps a focus on social justice might spark more effective evangelism. After all, their efforts to convert blacks were failing miserably as they encountered despair and rage. Increasingly, young evangelicals encountered "suspicion of the Christian faith as Whitey's religion to oppress the Blacks." "The door to Negro evangelism, while it is by no means completely closed, is slowly swinging shut," wrote Dan Orme, an associate editor for *Freedom Now* from Athens, Georgia. Evangelicals remained too preoccupied with "personal sins, but not racial injustice or economic exploitation." At a Baptist conference on race and religion in 1968, Bill Pannell told attendees that "old style evangelism is inadequate to meet the needs of the ghetto; we must meet human needs if we are to genuinely meet religious needs." By the late 1960s *Freedom Now's* constituents had surveyed the racial landscape and decided that converting souls by itself could not sufficiently level the terrain.[22]

Meanwhile, Alexander and like-minded evangelicals saw progress in the flurry of activism and civil rights legislation in the mid-1960s. Though many states remained recalcitrant in integrating public schools, others integrated quickly and peacefully. At Wheaton as early as 1962, students incensed by discrimination against black students integrated the city's barbershops by lobbying the local chamber of commerce and publicizing the injustice in local newspapers. These successes convinced an emerging evangelical left to bring, however belatedly, political power to bear on racial injustices. The assassination of King in 1968, an event that "pressed home a sense of urgency" for *Freedom Now* in tackling racism on a structural level, prompted Alexander to lament that "we had been fiddling while Rome burned." The first issue after King's death signaled an abrupt shift in tone and method: "The time for polite discussion is past. . . . It is time for you, for your political party, for your denomination to become involved in a massive action program."[23]

Prominent civil rights leaders reinforced Alexander's call. In 1965 activists in Selma stirred Frank Gaebelein, a noted evangelical leader and associate editor of *Christianity Today.* Covering the Selma march as a journalist, Gaebelein became "so keenly aware of the rightness of the march that I moved from the side [of the journalists] and joined the marchers as they walked out of the city and crossed the bridge over the Alabama River." Later in the year, at a 1965 meeting of the National Conference on Religion and Higher Education, evangelical participants were stunned by the myriad student projects

Figure 4. John Alexander, a vocal civil rights advocate within white evangelicalism, helped broaden the agenda of the evangelical left beyond race to issues such as poverty, housing, and fair trade. Courtesy of Mark Olson.

launched by mainliners. They were rebuilding burned-out black churches in the South and serving poverty-stricken residents of the inner city. One InterVarsity administrator, used to working with evangelical students at state universities, reported that these efforts made "our summer program of camp activities seem rather superficial." He was especially impressed with Paul Potter's work in SDS's Economic Research and Action Program (ERAP). Four years later, at the 1969 U.S. Congress on Evangelism organized by Billy Graham in Minneapolis, a prominent civil rights leader spoke to nearly 5,000 evangelicals. The Southern Christian Leadership Council's Ralph Abernathy encouraged evangelicals to acknowledge the systemic sources of racial inequality. He quoted the biblical prophets, exhorting the delegates to "let justice roll down like the waters."[24]

A chorus of black evangelicals concurred that inequality was built into the very foundation of America. William Bentley, a black Pentecostal preacher with a degree from Fuller Seminary and the president of the National Black Evangelical Association, criticized government priorities "that privileged the military budget over education, child care and poverty relief." Black America, wrote Tom Skinner, would not follow a "white Christ," by which he meant a "defender of the American system, president of the New York Stock Exchange, head of the Pentagon, chairman of the National Republican Committee, a flag-waving patriotic American—and against everything else." In fact Jesus himself "would probably agree with many of the radicals of today—even groups like SDS and Yippies—as they tell how corrupt the system is." John Perkins, whose focus on evangelism in the early 1960s in rural Mississippi precluded social work, began in the late 1960s to endorse economic redistribution. Frustrated with lack of progress since the passage of the Civil Rights Acts—segregation persisted and more than half of black families in Simpson County lived under the poverty line—Perkins issued a document entitled "Demands of the Black Community." It insisted on 30 percent black employment in all businesses, desegregation of public spaces, a minimum-wage campaign for domestic workers, paved streets in black neighborhoods, removal of the police chief, and an overhaul of arrest procedures. Perkins's new focus signaled an important shift in young black evangelical thought: true reconciliation could come only through cultural equity and more equitable distribution of economic resources.[25]

A broadening of evangelical vocation added to the insistent chorus of black evangelicals urging attention to structural inequities. Nearly every contributor to *Freedom Now* held a job in education or social services. The fields of sociology and social work grew substantially at evangelical colleges in the 1960s and 1970s. Many in the evangelical left armed themselves with dog-eared copies of the literature of the progressive and New Left movements. They read *Soul on Ice* (1967), Black Panther Eldridge Cleaver's collection of lyrical essays on racial liberation. They studied *The Other America* (1962), Catholic socialist Michael Harrington's exposé on poverty in the United States, as well as the Kerner Report (1968) on race riots. Each suggested the need for corporate, not merely personal, responsibility.[26]

Growing numbers of younger evangelicals began to speak of "cultures of poverty," the psychological damage of institutional racism, and the inequities of economic structures leading to urban rioting. Of the Kerner Report, Trinity Evangelical Divinity School student Jim Wallis wrote, "I must have read that report at least five times, studying its more than six hundred pages with a thorough intensity. It completely confirmed my experience of the black community. The causes of urban violence were poverty and its accompanying miseries: bad housing and inadequate education, lack of medical care, high unemployment." Taking social scientific studies seriously inevitably led young evangelicals away from the traditional evangelical notion of evangelism as the engine of social change. Instead of understanding racism as a long series of personal white-on-black abuse, they increasingly thought of racism as built into economic, social, and cultural systems. Charles Taber, a Bible translator with a Ph.D. in anthropology and linguistics, cited scholarly studies showing that speaking a black dialect supplied a "sense of identity, personal worth, and belonging to one's social worth." Neta Jackson, a Wheaton graduate and member of the Reba Place intentional community near Chicago, objected to the psychological implications of evangelical publishers' portrayal of sin as black and spiritual purity as white. James O. Buswell, III, an evangelical anthropologist, urged authorities to place blacks in positions of power to help fight the Sambo myth. Newly attentive to white economic and cultural hegemony, evangelicals associated with *Freedom Now* were suggesting that social structures were conspiring against black social advancement.[27]

Soon Alexander was devoting entire issues of the journal (renamed in 1970 from *Freedom Now* to *The Other Side*) to poverty and other topics previously considered peripheral to racial justice. The magazine's new name reflected the broadened agenda. Other minority groups—migrant workers, prisoners, POW's, political and religious dissidents in Russia, the elderly, orphans, widows, the unemployed, and Vietnamese peasants—were, like blacks, victims who lived on "the other side." Social engineering, protest, and politicking were necessary, given the culpability of structures in abusing the oppressed. Hostility toward Richard Nixon and his racially tinged campaign for "law and order" grew in *The Other Side* circles. One correspondent reported on his participation in the Poor People's Campaign, a march by a "multiracial army of the poor" led by King (who was killed midway through the Campaign) from Mississippi to Washington, D.C., over the course of several months in 1968. Sixty Wheaton students, led by Alexander and the college's Social Action Forum, marched in Chicago's western suburbs in solidarity with the Campaign. Likewise, *The Other Side* urged busing white and black children to ensure integrated schools and constantly complained about the lack of federal funds for Upward Bound, Head Start, the rural South, and the inner city.[28]

Similar critiques began to pervade other quarters of moderate evangelicalism. Charles Furness, a social worker in Newark, New Jersey, asserted that race riots were rooted in intolerable economic conditions. The Christian World Liberation Front, an evangelical intentional community in Berkeley, California, virulently criticized white flight, spoke of racism as "embedded" in American society and religion, and compiled bibliographies on "race and poverty." Ka Tong Gaw, Wheaton sociology professor and associate pastor of the racially integrated Circle Church in Chicago, regularly taught students and parishioners about the connection between racism and economic injustice. Evangelical sociologist David Moberg released a popular book, *The Great Reversal: Evangelism Versus Social Concern*, that denounced "social sin." Articles treating the structural sources of poverty appeared even in the conservative *Christianity Today*.[29]

Despite leading evangelicalism toward a new consideration of structural inequality in American society, advocates for racial justice nonetheless occupied an isolated position on the political spectrum. In the early 1960s, numbers of evangelical students traveled south to participate in Freedom Summer, but their diffuse presence in the midst of white mainline, black Protestant, and northern Catholic solidarity went unnoticed. In the mid-1960s, evangelicals associated with *Freedom Now* still felt profound ambivalence toward Martin Luther King, Jr.'s activism. In the late 1960s, some mimicked the symbols of Black Power, but could not in the end deny New Testament norms and early movement ideals of beloved community. Some worked with mainline groups on issues of economic racism and community development, but their contributions were overshadowed by the bureaucracies of more established traditions. At every turn, Alexander and his circle of black activists found themselves out of step with dominant streams of racial rhetoric and activism. They fit neither with the law-and-order Republicanism embraced by Nixon nor with the emerging stridency of the civil rights movement in the late 1960s. Indeed, two years before the Chicago Declaration, a frustrated Alexander noted his uncertain position in the evangelical landscape: "The most frequent criticism made of *The Other Side* is that it parrots liberal, secular thinkers. Frankly I have difficulty understanding the criticism. How many secular magazines are there which, like *The Other Side*, present the plan of salvation in more editorials than not?" Dismissed by leftist activists as disturbingly late in joining the movement and by mainstream evangelicals as disturbingly activist in orientation, the embattled Alexander occupied an awkward political location.[30]

* * *

Soon, however, *The Other Side* joined other politically progressive evangelicals also emerging from a passively conservative, individualist posture. When the evangelical left convened in Chicago in 1973, John Alexander was there. So were an impressive number of black evangelicals associated with Alexander, such as William Bentley, John Perkins, and William Pannell. Others included Ruth Bentley, on staff at the University of Illinois-Chicago; Clarence Hilliard, pastor of the interracial Circle Church in Chicago; and Wyn Wright and Ron Potter of Voice of Calvary. These individuals were instrumental in constructing the Chicago Declaration's opening confession about the most critical issue of the postwar era: "Although the Lord calls us to defend the social and economic rights of the poor and oppressed, we have mostly remained silent. We deplore the historic involvement of the church in America with racism and the conspicuous responsibility of the evangelical community for perpetuating the personal attitudes and institutional structures that have divided the body of Christ along color lines."

While this tardy contribution failed to shape significantly the national debate on civil rights, Alexander did lead the way among those seeking to add a structural component to evangelicals' undeveloped social theory. By the early 1970s evangelical debates over race had expanded to crime, housing, and economic structures. From an emphasis on individual actions to help disenfranchised southern blacks emerged a holistic effort to raise the psychological, economic, and political health of a race. From structural considerations about race would emerge larger debates over capitalism, peace and war, gender, simple living, and participatory democracy. And from these debates emerged evangelicals willing to take political action on behalf of "the other side of the world's affluence, the side of America that is hungry, defeated, and suffering." Deeply distressed by the failure of evangelicalism in the civil rights movement, some vowed not to repeat such a moral lapse. "While I was sitting comfortably in my living room," wrote Alexander, "King laid down his life for garbage collectors. Nothing but the blood of Christ can atone for this sin of mine." This lament would inspire evangelical progressives toward ever more substantial dissent—soon against U.S. imperialism in Southeast Asia.[31]

CHAPTER 3

Jim Wallis and Vietnam

America was wrong—wrong in the ghettos and in the
jungles of Southeast Asia.

—Jim Wallis

Like the rest of the nation, evangelical opposition to the Vietnam conflict developed unevenly. John Alexander and his father Fred, who agreed on civil rights, spent hours arguing over Vietnam in the late 1960s, agreeing only that "factual issues in Viet Nam are very complex, and we do not feel that Christians are in any special position to decide what the facts are." When *The Other Side* finally did come out firmly against the war in the early 1970s, the magazine received "a lot of negative reaction from people who had been supporting us on other issues."[1]

Protestants in general were reluctant to join antiwar activism. Many mainline leaders, stridently anticommunist during the Cold War, supported intervention in Vietnam as a means of halting Russian and Chinese advances. Dissent grew only after a group of prominent mainline spokesmen— among them Yale's William Sloane Coffin, Jr., Stanford's Robert McAfee Brown, Union's Reinhold Niebuhr, Hartford's Peter Berger, and Martin Luther King, Jr.—spoke out against the war around the time of the Tet Offensive in 1968. Fundamentalists mostly fulminated against the emerging mainline dissent. Convinced that the United States was a bulwark against communism, John R. Rice, a prominent Baptist pastor and editor of *The Sword of the Lord*, declared that American troops "would be carrying out the command of God." Most prominent neo-evangelicals, similarly unimpressed with emerging mainline critiques of American foreign policy in the late 1960s, maintained a moderate pro-war stance, even after the Tet Offensive and troop escalations. "What special wisdom do clergymen have on the military and international intricacies of the United States government's involvement in Viet Nam?" asked Carl Henry. "None" was his answer. Mainliners might "speak piously about our difficulties in Viet Nam, but a vocal and uninformed piety is worse than silence." Though misgivings grew in the early 1970s, the most prominent neo-evangelicals followed Henry's lead. Billy Graham, *Christianity Today*, and the National Association of Evangelicals, three exemplars of neo-evangelicalism that were convinced by long-held theories of dominos and containment, conceded that intervention was justified and worthy of support.[2]

Despite charting a middle course between criticism of the war and fundamentalist jingoism, evangelical heavyweights such as Henry soon faced dissent from within. As early as 1966, contributors to the Grand Rapids-based *Reformed Journal* questioned whether Vietnam satisfied the criteria of a just war. In 1968 InterVarsity Christian Fellowship offered a Mennonite pacifist dozens of pages in its magazine to question the morality of Christian involvement in the military generally and in Vietnam specifically. An InterVarsity student at Portland State College, worried about the souls of Vietnamese innocents, wondered, "How can one witness with a bullet and a bomb?" Members of the Post-American intentional community in Chicago explained that opposition to Vietnam was their defining issue, one that engaged them on "a basic, deep, personal emotional level." Its members anguished over the helicopter gunships that spread machine gun fire, explosives, and napalm in the Vietnamese countryside, defoliating forests and jungles and rice paddies. Most antiwar evangelicals, even scholars who debated just war theory, responded primarily out of visceral revulsion over the images of spilled blood that splashed across their 13-inch television sets. Unmoved by the Cold War insistence on resisting communist advances in faraway places, growing numbers of evangelicals mobilized politically after watching friends return from Vietnam in body bags.[3]

Dissenting evangelicals also added a deeper grievance. By the end of the 1960s, antipathy toward the Vietnam War—initially grounded in the instinctive sense that dropping napalm onto civilian villages was evil—had matured into a critique of American society, civil religion, and evangelicalism itself. "Finally," wrote Post-American leader Jim Wallis, who would become one of the most important faces of the evangelical left over the next decades, "the alienation from the church that my confrontation with racism had begun was completed by Vietnam." Judging that "America was wrong—wrong in the ghettos and in the jungles of Southeast Asia," Wallis saw civil rights and antiwar protest as God's instruments of justice. The most strident antiwar evangelicals not only picketed ROTC activities and joined national Moratorium Day protests, but also proffered New Left critiques of the American economic and political systems. Indeed, for angst-ridden students such as Wallis, afflicted in the early 1970s with alienation over Vietnam, the "sixties" came in a belated but accelerated rush.[4]

I

Few observers of Jim Wallis's evangelical conversion in the American heartland would have predicted his Post-American future. On a Sunday evening in the early 1950s, the six-year-old Wallis was spiritually stricken. A visiting evangelist jabbed his finger at the youngster perched on a front-row pew and declared, "If Jesus came back tonight, your mommy and daddy would be taken to heaven, and you would be left all by yourself." Frightened, Wallis sat quietly in the back seat of the family station wagon on the way to the family's FHA-financed, three-bedroom home in suburban Detroit. Once there his mother told the boy that God loved him and "wanted him to be His child." Nodding his head, young Wallis—future war protestor and founder of the leftist tabloid *Post-American*—was born again. Following this moment of crisis, Wallis's childhood progressed in idyllic fashion. His father, a World War II veteran and engineer for Detroit Edison; his mother, a homemaker; and four siblings offered him "an abundance of warm affirmations, constant kudos, and great expectations for success." They all attended an evangelical Plymouth Brethren congregation that opposed movie-watching, maintained a staunch theological conservatism, and warmly embraced its small circle of members.

Wallis, however, rebelled against the suburban pieties of his youth. As a teenager in the throes of the 1960s, he did not want to be "just another white kid from everything that was 'middle' about America." "We were from Michigan," he later explained. "We were middle-class. We were Christians. We lived in a nice suburban Detroit neighborhood and my brother and sisters and I all went to good schools. The world looked fine to us. My parents believed that we lived in the best city in the best state in the best country in the world." But young Wallis wondered why the only blacks he saw in his church were missionary converts from Africa, never from nearby inner-city Detroit. He began asking questions at his church, whose members stiffened in resistance to his tight pants, long hair, and, most of all, his uncomfortable questions. Upon getting his driver's license, he ventured into downtown Detroit in search of answers. As he wandered the streets full of exotic ethnic groups and militant advocates of Malcolm X, Wallis sensed that "life seemed more real there, more human, and more interesting than in the suburbs, which now felt so artificial and isolating to me." The summer before he began college, a factory job centered his attention on the economic injustices and racial brutalities of postwar Detroit. Amid the riots of 1967, a shocked Wallis observed "the terror of a city at war, saw the devastation, and listened to the anger and despair of black friends and co-workers. . . . The response of the police was unrestrained brutality that knew no bounds." Instead of seeking help from a policeman if he encountered trouble, as Wallis's mother had taught him to do, a black co-worker had been instructed by his own mother to "quickly hide down a stairwell or behind a building. Just don't let him find you! After he passes by, it's safe to come out and find your way home." Detroit, Wallis recalled, "was my baptism of fire, teaching me how racism had betrayed the ideals I had been taught as a child."[5]

Wallis's politicization continued at Michigan State University, where he studied from 1967 to 1970. A stint in student government soon led to involvement in MSU's chapter of Students for a Democratic Society, a New Left student organization in the 1960s that marshaled participatory democracy and direct action in its critique of American politics and society. He joined students up in arms over the university's heavy-handed treatment of protesters, revelations of campus ties to defense contractors and the CIA, the May 1970 shootings of Kent State University students by the Ohio National Guard, and the U.S. incursion into Cambodia. By his senior year Wallis enjoyed a national profile and claimed he could activate 10,000 protestors in a few hours' time. He was a key organizer in the national student strike in the spring of 1970. But when leather-clad Weathermen and SDS comrades smashed the East Lansing City Hall, his commitment to the movement collapsed. The secular radical movement, he decided, was grounded only in "humanistic platitudes," and its logical end was moral confusion. Wallis watched in horror as the movement degenerated into violence and fragmentation. Evangelical radicals, who would coalesce in the early 1970s, could never ally with SDS. Inspired by early iterations of the New Left, leftist evangelicals were left utterly alienated by the "days of rage" that engulfed

Figure 5. Jim Wallis, founder of the Post-American community, launched his life of activism as a member of Students for a Democratic Society at Michigan State University. Courtesy of Sojourners, Washington, D.C.

the movement in Chicago, Berkeley, and New York at the turn of the decade.[6]

Soon after rejecting the radicalized New Left, Wallis turned back to his abandoned childhood faith. "I started reading the New Testament again," he recalled, "which I hadn't done in many years, just on my own. What I began to see in the first three Gospels was a Jesus who stood with the poor and marginalized and who taught his followers to be peacemakers, a Jesus I had never heard much about in church but was now rediscovering." This spiritual awakening, coupled with admiration for nonviolent Martin Luther King, Jr., and the faith-rooted origins of the civil rights movement, led him to theological training at Trinity Evangelical Divinity School, a rapidly growing conservative evangelical seminary in the northern suburbs of Chicago. Days before the fall semester began in 1970 and shortly after watching MSU's SDS chapter dwindle to a small circle, Wallis drove around the southern tip of Lake Michigan in his Ford Falcon. Combining his revived evangelical faith with a radical critique of American politics and international policy, he intended to "take on the evangelical world with Jesus and the Bible."[7]

Wallis quickly provoked the conservative campus into heated debate about the war in Vietnam. Every Wednesday at noon, students and faculty met for lunch and debate at The Pits, a small café in the basement of the administration building where polite discussion often spiraled into heated arguments between just-war advocates and pacifists. Wallis, a noisy student with a bushy red beard, was "the archetype of a prophet," a classmate remembers, and often served as the lightning rod in these debates. His fellow students would "sit there with mouths agape getting really mad at him" as he charged Trinity with having departed from biblical ideals.[8]

With unrelenting appeals to Scripture, the young firebrand managed to persuade many of his classmates. Jonathan Bonk, a student from an Evangelical Free church in Manitoba, found compelling Wallis's emphasis on peacemaking, prayer, and radical generosity as preached by Jesus in the Sermon on the Mount. Wallis ripped out all the pages in the Bible that dealt with money and poverty, leaving only a tattered shell remaining, to make his point that social justice mattered. While others in the New Left made their case using sociological arguments, Wallis "made it theological" and insisted on scriptural justification for arguments. This was a tactic that convinced disenchanted conservative divinity students to rally around his leadership. The "Bannockburn Seven"—named for the wealthy section of Deerfield where Trinity was located—rallied first against stringent campus standards. When the faculty rejected a 93 percent student vote urging loosening campus parietal rules, Wallis and his friends released a manifesto. "At Trinity—Students Are Niggers," a document that borrowed from Jerry Farber's underground essay "The Student as Nigger," charged that the school "will become either a center of progressive evangelical thought, or a fundamentalist enclave of legalism, sell-out religion, and reactionary thought. The choice is yours." They invited the *Chicago Tribune* to observe a mock funeral in front of the administration building, where they played Taps, built a makeshift graveyard, and "buried student opinion." They particularly targeted eminent evangelical theologian and dean of the seminary Kenneth Kantzer, who told protesting students seeking reform "outside the framework of legitimately elected student government" to consider themselves "not welcome." Faculty, he reasoned, had come from the "greatest universities on earth, prepared to write volumes on the decisive theological issues of the day"; instead they were getting "tied up for significant amounts of time debating whether visiting hours for girls should be from 3–12 or 4–11 on Saturdays and Sundays."[9]

The Bannockburn Seven quickly broadened their agenda beyond campus rules to critique evangelical nonengagement with broader social issues. Bob Sabath felt "deep alienation from the church," telling a Milwaukee newspaper reporter that "I felt the evangelical church had betrayed me, betrayed itself. It was not dealing with those questions of racism, war, hunger. I was in fact contributing to them." In a "Deerfield Manifesto," written in late 1970, the seminarians stated that the "Christian response to our revolutionary age must be to stand and identify with the exploited and oppressed, rather than with the oppressor." By the summer of 1971, Wallis and his compatriots had formed the People's Christian Coalition (though they more often called themselves the "Post-Americans," for the magazine they edited) to address violence, race, poverty, pollution, and other "macro-ethical subjects." They met regularly for prayer, Bible reading, sociological study, celebrations called "God parties" (which always opened with a rendition of Three Dog Night's "Joy to the World"), and demonstrations against the war. As the Coalition rapidly grew and took up more of their time, they finally stopped taking classes at Trinity. But their common "alienating seminary experience," as Sabath put it, continued to bind them together. In early 1972, 25 Trinity classmates launched an intentional community, located initially in an apartment building in Rogers Park on Chicago's north side and then in the impoverished Uptown area.[10]

The seminarians' most enduring legacy came from their tabloid, which featured a signature blend of evangelical piety and leftist politics. The first issue of the *Post-American*, issued in the fall of 1971, featured a cover of Jesus wearing a crown of thorns and cuffed with an American flag that covered his bruised body. America, the depiction implied, had re-crucified Christ. Inside, "A Joint Treaty of Peace between the People of the United States, South Vietnam and North Vietnam" declared that the American and Vietnamese people were not enemies and called for the immediate withdrawal of U.S. troops. The "American captivity of the church," it continued, "has resulted in the disastrous equation of the American way of life with the Christian way of life." For Wallis, the publication of the *Post-American's* first issue was a deeply spiritual moment. Having stayed up all night editing, returning proofs to the printer, and hauling stacks of freshly printed issues back to his small apartment, he paused in the early morning hours. He placed a copy on his bed, dropped to his knees, and began to pray. Strong feelings of "gratitude, expectation, and bold, confident faith" rushed over him as he reflected over the long journey that had led him to this point. "The gospel message that had nurtured us as children was now turning us against the injustice and violence of our nation's leading institutions and was causing us to repudiate the church's conformity to a system that we believed to be biblically wrong."[11]

For a group of evangelical seminarians raised in the evangelical heartland, this was an audacious declaration. And they proclaimed it widely. The Post-Americans distributed 30,000 copies of the first edition, printed with $700 in pooled money. They blanketed 15 colleges and seminaries in the Chicago area and sold copies for 25 cents in Old Town, New Town, and downtown Chicago. Within a few months, they had sold 225 full subscriptions. The real growth potential, however, lay in the thousands of other disillusioned evangelical students across the country. They borrowed mailing lists and took their searing critique on the road in an attempt to awaken sleepy evangelical campuses. In spring 1971 Wallis received a rousing reception when he told students at an American Association of Evangelical Students conference that their "hearts were larger than the narrow faith they had been given." Wallis and Clark Pinnock, his mentor and a professor at Trinity, traveled to the University of Texas at Austin under the auspices of InterVarsity to preach and condemn the war on the streets. One 16-day trip in 1972 took the Post-Americans to evangelical campuses, major universities,

The POST-AMERICAN

Fall 1971
Vol.1 No.1

Voice of the People's Christian Coalition

. . . and they crucified Him

Figure 6. The first issue of the *Post-American* featured Jesus wearing a crown of thorns and cuffed with an American flag. Courtesy of Archives and Special Collections, Wheaton College, Wheaton, Illinois.

intentional communities, and churches in northern Indiana, lower Michigan, northern Ohio, central and eastern Pennsylvania, and up the East
Coast from Washington to Boston. They brought copies of their magazine,
distributed reading lists full of New Left writers, and offered free university
courses on Christian radicalism, the New Left, women's liberation, and racism. They gained even more publicity when Mark Hatfield, a U.S. Senator
from Oregon, and John Stott, Britain's leading evangelical figure, endorsed
them. Within two years, 1,200 people had subscribed to the *Post-American*;
within five years, nearly 20,000; by the 1980s, 55,000. The Post-Americans had
clearly tapped into a substantial market of angst-ridden evangelicals searching for authentic faith.[12]

II

The Post-Americans' impatience with traditional politics and their search
for authenticity borrowed explicitly from the New Left. For the Post-
Americans, both conservative and liberal Christianity had failed. The conservative evangelical journal *Christianity Today* espoused ambivalent civil
rights and pro-war positions, while the mainline journal *Christian Century*
embodied a soft, compromising, and spiritually vacuous liberalism. These
establishment institutions never understood "the depth of rage and anguish
involved in those who broke with the mainstream of American politics because of Vietnam. The protests of the New Left were never taken seriously."
Even after the war, the *Post-American* observed, the *Century* remained "sub-
dued but unchanged in its support of the American covenant." It was this
outrage over liberal hesitancy that characterized both the Post-Americans'
and the New Left's critiques of American politics. The Post-Americans and
SDS alike mocked liberal optimism that education, America's essentialist
creed of equality, and gradualist politics would gradually end segregation
and achieve military victory in Southeast Asia. Liberalism's ponderous efforts betrayed its complicity in an unholy trinity of big business, the media,
and government bureaucracy. In many ways, the Post-Americans were nicely
positioned to find this critique plausible, given their roots in antimodernist
fundamentalism. They easily combined their distrust of big government,
skepticism of science and rationality, and faith in the efficacy of prayer and
healing with the New Leftist thought they encountered at state universities.
The Post-Americans charged that the American power structure maintained

impoverished commitments to unlimited economic growth, big government, technology, and global dominance.[13]

Evangelical radicals, like secular leftists, vociferously attacked the concept of unlimited economic growth, an important marker of postwar liberalism. In the 1930s British economist John Maynard Keynes suggested that if the government correctly regulated economic structures through managing the supply of currency and the flow of government spending, a permanent and unlimited pattern of economic growth could prevail over the cyclical patterns of boom and bust that had characterized much of American history. While the Post-Americans, citing New Left voices Herbert Marcuse and Charles Reich, did offer economic critiques of unlimited growth, their most insistent opposition came on moral grounds: at its base, Keynesian economics merely justified corporate greed. The Post-Americans denounced Proctor and Gamble, Ford, AT&T, and Westinghouse for perpetuating the "liberal-industrial scheme" of unlimited economic growth. "We protest," Jim Wallis declared in an exemplary critique of liberalism, "the materialistic profit culture and technocratic society which threaten basic human values." From 1973 to 1978, the *Post-American* printed over one hundred articles on the poor and disenfranchised, many of which explicitly blamed consumer culture and big business for their economic plight. The liberal scheme of consumption to stimulate the economy was a telling symbol of prosperity gone awry.[14]

Objections to faith in science and to the "spirit-deadening assembly-line routine" of technology pervaded Post-American skepticism about unlimited growth. Technology gave the "powers and principalities," as Wallis called governments, corporations, and other brokers of power, an even more insidious means of wielding control over "the people" than traditional uses of power. French philosopher Jacques Ellul's meditations on "technological tyranny" mediated the New Left social thought of Charles Reich, William Domhoff, and C. Wright Mills for evangelical radicals. Ellul, a Reformed Protestant admired for his personal piety and resistance to the Nazi regime in France, contended that science and technology desacralized and replaced Scripture. The Post-Americans found many specific products to criticize based on Ellul's social theory. One of their most compelling examples was infant formula. From all appearances it seemed like a technology that could help dry mothers or orphaned babies. Instead, it led to costly dependence on American companies, intent only on increasing their consumer base and the reach of their economic empires. Given the need for clean water, sterilization, and the formula itself, contended the Post-Americans, offering classes on techniques of breastfeeding would be simpler and less disruptive to cultural norms. The ties between technology and big business led many New Leftists to despair about "the technocracy," a term used with regularity among evangelical radicals. The technocracy perpetuated a bureaucratic maze that threatened to extinguish human autonomy and creativity.[15]

The collusion of big business and technology, contended evangelical leftists, necessarily resulted in American imperialism. The tremendous appetites of corporations, though somewhat sated by a booming economy and new technologies, required ever-expanding markets that spilled outside American borders. The United States nurtured an "expansionist thrust," maintained Wallis, who drew from the scholarship of New Left historians, especially William Appleman Williams's primer of revisionist history *The Tragedy of American Diplomacy*. The Post-Americans also assigned Gabriel Kolko's *The Roots of American Foreign Policy* and Merlo J. Purcy's *The U.S.A. Astride the Globe* in their free university courses. American attempts to contain communism and spread democracy around the world, the Post-Americans argued, did not truly democratize the world, but rather betrayed American economic self-interest and an attempt to solidify its imperial dominance. Richard Barnet, a *Post-American* contributing editor with close ties to Inter-Varsity and the evangelical Church of the Saviour in Washington, D.C., argued that expansionist national security managers and their collusions with multinational corporations were exacerbating America's inherent imperialist streak. They had generated dozens of American military interventions—one every eighteen months—from 1948 to 1965. The Vietnam War was not an "aberration," concurred Wallis, "but in fact only the most current example of a long and bloody record of U.S. interventionism."[16]

Drinking deep from the wells of revisionist history and New Left sociology, evangelical radicals eyed conspiracy at the highest levels of the United States government. Art Gish, a Post-American ally who sought to merge the "old, old story" with the New Left, argued that Vietnam, racism, and poverty exposed an "evil system that forces men to do evil deeds." The demand for increased corporate profits, evangelical radicals believed, drove unjust distributions of humanitarian aid, sparked wars that killed millions in Southeast Asia, and imposed jarring systems of technology on developing nations. They spoke of "Amerika" or "the American way of Death," corrupting patriotic phrases to express their anger toward the nation. Mourning American abuse of the world's disenfranchised, they compared America to

Babylon or Rome. "god is an american," read the satirical cover of the Fall 1972 issue of the *Post-American*, "and Nixon is his prophet." The bitter taste of a fallen nation remained on lips of evangelical radicals, evidence of a formative encounter with the New Left.[17]

III

The rhetoric of the *Post-American* pointed not only to evangelical appropriation of New Left social critiques, but also to a radical political style. This new style sharply contrasted with the mid-century neo-evangelical inclination to court establishment structures. The church "forsakes the spirit of Christ," an editor of *Christianity Today* had argued in 1967, when it uses "picketing, demonstration, and boycott." Dissent, evangelical radicals countered, was necessary to correct the status quo. Spiritual resources should be used to judge, not merely legitimate current conditions. The Post-Americans dismissed decorous evangelicalism as passé, even immoral, in the face of social injustice. Their protests, reflecting the New Left's demonstrative methods, such as guerrilla theater, picketing, leafleting, and direct confrontation, marked a profound departure from evangelical quietism.[18]

Evangelical radicals used these new tactics to confront mainstream evangelicals at Explo in 1972. Staged by the conservative student ministry Campus Crusade, Explo was a religious rally held in Dallas's Cotton Bowl that attracted nearly 85,000 high school and college students. Signs of the establishment predominated. Students attended seminars on "How to Live with Your Parents," listened to speakers Bill Bright and Billy Graham, and joined in patriotic rituals. A small minority of Explo participants, however, viewed the spectacle with distaste. Jim Wallis and the Post-Americans joined forces with an evangelical commune from Berkeley, California, and a group of Mennonites to condemn the displays of civic religion as a "truncated and domesticated gospel." Sharon Gallagher of the Christian World Liberation Front told a *New York Times* reporter, "The whole thing reminds you of the Roman Coliseum. Except in those days the Christians weren't in the stands. Something's changed." Several hundred or so evangelical radicals set up literature booths and wore black armbands to protest the war. Wallis quizzed Billy Graham at a press conference about his close ties with Nixon and his tacit approval of the war. Others wore sandwich-board signs that read "The 300 Persons Killed by American Bombs Today Will Not Be Won in This

Figure 7. The Post-American intentional community in 1975 moved to the Columbia Heights section of Washington, D.C. under the new name of Sojourners. Courtesy of Archives and Special Collections, Wheaton College, Wheaton, Illinois.

Generation" (a variation of the convention's theme, "Win the World for Christ in This Generation"), "Choose This Day—Make Disciples or Make Bombs," and "Love your Enemies or Kill Your Enemies." During a military ceremony, they stood under the stadium's scoreboard, unfurled a banner—"Cross or Flag, Christ or Country"—and chanted "Stop the War!" The protest attracted Dallas policemen and the major news outlets, but not the explicit support of most Explo participants, though many smiled and said "Right On" or "Amen" as they walked by the booths of the antiwar contingent. One journalist wrote that Campus Crusade, like the federal government, was "perfectly able to swallow up dissent."[19]

Renaming themselves Sojourners (a biblical allusion that more clearly transcended the American context of the group's founding name and reflected its commitment to community) and moving in 1975 into a dilapidated neighborhood in the northern section of the District of Columbia, the Post-Americans continued their program of contentious dissent. They pledged to move more intentionally toward "nonviolent direct action." "Our resistance to evil," one statement read, "must never be passive but active, even to the point of sacrifice and suffering. . . . We therefore refuse military service, military-related jobs, war taxes, and will engage in nonviolent direct action and civil disobedience for the sake of peace and justice as conscience dictates and the Spirit leads us." Continuing to rely on *The Organizer's Manual*, which had been an influential resource within the New Left, the Post-Americans traveled across the Eastern seaboard protesting nuclear weapons on site at munitions factories. They agitated for tenants' rights, forming the Columbia Heights Community Ownership Project to protect homes from speculators. In a dramatic protest against real estate speculation and gentrification, the *Washington Post* reported, Post-American members squatted in an apartment building, an act preceded by a march with banners as Third District policemen watched. They staged hundreds of other similarly theatrical protests in the last half of the decade, over forty in the first six months of 1977 alone. Thus even as nonviolence remained an absolute virtue for evangelical radicals, that nonviolence grew more demonstrative.[20]

Through the 1970s evangelical radicals sought to develop clearer principles of active peacemaking. A "Task Force on Evangelical Nonviolence" urged evangelicals to learn from the experience of women seeking to win the right to vote, from black Christians in the South, and from those who tried to thwart invasions in Europe. Several InterVarsity chapters sought to transcend both the law-and-order stance of most evangelicals and the violence of radical leftist groups. The Columbia Presbyterian Medical Center chapter in New York City, for example, pledged to pursue nonviolent means of quelling campus unrest, even physically injecting themselves between opponents in violent demonstrations. Public dissent to social injustice, evangelical radicals believed, should be carried out in a thoughtful, not haphazard or emotional, fashion. They carefully chose corporations to boycott. They published task lists, wrote guidelines on how to negotiate with the press and the police, played strategy games, engaged in scenario-writing, and conducted "force-field analysis." One manual disavowed name-calling or the use of hostile words. Richard Taylor of the Philadelphia Life Center told nonviolent demonstrators to pray for their attackers and to recognize that "police and others are beloved children of God—Christ died for us all." Furthermore, he urged activists to "get the facts right," maintain a humble spirit while protesting, seek spiritual guidance, engage in regular disciplines of prayer and group worship, place a priority on public education, and engage

policymakers in good faith negotiations. Evangelical radicals, responding to
New Left excesses, did not observe these priorities in the violent Weathermen of the early 1970s.[21]

Even as they sought to retain evangelical piety and a sense of humanity
toward oppressors, evangelical radicals did not hold back their insistent
critiques. They calculated how protests could be carried out to the greatest
effect. Many learned from and worked alongside Catholic antiwar activists
from Jonah House in Baltimore. Philip Berrigan, a Catholic, and Ladon
Sheats, an evangelical from East Texas and former IBM executive, crashed
the fiftieth anniversary celebration of Pratt and Whitney, a corporation that
built engines for fighter jets. On October 5, 1975, Sheats marched up a platform that displayed a jet fuselage, poured his own blood into the cockpit,
and then wrote the word "death" in blood on the equipment. In a "statement
of conscience" to the judge at his trial (and then reprinted in the evangelical
satire magazine *Wittenburg Door*), Sheats explained that the U.S. "is controlled by a power consortium of the Executive Branch, Pentagon, and
Multi-national Corporations. They control our destiny. Their music is profits and their dance is death." At Calvin College in Grand Rapids, Michigan,
students angry about residence policies hanged the dean in effigy and
painted "End the War" in four-foot, whitewashed letters high on the wall of
an academic building. At Wheaton, students reenacted death scenes from
Vietnam, carried coffins to the city's draft board office, mocked cadet rifle
drills with displays of toy machine guns, offered bitter commentary on the
college president's support for the war, and wore nooses over their heads at
demonstrations. Richard Taylor urged evangelicals to act as Jesus would if
he lived in modern-day America. He suggested picketing wealthy churches
with "Repent" signs; jack-hammering concrete city plazas; planting tomato
vines in the cracks; agitating against the "great American steak religion";
and performing "socio-dramas" that illustrated the torture techniques used
in Russian prison camps. Holding few illusions about short-term policy
gains—"Major social evils and injustices," explained Taylor, "will rarely, if
ever, be overcome by one beautiful demonstration"—they consoled themselves with the logic that prophetic action had value in itself.[22]

The evangelical encounter with the New Left significantly widened the
range of social activism in a tradition previously marked by apoliticism
and passive ballot punching. Even *Christianity Today*, the most influential
magazine of the evangelical establishment, printed an article in 1978 by Ron
Sider suggesting the use of blockades as a form of nonviolent intervention.

Soon evangelicals on the right would co-opt that very strategy to use at abortion clinics. These methods, however, were rooted partly in the activism of the New Left, mediated by the Post-Americans who pioneered the postwar incarnation of the gospel as public drama.[23]

IV

The Post-Americans also echoed the New Left's polarizing rhetoric, heeding the call of movement intellectual C. Wright Mills "to serve as a moral conscience and to articulate that conscience" in words. In his 1958 "Pagan Sermon to the Christian Clergy," Mills had told spiritual leaders they were operating in "moral default" by not speaking out against the madness of the nuclear arms race. Christians, he implied, should feel the burden of moral imperatives in ways that secular leftists could not. The Post-Americans complied with Mills's admonition, speaking out with spiritual language and moral clarity not only against nuclear weapons, but also against poverty, sexism, imperialism, and the very structure of American society. Helping to break the mid-century evangelical hesitance to tie faith closely to politics, the Post-Americans not only extended the limits of activism but also applied moralistic, absolutist rhetoric to social issues.[24]

This point must be stated carefully, for mainstream evangelicals did occasionally use a language of stark dualism toward political ends. Billy Graham, for instance, emphatically denounced communism at evangelistic crusades in the 1950s. But on most domestic issues, neo-evangelicals practiced moderate speech in order to earn a respected place in civil discourse. The Post-Americans, however, began to sound more like their fundamentalist grandparents than their neo-evangelical parents in their abundant use of apocalyptic language. Their recovery of words such as "satanic" and "demonic," however, was as indebted to the moral rhetoric of the New Left and the counterculture as much as to fundamentalism. Though some sectors of the New Left exhibited hostility toward faith, the movement nonetheless nurtured an ethos that resonated with many characteristics of conservative religion, particularly in the movement's search for meaning and authenticity, its demand for total commitment, and its view of the world as divided between light and darkness. InterVarsity's president John Alexander wrote that leftist radicals "almost consider themselves today's Christians, the only ones dedicated to Christ's concern for the peopleness of people. They are the righteous. The segregationists and inactive are the sinners." Moreover, some in SDS nurtured hope of a revolution that would reconfigure cosmic history, not unlike the Christian conception of the "Second Coming." There was, according to one young evangelical, a "sureness that a Judgment Day is coming to help the Oppressed." Imbued with this apocalyptic sensibility, the New Left denounced attempts to implement social justice through the rational application of science, technology, and education. John F. Kennedy's liberal strategy of applying steady and incremental pressure on southern states was especially abhorrent to SDS. The New Left instead echoed the call by the Student Nonviolent Coordinating Committee for a theologically pessimistic, activistic role in forcing an immediate end to the sin of segregation. Some northern evangelicals, themselves believers in original sin and tied ecclesiastically to the abolitionists of the nineteenth century, identified with this religiously saturated call for an end to segregation. Though evangelical radicals' belated response failed to help shape the movement against segregation, the inspiration of civil rights action decisively drove them past liberal perspectives and restrained speech.[25]

Evangelical radicals extended moralistic civil rights rhetoric to global and cosmic realms. Questions of international economics, explained writers in *The Post-American*, were moral, not merely technical or managerial. Evil itself resided in bureaucratic capitalism and the military-industrial complex. Jim Wallis refused to use liberal language of "mistake" or "blunder" to describe the Vietnam War. Instead he called it a "lie . . . a crime and a sin . . . that continues to poison the body politic." Wallis's colleague Bob Sabath developed theological categories to reflect this dualistic rhetoric. Describing American power as a satanic principality, Sabath coupled the Apostle Paul's description of "principalities and powers" with leftist fears of government power and economic bureaucracy. He expounded Romans 13, a scriptural passage that urged submission to governing authorities, in the context of the thirteenth chapter of Revelation, a passage that declared open resistance to the Roman Empire. "Here was the Christians' first dictate against the hellish iniquities and arrogant nationalism of the world's most powerful nation," explained Sabath. In only thirty-five years, the early church had transformed from a law-abiding people, suggesting that "even a legitimate state . . . is always in danger of becoming satanic. There is an inevitable drift toward the demonic." Wallis grounded this hermeneutical judgment in the creation account. Supernatural beings had been created for human good, he suggested. But they had revolted. Consequently, they have "an ever-present tendency to usurp God's intended purpose for them and hold humans in bondage to their pretentions to universal sovereignty." For evangelical radicals, good and evil were not abstract categories; they came to life in supernatural demons that infested both historic and modern institutions.[26]

The Post-Americans interpreted evil in very specific ways. They saw demons at work, for example, in the concentrated power of elite Latin American oligarchs. Unlike many in the New Left, they saw evil in the totalitarian regimes of Stalin and Mao. But like the New Left, they concentrated most on the "United States of Babylon." Bible study notes from the early years of the Post-American community encouraged followers toward "resistance to the principalities of death" in the administration of Richard Nixon and corporate America. Structural injustice in America, explained member Boyd Reese to the InterVarsity chapter at SUNY-Binghamton, could be blamed on "principalities and powers." Member Joe Roos suggested that Watergate and the Vietnam War, which represented America's "pinnacle of arrogance," confirmed the role of Satan in temporal affairs. "The prince of this world," Roos explained, "encourages and delights in the consequent suffering and moral decay." That the Post-Americans' vitriolic attacks on the power elite of America were met with equally contentious responses from members of the establishment—"We've been the most assailed by people and institutions of wealth and power," several members boasted to a *Washington Post* reporter in 1976—only confirmed their sense of embattlement at the hands of the principalities. A controlling metaphor of warfare between good and evil—"The church of Jesus Christ is at war with the systems of the world"— characterized evangelical radical conceptions of American society.[27]

If the Post-Americans suggested that America had succumbed to the forces of evil, they nonetheless predicted ultimate victory. The cosmic war between good and evil would be won through the crucifixion, resurrection, and ultimate triumph of Christ. The cosmic implications of Christ extended beyond "the liberal . . . theology which reduced Jesus to a Galilean boy scout." Ultimately, explained Boyd Reese, Christ would "defeat the demonic nature of American power brokers, thus offering hope for social justice that secular messianisms could not." Since there were "spiritual as well as political dimensions to the struggle for justice, with praying together one of the most radical political actions people can take," Reese explained, "it will not be long until American power will have to answer to Christian prayer and protest." Evangelical radicals fought alongside God as foot soldiers in a battle against American principalities that would soon be won.[28]

The Post-Americans thus readily appropriated radical rhetoric and activism toward both evangelical and leftist ends. Wallis, in fact, sought to integrate the two movements. He envisioned a mass of evangelical activists filling the ranks of the fragmenting and increasingly violent New Left. These activists—equipped with spiritual resources to nurture justice, compassion, and community—would recover the best virtues of the old New Left as they usurped the movement's recent forms. Evangelical radical appeals to Jesus over Marx, Mao, and the Weathermen were not evidence of an evangelistic ploy, as some critics believed. Even as evangelical radicals tried to convert secular leftists, they made common cause with leftists on issues such as the Vietnam War and nuclear proliferation. Their multiple agendas blended together, blurring lines between politics and faith. This was precisely the point—to tie the sacred to the temporal so closely that the two were indistinguishable.

This integration of the sacred and temporal by evangelical radicals points to developments in broader evangelicalism. Carrying on fundamentalist and leftist traditions of contentious political behavior, evangelical leftists prefigured the political style of the religious right. Jerry Falwell, Pat Robertson, and Operation Rescue's Randall Terry, though adopting a very different political perspective from Wallis, benefited from his precedent. After Robertson declared at the National Association of Evangelicals' fortieth annual convention in 1982 that "we must be prepared for radical action against the government," a key member of the evangelical left wondered, "How is it that respectable Evangelicals can be flirting with radical activism?" The answer, ironically enough, lay in part with evangelical radicals on the other end of the political spectrum. Modeling an activist method and an absolutist, moralistic style, the Post-Americans helped show the way for other evangelicals to bridge the New Left and the religious right.[29]

* * *

Ironically, the antiwar activism of Wallis has been acknowledged least by his political allies. Despite their active presence and clear resonances with the New Left, evangelical radicals cannot be found in histories of the modern American left.[30] New Left historiography, while increasingly less circumscribed in recent years by rigid boundaries and a master narrative of declension with SDS at the center, has found little room for the incongruities of evangelical radicalism. The literature's preoccupation with the declension of certain "pure" forms of the New Left often leaves out many leftists who, after the disintegration of SDS, did not join the Weathermen, drop out, or face co-optation by the right. Many worked in such unlikely sites as business and professional circles, non-elite universities, small towns, and mainline religious denominations. The Post-Americans, for example, embraced traditional spirituality and repudiated SDS's spiral into violence, fragmentation, and authoritarianism. Yet, significantly, they shared SDS members' profound sense of dislocation and critique of traditional society. In fact, some, denouncing the illiberal turn of the movement, characterized themselves as the true carriers of the movement. During the 1973 Thanksgiving Workshop, Wallis claimed to represent the *real* New Left. His audacity, no doubt, hurt his standing in leftist circles, if he was noticed at all.[31]

As the Post-Americans coupled New Left sociology and *Christianity Today's* theology, they enjoyed surprising resonance within evangelical institutions. Fellow travelers at Wheaton College, Calvin College, InterVarsity Christian Fellowship, and Fuller Seminary shared Wallis's critique of Christians "whose god is American, white, capitalist, and violent; whose silent religion and imagined neutrality goes hand in hand with 'nigger' and 'napalm.'" Even Leighton Ford, an evangelist and close colleague of his brother-in-law Billy Graham, echoed these themes, if in slightly muted terms: "We've seen the burned out ghettoes . . . the rural slums . . . the bodies at Kent State . . . the stupidity and greed that has killed Lake Erie. No longer can we labor under the illusion that God is our great white father and that Jesus Christ wears red, white, and blue." More than a few respected mainstream evangelicals like Ford would go on to sign the Chicago Declaration, which challenged "the misplaced trust of the nation in economic and military might—a proud trust that promotes a national pathology of war and violence which victimizes our neighbors at home and abroad." The antiwar impulse of evangelical radicals—represented in Chicago by Post-Americans Joe Roos, Wes Michaelson, Boyd Reese, and Jim Wallis—animated these words and hardened the new evangelical attention to social injustice begun by the civil rights movement.[32]

CHAPTER 4

Mark Hatfield and Electoral Politics

We must be prepared to hear God's word of judgment
upon our nation, for hope comes only when we
acknowledge our fallenness and repent. But then, we
must also offer a word, and an example, of hope and
renewal.

—Mark Hatfield

On a Monday morning in 1971 soon after the first issue of the *Post-American* was released, Jim Wallis took a telephone call from Senator Mark Hatfield, a Republican from Oregon. "Is it true," asked the senator, who over the weekend had perused the provocative tabloid, "that there are other evangelical Christians against the war?" This brief exchange sparked a long and unlikely friendship between the long-haired radical and the silver-haired politician voted the best-dressed man in government. Wallis would go on to draft pieces of legislation for Hatfield's staff and offer spiritual support to Hatfield himself. The Senator in turn would invite Wallis to Washington and then introduce the Post-Americans to the corridors of power when they moved to the nation's capital four years later. On one memorable occasion, Hatfield, with a glint in his eye, led Wallis and a ragtag group of Post-Americans into the Senate Dining Room for a meal. Hatfield became a patron and critical ally who offered the Post-Americans and other young members of the evangelical left a measure of credibility. "They are among the finest young people I have ever met," wrote Hatfield to a prospective landlord for the Post-Americans, "and I can assure you of their unquestioned integrity, high character, and responsibility." Wallis's father, returning the compliment in a letter to a critic of his son, wrote, "Is not Mark Hatfield, for instance, who is a U.S. Senator, an *authority* in this land? He, as you know, is a real Evangelical."[1]

Even conservative critics could not deny Hatfield's evangelical credentials. He could pray with the passion of a Southern Baptist, ruminate about the integration of faith and learning with a starched Wheaton evangelical, and rail against civil religion with an evangelical radical like Wallis. In fact, Hatfield's ability to bridge divides in the evangelical world—between old and young, radical and conservative—suggested the broader promise of the evangelical left as it emerged in the early 1970s. Hatfield, who showed the way for many evangelicals into the world of organized mainstream politics, stood as an exemplar of progressive politics and evangelical piety. He was regularly cited as a model politician and man of God during his meteoric rise from Oregon state legislator to two-term governor to U.S. senator to vice-presidential contender. His popularity and influence in evangelical circles, even as he pushed for civil rights legislation and against the Vietnam War and capital punishment, underscored the flexibility of evangelical politics and the fluidity of political parties before both hardened in the late 1970s.

I

The hard work but relative security of the lower middle class marked Hatfield's early years. Born on July 12, 1922, to a schoolteacher mother and a blacksmith father who worked for the Southern Pacific Railroad, Hatfield grew up in the logging town of Dallas, Oregon. The texture and rhythm of his days revolved around lumber. He played amid the rugged beauty of the mountains and lush forests of the Pacific Coast Range between the ocean and the Willamette Valley. A whistle in the town's fire station blew at noon and five o'clock to signal that it was quitting time—and that the women had better have a meal ready soon. Insulated by a small family size and two secure jobs, Hatfield's family weathered the Great Depression with relative ease. There was always plenty to eat, and they had enough money to send young Mark off to Willamette University in the state capital of Salem. The Hatfields were also politically active as faithful Republicans. At ten years old Hatfield pulled wagons full of Herbert Hoover campaign literature door to door. As a teenager he devoured Hoover's *The Challenge to Liberty* (1934), an attack on Franklin Roosevelt's "imperial presidency." He mourned the end of Prohibition and denounced federal consolidation of power in the New

Deal. As a college student at Willamette, he worked for the Oregon Secretary of State and as a tour guide at the Oregon State Capitol Building. Hatfield, who had a key to the governor's office, sometimes went in and sat in the governor's desk chair, dreaming of a glorious career in politics. In his senior year the future governor ran for student body president. He lost, for the last time in what would become a remarkable forty-five-year run in political office.[2]

If prosperity launched Hatfield on a trajectory of political success, tragedy and war pushed his politics in a progressive direction. When Hatfield was seventeen, his car struck a young woman crossing the road, killing her. His journey through the court system, which found him civilly, but not criminally, liable, encouraged his progressive views on criminal rights and his animus against "law and order" rhetoric in the late 1960s. Hatfield's navy service in the South Pacific in World War II after college graduation similarly transformed his views on diplomacy. His job as a lieutenant was to ferry loads of Marines on the USS *Whiteside* ashore at Okinawa and Iwo Jima—and then return the dead and wounded to the battleship. The whistle of bullets, the noise of 16-inch guns, a near hit from a Kamikaze pilot, and the gaping wounds of his comrades shattered Hatfield's innocence. Months later he was among the first Americans to see the devastation of the nuclear strike on Hiroshima. "Here were people dehumanized in my mind throughout the war, thinking of them as one vast, massive enemy, not human, not like any of us," wrote Hatfield. "Now on their shore, I knew the brilliant truth. They were exactly like us, suffering, afraid—human. Oh, so human. As the adults relaxed and smiled, as my lunch was completely given to the children, my loathing vanished. I stood awash, clean in an epiphany which has never deserted me. Hatred had gushed out, transmuted into the powerful balm of compassion." Before returning home, Hatfield sailed to Haiphong in Indochina, where he witnessed what he described in a letter to his parents as the "wealth divide between the peasant Vietnamese and the colonial French bourgeoisie." This he blamed on French colonizers, a conclusion that would later inform his contrarian stance on the Vietnam War.[3]

After studying political science at Stanford University in the late 1940s, Hatfield settled in as an assistant professor at his alma mater in Salem. His participation, however, in the local Cancer Society chapter, the local Radio Free Europe committee, and the Citizens Committee for the Hoover Report— and his speeches at any Rotary, Kiwanis, union hall, or grange that would have him—pointed to political ambitions. At age twenty-eight, to the accompaniment of a student brass band playing "Battle Hymn of the Republic,"

Hatfield filed as a candidate for the state legislature. After an energetic 1950 campaign, he beat out a field of six to win a term as the representative of Marion County in Oregon's lower assembly. For the next several years, Hatfield, still a bachelor, taught political science at Willamette College in the mornings, walked across the street to the Oregon Capitol Building for legislative sessions, and then returned to his parents' home to sleep at night.[4]

Hatfield's faith deepened as his political stature rose. Raised in an apolitical Baptist church that discouraged his youthful enthusiasm for politics, Hatfield had soured on institutional Christianity. When a member of Willamette's InterVarsity chapter asked about his religious philosophy, Hatfield could only mutter something about the Golden Rule. Jarred by his own lack of spiritual depth, Hatfield made a decision that reoriented his life. Declaring that he "wanted to live the rest of my life only for Jesus Christ," he asked God to "forgive my self-centeredness and to make me his own." Hatfield's conversion experience did not lead him in a typical direction to the right or toward apoliticism, despite new pressure applied by his old Baptist church. "Oh, Brother Mark," several members cautioned, "we're so glad to see you squared away with the Lord. Now you'll get out of that horrible slime of politics. . . . God has called you to preach, Brother Mark. We want you to go to seminary." He instead immersed himself in state politics, convinced that, for him, the demands of faith required public service. After winning reelection as a state representative in 1952, Hatfield then won election as Oregon's secretary of state. In 1958, at thirty-six, he became the youngest governor in Oregon's history. In 1962, a year when Democrats swept offices statewide, he won a second term. Hatfield, described by political observers as "a verbal spellbinder," dark and "too handsome, almost, for his own good," shot to prominence. Only his state's geographic isolation held him back from national office.[5]

As Hatfield's meteoric rise in Oregon politics progressed, it became increasingly clear that he represented a progressive wing of the party of Lincoln. To be sure, he was still a Republican. In fact, Hatfield was an unambiguous social conservative on abortion before the party itself became more consistently pro-life. He was also an anti-New Deal fiscal conservative. But his populist call for "genuine political, economic, and ecological self-determination" meant reducing "excessive concentration of power" everywhere, not only in the executive branch of government and labor unions, but also in big corporations and the military. Hatfield's emphasis on decentralization, voluntarism, compassionate globalism, political localism, and populist electoral measures such as the recall, initiative, and referendum in fact dovetailed nicely with Oregonian tradition. Hatfield often cited his state's historic leadership in women's suffrage, child-labor laws, worker benefits, and the progressive income tax. He opposed a state sales tax, arguing that it was a regressive tax that hit low-income earners disproportionately. He sought and received labor support, earning the endorsement of the Teamsters in his 1952 run for the governorship. Hatfield's leadership of the Young Republicans in Oregon in 1949 resulted in a platform that included aid to the poor and elderly, taxes on the timber industry to fund environmental research, and an end to racial discrimination. Dismissing the racial overtones that plagued much of the growing conservative movement at mid-century, Hatfield joined the NAACP. In 1953 he successfully introduced a bill that prohibited discrimination in hotel accommodations well before national and most state initiatives. Most Oregon evangelicals supported these initiatives; after all, they came from a governor who regularly stopped his state vehicle to kneel on the roadside to pray.[6]

Hatfield's political nonconformism delighted many of his constituents, who had been raised in Oregon's rich history of bipartisan, independent politics. But it also confounded the media and infuriated conservative critics. One bemused *Los Angeles Times* columnist, after meeting the thirty-two-year-old Hatfield for the first time, wrote that "I would judge from talking with him that he thinks it's wrong to be a conservative and is a little worried lest, by gum, he is. And to compensate for this anxiety, Mark wants the world to know that he's a Republican with an L—a liberal Republican." He "works both sides of the street," one critic of the governor told the *Portland Oregonian*. "One Sunday he will give us as liberal a speech as you will want and the next Sunday will come out with a fundamentalist talk." Nor did Hatfield's combination of political progressivism and religious piety play well in rightist wings of the national Republican Party, which was in the midst of a conservative revival sparked by the rising prominence of Catholic intellectual William F. Buckley and the *National Review*, the student activist organization Young Americans for Freedom, and libertarians Friedrich Hayek and Ayn Rand. This burgeoning conservative movement attacked Hatfield's numerous resolutions in support of civil rights bills at National Governors Conference meetings in the early 1960s.[7]

Hatfield's progressive politics decisively cast him on the side of Nelson Rockefeller in the contentious Republican wars that pit the New York governor against Barry Goldwater, U.S. senator from Arizona and author of *Con-*

science of a Conservative (1960). Hatfield, who was often mentioned as a favorite for a vice-presidential spot should Rockefeller be nominated in 1964, considered himself as something of a "Rockefeller agent of the West," according to one newspaper report. Concerned that the far-right movement might eclipse moderate sectors of the party, Hatfield denounced Goldwater at the 1963 Western Governors' Conference in his rival's home state of Arizona. Hatfield declared, "I have no doubt there are men engaged in the fantasies of sitting in the White House . . . and engaging in a blood bath in carrying out their hate campaigns. [This] would mean the literal destruction of the minorities—Jews, Catholics, and Negroes. I have no time for the extremists' or fanatics' right-wing infiltration of the Republican Party." As the Republican convention approached, Hatfield actively opposed Goldwater's nomination, engineering a decisive 33-18 percent victory for Rockefeller over Goldwater in the Oregon primary.[8]

Hatfield kept up the assault even as Goldwater was securing the nomination. In a combative keynote address at the 1964 Republican National Convention that earned headlines across the nation, Hatfield took aim at many in the convention hall: "There are bigots in this nation who spew forth their venom of hate. They parade under hundreds of labels, including the Communist Party, the Ku Klux Klan, and the John Birch Society." He then called for increased funding of social programs to help the hungry and the elderly; equal opportunity for minorities in education, employment, and housing; and a stop to the still-small American intervention in Southeast Asia. The speech received raucous applause from the Oregon and East Coast delegates but boos and lukewarm applause from others. A bomb threat during the speech prompted an Oregon state trooper to crawl under the platform to check for explosives. The next day, as Republican headquarters was barraged by telegrams calling Hatfield "a traitor to Republicanism" and "a Communist sympathizer," Goldwater won the nomination. The conservative movement had turned into a juggernaut, capitalizing on Cold War fears, white opposition to the civil rights movement, and impressive ground troops from the John Birch Society. The end of liberal Republicanism, crowed conservative theorist Russell Kirk, was at hand. Though an exaggeration, since moderates would soon purge many leading Goldwaterites from the GOP after the candidate's disastrous loss in the general election, Republican moderates like Hatfield nonetheless were caught in the middle. They were wary of the rapidly expanding welfare state presided over by the Democrats, yet estranged from many in their own political party.[9]

The most salient aspect of Hatfield's political identity came to be his views on foreign affairs. In the years following his convention speech, Hatfield questioned whether Vietnam conformed to just war standards of macro-proportionality just cause, and last resort. "Christian doctrines allowing for just wars," he wrote, "would clearly prohibit what we were doing there." These convictions, he explained, were rooted in spiritual sources emanating "intuitively, emotionally, from my depths." He felt "a deep inner peace" that "flowed from seeking God's will," despite the political risk of being one of the first nationally prominent politicians to dissent from the burgeoning conflict in Indochina. At the 1965 National Governors Conference in Minneapolis, Hatfield cast the lone opposing vote against a resolution supporting U.S. military presence in Vietnam. Remarkably, Hatfield cast this vote despite being flown to Washington on Air Force One by President Lyndon Johnson to hear the pro-war case from secretary of defense Robert McNamara, secretary of state Dean Rusk, and a battery of top military generals in the White House's East Room. After a full dose of the "Johnson treatment," the recalcitrant Hatfield declared that "the U.S. must exhaust all avenues toward peace. We have no moral right to commit the world and especially our people to WWIII unilaterally or by the decision of a few 'experts.'" Peaceniks in Portland began to cheer when a car with a Hatfield sticker passed by.[10]

Hawks found Hatfield's views—and unusual set of constituencies—repugnant. Robert Duncan, Hatfield's Democratic opponent for the U.S. Senate in 1966, sought to exploit the state's overwhelmingly pro-war sentiment. At the time, three-quarters of Oregonians supported the war. According to one journalist, Vietnam reignited "smouldering resentments against Hatfield among conservative Republicans—against his pro-labor positions, his national ambitions, his debonair elegance." Though his antiwar position damaged his appeal, the immensely popular governor still managed to eke out a 24,000-vote win. Hatfield joined a coterie of other Senate doves, including Mike Mansfield of Montana; Harold Hughes of Iowa, another outspoken evangelical who went on to nominate the antiwar Eugene McCarthy at the 1968 Democratic National Convention; and J. William Fulbright, author of *Arrogance of Power*.[11]

On his arrival in Washington, Hatfield promptly ratcheted up his antiwar rhetoric. He published a book, *Not Quite So Simple* (1968), that articulated his many criticisms of the war. In an 18-month period between 1967 and mid-1968, he gave over 150 antiwar speeches that pitched a three-point plan to resolve the conflict: de-Americanize the war, stage an all-Asian peace conference, and establish a "Southeast Asia common market." He introduced a bill to abolish the draft and create an all-volunteer military. He appeared with William Sloane Coffin, the liberal Yale chaplain-activist, at antiwar rallies. In a speech at Harvard, Hatfield explained that the United States had confused nationalism with communism and that, to keep the war going, the Johnson administration had begun lying to the nation. These activities belied the location of his seat assignment in the Senate chamber—on the far right of the Republican side of the aisle.[12]

Hatfield's antiwar activities had confounding electoral implications. Peace activists tried to tap Hatfield as a peace candidate for president in 1968. He declined to enter the New Hampshire primary, but then offered his support to the Democratic Eugene McCarthy. In fact, he wore a McCarthy button under his lapel early in the campaign and urged his friends to switch party registration so they could vote for McCarthy. After the hawkish Hubert Humphrey won the Democratic nomination, however, Hatfield threw his support to Richard Nixon, who, after a series of private meetings, seemed to be the least pro-war of the other candidates. Vietnam, which Hatfield called the "overriding issue" of the campaign, trumped his alliance with Rockefeller, whom Hatfield had supported for more than a decade. Hatfield found Rockefeller's answers to his queries unsatisfactory, convincing him that the New York governor had "adopted the basic premises" of the Johnson administration and did not grasp the seriousness of the "mystique of violence that pervades our entire society and erodes our national soul." In return for Hatfield's support, Nixon (with encouragement from Billy Graham, who was present during the vice-presidential deliberations at the Hilton Plaza in Miami) considered Hatfield as his running mate. A Miami newspaper predicted a Nixon-Hatfield ticket on its front page during the 1968 Republican National Convention, and ABC's Peter Jennings was on hand at Hatfield's hotel in case he was chosen.[13]

The Nixon-Hatfield relationship, however, deteriorated rapidly after Nixon's victory over Humphrey. The war, Hatfield repeated over and over, was not only a "war of miscalculation," but also "a singular moral catastrophe." Hatfield attacked defense costs, decried the burgeoning power of the Pentagon and the White House's refusal to submit to congressional oversight, voted to repeal the Gulf of Tonkin Resolution, and called for a day of education and protest. When Nixon announced troop withdrawals, Hatfield introduced a bill that would accelerate the process. Most significantly, in 1970 he cosponsored an "amendment to end the war," which proposed to withdraw from Cambodia in 30 days, remove troops from Vietnam by June 30, 1971, and limit tax monies to the systematic withdrawal of troops. The intent of the Hatfield-McGovern Amendment was to aim "straight at Nixon" by "vetoing the war." The amendment, which lay relatively dormant until the Kent State massacre on May 4, 1970, was finally defeated by a 55–39 vote on September 1, 1970. But it did accelerate antiwar activism, and Hatfield, called "the grooviest senator in the nation" by a student protestor, became the darling of the antiwar student movement as he spoke in favor of amnesty at university rallies.[14]

Hatfield also challenged the White House on a number of domestic issues. He opposed, for instance, Nixon's veto of an appropriations bill for health, education, and welfare programs. Hatfield also helped block two of Nixon's nominations to the Supreme Court. Clement Haynesworth and Harrold Carswell, both conservative Southerners nominated to help swing southern white Democrats toward the Republican Party, fell under scrutiny by opponents of Nixon's "southern strategy" to exploit concerns over the size and interventions of the federal government in racial integration. Concerned that Carswell had incorporated a segregated country club and that he had been biased against civil rights attorneys in the early 1960s, Hatfield told Nixon in a telegram that "the name of G. Harrold Carswell has become a symbol of despair, distrust, and disillusionment." In an interview with the *Washington Post*, Hatfield said, "I'm not going to sacrifice my conscience. My vote is going to be no even if I have to vote that way 9 or 10 times until they appoint someone with a twentieth-century viewpoint." True to form, he cast a GOP vote against the nominee. In a tense Senate chamber Carswell went down to defeat.[15]

Hatfield, aware of his maverick voting record, wondered aloud about his political future. "How many times can you vote against the President," he mused to the *Washington Post*, "and still stay on the ball club?" Unpredictable and difficult to categorize, Hatfield only inconsistently voted as a rank-and-file Republican on economic and social issues. His staff contained more Democrats than Republicans, and the senator was courted as a potential running mate for the Democratic nominee George McGovern in 1972. But few questioned his Republican credentials, which were deeply embedded as a matter of identity more than policy adherence. Not many conservative critics called for Hatfield to leave the GOP as he became one of the most powerful Republicans in the Senate. He would eventually chair the Appropriations Committee and serve as the ranking member of the Energy and

Natural Resources Committee. If Hatfield's resilience could be attributed in part to his adroit political instincts in a progressive state, his brand of politics was possible only in an era before the late twentieth-century culture wars. As Republican intramural contests over Supreme Court nominees demonstrate, the senator's dissenting politics reflected the relative flexibility of party politics during the 1960s and early 1970s. Hatfield persisted, even flourished, under a Republican umbrella that included both Rockefeller and Goldwater.[16]

II

Despite his strong antiwar activism, Hatfield continued to be a welcome presence among many evangelicals. He traveled the evangelical circuit in the 1960s and 1970s, speaking at countless graduations and symposia. He served on boards of evangelical institutions and published books with evangelical publishers. Letters asking for donations to Hatfield's re-election campaigns circulated across the country in evangelical circles. He cultivated close relationships with Billy Graham, Bill Bright's Campus Crusade, Inter-Varsity Christian Fellowship, Carl Henry and *Christianity Today*, and the Southern Baptist Convention. Such close ties suggest the presence of a liberal faction within establishment evangelicalism. In the early 1970s, America's best-known evangelical politician stood as proof of evangelicalism's unsettled political future. In a period of remarkable fluidity, it really did seem as if evangelical politics could take any number of directions.[17]

Hatfield's politics thus inspired a diverse range of responses from evangelicals. Many political moderates admired his legislative work. Robert Linder, an InterVarsity leader and professor of history at Kansas State University, explained that Hatfield "provided the spark of leadership" and "had the voice of authority" to "put into words what we were thinking." His stature convinced some evangelicals, many of whom felt a spiritual kinship with the senator, to oppose the war. And yet many, especially hard-line conservatives, did not. After an antiwar speech at the 1969 U.S. Congress on Evangelism, Hatfield received a letter that read, "I heard you speak at the Men's Fellowship at my church a year ago and at that time you believed in Jesus Christ as your personal Lord and Savior. Now because you won't support the boys in Vietnam and you're fighting President Nixon who has been placed there by God, I know that you're not." In the early 1970s a gradually politicizing Bill Bright of Campus Crusade discontinued his advisory board, which Hatfield served on, partly because of complaints about "so-called Christians like Mark Hatfield." The hostility from an outspoken few in his own spiritual tradition sent the senator into a personal tailspin, wondering if his spiritual and political lives could somehow be resolved. "Continually," he lamented, "it seemed as though I was becoming a divisive force within the evangelical community, a role I had no desire to play. Yet, I felt compelled to say what was on my heart, without compromising any convictions." Being an evangelical moral crusader proved exhausting and politically isolating, and a downcast Hatfield nearly resigned from the Senate in 1970.[18]

At his most disquieted, Hatfield encountered several progressive evangelical groups that gave him hope and persuaded him to carry on his political career. The senator, born into a tradition of fundamentalist localism, felt especially strong kinship with the Post-Americans, grounded as they were in populist, antiliberal activism. Listed as a contributing editor on the masthead, Hatfield contributed numerous articles to the *Post-American*. Wes Michaelson, who worked among the Post-Americans in Washington, served as Hatfield's chief aide and ghost-wrote his memoir *Between a Rock and a Hard Place* (1976). Hatfield and Wallis met regularly in the Senate building for prayer and political collaboration, out of which came the most audacious speech of the senator's career. On February 1, 1973, in front of Nixon, Henry Kissinger, Billy Graham, and 3,000 others at the National Prayer Breakfast, Hatfield called the Vietnam War a "national sin and disgrace." It was a brazen assault on the President, according to UPI reporter Wesley Pippert, that essentially reenacted "one of the most dramatic confrontations since the Prophet Nathan told King David, 'You are the man!'" White House officials, infuriated at his remarks, put Hatfield on the White House "enemies list." The *New York Times* ran a 22-paragraph story on the breakfast that devoted just two paragraphs to Nixon's remarks and 12 to Hatfield's. The *Times* would have been even more fascinated had they known that much of the text—parts taken nearly word for word from a manuscript written by Wallis— had been sent to Washington from a Chicago Ford dealership, which possessed one of the few fax machines that the Post-Americans could use.[19]

If Hatfield's alliance with the Post-Americans took place at the margins of evangelicalism, an encouraging experience at Fuller Theological Seminary occurred at the movement's heart. In 1970 Hatfield witnessed a series of antiwar gestures as he gave the commencement address at Fuller. One-third of the graduating class, which cheered as he walked into the room,

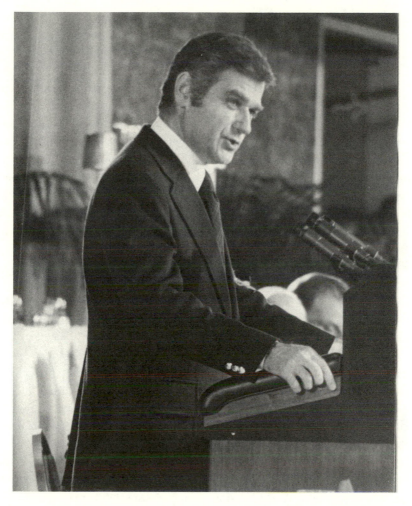

Figure 8. Senator Mark Hatfield, an antiwar Republican senator from Oregon, confronted President Richard Nixon at the 1973 National Prayer Breakfast, calling the Vietnam War "a national sin and disgrace." Infuriated administration officials put Hatfield on an "enemies list." Courtesy of the Archives of the Billy Graham Center, Wheaton, Illinois.

wore black bands on their gowns to signify opposition to the war. Students in a balcony unfurled a banner that read, "Blessed are the peacemakers. We're with you, Mark." The speech that followed, entitled "American Democracy and American Evangelicalism—New Perspectives," affirmed the demonstrating students, many of whom would soon join the emerging evangelical left. Hatfield began his speech, which distilled the senator's socioreligious thought, by reading excerpts of his hate mail. These critics, the senator continued, represented "a theological 'silent majority' in our land who wrap their Bibles in the American flag; who believe that conservative politics is the necessary by-product of orthodox Christianity; who equate patriotism with the belief in national self-righteousness; and who regard political dissent as a mark of infidelity to the faith." Fuller's mandate, Hatfield admonished, was to offer a social and ethical alternative to the "Biblical Nationalists." Fuller's evangelical leadership should revolve around three pressing issues—war, race, and the distribution of wealth—all moral, even spiritual, obligations that could return evangelicalism to the "entirety of the gospel."[20]

Fuller's commencement that year proved transformative for both the senator and the seminary. For Hatfield, the Fuller visit was renewing. "There was an inner urge of joy, peace, and strength which I vividly recall to this day. These brothers and sisters were really with me; their acceptance created a sense of spiritual solidarity. . . . It demonstrated to me that there were countless evangelicals, who because of their faith in Christ, could not condone the immoral and barbarian violence our nation was inflicting throughout Indochina." The surprisingly encouraging response, Hatfield explained later, helped reverse his waning desire to remain in politics. For the seminary, the Hatfield visit stimulated a lively debate. An antiwar faction, made up largely of students and faculty from the School of Theology, squared off against the School of World Mission, which viewed the war as an opportunity to spread the gospel in Southeast Asia. Dozens of Fuller students participated in antiwar protests at the Pasadena post office, and theologians Fred Bush, Jaymes Morgan, and Paul Jewett wrote articles condemning American military intervention. These activities provoked evangelism expert Ralph Winter, who took antiwar activists to task. "How useful is an orgy of confession?" he wrote. "An ascetic self-abuse can all too easily substitute for constructive action." Winter's salvo, in turn, generated a stiff backlash from students and faculty in the School of Theology. A lively exchange of missives on the campus bulletin board followed. Hatfield's visit, coming in the middle of this controversy, elicited both a storm of protest and a groundswell of support. The antiwar faction, led by students Jay Bartow, Randy Roth, and Robert Johnston, wrote a petition expressing "their deep distress over the War in Indochina." "Our understanding of God's Word and its bearing on this question," the statement read, "compels us to speak in support of the Hatfield-McGovern amendment." About a third of the student body and half the faculty signed the petition a week before Hatfield's commencement address.[21]

Hatfield proved equally polarizing in other sectors of evangelicalism. In early 1974 Wheaton College's president Hudson Armerding barred Hatfield from speaking in chapel, relegating him to an auxiliary building. This infuriated hundreds of admirers, one of whom expressed enthusiasm for Hatfield's "reputation as an evangelical legislator" with "high ideals" working in Washington, a place where "nothing good could come out." Students and faculty already participating in regular anti-ROTC and antiwar protests on Wheaton's campus surmised that conservative donors had pressured Armerding. The president's move backfired; it inflamed many faculty and students, who turned out in great numbers to give Hatfield standing ovations whenever he visited campus to give an address. After one visit, the student newspaper's headline read "He Came; He Spoke; and We Were Conquered." Hatfield's experience at Wheaton—marked by generational, political, and institutional cleavage—highlights the multidirectional mobilization occurring within evangelicalism in the early 1970s.[22]

Even as more evangelicals grew uneasy over Nixon's war policies, Hatfield's antiwar leadership did not result in broad-based antiwar activism. Most evangelicals who harbored dissenting views refused to speak out or march. Billy Graham, for example, newly distressed over the Cambodian incursion in 1970 after initially praising Johnson's escalation a few years earlier, refused the many entreaties of young evangelicals to condemn the war. "What can people expect me to do?" he rhetorically asked. "March in protest? Carry a sign? If I do that, then all the doors at the White House and all the avenues to people in high office in this administration are closed to me." Graham, in fact, sought to preserve such access by condemning Hatfield in a phone call with Nixon on the evening of February 21, 1973. In White House tapes an obsequious Graham can be heard telling the President how "terrible" and "embarrassed" he was when Hatfield condemned the war at the Presidential Prayer Breakfast. "To use a platform like that in your presence at a Presidential prayer breakfast," said Graham, "which we leaned over backwards all these years to keep non-political, and to get up and do a thing like that was just inexcusable. And if he has any part in it next year, I don't intend to go." The political aspirations and reluctance of evangelicals to question authority stood in the way of a massive antiwar push.[23]

This conservative pressure discouraged the many moderates with misgivings about the war from articulating their doubts publicly. It also tamped down the edgier elements of evangelical dissent. Only later would Hatfield enjoy the "heartwarming experience" of finding that among the 90,000 readers of InterVarsity's magazine "there were many who were conservative theologically who totally agreed with my stand." But their antiwar dissent remained muted by a still-dominant ethos of pietist personalism. "For all our pompous talk," editorialized one moderate evangelical journal, "we were not there to help the Hatfields who fought alone. We hid our light while Viet Nam died. Many of us even waved flags. Repent all of us."[24]

III

As his critique of Vietnam enjoyed a wider audience, the senator, buoyed by his relationship with the emerging evangelical left, deepened his critique of American society. "Our involvement in Indochina was mistaken, got out of hand," explained Hatfield, "and raised questions about our national character." He argued that the war had laid bare American abuses of imperialism for economic gain, infringements on domestic freedoms, and the idolatry of presidential power. The war also exposed evangelicalism at its worst: a tradition with a watered-down faith willing to baptize whatever the nation did. To be sure, Hatfield explained as the war ground to a stalemate in the early 1970s, civil religion was not uniquely evangelical or American. But American evangelicals certainly had added a "moral and religious tone" to a crusade against "communism abroad and corruption, bureaucratic regimentation, and creeping socialism at home." Hatfield denounced this "tendency to enshrine our law and order and national righteousness," a very different impulse from biblical faith, which rests on "the ultimate authority of Jesus Christ." Evangelicalism, declared Hatfield in mainstream and progressive evangelical magazines alike, had succumbed to a pernicious civil religion, unwilling to assume a prophetic posture in the face of America's sins.[25]

Growing numbers of other evangelicals, often drawing on insights from sociologist Robert Bellah, also denounced evangelicalism's conflation of faith and nation. As Vietnam wore on and the Watergate scandals emerged in

1973, the evangelical left denounced American spirituality as inauthentic, bland, and preoccupied with communism. Civil religion sacralized the status quo, Fuller professor Jack Rogers suggested. He faulted evangelicals for obsessing about the struggle between communism and democracy when the "real issues" were between "rich and poor, strong and weak, and white and nonwhite." Nixon's policies—baptized, they felt, by Billy Graham who all-but-endorsed Nixon in 1972—perpetuated this preoccupation with communism and exposed "the pernicious nature of this civil religion—the religion of Americanism." Graham himself, according to evangelical critics, was the most egregious offender. In a July 4, 1970, sermon at an Honor America Day rally in Washington, D.C., the evangelist urged Christians to honor the nation. "On that day," wrote evangelical antiwar historians Robert Linder (Kansas State), Richard Pierard (Indiana State), and Robert Clouse (Indiana State), "honoring America and God was implicitly synonymous with sustaining Nixon's aims in Southeast Asia."[26]

The nation, continued progressive critics, in fact had never been authentically Christian. Debunking the myth of Christian America in a 1973 commencement address at Messiah College in Pennsylvania, Hatfield contended that American history revealed a superficially religious nation. "The development of America has been a story of shameful deeds committed in the name of the nation," wrote Linder and Pierard. Deists had founded America, they argued, and any sort of evangelical consensus that might have emerged in the nineteenth century had waned in vitality. These historical realities ought to keep at bay "Christian jingoism" and views of America as a "messianic policeman" who would "remake the world in its own image." Another critic wrote, "If we don't eliminate American 'Independence' celebrations, we should, at the very least, see them in their limited, relative, provisional, temporary context. . . . A year of sackcloth and ashes would be better than a year of Disneylike parades."[27]

According to Hatfield, America's egregious failures demanded repentance. The senator ended his National Prayer Breakfast censure of Nixon with these words: "Today our prayers must begin with repentance. . . . We must turn in repentance from the sin that scarred our national soul." A year later in Senate chambers, Hatfield proposed such a process of repentance, formalized in a national day of humiliation. Modeled after Lincoln's "Proclamation of a Day of Humiliation, Fasting, and Prayer" in 1863, Hatfield's proposal called for Americans to "confess our national sins." Thomas A. Carruth, a professor at Asbury Theological Seminary, rented a "wide-area telephone line" to lobby Congress to pass the resolution. Though the bill itself languished in the House after passing the Senate, thousands of congregations observed the day of repentance.[28]

Hatfield's resonance with the New Left, disgust with the Vietnam War, and distaste for civil religion, however, did not mean that he went all the way with his most radical evangelical comrades. Unlike the Post-Americans, Hatfield never corrupted patriotic phrases—such as "Amerika" or "the American Way of Death"—to express contempt toward the nation. He still saw redemptive potential in the nation and sought to engage American political culture constructively. This impulse, even as he criticized the nation, made Hatfield significant and representative of growing evangelical trends. He sought to repair the nation, to invest it with spiritual resources. He worked his way up state and national political structures, seeking justice from within a corrupt system. Like the religious right that would follow, Hatfield balanced revulsion toward a fallen nation and a compulsion to reshape it.[29]

A cadre of progressive evangelical politicians echoed the senator's view that politics was "a legitimate expression of Christian faithfulness" on par with "full-time Christian service." The roster was surprisingly large in the 1970s. Among many others, Michael Haynes served as a three-time Democratic state legislator in Massachusetts, member of the state parole board, and founder of the Evangelical Committee for Urban Ministries in Boston. Iowa's Democratic senator Harold Hughes, Hatfield's closest confidant in the Senate and an outspoken evangelical Methodist, helped expose the unauthorized bombing of North Vietnam and the secret bombing of Cambodia, authored the Hughes-Ryan Amendment forbidding covert operations by the CIA, reduced military aid going to South Vietnam, and took a "pro-life" position on abortion, capital punishment, and poverty. Paul Henry worked on environmental concerns as staff director for the House Republican Conference and as a member of the Michigan State Senate and the U.S. House of Representatives. Don Bonker, an outspoken evangelical from the state of Washington in the U.S. House of Representatives, worked on equitable foreign trade, environmental issues, and human rights. Stephen Monsma, a political scientist at Calvin College and a Democratic member of the Michigan Senate, chaired a natural resources subcommittee and led passage of the environmentally friendly "bottle bill." Evangelical Free Church-affiliated John B. Anderson, who as an independent went on to challenge Ronald Reagan and Jimmy Carter for the presidency in 1980, had earlier voted for the Open Housing Act, pushed for the War on Poverty, and opposed the Vietnam War.[30]

*   *   *

All these politicians, many of whom preceded Jimmy Carter in national politics, saw their work on military, poverty, and environmental matters as an outgrowth of Christian vocation. That faith could bring about political redemption was a message articulated in the 1960s and 1970s clearly, insistently, and powerfully by evangelicals on the left as well as the right. Senator Mark Hatfield, who would send a high-spirited telegram to delegates gathering in Chicago for the Thanksgiving Workshop in November of 1973 and then enthusiastically sign the Chicago Declaration, was his era's most important example of a distinctly evangelical partisan politician.[31]

CHAPTER 5

Sharon Gallagher and the Politics of Spiritual Community

In Berkeley, Washington, Havana, Peking, Moscow,
Paris, Hanoi, Saigon and other locations all over the
world there are people who have received Jesus into their
lives and become members of God's family. . . . He will
teach us how to share mutually such problems as
income, childcare, housing, and education. Among His
people in Berkeley, He will promote alternatives to the
stifling elitism, egoism, and sectarianism which rightly
turns people away and destroys unity.
—first issue of *Right On*, distributed on
Telegraph Avenue in Berkeley in 1969

By the early 1970s political activists, evangelical and secular alike, despaired over the futility of their protests. Racial conflagration persisted, despite the work of Martin Luther King, Jr., and *The Other Side's* John Alexander. Big business remained big, despite New Left critiques by Tom Hayden of Students for a Democratic Society and Jim Wallis of the Post-Americans. The war continued, and Richard Nixon coasted to an easy second victory, despite Senator Mark Hatfield's efforts. As America's cultural and political elites reigned unimpeded, activists felt as if they had exhausted established methods for political change. In 1972 Tom Skinner, the fiery black evangelist so critical of American structures at Urbana '70, explained that he had never seen someone actually get in the system, work themselves way up to a position of power, and then transform that system. "By the time you've done that," said Skinner, "you've had to prostitute yourself on the way up and you forgot what you came there for. . . . You see, the system is essentially too evil to change—it cannot change." Society still needed "radical, revolutionary" efforts to defeat the technocracy.

But not violent efforts, cautioned activist evangelicals. As much as they shared the New Left's practice of participatory democracy and its radical social critique, they criticized its descent into violence. Skinner, for example, condemned attempts to "blow the whole system up, just bomb it out, pick up guns, take to the streets and wipe out the entire establishment and start all over." The "technocracy is so powerful and resilient," he explained, that any such revolution would fail:

> The so-called radical plants a bomb underneath a General Motors plant and blows it sky high and then wipes his hands and says we got General Motors. The truth of the matter is that he hasn't touched General Motors. Tomorrow morning the executive committee of General Motors will call an emergency meeting, they will find a new location and build a new plant; they will double production facilities in the existing plant to make up for the one that was bombed out. The insurance will cover the rebuilding of the new plant and what that doesn't cover will be written off of next year's income tax. So you haven't really touched General Motors, you've simply inconvenienced them. Inconveniencing the system is not the way to radically change it.

Disavowing both liberal and New Left approaches (political conservatism was even less of an option), Skinner proposed a new strategy of social change. Spiritual revolution grounded in historic Christianity would sweep aside established political categories. This "third way" would transcend categories of right and left by establishing micro-communities of authenticity, peace, and justice directed by Jesus. "Have some people who can get together and begin to produce live models of what the world ought to be," suggested Skinner. Such a community would be a "new order," a "beloved community," a "forever family," "a Third Force," as those in the evangelical left variously called this third way. "What Jesus has in mind is, through a radicalized group of people, to produce a new community, a new order of things that will be a live model, on earth, of what is happening in heaven. So when the lonely and the despondent, the unloved, the despised, the hated stand up and say, 'Where has the love gone?' the new order, the new

Figure 9. The staff of *Right On*, the monthly tabloid of the Christian World Liberation Front, sits on the steps of Dwight House in 1971. Courtesy of *Right On/Radix*, Berkeley, California.

community, stands up and says, 'Over here! Love is practiced among us. We are the epitome of love, we live it out.' "[1]

This communitarian vision of radical love inspired a young college student named Sharon Gallagher. Joining a motley group of street people, radical leftists, and disaffected evangelical students amid the Sixties counterculture, Gallagher helped build an intentional community in Berkeley. The Christian World Liberation Front (CWLF), one of dozens of evangelical communes (and thousands of Jewish, Buddhist, Catholic, and secular communes) throughout the United States, sought to construct an alternative path of spiritual fervor, social egalitarianism, and local community. Occupying nearly half a dozen communal houses that dotted the Berkeley flatlands, CWLF published a magazine that printed tens of thousands of copies a month, regularly leafleted the UC-Berkeley campus, ran an organic farm in Northern California, launched a free university, and protested against Richard Nixon, the Vietnam War, and nuclear power plants. All the while, members of "God's Forever Family," as CWLF sometimes called itself, met every Saturday evening to pray and sing songs such as "They Will Know We Are Christians by Our Love." In their rejection of "hackneyed categories of Left and Right" and pursuit of a third way of authentic spirituality, Gallagher and her colleagues add complexity to the usual narrative of postwar evangelicalism that features suburban southern Californians who embraced the defense industry and the Reagan Revolution. CWLF, repudiating conventional politics, sought to overcome the dehumanizing forces of the technocracy by pursuing a new politics of spiritual community.[2]

I

Sharon Gallagher's fundamentalist background in the Plymouth Brethren Church belied her future as a progressive evangelical. Raised in the San Fernando Valley in the 1960s, she was carted by her minister father and mother all around southern California. In Watts her father sometimes preached to a black chorus of encouraging "Amens" and afterwards settled down to an afternoon meal of chicken, sweet potatoes, and pies. On other Sundays she visited Hispanic congregations in the barrios of Los Angeles. Her home church was less exotic, full of first- and second-generation Scots Irish stiffly proud of their plain clothing and lack of choirs, robes, a pastor, and other accoutrements of "worldly churches." Together members of these congregations refused to visit movie theaters in quiet witness against the "cultural waste-land" of nearby Hollywood.

Increasingly, however, the most salient element of Gallagher's childhood was her suburban location. Bored with high school and wishing to test the limits of her religious tradition, she entered and won a beauty contest, then started modeling. At Westmont College, an evangelical liberal arts school in Santa Barbara, suburban expectations heightened. "We were mini-skirted, sports-car conscious," she wrote, recalling the wealthy evangelical students there in the late 1960s. "As a female student I knew that how I looked was my identity, that what I wore was more important than what I thought. My value was determined by who I dated." The standards, she concluded, were more "middle-class American" than Christian. When as a junior she visited an evangelical commune called the Christian World Liberation Front six hours to the north in Berkeley, she marveled at their generosity and social consciousness. Instead of scoffing at "those people," as students at Westmont sometimes referred to hippies and drifters on the streets of Berkeley, CWLF was "sharing God's love with them, giving them food, shelter, and the gospel." After graduating in 1970, she drove north to join the maelstrom of Berkeley politics and to indulge in films, art museums, and edgy music, all cultural delights forbidden by her fundamentalist church. Gallagher was welcomed as a thoughtful and engaging addition to CWLF.[3]

CWLF drew dozens of other evangelical students similarly discontented with the cultural idiosyncrasies, isolationism, and middle-class ennui of their tradition. "Far from being a white, middle class, Gentile, Nordic war god, born in Kansas City—who defends the 'American way of life,'" read a typical 1972 article in CWLF's tabloid *Right On*, "I found that He was a Jew, probably black by Western standards, poor, a conscientious objector, born in a ghetto in the Middle East, and a defender of truth and justice." Another member, disillusioned with pressures at home, declared, "My parents suck wind. They wanted me to be a doctor like my father. They gave me every-thing I ever wanted except love and time from their 'busy schedules.' I got plenty sick of seeing people work their asses off for nothing but money. Big-ger cars, bigger houses, bigger. They want me to be like them in every way. For a steady job I have to have: Haircut, their clothes, degree." Yet another articulated her grievances in free verse: "We left our parents squabbling over their strength, comparing laundry . . . we left that small town . . . and car-ried no schedules." Donald Heinz, a religious studies scholar who spent time as a participant-observer within CWLF in the early 1970s, noted that "it was

Figure 10. Sharon Gallagher joined the Christian World Liberation Front in 1971, edited *Right On*, and helped launch the evangelical feminist movement. Here Gallagher, on left, works with art director Nancy Bishop on an early issue of the magazine. Courtesy of *Right On/Radix*, Berkeley, California.

of immense importance, especially in the early years of CWLF, for its followers to know that Jesus was not middle class. To have freshly stolen him back from the churches, where he had been kept for years, was a major cause of group cohesion and strength." Disaffection with middle-class culture attracted Gallagher and hundreds of other evangelical students to Berkeley in search of something more authentic.[4]

Many of these disenchanted students who joined in the early 1970s were startled to learn the story of CWLF's origin. Launched in 1969 as an experimental evangelistic outreach to street people and radical students near the volatile University of California-Berkeley campus, CWLF came from two unlikely sources. One, shockingly, was a conservative student ministry. Campus Crusade for Christ resonated with right-wing political causes, pursued evangelistic outreach to the "straight, fraternity-sorority crowd," and forbade male staffers from growing long hair. Its founder, Bill Bright, would become a key figure in the rise of the religious right. A second source was the Jesus Movement, a countercultural grassroots spiritual revival originating in southern California that developed a reputation for anti-intellectualism. CWLF's founder Jack Sparks, a former Penn State statistics professor, harnessed the best of these traditions, turning CWLF into a dynamo of youthful enthusiasm, thoughtful social concern, and evangelical spirituality. A mere two years old when Gallagher joined, CWLF was enjoying spectacular growth and stunning prominence. *Right On* rapidly spread through networks of evangelical churches and colleges. Newspapers with a national profile, such as the *Los Angeles Times* and *New York Times*, printed multiple feature stories about CWLF's exploits.[5]

Media outlets were drawn to the incongruity of CWLF's explicit evangelical spirituality in the midst of such a profoundly leftist environment. After getting tear-gassed in a street riot on his first day in Berkeley, Sparks jumped headlong into the fray. He became "Daddy Jack" and exchanged his academic suit and short hair for overalls, long hair, and a beard. Sparks did not, however, trade in his evangelical faith for the Eastern syncretism so popular on Berkeley streets. He co-opted signature issues and borrowed unorthodox methods and language from the left in order to preach Jesus crucified and resurrected. Political wars, racism, imperialism, poverty, and the population explosion, Sparks proclaimed, were rooted in spiritual oppression, which could be relieved by a man "who has all the answers we need— someone who loves YOU." Within months of his 1969 arrival, Sparks's sermons had caused a stir, no small accomplishment in Berkeley.[6]

Using revolutionary language as an evangelistic tool, Sparks renamed the fledgling Campus Crusade chapter in a blatant rip-off of the Third World Liberation Front, an activist group launched in 1968 at UC-Berkeley. CWLF also went by the "Christian Revolutionary Medical Committee" when publishing a handbook on what to do when tear-gassed at a protest. The "People's Committee to Investigate Billy Graham" took busloads of Berkeley students and street people to a crusade in Oakland. The "Christian Revolutionary Art Center" advertised sweatshirts with slogans such as "Jesus the Liberator" and "Wanted: Jesus Christ." Whatever its name, CWLF tirelessly launched energetic campaigns. In July 1969, *Right On*, preaching liberation from "exploiters" and "rich men," rolled off the press. During the fall semester of 1969, CWLF became an official Cal student organization and promptly blanketed Berkeley with tens of thousands of tracts entitled "Moratorium on Internal Wars" and "Jesus in Berkeley." Another leaflet mimicked the countercultural style, even as it disparaged some elements of the Berkeley Liberation Program. BLP's manifesto featured a clenched fist overtop thirteen demands, the last of which read, "We will unite with other movements throughout the world to destroy this motherfuckingracistcapitalistimperialist system." CWLF's version—thirteen demands labeled "New Berkeley Liberation Program"— also criticized high rent, war, environmental degradation, oppression, and racism. But it also implied that radical politics was not a magic elixir. In fact, CWLF urged the tract's readers to "RADICALIZE THE REVOLUTIONARY MOVEMENT!" Jesus, the tract read, had proclaimed a spiritual revolution to bring about fundamental change: "Accept Him as your Liberator and Leader; then join others of his Forever Family here to change this world."[7]

CWLF's appropriation of revolutionary rhetoric infuriated Berkeley left- ists, who saw evangelism, not their shared social critique, as CWLF's most operative ambition. Richard York, a long-haired Episcopal priest who ran the Free Church of Berkeley, told the *Los Angeles Times* in February 1970 that CWLF "only looks like part of the radical movement." York speculated that many of their members "are not converts off the street but fundamentalist college students. They put on hippie clothes to go over to Telegraph." An edi- torial in the *Daily Californian*, UC-Berkeley's student newspaper, worried that faith, especially of the Christian variety, might function as a pacifying diversion from total resistance to Nixon and the war. The "Krishna Krazies" and "the little Buddhist ladies" were merely "a manifestation of our time, like dope and rock music." But groups like CWLF were in a different category altogether. "What riles me," exclaimed the editorial, "is the Goddam Christians!"[8]

CWLF, to be sure, provoked much of the bile. Ahead of leftist activists in October 1969, CWLFers reserved the steps of Sproul Hall for a lecture by Chinese refugee Calvin Chao on the evils of Mao and the virtues of Christ. Wanting the steps of Sproul for themselves on Moratorium Day, inflamed antiwar activists and Maoists set up an amplifier next to Chao, threw rocks into the crowd, and set fire to the nearby ROTC building. CWLF also sought to infiltrate SDS. At a 1970 regional meeting of SDS in Berkeley, CWLF nearly hijacked the proceedings. After one young evangelical declared, "I propose that—along with politics—Jesus Christ be discussed as the ultimate solution to the problems facing the world," two dozen CWLFers applauded and tried to force a vote on the resolution. The irate SDS regional chair yelled, "We will not discuss issues of a nonpolitical nature." Members of CWLF shouted back that they were in fact political revolutionaries, but that they followed "God, not men." They subsequently staged a sit-in front of the platform, demanding that SDS "live up to its middle name and permit all views to be heard." Screaming "Pigs! These are pigs sent by the American government!" SDSers rushed the two dozen evangelical protesters, shoving, kicking, and dragging them out the doors of the meeting hall. The next year, after *Right On* had peppered radical underground tabloids with insults, *Ramparts*, the brash muckraking monthly from San Francisco, responded. It described the faith of the CWLF as only for "the fearful, the guilt-ridden and the childish, for those unprepared to dive, to make their faith leap into a political reality or mystical depth." Calling articles in CWLF's tabloid *Right On* "nothing but half-baked and awkward attempts at political relevancy," *Ramparts* argued that the evangelical commune was instead a front for political conservatives, that they were run by "right-wing sugar-daddies." CWLF, denying right-wing associations, responded by accusing SDS and Black Power advocates of male chauvinism, sexual deviance, and hypocrisy in demanding ideological conformity.[9]

Mutual hostility between *Right On* and *Ramparts*, however, gave way to a growing amount of shared social and political space. In fact, dozens of students and street people on Telegraph Avenue began to embrace "Jesus the Liberator." In 1970 members of CWLF rejoiced at the news of "a number of new brothers and sisters who've become Christians recently, including Greg, Wayne, Dave, Ricardo, Carol, Jackie, and others." Even more were converted during confrontations on the street. Within hours, CWLF would baptize the new converts in Sproul Plaza's Ludwig's Fountain. Among them was David Fetcho, a writer for the *Berkeley Barb*, practitioner of Ananda Marga, and an instigator of the People's Park demonstration. Another convert was "Susan," an SDS activist who read an article in *Time* magazine that described CWLF as "brazenly co-opting the Movement in the name of Jesus." The disillusioned daughter of a Republican "middle-class bag with a pool and all the rest," Susan angrily drove a bus straight to Berkeley to "find out who in hell these people were and rebuke them." But no matter how strident her rebukes, "no matter what I did, it was love toward me." Members of CWLF allowed her to park her VW bus in the driveway of one of their community houses and invited her to meetings where they talked about authentic love. "I went up to the leader after it was over. How can I find that kind of love? He told me to ask Christ into my life and asked me if I wanted to pray with him." A short time later "I had an immediate awareness of supernatural presence. . . . I had been horribly lonely, even in the presence of other people. I have a sense of not being alone anymore." Susan, like Weathermen Randy Berdahl and Jim Fox, had gotten "saved." By early 1970, less than a year after Sparks moved to Berkeley, thirty people lived in three community houses. By 1972 *Right On* enjoyed a circulation of over 50,000. By 1974 CWLF had nearly 200 members in "God's forever family" and a staff of 30 that oversaw its mushrooming programs.[10]

As Berkeley leftists joined the former Campus Crusade chapter, CWLF turned more authentically countercultural. Rhetoric initially utilized for evangelistic purposes evolved into deepened expressions of angst over middle-class conservatism. Susan, after converting to evangelical faith, retained her leftist politics. She worked with farm workers and helped write new tracts that expressed her continuing left-wing commitments. One read "OFF ROTC— Out of Viet Nam." Another urged Berkeley residents to come to a meeting in which CWLF would plan action against poverty, Nixon, and "tyrannical forces and powers." At Christmas members put Santa Claus on trial for "economic imperialism." No friend of the Vietnam War or Richard Nixon's politics, CWLF protested the president's appearance in San Francisco by distributing antiwar leaflets and waving signs that read "Turn to Jesus, Mr. President." Other members picketed military bases to protest Vietnam, Sears for failing to offer health insurance, the Soviet embassy for persecution of Jews, and flesh merchants in Manhattan for exploiting women "in a male chauvinist fit of lust and greed." In front of hundreds of spectators at Sproul Plaza, CWLF's street theater department regularly performed caustic, satirical skits denouncing the dehumanization of the University of California bureaucracy and the institutional evil of the U.S. "secular superstate." "There were so many protests," remembered Sharon Gallagher, that "it was a blur." *Ramparts*, in its 1971 denunciation of CWLF, overlooked evidence that faith animated not only members' evangelism, but also a politics that was turning increasingly leftist.[11]

As an organization, CWLF used a strategy of co-belligerency, generally conducting demonstrations within demonstrations. Members often affirmed the causes of leftist protesters, sometimes chanting along, sometimes chanting alternative slogans. Like secular leftists in Berkeley, CWLF condemned landlords for their greed in charging exorbitant rents. But in a leaflet entitled "Why Your Landlord Makes Money" the group asserted that in addition to the coercion of public denunciation, the spiritual regeneration of landlords would make the biggest difference. "Pray for your landlord," CWLF urged, "that his entire being, including his warped sense of values, will be changed as he gets into Jesus." Similarly, during San Francisco's Mobilization Parade on November 15, 1969, 200 CWLF members marched with 150,000 other protesters and distributed 60,000 leaflets urging an end to the war. But they also declared that Jesus was the real solution and condemned the most radical protesters for trying to destroy American society with violence. CWLF, evolving rapidly amid the tumultuous atmosphere of Berkeley, emerged as a mix of leftist politics and evangelical spirituality.[12]

As their political dissent became more explicit, CWLFers erased signs of their Campus Crusade affiliation. Sparks would later say that "the work I was doing was too hot for [Crusade] to handle." Though CWLF continued to promote spiritual liberation through Jesus Christ rather than political liberation through Mao, its language and grievances, especially as more radicals converted, increasingly mirrored those of the New Left. Campus Crusade thus became a victim of its own evangelistic success. When the new emphases frayed relations between CWLF and its well-scrubbed middle-class sponsors, the organizations parted ways. The divorce, while amicable, was so pronounced that most members in the 1970s were oblivious to the group's origins amid the increasingly motley crew of leftist radicals, street people, students on drug trips, recently released mental patients, and adherents of marginal cults. David Gill, who joined in 1971 and became coeditor with Sharon Gallagher of *Right On*, was appalled to discover that "some right-wing Crusade types" had founded CWLF.[13]

II

If CWLF's politics were transformed, the foundations of their faith were not. Like others in the emerging evangelical left, members of CWLF grounded their activities in Christian spirituality. Biblical allusions and spiritual disciplines coursed through their daily lives. Battling an evil war and a bureaucratic society that failed to stamp out poverty and racism, they felt a deep existential sense of human sin and social depravity. At the same time they believed in Jesus Christ as the bridge between the depravity of the earth and the integrity of the divine. Authentic spirituality, CWLF contended, attended to these realities and helped to confront the plastic, authoritarian culture of the technocracy.

Even as CWLF sought to retain authentic spirituality, it exploded the cultural boundaries of established evangelicalism. As part of the growing Jesus Movement, members pushed against old denominational allegiances and experimented with Pentecostal and contemplative modes of worship.

They nurtured the language of the streets, dismissing legalistic fundamentalism in favor of a freer, more spontaneous faith. Men arrived at prayer meetings wearing beards and blue jeans. Women wore peasant skirts. When meetings finally got started—epidemic lateness and socializing characterized their gatherings—members raised their arms and sang enthusiastically. They played guitars instead of pianos and organs. They sang "Kum-ba-yah, My Lord" and "Pass It On," songs inspired by both orthodox doctrine and a countercultural style. Instead of sitting in pews, they perched on folding chairs or sat cross-legged on the floor. Leaders eschewed formal sermons in favor of more casual "teachings" or group sharing that often veered in tangential directions. For the celebration of communion, CWLF served Spanada wine—not grape juice—in Dixie cups. For countercultural evangelicals from conservative evangelical congregations who "just wanted to stand up and scream at the top of my lungs" at the "repetitious absurdity" of formulaic evangelical congregations, these new styles were refreshing in their end run around traditional worship forms.[14]

The relaxed mode of worship and dress extended to language. Many in CWLF defied their parents' censure of profanity. While they never swore in God's name, vulgarities sprinkled *Right On*, internal documents, and daily speech. CWLF also applied colloquial language to Scripture. In *Letters to Street Christians*, the group's translation of the Apostle Paul's letters to the early church, "two brothers from Berkeley"—Jack Sparks and staffer Paul Raudenbush—explained that they wanted "to get the New Testament down for right where kids are today. . . . 'Cause of that we had to get away from formal language and dusty religious rap. Dig it." *Letters* rendered James 2:17–20 as "Brothers and sisters, why say you trust in Jesus when you don't live like it? You're just jiving Him and yourself, and that isn't the kind of faith that makes you a member of God's forever family. . . . You say you believe in God. Right on! So do all the devils in Hell, and it really freaks them out. You'd better dig it: a plastic trust without action is dead. Dig?" This "hippie Bible," as it was known, sold over 100,000 copies in 1970 alone.[15]

Francis Schaeffer, an American émigré in Switzerland, provided a theological rationale for much of CWLF's cultural engagement. In 1955 Schaeffer founded L'Abri Fellowship, a retreat center in a beautiful valley of the Swiss Alps, as a bastion of Calvinist orthodoxy. Initially he restricted music, film, and other exposures to the secular world. By the late 1960s, however, Schaeffer had turned into a hippie guru who blended a countercultural style with traditional defenses of the faith. The bucolic setting of L'Abri and Schaeffer's growing reputation as a thinker willing to take on all philosophical comers attracted youths traveling from India to the West still high on opium as well as earnest evangelical students traveling east from America. They all came in search of resolution to existential questions. In knee-high Swiss knickers, a beige Nehru jacket, long hair, and a white goatee, Schaeffer engaged them through rambling lectures delivered in a high-pitched voice and exchanges over modest meals of soup, cheese, and bread. By the early 1970s Schaeffer, known now for his key role in the formation of the Christian right, had risen as the most influential apologist for the faith among many members of the emerging evangelical left.

Following graduation from Westmont in spring 1970, Sharon Gallagher traveled to L'Abri. During four transformative weeks, Schaeffer and others, including Os Guinness, introduced her to the exotica of the counterculture under the guise of criticism. In fact, according to Schaeffer's son Franky, many luminaries of the sixties counterculture, among them Mick Jagger and Keith Richards of the Rolling Stones, Paul McCartney of the Beatles, Jimmy Page of Led Zeppelin, blues-rock guitarist Eric Clapton, folk artists Bob Dylan and Joan Baez, and drug guru Timothy Leary had encountered Schaeffer. Many of them had visited L'Abri. According to Schaeffer, these figures, while flailing about unsuccessfully for a sense of the transcendent, were helping the evangelical cause by "tearing down the wall of middle-class empty bourgeois apathy." As he taught Gallagher at L'Abri, "you don't hide from culture, you transform it. You go watch a movie and then critically engage it." Gallagher, inspired to join CWLF and write movie reviews for *Right On* "since no other Christian magazines were doing this," delayed her entrance to a Ph.D. program in psychology at the University of Southern California. She transplanted Schaeffer's strategy to Berkeley, where CWLFers fraternized with the dynamic personalities of the counterculture. As coeditors of *Right On*, Gallagher and David Gill interviewed Black Panthers Bobby Seale and Elaine Brown. After *Right On* became a magazine called *Radix*, Gallagher also interviewed Eldridge Cleaver, Noel Paul Stookey (of Peter, Paul, and Mary), Arlo Guthrie, and Theodore Roszak. She sat next to, and befriended, activist Abbie Hoffman in the "alternative press" section at the 1972 Republican National Convention. Meanwhile, contributing editor Steve Turner interviewed John Lennon and Yoko Ono for *Right On* in London. By the early 1970s, CWLF had become an authentic contributor to the Berkeley counterculture.[16]

Francis Schaeffer, who declared that *Right On* was uniquely positioned to "make a clear distinction between the contentlessness of much of the

Figure 11. The Christian World Liberation Front sought to critically engage popular culture and contemporary politics. Here Sharon Gallagher and *Right On* co-editor David Gill speak with Black Panthers Elaine Brown and Bobby Seale in Oakland, California. Courtesy of *Right On/Radix*, Berkeley, California.

Jesus Freaks and something solid built on sufficient content and reasoned comprehension," was the inspiration for much of the group's cultural literacy and social activism. CWLF members, for example, read *The God Who Is There*, Schaeffer's 1968 indictment of the torpor of twentieth-century Western thought. Blaming Hegel's notion of synthetic truth as the precursor of philosophical relativism, Schaeffer led readers on sweeping journeys explicating the deficiencies of modern philosophy. Søren Kierkegaard was a particular target of abuse from Schaeffer for his suggestion that a "leap of faith" was necessary to overcome the paradoxes inherent in Christianity. Western philosophy had abandoned the Reformation synthesis of reason, truth, and faith, Schaeffer expounded, in favor of a soft "new theology" that denied "the God behind truth." Philosophers had separated the "lower story" of natural revelation from the "upper story" of divine revelation. This separation, marked by a "line of despair," left the "upper story" unhinged and susceptible to mysticism, despair, and the nihilism of modern existentialism. Conservative evangelical faith, rooted in verifiable natural theology, alone offered the truth that the counterculture sought in vain. Christians, he had told Wheaton students in 1965, can and should "rationally prove the authority of the Bible." This contention in itself was not innovative. Evangelical scholars had been denouncing philosophical relativism since before

the fundamentalist-modernist controversies of the 1920s. Schaeffer, however, emphasized evangelical rationality as an evangelist and a cultural critic.
While most evangelists conducted altar calls, Schaeffer sought to marshal
secularism against itself through an analysis of modern culture. Out of a
tradition that often demanded distance from contemporary culture, Schaeffer spoke with fluency of Van Gogh, Henry Miller, the Beatles, and Federico
Fellini, describing their common cries of despair sympathetically, but also
showing how they contributed to modern ailments such as environmental
degradation, racism, and "plastic culture."[17]

While evangelical scholars eventually dismissed Schaeffer's analysis of
philosophy, culture, and literature as lightweight, students unversed in high
or popular culture were drawn like moths to light. For Wheaton students
struggling with their college administration for permission to watch the
movie *Bambi*, Schaeffer's calm, didactic discussions of Fellini felt both incongruous and liberating. Schaeffer's riffs on John Cage and Salvador Dali
thrilled culturally literate students worried about the intellectual integrity
of evangelical scholarship. Thousands of evangelical youths—among them
numerous readers and members of CWLF—made their way through the
Swiss mountains to L'Abri. They were, as Schaeffer described in *Right On*,
"young people with strong evangelical backgrounds who say, 'No one has
given us any intellectual answers, and we haven't seen much reality. You are
our last hope. We're ready to throw the whole thing over.'" Those who did
not make the journey heard Schaeffer speak at their evangelical college
campuses—or read one of the over 2.5 million copies of Schaeffer's eighteen
books distributed by InterVarsity Press between 1965 and 1975.[18]

CWLF mimicked Schaeffer's attempts to prove the faith. *Right On* devoted extensive space in 1971 to Christian apologetics, contending for the
existence of God and proofs of Noah's ark and a worldwide flood. Members
also went on the offensive against popular Eastern spiritualities in Berkeley.
They nurtured an exclusive faith, asserting that Christianity was the true
religion and that all others were false. Three former hippies who had dab-
bled in Eastern mystical religions started a branch ministry of CWLF called
the Spiritual Counterfeits Project (SCP). SCP took on a host of "false religions," protesting events led by Sun Myung Moon, Guru Maharaj Ji, and
Maharishi Mahesh Yogi and legally challenging the use of Transcendental
Meditation in public schools. In 1976 SCP filed a civil suit in the U.S. District Court of New Jersey against the New Jersey public schools for including the practice of transcendental meditation in the curriculum. Spirituality

in CWLF, despite its exuberant forms and its indebtedness to a counterculture imbued with mysticism, thus remained startlingly preoccupied with rational proofs of the faith. This posture reflected CWLF's location next to UC-Berkeley and a dozen competing religions—and how embedded CWLF was in a long evangelical tradition of apologetics. CWLF sought both to nurture a thinking faith among young evangelicals and to establish the veracity of the Christian gospel in the modern American university.[19]

CWLF's sense of embattlement—seen in its use of the judiciary to oppose Eastern religions—extended its methods toward confrontation and exuberant expression. At the Democratic National Convention in Miami in 1972, CWLF unfurled a huge banner in the arena that read "Serve the Lord, Serve the People." In a reprise of the Merry Pranksters' tour chronicled in Tom Wolfe's *Electric Kool-Aid Acid Test* (1968), a group of CWLF members set off on their own cross-country tour of 23 states. For over two months in 1973, they visited churches and universities in a large van and picked up new converts along the way. A sound and film crew led by noted documentary filmmaker George Landow came too. The result was the 13-minute cinema-verité style "A Film of Their 1973 Spring Tour Commissioned by Christian World Liberation Front of Berkeley" (1974) that utilized stroboscopic editing and rapid-rhythm shots that ran no longer than three frames. Despite its conventional evangelical origins, CWLF pioneered a new public style, as the staccato effect of "A Film" suggested. Borrowed from the counterculture in Berkeley, CWLF's bombastic language, street theater, breadth of audience, overblown cartoons, and sheer volume helped usher in a new confrontational style—in political protest and in evangelism alike. Significantly, and without pausing to notice, CWLF was accelerating a new era of evangelical cultural engagement.[20]

All the while, the community remained solidly evangelical in its spirituality. Members practiced traditional spiritual disciplines of prayer, worship, and Bible reading. "You must come to know Jesus *existentially*, that is, in your own life-experience," wrote Sharon Gallagher. They wrestled with age-old questions of theodicy. Following the biblical injunction of I Peter 3:15, CWLF members were "ready to give the reason . . . concerning the hope that is within you." Spiritual concerns nearly always trumped political concerns for most other third-way evangelicals too. "Christians derive strength in the inevitability of Christ's victory," wrote Post-American Dennis MacDonald in 1972. "They find their hope and identity in the coming order when all will be new, when men will learn war no more, when justice will flow like water

and when love will be law." Rationally defending theism, spreading the message of Christ's salvific work on the cross, and practicing prayer and worship
thus grounded their community in faith. At the same time, CWLF reformu-
lated these traditional messages of evangelical spirituality. Members discouraged cultural separation and the blind preaching of the gospel in favor of
befriending nonbelievers and modeling a new society. Suggesting that authentic faith should result in a politics that was "ultimately far more revolutionary" than either mainstream evangelicalism (which by the mid-1970s
was preoccupied by debates over biblical inerrancy) or the radical left, this
segment of the emerging evangelical left sought to pioneer a third way rooted
in spirituality.[21]

III

If the emerging evangelical left valued faith, it also cultivated faith in community. Disillusioned by the size of burgeoning evangelical congregations in
suburban Chicago that had succumbed to the technocracy, professional editor and occasional *Right On* contributor Lane Dennis moved to the woods of
Michigan's Upper Peninsula to escape the "mass world with its impersonal
power." The technocracy was "extremely dehumanizing," he lamented, and
had concocted a poisonous cocktail of insidious consumerism, fragmented
relationships, authoritarianism, ecological collapse, and spiritual lethargy.
But Christ offered a third way of "radical communion with fellowman" that
in important respects resembled the secular cooperative living movement.
The more strident advocates of the third way suggested that only communal
living—with its intimate relationships, egalitarian temper, simple living, and
ecological sensitivity—could challenge the life-draining technocracy. "Each
new defection from the old," wrote Dennis, "loosens the grip of official
consensus. Each new community points to what life can be." In fact, echoed
CWLF founder Jack Sparks, "Community actually represents the only effective way to fight the bondage of the economic bureaucracy." Spiritual communities of "loving defiance" could point to a new social order grounded in
authentic relationships, faithfulness to Jesus Christ, egalitarian structures,
and grass-roots activism. Like social analyst Charles Reich, whom CWLFers
often cited in the pages of *Right On*, they believed that "the only way to destroy the power of the Corporate State is to live differently now." Jesus, they

maintained argued, "came to change the system" of the establishment and the radicals by establishing this "third way" of spiritual community.[22]

Abandoning mass structural transformation in order to create these communities led many third-way evangelicals to embrace the small-is-beautiful impulse so prevalent in the broader counterculture. "Small scale culture—based on intimacy, sympathy, trust, and face-to-face relationships—has increasingly been replaced by the mass world with its impersonal power relationships," wrote Dennis in 1973. Watergate loomed large in the imaginations of third-way evangelicals. Worried about computer files, closed-circuit television, cashless monetary systems, and army surveillance, Sharon Gallagher noted that "in our age technology has enlarged the possibilities for destruction and infringement of personal freedom." Railing against mass production, plastics, large supermarkets, suburbs, large-scale evangelism, and mega-churches, these evangelicals despaired at their own complicity. They recognized that each time they purchased a commercial product, watched a movie, even left their hometown communities to pursue education and jobs, they were perpetuating mass culture. Objections to faith in science and to the "spirit-deadening assembly-line routine" of technology pervaded their rhetoric. "The spiritual revolutionary is not enamored with either social or physical sciences," stated CWLF's 1970 "Revolutionary Catechism." "He knows only one true science: the science of the application of God's love to people." This ideal, however, was difficult to imagine after even the most heroic attempts to break the technocracy through mass politics in the 1960s had come to an ig-nominious end. American bigness was hegemonic.[23]

In defiance of mass culture, CWLF and other third-way evangelicals lived small and locally. They tended their souls, as historian and social critic Theodore Roszak suggested in *Where the Wasteland Ends* (1973). They sought true fulfillment in the "do-it-yourself" approach of forming food cooperatives, raising rabbits, tilling gardens, and most of all, fully participating in community life. At Rising Son Ranch, CWLF's organic farm in the rolling hills of southern Humboldt County in northern California, members could "meet the needs of the whole person." "Living quietly out in the woods, tending gardens, sharing meals, and meeting daily to read the Word," explained one of the ranch's leaders, residents "have found the peaceful communal situation they had long desired." Back in Berkeley, members lived communally by sharing resources. Those with extra clothes left articles on the porches of the many CWLF houses for others to take. During worship services, members passed a hat in which those who had extra money added to the collection. Those who needed support emptied the hat. Sharon Gallagher was one of many members who occasionally checked out one of the communal cars at the CWLF office to take visiting guests to the airport or to run other errands.[24]

Third-way evangelicals coveted the closeness, smallness, and earthiness of these communal practices. In CWLF's first five years of existence, people lived together in more than half a dozen buildings, including Dwight House, Grove House, Stuart House, Benvenue House, Roosevelt House, House of Pergamos, Richmond House, and a set of apartments called "God's Love." Members of Dwight House at first advertised their house as a "crashpad" and welcomed people from the street. Seeking to resocialize new converts out of drug use or reprogram them out of Eastern spirituality, CWLF immersed them into a "new meaning system." The system, according to participant-observer Donald Heinz, included "the benevolent warmth of Jack Sparks, living in a Christian House, a continual religious interpretation of all that is happening through prayer, putting one's life under a new norm through private and group Bible study, and, not least important . . . the mutual conversations and consolations that occur in Christian community." Third-way evangelicals termed this spiritual commitment "discipleship," a process that sought to circumvent the fragmentation of modern commuter lifestyles.[25]

The process of discipleship gradually formalized into a rigorous schedule. CWLF's weekly calendar revolved around a group worship service called the "Family Celebration." On Saturdays at 7:30 p.m. young people sprawled across stained, overstuffed couches filling the large living room of Dwight House at 2736 Dwight Way in Berkeley. CWLF's weekly calendar also included a class on the Old Testament at 4 p.m. on Sundays, a "Bible Rap" at 2 p.m. at Ludwig's Fountain on the UC-Berkeley campus during the week, an evening study at 7:30 p.m. on campus, a Wednesday class on "Genesis in Space and Time" at 4 p.m., a Wednesday evening forum called "The Loaded Questions" at 7 p.m., the Thursday evening "Androclean Forum" in Oakland, and a Friday evening "Covenant House Discussion" at 7:30 p.m. The tightly structured schedule reflected an increasingly disciplined community life. After the initial haphazard leadership, lax rules, and inevitable chaos of 1969 and 1970, CWLF imposed stricter rules governing drug use, smoking, house maintenance, and cooking. The "house meetings" held twice a month and more frequent worship services, at first optional, became expected parts of community life. Failure to conform to CWLF standards of piety sometimes resulted in excommunication when members were found to be "living in sin." But patterns of control remained couched in the language of servanthood, discipleship, and close community. "After five years we see a broad fellowship, deep roots in the community, a family that seems to belong here, the feeling that we belong in Berkeley. We're part of what this community is. What we sought within it, a community of believers, has happened," declared founder Jack Sparks.[26]

In addition to cultivating close community, third-way evangelicals also experimented with egalitarian methods of governance. Against the bureaucratic structures of technocratic America society, community living offered the opportunity to form authentic democratic structures that gave a voice to the voiceless. At a festival sponsored near Rising Son Ranch, ushers wore the designation of "Servant" on armbands. CWLF informalized or entirely dropped what they called "titles of distinction," following the lead of Art Gish, a *Right On* contributor and Church of the Brethren evangelist. Gish's *Beyond the Rat Race* (1973) and *The New Left and Christian Radicalism* (1970), both influential in CWLF in the early 1970s, argued that titles perpetuated inequality and authoritarianism. Using "Mr." and "Mrs." created generational barriers. Using "pagan titles" like "professor" or "doctor" set people "apart from others." Using "Reverend" violated the notion of the "priesthood of all believers." "Either everyone should be given these titles," wrote Gish, "or no one." Even Jack Sparks, the charismatic leader of CWLF who came as close to an authoritarian leader as any among third-way evangelicals, was known as "Daddy Jack."[27]

Third-way evangelicals extended their egalitarian claims beyond language to leadership and vocation. While Sparks retained considerable influence because of his charisma and status as a founder of CWLF, his leadership was not "flamboyant," according to Heinz. Rather, the group nurtured a "cult of improvisation" in which anyone was free to speak at meetings. Those who led large ministries, called elders, did not hold much power in the very fluid organizational structure. Perhaps most telling regarding the egalitarian claims of third-way evangelicals was their treatment of women. Gish encouraged married men to stay home to raise children while women entered the workforce. He advised men to wash dishes and women to fix cars in order to break down hierarchies of vocation and gender. Sharon Gallagher, after reading Betty Friedan's *Feminine Mystique*, began to begrudge mail addressed "To the Editor. Dear Sir" or to "Mr. Sherren Gallagher." Such slights led Gallagher, like early leaders of the National Organization for Women, to create consciousness-raising groups. She occasionally refused to take notes in meetings and successfully agitated for women elders and preachers in CWLF. In feminism, Gallagher said, she "found a name for the anger, rebellion, and loss of sense of self I had felt in college. As I reread the Bible, whole passages of Scripture became clear to me in new ways. I discovered passages that I had never heard theologized upon by male theologians." Newly committed to "biblical feminism," she helped found the Bay Area Evangelical Women's Caucus and the national Evangelical Women's Caucus and later, with Ginny Hearn, edited its monthly newsletter *Green Leaf.* She also joined feminist protests, including the 1975 United Nations-sponsored International Women's Conference in Mexico City. Gallagher's commitment to "biblical feminism" extended the egalitarian impulse within CWLF.[28]

CWLF also fought class inequities. Members regularly quoted Jesus' words that it is easier for "a camel to go through the eye of a needle than for a rich man to enter into the kingdom of God." The group's "Open Statement to the Hearsts and the SLA," while condemning the Symbionese Liberation Front's kidnapping of the nineteen-year-old newspaper heiress Patty Hearst in 1974, nonetheless argued that her fate resulted from "the sins of the upper class of which the Hearsts are a part. They are part of an unjust establishment which allows some to have millions and others to live on the brink of starvation, and which drives some of its young people to extreme acts in the attempt to redress the imbalance." *Right On*, praised by Post-American Jim Wallis for this "uncomfortably Christian" statement, insisted that the church-going Hearsts should have "done what Jesus commands them to do as one of his would-be wealthy followers—that is, give their riches to serve the poor." For its part, CWLF offered no-tuition classes in a "free university" intended to educate the poor as well as to sidestep the bureaucratic nature of university culture. Led by David Gill and Bernie Adeney, The Crucible (a predecessor to New College Berkeley, which became an affiliate of the Graduate Theological Union), featured fewer lectures, more discussion, and marginalized topics and texts typically unavailable at traditional colleges. It offered classes as diverse as "History of the Radical Church," "Liberation and the Christian Sister," and "Introduction to New Testament Greek." The Crucible was the most successful of the evangelical free universities in the early 1970s, but it nonetheless failed to attract blue collars. In this way CWLF's preferential view of the poor reflected the political left's failed vision of the sixties. SDS's attempt to create egalitarian political structures— what the Port Huron Statement called "participatory democracy"—to give the poor more power, in the end proved to be the pipe dream of a white elite.

CWLF's vision fared little better, though members insisted that its mere existence as an alternative society steeped in egalitarianism, spiritual authenticity, and generosity was in itself a successful challenge to the technocracy.[29]

* * *

This Christian commune in Berkeley represented a larger groundswell. Jim Wallis also was trying to build an all-encompassing, anti-technocratic community. The Post-Americans scheduled activities for every evening of the week. This "chiefless community" pooled their paychecks, leveling individual wealth by distributing allowances of $200 per month. Decisions about issues as practical as finances, as mundane as home maintenance, and as sensitive as sex and the discipline of children were hashed out in regular evening discussions. Speaking of the "class bias of God," the Post-Americans organized a free university, formed a food cooperative, and led a housing reform movement.[30] In addition to CWLF and the Post-Americans, dozens of other evangelical intentional communities formed across the nation in the 1970s.[31] Anabaptist, charismatic (both Protestant and Catholic), and Jesus Movement-oriented evangelicals, typically with fewer ties to mainstream evangelicalism and less of a political profile, established hundreds more.[32] The third-way impulse also subtly shaped the broader evangelical consciousness on issues such as poverty as well as the living habits of millions of moderate evangelicals. Senator Mark Hatfield affirmed CWLF on several occasions, speaking of the limits of politics and the importance of prophetic single-issue activism on Vietnam and global hunger. Jimmy Carter, in his infamous 1979 "malaise speech," echoed themes of the evangelical third way when he mourned the American tendency to "worship self-indulgence and consumption" and to define identity by "what one owns, not by what one does." Despite criticism, Carter's poll numbers rose after the speech. The third way both reflected and drove an American preoccupation with authenticity in the 1970s. And among evangelicals, the third way dramatically expanded the definition of "politics" to include cultural criticism and lifestyle.[33]

The most rigorous forms of the third way enjoyed surprising staying power. CWLF, for example, continued its communal arrangements and substantial local activism well into the 1980s under the new banner of the Berkeley Christian Coalition. Many Catholic Worker communities, inspired by activist Dorothy Day and similarly motivated by communitarianism, voluntary poverty, and hospitality, persisted far longer. That Catholic and

Figure 12. Third-way evangelicals borrowed their casual, yet intense, style from the counterculture. Here members of the Sojourners community, dressed in blue jeans and peasant skirts, lift their hands as they sing a chorus. Courtesy of Archives and Special Collections, Wheaton College, Wheaton, Illinois.

evangelical communities alike were grounded in divine transcendence and sacred texts and lived out in "the church" seems to have contributed to the greater persistence and intensity of third-way communities, compared to many of their secular counterparts. Despite the movement's ultimate failure in sparking a swell of small communities that ultimately transformed society, it was only a relative failure in comparison with the thousands of secular utopian communities that fizzled within months or years of conception. Moreover, most third-way evangelicals, gravitating toward urban centers to address race and poverty, took the reverse trajectory of many New Leftists who abandoned urban problems for the countryside.[34]

Still, the emphasis on spiritual community left third-way evangelicals vulnerable to criticism from the likes of Carl Henry. Mainstream evangelicals accused CWLF of relapsing into the religious insularity and social quietism of early twentieth-century fundamentalism. These critics were correct about CWLF's circumspection about the prospects of restructuring American capitalism through electoral politics. They were correct in pointing out the third-way rejection of mass politics, rooted in profound disillusionment over the elections of Nixon, the rejection of McCarthy at the 1968 Democratic Convention in Chicago, and the persistence of the Vietnam War. "We are becoming more pastoral," wrote Wallis. "The new front is spirituality."[35]

Third-way evangelicals themselves, however, disagreed with charges of apoliticism. "The reality of God and a relationship to Jesus as Lord cannot be divorced from the reality of political and socio-economic conditions around us," wrote Gallagher in *Right On*. Living in small, egalitarian communities, the Post-Americans insisted, was in itself an act of defiance against the bureaucratic technocracy. A non-vote in electoral politics, like Post-American Wes Michaelson's write-in ballot cast for Donald Duck in the 1976 election, was as much a political stand as a vote for a "lesser of two evils." The thoughtful abstinence from mass politics by "cells of dissent" clearly challenged the establishment and functioned as a call for more radical political change. CWLF's David Gill wrote, "Drop out? No, if that means withdrawal and disengagement. But yes, if that means joining with brothers and sisters in a common and unified witness and life-style radically other than the options thrown up by the world-system." "We must go beyond the system," Gill would later write, "creating a new politics built from the grass-roots of the local church: our primary community."[36]

Gill's "new politics" point to another way in which third-way evangelicals persisted in politics: they narrowed their focus from the national to the local level. Gallagher warned of "close allegiance with any world political system or nation state." Redirecting political energies, they sought to soften the harshest elements of the economic system. The Post-Americans, for example, launched housing reform and food cooperative initiatives, and CWLF started a free university. The Chicago Declaration, which Gallagher helped draft at the 1973 Thanksgiving Workshop, bore evidence of this new local thrust: "We propose that Christians across the country form coalitions on the local level which would concentrate on specific problems in their communities. These coalitions would serve as means of social witness and focus on issues of social justice and righteousness."[37]

Thus third way evangelicals—even in their refusal to align with the New Left, liberalism, or conservatism; even in their isolationist tendencies; even in their boycotts of electoral politics; even in their new emphasis on spirituality and community living—paradoxically persisted in their political thrust. They were building micro-societies that would prefigure coming justice—that of Jesus' second coming, but also of a more just and humane society. They reasoned that a corrupt world obsessed with bigness could be reached only by creating alternative social structures that would shine as a beacon to the world. Francis Schaeffer's disciple Os Guinness suggested the political nature of their project when he urged Christians to build close-knit communities that would "forge solidarity with those who suffer." This prophetic task demanded not a "quiet in the land" approach, but a rational and social toughness "beaten out by the hammer of transcendent truth on the anvil of empirical reality." Gallagher concurred, "We've found that working in a community encourages and strengthens us in being in the world but not of it." The third way sought to transform politics by transcending electoral politics or to invert national politics by emphasizing local politics. Politics was a spiritual quest; as for all social activists, the personal and the political can never be truly separated. To judge that they can be separated, third-way evangelicals argued, only revealed a lack of political imagination.[38]

That the third way retained the subtle political edge of disillusioned evangelical leftists complicates the standard narrative of American political radicalism, which treats "the seventies" as a decade of declension, of unremitting spiritual inwardness and political apathy. "The perfect Seventies symbol," one critic said, "was the Pet Rock, which just sat there doing nothing." A closer examination shows that, at least in the case of third-way evangelicals, politics was instead re-formed. The third way, rather than undercutting political engagement, actually intensified the entanglement of religion and politics. "The recovery of the church's identity in the world is most basic to its political responsibility. . . . The church is thus an inexhaustible revolutionary force in the world," wrote Jim Wallis. Critics who understood this sector of the evangelical left as a relapse into the apoliticism of the fundamentalists were wrong. Instead, it left a broadly influential political legacy. For millions and then tens of millions of evangelicals, these members of the Jesus Movement helped point the way in tying faith closely to politics as they sought to shape the nation through churchly dissent. The consequence was the armies of evangelicals who mobilized first on behalf of Jimmy Carter in 1976 and then for Ronald Reagan in 1980. The mobilization did not end up where third-way evangelicals wanted it to go, but they helped set it in motion.[39]

PART II

A Broadening Coalition

CHAPTER 6

Samuel Escobar and the Global Reflex

Christians in the Third World who contemplate the
so-called West expect from their brethren a word of
identification with demands for justice.
—Samuel Escobar at the International Congress on
World Evangelization in Lausanne, Switzerland

As the Thanksgiving Workshop of 1973 approached, the progressive evangelical coalition consisted primarily of Americans with roots in Billy Graham-
style revivalism. Sharon Gallagher's communitarianism, Mark Hatfield's
electoral savvy, Jim Wallis's antiwar activism, John Alexander's civil rights
advocacy, and Carl Henry's social engagement formed the basic architecture
of an emerging evangelical left. But it took the contributions of people from
non-American contexts previously on the margins of neo-evangelicalism
to launch the movement. Non-Anglo ethnic groups—including Dutch Reformed, Swiss-German Anabaptists, Latin American Christians, and other
third-world evangelicals—added trenchant critiques of social passivity and
shaped the course of evangelical politicization.

These international encounters forced American evangelicals to think
more critically about their own heritage and assumptions. If travel to Marxist countries by SDS leaders in the 1960s encouraged radicalization of the
New Left, exposure to the third world pervaded the evangelical left even
more. C. Peter Wagner, a scholar of missions, noted in 1966 that "on mission
fields such as Latin America, where people are deeply involved in one of the
most explosive and widespread social revolutions in history, the relation
of the Church to society is a top-priority issue. There is no pulling back.

Christians, like everyone else in Latin America, are caught in a whirlpool of rapid social change, and they demand to know what the Bible has to say to them in this situation." Interpreting the Bible for themselves—and increasingly for American evangelicals—substantial numbers of non-Western converts and missionaries offered sharp criticisms of American politics, culture, and capitalism. These critiques turned many on the emerging evangelical left toward Vietnam protests, civil rights, and a more tempered nationalism. By the 1970s, these progressive interests—and a more resolute global concern generally—had become important markers of the evangelical left.[1]

The story of Peruvian evangelical Samuel Escobar exemplifies this global reflex. Escobar was one of the founders of the Latin American Theological Fraternity and served as its first president. He also shaped moderate evangelical politics in North America as a key figure in InterVarsity Christian Fellowship. Escobar represents a significant evangelical stream in Latin America that has been obscured by a preoccupation with liberation theologians and right-wing Pentecostals. The strident ethos of campus radicalism may have turned evangelical students toward the left, but many were already being primed by progressive evangelicals from around the world.[2]

I

Samuel Escobar, perhaps the staunchest critic of American evangelical social conservatism, was born in Arequipa, Peru, a city noted for its colonial-era Spanish architecture and spectacular snow-capped Andes mountain peaks. While the number of Latin American Protestants would increase at mid-century, in the 1930s Escobar's hometown (called the "Rome of Peru" for its spectacular religious processions) was still dominated by Roman Catholicism. Escobar's parents, affiliated with Iglesia Evangélica Peruana, were religious minorities much more concerned with biblical fluency and spiritual piety than with politics. In fact, Peruvian evangelicals, often branded by their opponents as conspirators with communists, liberals, Masons, and the CIA, were politically marginalized in this era. Escobar grew up deeply aware of the cost of being a minority evangelical. As a child, he worried about martyrdom by fire and stones.[3]

Escobar's turn away from apolitical piety began during high school in the late 1940s. He began to drink deeply from the wells of Peruvian literature and political activism. One of his favorite authors, Manuel González Prada, known for his striking critique of the Catholic Church—which he said "preached the Sermon on the Mount and practiced the morals of Judas"— called for Indians, workers, and students to join together in reforming Peru. Escobar also read Ciro Alegría, an advocate for Peruvian Indians; César Vallejo, whose poetry and novels depicted Peruvian "democracy" as a farcical pawn of international corporations; and Víctor Raúl Haya de la Torre, founder of the Pan-Latin American reform movement Aprismo. Escobar also learned that the earliest evangelical believers in Latin America were not politically indifferent or conservative. In the late nineteenth century they had fought for religious freedom and against poverty. Transformed souls, Latin American evangelicals had assumed during that era, would trigger social transformation. Not until much later did evangelicals abandon these commitments. Early models of socially active evangelicalism inspired Escobar to transcend contemporary evangelical quietism. "My fledgling Protestantism," he wrote, "began to perceive the possibility of a different, more authentic, Christianity that was both deeply biblical and Latin American."[4]

Escobar's conviction intensified over the next decades. In 1951 Escobar entered San Marcos University in the Peruvian capital of Lima. His alienation from the establishment, nurtured as a minority evangelical in Arequipa and extended by reformist literature, deepened at San Marcos. Surrounded by currents of Marxism and existentialism, he could not help but notice glaring inequalities. "The misery of the Peruvian interior, the brutal contrast between waste of the wealthy and malnutrition of the poor, the corruption and military coups and bullying in the service of the economic 'liberals,'" he noted, "were so obvious that any observer could tell that an urgent change was needed." Hundreds of thousands of political deaths and disappearances, massive urbanization, and religious transformation at mid-century marked a period of profound volatility. University students denounced the political regimes that perpetuated these disturbing trends.

And yet if Escobar counted himself among these student critics, he could not assent to the ideological materialism and party-line atheism of Marxism. During his first year at the university, he underwent a spiritual revival and was baptized. He joined the International Fellowship of Evangelical Students (IFES), a collection of global InterVarsity affiliates, and encountered the writings of evangelical theologian Carl Henry. He also eagerly participated in church work. "In this intense contact with simple people

week after week," Escobar later wrote of his Sunday School teaching and
street evangelism, "I learned to translate the great ideas that I drank from
books in the university into simple messages understandable for persons of
the middle class or the urban proletariat which were my brethren in Christ."
Increasingly he felt compelled to integrate social and spiritual concerns
amid "the ecstasy and agony of revolutionary times."[5]

He did so squarely within the evangelical orbit. In 1959 Escobar accepted a position with IFES to work with evangelical students on Latin
American university campuses. This introduced him to other networks of
European, American, and Latin American evangelicals who shared his
combination of evangelical piety and concern for social justice. He met and
read books by promoters of moderate, nonsectarian forms of British evangelicalism such as F. F. Bruce, James Packer, John Mackay, and John Stott.
To Escobar's astonishment, most of these new contacts left decisions "entirely in the hands of Latin Americans who had taken the lead there. This
type of non-paternalistic missionary praxis was really something new for
many of us." He also worked closely with Latin America Mission (LAM), a
vast network of neo-evangelical missionaries, radio stations, medical clinics, seminaries, publications, and camps. Escobar helped LAM, which had
been administered by North Americans since its founding in 1921, to "lati-
nize." In 1971 LAM turned over all administrative power to Latin Americans. Escobar took advantage of this latitude. He absorbed proto-Vatican II
themes of indigeneity and the laity from Catholic sources. He read Paulo
Freire, author of the seminal *Pedagogy of the Oppressed* (1968) and pioneer-
ing educator of the urban poor. In fact, he would go on to pursue doctoral
research on Freire at Madrid University in Spain. All the while, Escobar
worked at a dizzying pace throughout South America, visiting churches,
training young people, forming university groups, editing IFES's *Certeza*,
and coordinating writing in Spanish by Latin Americans.[6]

In these roles Escobar became a key voice for new Latin American leaders. He nurtured indigenous networks and theological production "from the
underside." He also spoke Latin American truth to North American power.
The Congreso Latinoamericano de Evangelización (CLADE), held November 21–30, 1969, in Bogotá, Colombia, troubled Escobar because of its
conservative North American ethos. Financed by LAM, the Billy Graham
Evangelistic Association, and the National Association of Evangelicals, planners of CLADE excluded several of Escobar's Latin American allies. "We are
not going to invite a few selected ones that we know are cooperating with the

Communist forces, are extremely liberal in theology, or would in any other way be a complete detriment to the cause of evangelism were they to attend the Congress," wrote former missionary and present NAE general director Clyde Taylor to evangelist Billy Graham in 1968. After the 920 attendees from 25 countries arrived in Bogotá amid the fanfare of a public procession with singing and the waving of national flags, C. Peter Wagner, an American missionary in Bolivia, handed out copies of his new Spanish-language book entitled *Latin American Theology: Radical or Evangelical?* In it Wagner decried the "new radical left" and propounded a "church growth" formula over social action. CLADE, felt Escobar, had been organized, planned, and executed by Americans who completely ignored the social implications of the gospel.[7]

If Wagner's book evoked enthusiasm among many North Americans, it provoked "indignation" among most Latin American attendees, who felt betrayed by this sudden display of de-latinization. Here, they noted, was an opportunity to speak back to an evangelicalism failing to promote social transformation. Rather than articulating an indigenous expression of North American free enterprise as CLADE planners wanted, Escobar instead delivered an address entitled "La Responsabilidad Social de la Iglesia." In front of a majority Latin American crowd, he declared that "one could be profoundly evangelical doctrinally as well as relevant and committed socially." The Gospel, he continued, should not be "reduced to the advantages, conveniences and interests" of a "middle-class ideology." Explaining that a conservative social agenda was being imposed on them by their North American benefactors, Escobar and others vowed to limit their dependency on foreign missionary aid and to confront "Anglo" theologies.[8]

As Escobar concluded his address, he received a "thunderous" standing ovation from the audience. To U.S.-educated Salvadoran Emilio Antonio Núñez, the speech was "a bomb to those who have not given a thought to the task of reflecting upon the social implications of the Gospel and who preach only a gospel of individual salvation." Brought together by their North American benefactors to affirm social conservatism, regional leaders of Latin American evangelicals instead were "gleefully discovering each other" as mutually "tired of the evangelical centers of power in North America telling us how to think, who to read, and what it mean to be evangelical." In ad hoc meetings in CLADE's final days, they plotted a new path. Instead of indoctrination by North Americans "whose programs and literature were a servile and repetitive translation forged in a situation

Figure 13. During his 1969 address at the Congreso Latinoamericano de Evangelización in Bogotá, Colombia, Samuel Escobar criticized American planners who "reduced [the gospel] to the advantages, conveniences and interests" of a "middle-class ideology." Latin American disillusionment at this event led to the founding of the Latin American Theological Fraternity. Courtesy of Samuel Escobar.

completely alien to ours," it was time, Escobar declared, "to start reflecting the faith as grownups and on our own." In a parting shot, entitled "An Evangelical Declaration of Bogotá," the Latin Americans pledged to pursue the social responsibilities of the church in a continent suffering from "underdevelopment, injustice, hunger, violence, and despair." These words sparked a new organization that would shape the North American evangelical left.[9]

One year later, on December 17, 1970, in a fertile valley in rural Cochabamba, Bolivia, 25 Latin American evangelical leaders formed the Fraternidad Teológica Latinoamericana (FTL), known in English as the Latin American Theological Fraternity. On one hand, the gathering in Cochabamba displayed explicitly evangelical themes. Delegates questioned liberation theology, a mid-twentieth-century Latin American movement that interpreted Scripture particularly in terms of freedom from economic and political injustices. Founding member René Padilla worried that the liberation theology espoused by the organization Church and Society in Latin America represented a "secularized Gospel, the dominant tones of which coincide with notes of Marxist tone." Escobar, elected FTL's first president at Cochabamba, contended that liberation theology was overly optimistic, humanistic, and idyllic. Others worried about its propensity for violent revolution. FTL also kept from its evangelical origins the basic conviction that Latin America needed evangelization.[10]

On the other hand, the Cochabamba delegation diverged from North American evangelicalism by taking liberation theology seriously. FTL acknowledged the social conditioning of theological work and thus the need to be self-critical. It also recognized that some liberation theologians had done good biblical work calling attention to realities like poverty, injustice, and oppression. These were important themes in biblical teaching and been excised from the evangelical canon. Along with liberation theologians, FTL criticized North American imperialism and the impulse to conflate capitalism and faith. Despite their own reservations about liberation theology's dismissal of the importance of personal conversion, members had little patience when North American evangelicals demonized liberation theology. "The versions of some North American conservatives about the ecumenical world," complained Escobar, "were simplistic and sometimes intended for evil." American conservative evangelicals, he continued, did not sufficiently recognize the gravity of global poverty and its structural roots. In time, FTL's self-conscious effort to unite some elements of liberation theology and evangelical identity coalesced around "contextualization." This approach to hermeneutics stressed sin both in social terms (like liberation theologians) and in personal terms (like American evangelicals). Escobar and his colleagues wanted to take the insights of liberation theology without the violence. They wanted to appropriate evangelical doctrine without North American worship styles, dispensational theology, and commitment to unfettered capitalism. FTL, in the words of one Latin American theologian, became "an evangelical variant of the Latin American theological ferment of the decade." With roots in a colonial underclass and North American conservative revivalism, FTL sought to negotiate a middle path between the "left-wing fundamentalism of naïve Marxism" and a "blind, pro-military anticommunism."[11]

The relative sympathy with which most FTL members treated liberation theology signaled a clear break from the political sensibilities of many evangelicals. Indeed, FTL's earliest history reflected the uneasy relationship it had with these sectors of North American evangelicalism. Many of FTL's first meetings—including its founding sessions in Cochabamba—were financed by North Americans, including the unlikely National Liberty Foundation, whose founder was a large donor and board member of the conservative Campus Crusade for Christ. Though Latin Americans expressed gratitude for financial help and interest, they also resented North American interference. Wagner, for instance, arrived at Cochabamba bearing an uninvited draft of an FTL constitution. "He presented it translated and printed in paper with the name of the FTL, even before there was any FTL," explained a member. "He wanted the FTL to adopt that declaration as its own." Wagner's attempts to foist biblical inerrancy and attach theological constraints to financial gifts prompted Escobar to maintain that "foreign intervention in different ways was really militating against what we were trying to do: that is, to have our own theology . . . our own definition of who is an evangelical."[12]

In 1972 FTL redoubled its push for independence. In January, the Evangelical Fellowship of Mission Agencies threatened to withdraw financial support if FTL member José Míguez Bonino was invited to give a paper at a conference in Lima, Peru. FTL's executive committee responded, "You are not going to tell us who to invite and who not to invite. This is the FTL [emphasis on the L]. If you want to help us, we are thankful for that. We need the money, but we do not accept any conditions attached. We maintain the invitation to Míguez Bonino." In the end, Bonino could not participate for health reasons. But FTL recognized its financial dependence and sought to diversify its funding stream. With new sources of help from progressive, evangelical, mainline, and international organizations, FTL grew rapidly. In one year alone FTL sponsored four regional consultations, in Argentina, Brazil, Peru, and Mexico. Regional and continental meetings continued through the 1970s, and the membership of prominent Latin American leaders grew to nearly one hundred. By the late 1970s FTL was producing a journal called *Boletín Teológico*, printed in both Spanish and English.[13]

That *Boletín Teológico* was printed in English points to another of FTL's key ambitions. In addition to securing independence, FTL intended to speak back to American evangelicalism on issues of politics, missions, and biblical interpretation. Like Escobar, two other FTL members—René Padilla and Orlando Costas—found themselves uniquely positioned to straddle the North and South American continents. Although trained in the United States and Europe, they had experienced Latin American inequality. They were able to articulate in devastating fashion, using North American idioms and logic, the role of the United States in exacerbating those inequalities.

Padilla was born the sixth of eight children in 1932 in Quito, Ecuador, to parents converted by American evangelical missionaries. In the late 1930s the family moved to Bogotá, Colombia, where Padilla's evangelist father moved from neighborhood to neighborhood starting new churches and preaching against the Catholic Church. In 1944 they relocated back to Ecuador, where his father worked for the evangelical radio station HCJB. Connections with American evangelicals there led to an invitation for young René to attend Wheaton College. During college from 1952 to 1955, he joined InterVarsity, befriended Mexican migrant workers, and dodged the U.S. military draft. After graduating from Wheaton and marrying an Inter-Varsity worker, Padilla was hired by IFES to start InterVarsity chapters at universities across Latin America. He also pursued doctoral studies at the University of Manchester under noted New Testament scholar F. F. Bruce. Padilla, known in Latin America as an aggressive advocate for evangelical literature in the Spanish language, worked through the 1960s and 1970s with IFES's *Certeza* and Editorial Caribe, the publishing arm of Latin America Mission. Crucially for the history of American evangelical politics, Padilla also circulated widely in North America, where he told evangelical audiences about the fusion of evangelism and social action that was taking place in Buenos Aires, Argentina, among drug addicts and slum dwellers.[14]

Orlando Costas, born in Puerto Rico, moved to Bridgeport, Connecticut, with his family as a young boy after his father's grocery business failed. Encouraged by friends and teachers to forget his native language and culture, Costas immediately felt the sting of North American ethnocentrism. "For three years I suffered the impact of a strange cultural environment, full of hostility and prejudice," remembered Costas. After initially rejecting his parents' evangelical faith, Costas was converted as a teenager at Billy Graham's 1957 New York crusade in Madison Square Garden. He finished high school at Bob Jones Academy in South Carolina and attended a diverse set of colleges on his way to several graduate degrees: Trinity Evangelical Divinity School in Deerfield, Illinois, Garrett Theological Seminary in Evanston, Illinois, Winona Lake School of Theology near Warsaw, Indiana, Universidad Interamericana in Puerto Rico, and the Free University of Amsterdam in the Netherlands. Costas then split his pastoral and academic career between the United States and Latin America. In 1966 he began work as pastor of Iglesia Evangélica Bautista in Milwaukee, which sparked an interest in social activism. In 1967 he served on the Commission for Social Development of Milwaukee. In 1968 he founded a community newspaper

La Guardia, the Latin American Union for Civil Rights, and the Universidad del Barrio. In 1969 he was named by Wisconsin's governor to the State Commission on Human Rights in the Division of Industry, Work and Human Relations. As a key figure in the "War on Poverty" in Milwaukee, Costas learned much about political organizing from the African-American community and wrote a book, *La Iglesia y su misión evangelizadora* (1971), in which he articulated these new concerns as a holistic form of evangelism. In 1970 Costas moved to Costa Rica, where he served as dean of the Latin American Biblical Seminary and joined FTL. Along with Padilla and Escobar, Costas played an important role in the indigenization of LAM. All the while, he maintained a close interest in American evangelicalism as a contributing editor of John Alexander's magazine *The Other Side* and author of *The Church and Its Mission: A Shattering Critique from the Third World* (1974). Through the 1970s Costas taught missiology at numerous prominent seminaries in North America, including Fuller, Gordon-Conwell, Andover-Newton, and Eastern Baptist.[15]

Escobar, like Padilla and Costas, reversed the trajectory of American missionary activity and began to circulate in the North American evangelical world. Entering the English-speaking world for the first time, Escobar became General Director of InterVarsity-Canada from 1972 to 1975. He then resumed working with IFES in Latin America for the next 25 years, though he returned to North America frequently. A main speaker at InterVarsity's Urbana conventions in 1970, 1973, and 1981, Escobar earned praise from students for his "prophetic call to service" and his sustained attack on American evangelicals' defense of the status quo. In 1970 the *Los Angeles Times* reported Escobar as declaring at Urbana that "the people of the third world are increasingly repelled by the white, middle-class God represented by American culture." His workshop on "Social Concern and the Gospel," which attracted 1,050 students, outdrew nearly every other workshop. Escobar's influence continued in five books and well over 100 articles and book chapters by the early 1980s. He also participated in key international congresses on world evangelism in Berlin (1966), Bogotá (1969), Ottawa (1970), and Madrid (1974). Most significant was the International Congress of World Evangelization, held in July 1974 at Lausanne, Switzerland. Escobar's participation at Lausanne in fact represents the ways in which global evangelicals moved 1970s North American evangelicalism in progressive directions.[16]

Described by *Time* magazine in a lengthy article as "a formidable forum, possibly the widest-ranging meeting of Christians ever held," Lausanne attracted 2,700 evangelical leaders from 150 nations (at least half from the third world) for debate over methods of global evangelism. At least a dozen other members of the FTL attended, among them Robinson Cavalcanti, a political science professor from Rio de Janeiro, Brazil; Pablo Pérez, a missiologist from Mexico City; Héctor Espinoza of Mexico; Juan Carlos Ortiz, pastor of the largest evangelical church in Buenos Aires; Emilio Núñez, president of the Central American Seminary in Guatemala; and Jorge León, a psychologist who worked at a Buenos Aires YMCA. Several played significant roles at the international gathering. Escobar served on the program planning committee and helped draft the resulting Lausanne Covenant. Padilla and Costas delivered plenary addresses. Others gave papers and reports.

In multiple forums at Lausanne, FTL members sharply criticized a truncated North American conception of evangelization. First, they described North American evangelism as technique-driven and rooted in cold efficiency. Too often, contended Costas, evangelistic crusades became "a commercial, manipulative whitewash." Evangelism based on the "systematization of methods and resources to obtain pre-established results," stated Padilla, found precedent not in Scripture but in a "fierce pragmatism" that "in the political sphere has produced Watergate." Second, evangelical efforts to save souls as quickly and efficiently as possible served to baptize the conservative status quo. Escobar declared that "Christians, evangelicals in particular, oppose the violence of revolution but not the violence of war; they condemn the totalitarianism of the left but not that of the right; they speak openly in favor of Israel, but very seldom speak or do anything about the Palestinian refugees; they condemn all the sins that well-behaved middle class people condemn but say nothing about exploitation, intrigue, and dirty political maneuvering done by great multinational corporations around the world." North American evangelicals failed to understand the multidimensional aspects of the gospel. Yes, Jesus saved souls, but he also cared about bodies and social structures. Escobar, urging "discipleship in the daily social, economic, and political aspects of life," told Lausanne delegates to work toward social justice "as a sign of the kingdom and anticipation of the new creation." These Latin American statements reinforced a growing assertion from the North American evangelical left: that Christians should integrate their faith with issues of social justice.[17]

FTL's efforts electrified Lausanne delegates. Escobar's paper alone elicited more than 1,000 responses. Together, estimated delegate John A. Coleman of Australia, the papers by Padilla and Escobar had "probably been subject to more comment than all the other papers put together." The controversy broke into two camps. Carl Henry, a key Lausanne planner, distinguished between those who stressed "the primacy of evangelism in terms of personal regeneration" and "the champions of 'radical discipleship' like Samuel Escobar and René Padilla [who] underscored repentance from social sins and the need to call for a changed socio-political order." In short, did evangelism involve social as well as personal regeneration? C. Peter Wagner, Donald McGavran, and Ralph Winter, strong champions of the church-growth movement, felt that Lausanne's mission—to focus on personal evangelism—had been hijacked by the new stress on social concern. According to these critics, FTL's activities and the media's "disproportionate emphasis on the social aspects of the Christian mission" had obscured the main point. The "big picture," explained McGavran, was "evangelizing the three billion living with no knowledge of Jesus." Several of the sharpest critiques of Padilla and Escobar came from third-world delegates theologically trained in conservative seminaries in the West.[18]

Most third-world delegates, however, embraced the FTL agitators. Padilla was one of only three Lausanne speakers to receive a standing ovation, brought to an end only when Cliff Barrows, Billy Graham's song leader, began to lead a hymn. According to one observer, cutting off the applause with an American hymn was "no doubt an innocent enough action, but one which some construed to have deep political overtones!" One delegate called Escobar's address "vibrant, prophetic, and life-giving." Others hugged him and congratulated him. Spurred on by this unexpected resonance from delegates, Padilla and Escobar organized an ad hoc meeting that tried to compel the committee drafting the Lausanne Covenant to incorporate social action into their statements about evangelism. On Sunday evening, July 21, 1974, they led 500 delegates in a discussion of "the social and political implications of radical discipleship today." The resulting document, "A Response to Lausanne," described attempts "to drive a wedge" between evangelism and social action as "demonic." American conservatives bristled, but British evangelical John Stott distributed and endorsed the document, which was attached to the final Covenant. In addition, the Lausanne Covenant itself underwent telling revisions in the wake of third-world dissent. The first draft included one sentence on social justice; the second draft promoted simple living, international sensitivity, and social justice in a section that was larger than any other in the Covenant. Lausanne's executive chair, Australian Jack Dain, later recalled, "No one will ever know except the members the agonies through which we all passed . . . I can only marvel after grappling for hours with these matters we did come to a common mind."[19]

The Lausanne Covenant marked a decisive moment in neo-evangelical history. On a global stage, evangelicals from around the world took advantage of an extraordinary opportunity to speak directly to those from the United States. According to Escobar and Padilla, evangelicals from the third world spoke with prophetic wisdom and courage, seeking to deal "a death blow to the superficial equation of Christian mission with the multiplication of Christians and churches." At the 1966 World Congress on Evangelism, statements on social concern had been soft and hesitant. John Stott, for example, had proclaimed that "the mission of the Church . . . is exclusively a preaching, converting, and teaching mission." But at Lausanne, Stott amended his earlier formulation. Now, he told delegates, "I would express myself differently. . . . I now see more clearly that not only the consequences of the commission but the actual commission itself must be understood to include social as well as evangelistic responsibility." Billy Graham similarly declared, "If one thing has come through loud and clear it is that we evangelicals should have social concern. The discussion in smaller groups about the contemporary meaning of radical discipleship has caught fire." As the affirmations by these Anglo titans at Lausanne suggest, the political effect of this new thrust soon would be evident within mainstream evangelicalism.[20]

II

The FTL was far from alone in its call for North American social responsibility. In the mid-1970s evangelicals from all over the third world cultivated relationships initially established at Lausanne, and FTL helped to coordinate this broader global reflex. Its publications, printed in English in addition to Spanish and Portuguese, widely spread Latin American evangelical social thought. In the Caribbean FTL worked with Michael Cassidy, who in the 1980s would go on to found African Enterprise and become an instrumental figure in South African antiapartheid battles. Saphir Athyal, president of a seminary in Yeotmal, India, visited FTL members in six countries in 1971. In South Africa a group of students from Potchefstroom University, who

observers said resembled *Right On*, *Sojourners*, and *The Other Side*, except
with a strongly Calvinist bent, sympathized with FTL's efforts. In Britain a
magazine called *The Third Way* and Buzz Christian Ministries denounced
American-style evangelism. In the Philippines the Institute for the Study of
Asian Church and Culture published a socially aware journal called *Patmos*.
By the 1970s the American monologue was over. A swelling chorus of African, Asian, British, and Australian evangelicals had joined FTL's effort to
speak back to the United States. Their primary complaints centered on issues
of imperialism and social justice.[21]

American evangelical imperialism, according to critics, linked a valid
impulse to spread the Christian gospel with American cultural values. Many
evangelical missionaries and their converts decried this "syncretic confusion of Christianity and Americanism" with a strident, sometimes bitter,
voice. In 1962 a Middle Eastern student at an InterVarsity event declared,
"We are the generation of a part of the world where misery, sickness and
poverty are predominant, despite the fact that we have many resources. This
has been the result of 500 years of colonialism and imperialism. . . . Your
religion is serving the interest of the imperialist." In the wake of Lausanne
in 1974, Orlando Costas decried the use of the term "third world"; he preferred the term "two-thirds world," explaining that Latin America was not
third rate, only "non-affluent, economically, politically, and culturally dominated." Most non-American evangelicals were more ambivalent than Costas—
after all, Americans had brought them the gospel—but on the whole most
resented the American cultural, economic, and political trappings that came
with the gospel. They charged that American evangelicals had confused the
gospel with the American way of life, and then imposed that corrupted gospel
on the world.[22]

This broad charge came in several variants. First, non-American evangelicals worried about North American cultural and intellectual hegemony.
Escobar complained that nearly 80 percent of evangelical book titles in Latin
America were merely translations from the West—and poor ones at that.
"The western model of ministry imposed upon the Third World churches,"
asserted Jonathan T'ien-en Chao of Hong Kong, could be blamed for a failure
to develop indigenous leadership. Zimbabwean Pius Wakatama confirmed
that "the task of making disciples for Jesus Christ was often confused with
that of 'civilizing the primitive and savage tribes.'" There was a tendency to
regard all things traditional as pagan and most things Western as Christian."

Missionaries, Wakatama lamented to InterVarsity students at Urbana '73, forced converts to discard their own ethnic markers in the face of the "paternalistic attitude that views mature nationals as being like children who need to be constantly supervised." Specifically, international evangelicals complained that missionaries imposed Western notions of numerical success and highly rational methods of interpreting Scripture. Echoing Padilla's objections to "the technological mentality" at Lausanne, Wakatama said that American missionaries had tried to "understand and explain" the Trinity because the "Western man is dichotomistic and his philosophical bent is pragmatic rationalism. His tools are scientific empiricism. He wants to dissect, compartmentalize and quantify things." This approach, Wakatama continued, had corrupted the African "wholistic approach to life." The Zimbabwean in fact spearheaded the call for a "selective moratorium" on American missionary work in Africa.[23]

Some American evangelicals listened. One InterVarsity student, cooling in her zeal for overseas missions work, told the organization's president that the Urbana convention's "foreign mission emphasis seemed irrelevant during a time of prejudice, war, poverty and a whole gamut of social issues that is pressing in on the Christian student of today." Missions director David Howard wrote about the stark "anti-missionary feeling" at a 1973 InterVarsity weekend conference in southern California. Even Americans who persisted in missionary work took the global critique of American imperialism seriously. In 1972 Bill Conard, a missionary to Peru, wrote that "all too long I linked Christianity with U.S. democracy, but now I feel that U.S. democracy is probably not the answer for most of the world, and that—amazing enough—Christ's believers can well live under, and perhaps even participate in, a wide range of political ideologies."[24]

Conard's separation of Christianity and U.S. democracy points to a second critique from third-world evangelicals. Many resented evangelicals' imposition of American-style democracy and laissez-faire capitalism. In 1965 Wheaton College student Ayub Waitara of Kenya, like many international students at evangelical colleges, denounced missionary attempts to tie faith to anticommunism. He accused the United States of using Africa as a battleground against communism. "Political morality," Waitara asserted, was not "a Western monopoly." He told his classmates that Africans should "find something that preserves African moralities and sensibilities," something "outside of the ideological struggle between communism and capitalism." To insist on anticommunism, Waitara said, blinded the developing world to the gospel. At Lausanne Emilio Núñez, a theologically conservative evangelical from El Salvador, decried the "humiliations" and "exploitations" inherent in the gaping disparity in wealth. He would later accuse the United States of "tightly controlling the economic world, setting prices and determining markets, loaning massive capital at unbearably high interest rates, and at the same time imperialistically imposing a free-enterprise economy on Latin America."[25]

Crucially, members of the emerging evangelical left took such critiques seriously. In 1965 Wheaton student Fred Smith, challenged by Waitara and other African exchange students, wrote that many abroad "are becoming disillusioned with democracy, because we who should best represent it too often represent not democracy, but only anti-Communism or capital investment." InterVarsity and Latin America Mission administrators worried that conservative evangelical institutions such as the Billy Graham Evangelistic Association, *Christianity Today*, NAE, and Campus Crusade might band together to "form an anti-socialist block in the name of the Gospel." Such a move would not bode well for missionary work overseas. "In the Third World," wrote staffer Charles Troutman to an InterVarsity vice-president in 1976, "the idea of the free enterprise system is so utterly discredited, even among those who maintain it for personal advantage, that [Harold] Lindsell's union of the Gospel and capitalism is going to appear like childish stupidity." Institutions such as InterVarsity and LAM observed what less globally oriented evangelicals at home could not, which was the economic aggression of American corporations that often followed in the wake of missionary activity. Accusations of economic imperialism thus dominated the evangelical left's rhetoric in the 1970s. InterVarsity missionary Barbara Benjamin's description of Chiquita's rapid expansion and then sudden departure in Ecuador reflected the growing antipathy among the emerging evangelical left to the vagaries of free markets. Prompted in part by third-world evangelicals, the American evangelical left began to question the matrix that tied together faith, patriotism, capitalism, and democracy.[26]

The high mark of anti-American animus came in the 1970s. At mid-decade a group of Latin Americans launched a campaign to renegotiate the terms of the Panama Canal Treaty. In an "Open Letter to North American Christians," Orlando Costas and seven other evangelical leaders lambasted the United States for their "ignorance, greed, and ethnocentrism." Arguing that the U.S. had stolen, not purchased, the Canal, they maintained that the U.S. government had cut fees for American companies at the expense of Panama. They condemned continued colonialism in Latin America, charging that "your precious 'American Way of Life' . . . feeds in no small proportion on the blood which gushes 'from the open veins of Latin America.'" Members of IFES in Costa Rica echoed Costas:

> Panama has waited patiently while you procrastinated in the renegotiation of the treaty through the years of Vietnam, Watergate, and the recent elections. You condemn the relics of colonialism in Rhodesia and South Africa. Why are you so slow to see the "beam in your own eye?" During the construction of the canal more than 25,000 poor laborers from the Third World laid down their lives on the altar of the First World economic development—yet your politicians have the gall to boast "we built it"! Your senators have been swamped with letters from citizens blinded by ignorance, greed, and ethnocentrism. We exhort you as brothers and sisters in Christ to write your senators today, indicating your support for the new treaty as a step toward justice for Panama and better relations with all Latin America.

Prominent progressive evangelicals in North America published these statements in InterVarsity's *HIS* magazine, Sojourners' *Post-American*, CWLF's *Right On*, the Institute for Christian Studies' *Vanguard*, and the evangelical satire magazine *Wittenburg Door*. Each urged readers to lodge protests with their politicians.[27]

Increasing numbers of American evangelicals began to voice similar sentiments. In 1967 Calvin College students, encouraged by a Reformed synod statement from the Netherlands, argued that the United States "should stop the war in Vietnam without delay." For a decade, from the mid-sixties to the mid-seventies, the Wheaton student newspaper and InterVarsity's magazine printed more articles critical of U.S. foreign policy and corporations than articles in support. The more acerbic *Vanguard* and *Sojourners* magazines printed unremitting denunciations of U.S. policies. In 1973, for example, the *Post-American* printed articles entitled "America's Empire" and "How We Look to the Third World," both of which described the United States as a "status-quo-seeking, interventionist monolith." Tony Campolo, a sociologist at the evangelical Eastern College, decried the economic imperialism of the American conglomerate Gulf & Western in the

Dominican Republic. During trips to the Caribbean nation in the early 1970s, Campolo observed that the company "was largely responsible for creating an economically oppressive system there.... Gulf & Western bought up more and more sugar land, they were getting interest in the banking system, and they controlled the hotel industries. They were basically controlling the life of the people in a very negative way." Campolo, who lost a race for the U.S. House of Representatives in 1976 as a Democratic candidate from Pennsylvania, urged evangelicals to enter political life in order to stop economic imperialism. Encouraged by third-world evangelicals, who interacted closely with the Post-Americans, the Christian World Liberation Front, and Mark Hatfield, the emerging evangelical left sounded an insistent internationalist voice.[28]

III

As penance for their sins of imperialism, international evangelicals encouraged Americans to pursue a new agenda of social justice. At Urbana '73 Colombian Gregorio Landero, president of Acción Unida, an organization that sought to integrate evangelism and social concern, urged American students to redefine evangelism itself. It continued to be about winning the souls of nonbelievers, but true evangelism also demanded attention to global structures. "A new life can't come to them," Landero declared, "not truly, till both their bodies and their souls become well." Speaking in an era defined by environmental and political upheaval in Latin America—earthquakes, hurricanes, and repressive military regimes in Argentina, Bolivia, Brazil, Chile, Ecuador, El Salvador, Honduras, Panama, Paraguay, Peru, and Uruguay—he told students at InterVarsity's Urbana conferences inspirational stories of economic uplift. North American help in teaching crop rotation and starting micro-enterprises was lifting Colombians out of poverty and priming them to receive the Gospel. Your task, he told the students, is to "help mobilize the resources of the churches and to minister to their social needs."[29]

Third-world evangelicals pointed out the very long way their American counterparts had to go in regard to social justice, even within their own borders. Racial segregation topped the list. Missionaries in Pakistan and the Netherland Antilles cited nationals who perceived "something incongruous and contradictory about churches which send missionaries half-way around the world with the Gospel of Christ while refusing to worship with the colored people of their own community." At a 1966 NAACP meeting at Wheaton College, Kenyan Wilson Okite urged classmates to join the civil rights movement, mentioning that independence from colonial powers in Africa inspired him and many others to agitate for equality in America. At Calvin College, a missionary to Nigeria told students that Africans were closely watching the 1964 presidential election. That Goldwater might win, even with his retrograde views on civil rights, "shocks them," Harry Boer reported. Africans receive American missionaries more warmly, Boer explained, when the United States promotes civil rights. Howard Jones, an associate evangelist with Billy Graham, was amazed by Liberians' awareness of racial tension in the American South. "From the modern cities to the underdeveloped bush sections of the country, Africans plagued us with questions concerning Dr. Martin Luther King and the 1955 bus boycott in Montgomery, Alabama," Jones told InterVarsity students. "They quizzed us about the Emmett Till lynching in Mississippi and other racial disturbances." According to Jones, these racial disturbances, publicized by Radio Moscow and Radio Peking, impede "the progress of Christian missions in Africa, Asia and other parts of the world."[30]

International evangelicals also critiqued American habits of consumption. For many, travel in the United States confirmed stories they had already heard about American wealth. René Padilla remembered the "very luxurious buildings" he encountered when he arrived at Wheaton College as an undergraduate in the mid-1950s. Coming from a context of "suffering," Padilla was disappointed to discover a church with "no comprehension of poverty." Kenyan Peter Rucro, who studied at Wheaton in the mid-1960s, told his classmates, "The United States is a unique society bogged down with plenty, leisure and waste." InterVarsity chapters, many of which started programs to help international students adjust to American culture, heard the same critique. *HIS* magazine reported that nine-tenths of foreign students at the University of Michigan considered Americans "overly preoccupied with money." An Iraqi student studying in Minnesota said that Americans "are too busy running to live." An Egyptian said that the "U.S. looks like a car race."[31]

These critiques impressed North American evangelicals. One student told of his encounter in Brazil with a shopkeeper who condemned North American missionaries for living too extravagantly: "I hastily surveyed my reflection in a shop window. Fortunately, I was wearing old sandals. My pants and shirt were old. I hoped I might pass inspection." "How different," he reflected, "our lifestyle is from that of Jesus! Our Christian lives in North America and Europe are patterned more after Herod and Pilate than after Jesus and Paul." Increasing numbers of American evangelicals repeated this student's words. The Christian World Liberation Front distributed flyers in the early 1970s throughout Berkeley charging that the "rich privileged minority partys [sic] while millions die in Biafra." Herb McMullan of the *Post-American* wrote that "economic growth and available resources are finite. In this situation, the technological 'have' nations remain committed to exploitive robbery, monopolizing the raw materials available in the world, domestically accelerating commodity production and productive exploitation." Senator Mark Hatfield, who represented the United States at the 1974 World Food Conference in Rome, returned convinced of a global food crisis and appalled by the Ford Administration's dismissal of the Conference's recommendations. Charging that the State Department was giving aid on the basis of potential for future economic markets to sell American products, Hatfield in 1975 encouraged millions of evangelicals to lobby the government to pass the Food for Peace program which would remove political considerations from the distribution of aid. Taking cues from third-world evangelicals, the evangelical left maintained that American wealth was inherently unjust.[32]

Global concern extended far into mainstream evangelicalism. During the mid-1970s articles on global hunger proliferated in magazines such as *Christianity Today* and *Eternity*. Relief agencies, including World Vision, World Relief, Mennonite Central Committee, and Bread for the World, flourished. Evangelical contributions to developing nations, despite a moribund economy, quadrupled between 1969 and 1982. Other evangelical agencies sought to address structural roots of global poverty. Dominated at first by food delivery and emergency medical care, interest shifted in the 1970s toward theoretical, scholarly, political, ecumenical, and long-term approaches to hunger. Evangelical agencies developed urban food-for-work and leadership training programs; built roads, hospitals, and schools; established cooperatives, credit unions, and loan programs; started micro-enterprises for small industry; and taught new agricultural techniques. Some also urged acts of moral suasion, boycotts, selective investment, and shareholder resolutions in order to constrain American corporations. The trend would continue in the 1980s. Burgeoning development organizations grew even larger, and hundreds of others smaller initiatives—HEED, Jubilee Crafts, Tearcraft, Worldcrafts, The International Institute of Development, Society for Community Development, Partnership in Third World Ministry, and United Action Association—flew below the radar. Shaped by the insistent voices of third-world evangelicals, this new global vision countervailed the all-in embrace of capitalism and superpatriotism by the religious right.[33]

*   *   *

The Thanksgiving Workshop strongly reflected the global reflex. Organizers invited thirteen individuals from its "Third World Participant List." They offered a seminar on "Third-World Women." Samuel Escobar helped write the Chicago Declaration, which rhetorically bludgeoned American materialism and imperialism. "We must attack the materialism of our culture and the maldistribution of the nation's wealth and services," read the Declaration. "We recognize that as a nation we play a crucial role in the imbalance and injustice of international trade and development. Before God and a billion hungry neighbors, we must rethink our values regarding our present standard of living and promote a more just acquisition and distribution of the world's resources."[34]

As Escobar sat in the Chicago YMCA along with Carl Henry, John Alexander, Jim Wallis, and Sharon Gallagher, he reflected upon the great change in evangelicalism signified by this progressive document. Decades earlier, as a university student in Peru, Escobar had read in an Argentinian religious magazine about a book called *The Uneasy Conscience of Modern Fundamentalism*. The book's author, Carl Henry, sharply repudiated otherworldly fundamentalism and called evangelicals to address social inequality. At the time Escobar saw only glimpses of Henry's theory in practice. Little did Escobar realize that it would take the efforts of thousands of international evangelicals like himself during the intervening decades to answer that call. That he was now working alongside Henry on initiatives to reshape society gave him "real joy."[35]

This collegiality persisted through the 1970s as progressive evangelicals mobilized on behalf of global and domestic justice. More and more of them agreed in principle with *Post-American* contributor Clark Pinnock, who told critics of liberation theology not to "complain when the liberationist smuggles politics into the Bible when evangelicals have been smuggling politics out of the Bible for centuries." Third-world evangelicals, in acknowledging

the politics of Jesus, gave shape to the very social engagement that Henry
called for, but never fleshed out. Despite their participation in the civil rights
and antiwar movements, the evangelical left's critical posture toward their
own tradition and nation was never solely indigenous. Prophetic voices from
outside America's borders offered aid and inspiration to the politics of the
evangelical left.[36]

CHAPTER 7

Richard Mouw and the Reforming of Evangelical Politics

As a remedy for the pervasive influence of sin, the
redemptive work of Jesus Christ has cosmic implications,
and we are called to witness to the radical scope of his
reconciling power. . . . It is wrong to think that all of our
social and political problems will be solved simply by
changing individual lives.
—Richard Mouw in *Political Evangelism*

Postwar evangelicalism in the United States encountered an ethnic challenge from within its own borders as well as from without. In the 1960s and 1970s, several important voices from Dutch Reformed enclaves in southern Ontario, western Michigan, and northwestern Iowa joined the growing chorus of those critiquing evangelical political conservatism and apoliticism. Historically on the fringes of evangelicalism but moving steadily closer to the American evangelical orbit during the twentieth century, Reformed evangelicals infused the growing coalition with a theological rigor and a history of political activism brought from the Netherlands. They contended that Christ was Lord over all of creation—and that his followers had been charged with a cultural and social mandate to shape the nation's power organizations. By the early 1970s, as the Thanksgiving Workshop approached, Reformed evangelicals such as Richard Mouw and his colleagues at Calvin College in Grand Rapids, Michigan, were active in pushing neo-evangelicals toward pragmatic methods of progressive political reform.

I

Mouw's childhood reflected the slow movement of the Dutch Reformed community toward neo-evangelicalism. Baptized in 1940 as an infant in the First Holland Reformed Church of Passaic, New Jersey, Mouw grew up among first- and second-generation Dutch immigrants. Some in fact still worshiped in Dutch-language services on Sunday afternoons. But as Mouw's mother, a member of the First Holland congregation, cradled young Mouw in her arms and presented him for baptism as a "covenant child," his father, a more typical homegrown evangelical, looked on suspiciously from the front pew. The product of an irreligious family and a dramatic conversion experience in his teens while a hillbilly musician, Mouw's father prayed his son would "someday realize that only a personal faith in Jesus, and not the rituals of the church, could guarantee [his] eternal salvation."[1]

Although his father, who later became a Reformed minister, would change his mind about infant baptism, young Mouw grew up with a foot each in the worlds of neo-evangelicalism and ethnically Dutch Reformed theology. With his father, he smelled the sawdust in fundamentalist revival meetings. Vaguely anti-Catholic and stridently anti-mainline, he forged friendships with Wesleyan, Assemblies of God, and Christian Missionary Alliance ministers in the broad transdenominational world of mid-twentieth-century evangelical conservatism. He attended summer Bible camps with intricate dispensationalist end times charts on the walls. He read Moody Bible Institute devotional guides. Like millions of others in the 1950s, the teenage Mouw was overcome "with a profound sense that God was speaking directly to me" and made the long trek forward toward Billy Graham on the stage at Madison Square Garden to "make a decision for Christ." "Surrounded by thousands of people," he remembers, "I felt that I was alone in the presence of the Eternal."[2]

With his mother, Mouw was drawn toward Reformed theology because of weaknesses he perceived in fundamentalist evangelicalism. He was especially wary of its anti-intellectual, otherworldly, and separatist sensibilities expressed in slogans like "The only school any Christian ever has to enroll in is the Holy Ghost School of the Bible!"; "You don't need a lot of exegesis. All you need is Jesus!"; and "When you know that Christ is the answer, then you don't have to worry about the questions!" Attending the non-Reformed, evangelical Houghton College in western New York, Mouw found the atmosphere intellectually stunting and politically restrictive. The administration, for example, forced out a history professor who had planted a Kennedy-for-President sign on the front lawn of his home. Mouw did, however, find allies among some of his classmates who were inspired by Carl Henry's seminal tract, *The Uneasy Conscience of Fundamentalism* (1947), which critiqued fundamentalism's indifference to social ills. When Fuller Seminary's Edward John Carnell released *The Case for Orthodox Theology* (1959), Mouw and his classmates were similarly captivated. Their favorite chapter, entitled "Perils," explained that fundamentalism was "orthodoxy gone cultic"—and did so, according to Mouw, in a "tone that brought delight to the hearts of evangelical college students who were chafing under restrictions aimed at various forms of 'worldliness.'" They read snarky excerpts out loud to each other. "Fundamentalists, it so happens, are afraid of one another," read one passage. "If a fundamentalist is seen entering a theater, he may be tattled on by a fellow fundamentalist. In this event the guilty party would 'lose his testimony,' i.e., his status in the cult would be threatened. But when he watches movies on television, this threat does not exist. Drawn shades keep prying eyes out. One of the unexpected blessings of television is that it lets the fundamentalist catch up on all the movies he missed on religious principles." Carnell's point—that it was possible to leave fundamentalism without becoming a theological liberal—was liberating to Mouw. He found the possibilities of the new evangelicalism exciting. "I wanted to work hard at helping to fulfill it," he later explained.[3]

But Mouw, like many pioneers of the evangelical left, found the neo-evangelical trajectory too gradual. Despite his family's restrictions on dancing, playing cards, and attending the cinema, Mouw hitchhiked to a nearby town to watch *Moby Dick* in a movie theater. He read J. D. Salinger's *Catcher in the Rye* and identified with protagonist Holden Caulfield's existential angst. By the time he graduated from Houghton in 1962, he found mainstream evangelicalism's ambivalence toward the civil rights movement incomprehensible. Criticism of Mouw's academic ambitions by fundamentalist friends only fed his alienation. As he pursued further studies at Western Theological Seminary, a Reformed Church of America school in Holland, Michigan, and then entered a philosophy program at the University of Alberta in Edmonton, a family friend wrote him "expressing concern for his soul." (Citing the Apostle Paul's warning in Colossians 2 about not being corrupted "through philosophy and vain deceit," Mouw's friend spelled the key word "fool-osophy.") In Alberta, Mouw studied for the first time with non-evangelicals, including socialists and Trotskyites, who sparked his opposition to the growing American presence in Indochina. By the time he entered the University of Chicago in 1963 to pursue a Ph.D. in philosophy, Mouw was finding "secular sources to be more helpful than evangelical ones" as he wrestled with moral questions about civil rights and the Vietnam War.

At Chicago Mouw explored a host of political and religious perspectives. Drawn to religious traditions that forthrightly confronted the segregated South, Mouw attended ecumenical chapel services, Catholic masses, and liberal Protestant congregations. Watching television coverage of the March on Washington in 1963, Mouw found Martin Luther King, Jr.'s message of "justice that would roll down like a mighty river" to be profoundly biblical and morally superior to the dominant evangelical stance of caution. He read Harry Emerson Fosdick, a liberal Baptist whose 1922 sermon "Shall the Fundamentalists Win" had drawn the ire of Mouw's forebears, and Walter Rauschenbusch, whose book *Christianity and the Social Crisis* (1907) launched the Social Gospel movement. He also joined the political left, helping to occupy the administration building in 1967 as part of Chicago's "Ban the Bomb" movement. He joined Students for a Democratic Society, eventually becoming an organizer. Drawn by its political principles, he also resonated with its tone. The passion, intensity, and length of the "endless participatory democracy antiwar protest discussion groups," he remembered, "was not unlike the fundamentalism of my youth." All the while, however, he worked "very hard not to be an evangelical."[4]

Estranged from his bewildered, and sometimes hostile, fundamentalist family and friends, Mouw felt isolated. It was "a very lonely time spiritually," he remembered. He gained some sustenance from civil rights hymns at radical meetings and rallies. But in the end, secular and mainline sources of authority, while nurturing his new moral convictions, failed to satisfy Mouw "in the deep places" of his soul. He remembered the spirituality of his childhood—"those moments in those old revival meetings when the preacher would say every head bowed, every eye closed, look into your heart, do you really love Jesus? For me those were the most sacred moments of my life. Never since then have I experienced that sort of transcendence." His radical political commitments, by comparison, failed to satisfy.

Old gospel hymns finally bridged the chasm between evangelical piety and radical politics. Lyrics such as "Is all on the altar of sacrifice laid?" "I surrender all," and "Break down every idol, cast out every foe" seemed to connect social action with the ultimate demands of following Christ. "Why shouldn't our draft cards be placed on the altar of sacrifice?" Mouw asked. "Shouldn't Jesus be made the Lord of what we do when we enter the voting booth? Mustn't we surrender our racism, our fondness for military solutions, and our ethnocentrism to his control?" This line of questioning brought Mouw to spiritual crisis one afternoon in his Chicago apartment. Fiddling with the radio dial, he came across the Moody Bible Institute Chorale singing an old hymn: "There is a fountain filled with blood; Drawn from Immanuel's veins; And sinners, plunged beneath that flood, Lose all their guilty stains." Mouw was deeply moved:

> I felt like I was discovering for the first time the real power of an evangelical faith. Nothing I had been studying in recent years, both in my philosophy courses and in my personal search for a way of tying things together—no secular perspective, no social gospel theology, no tract on "political Christianity"—had the radical depth of the solution the Moody choir was singing about. *All* of our guilty stains! Not only the very real guilty stains of my personal life but also the stains of our racism and nationalism and militarism. I knew, in that very moment, that while I had to keep wrestling with many of the trappings of evangelicalism, I had no choice but to do so *as* an evangelical.

Assenting that "a real body came out of a real tomb on Easter morning," the young doctoral student began once again to draw inspiration from evangelicalism.[5]

In 1968, as he finished his dissertation, the newly revived Mouw accepted an appointment on the philosophy faculty at Calvin College in Grand Rapids. He reentered the evangelical world cautiously at first but was soon heartened by the discovery of numerous fellow travelers. "When we regathered after the evangelical diaspora of the '60s," Mouw recounted several years later, "we discovered that there had been a significant number of scattered, lonely and frustrated 'Evangelicals for Gene McCarthy.'" And so Mouw rejoined evangelicalism in the late 1960s with a renewed piety that energized his passion for social activism. Importantly, Mouw's position at Calvin, the top educational institution of the Christian Reformed Church, reflected a renewed connection with his Reformed roots, which in turn profoundly shaped his new evangelical activism.[6]

II

At mid-century Calvin College was emerging from ethnic isolation. The parents of many of Mouw's students had grown up speaking the Dutch of their immigrant forebears and still felt like outsiders in American society. Adhering to the theological principles of the acronym TULIP—total depravity, unconditional election, limited atonement, irresistible grace, and perseverance of the saints—Dutch Calvinists opposed the free will theory of salvation and the effervescent revivalism that defined many strains of American evangelicalism. But if some cultural distance between American evangelicals and Dutch Calvinists remained, the college's Reformed theology by definition encouraged engagement in broader social structures. Abraham Kuyper, a close second only to sixteenth-century John Calvin himself as a patron saint of Calvin College constituents, stressed the sovereign lordship of Jesus Christ over all spheres of human activity. Calvinism, he wrote, "did not stop at a church order, but expanded in a life-system . . . that is able to fit itself to the needs of every stage of human development, in every department of life." Kuyper credited Reformation innovations for the flowering of modern European civilization with its attendant advances in science, art, commerce, republican government, and industry. He modeled this vision of Reformed worldliness in a dazzling turn-of-the-century career as a philosopher-theologian, founder of the Free University of Amsterdam, hyperactive journalist, and prime minister of the Netherlands.[7]

Following Kuyper's lead, Reformed evangelicals in the mid-twentieth century contended that the "Gospel must not be confined to Christian institutions." They punctuated their rhetoric with words such as "all" and "every." In 1971, for example, Martin LaMaire, a commercial artist and member of a Christian Reformed congregation in Berwyn, Illinois, declared in John Alexander's *The Other Side* magazine that "Jesus Christ is the Ruler, Redeemer, and Reconciler of *all things*, including the political, social, educational, artistic, racial, economic, labor, management, and scientific dimensions of life." Against the American fundamentalist dismissal of the worldly arts of politics and high culture, Reformed evangelicals, often only a generation removed from Kuyper's Amsterdam, insisted that Christians ought to be in the forefront of intellectual and social thought.[8]

Calvin students sought to live out these continental convictions amid the cultural shocks of the 1960s. Troubled by the college's relocation from urban Grand Rapids to a suburban estate, many pointed out the hypocrisy of enforcing behavioral restrictions while abandoning their tradition's social and cultural mandate. "The faith of our fathers . . . is clearly out of date," editors of the student newspaper declared in a blistering 1966 editorial that exploded like a bombshell in the Christian Reformed community. Campus unrest percolated into the late 1960s, carried along, according to a college historian, by a "sizeable group brilliant in thought and expression, spiritually sensitive, and deeply concerned about fundamental social and theological problems." To college officials they were also "noisy, ill-mannered, and enamored with the tactics of overkill and shock." In 1970 these students presented a "Youth Manifesto" to the annual Christian Reformed synod. They complained about racism, male chauvinism, lack of support for conscientious objection to war, moralistic and sentimental sermons, and the denomination's "edifice complex" in the face of poverty. "We feel cheated, neglected, yet still hopeful," said writers of the Manifesto. "We ask that you reaffirm that not only is God's Word relevant to all of life, but begin to make a concerted effort to implement God's Word to all of life."[9]

A number of young professors also embodied this sense of disillusionment. One wrote an article entitled "I Am Not One of Us." Mouw noted that his own family had been "seduced away by American fundamentalism." Yet if many students and professors found Christian Reformed and Calvin College structures ossified, they were inspired by older Kuyperian categories. Mouw enjoyed his own Reformed catechesis in a weekly colloquium in the philosophy department. He also served as a contributing editor to the *Reformed Journal*, a magazine he described as promoting "a combination of sane orthodoxy and enlightened social concern." Mouw learned that his new colleagues at Calvin had supported civil rights in the early 1960s when his own fundamentalist contemporaries had not. They had praised King's March on Washington in 1963 and backed federal intervention in the South. The youthful Mouw, bringing along leftist inclinations nurtured in Chicago, was glad to join the faculty's ferment. Calvin ethicist Lewis Smedes served as the president of the Grand Rapids Urban League. Mouw and other faculty members joined the Grand Rapids NAACP. They brought civil rights activists James Farmer and Fr. James Groppi to campus. In 1968 Mouw helped mobilize student antiwar efforts and added his signature to 47 others in a faculty petition calling for a cessation to the bombing of North Vietnam.[10]

Mouw also began to preach to evangelicals outside Grand Rapids. His first book—written in 1973 as "a progress report on a personal quest"—typified the approach of a new guard that saw progressive social action as a legitimate Christian activity. In the aptly titled *Political Evangelism*, Mouw denounced the "political passivity that has often been the posture of a culture-denying fundamentalism." Evangelism, rather, should integrate personal salvation and political activism. The word of God should be made

Figure 14. Richard Mouw, author of *Political Evangelism* (1973), represented Reformed evangelicals associated with Calvin College at the Thanksgiving Workshops. Courtesy of Archives, Calvin College, Grand Rapids, Michigan.

"flesh" by making systems just. Challenging Carl Henry, Mouw explained that "it is wrong to think that all of our social and political problems will be solved simply by changing individual lives." Take the case of a Christian slum dweller who rents from a Christian slum landlord, he suggested. "Each has experienced the redeeming power of the gospel in a personal way, but the reconciliation they might experience together in Jesus Christ is severely hindered by the kind of social system in which they live. There are economic practices, laws, and prejudices woven into the very fabric of society." With its attention to social structures and its view of politics as a legitimate religious calling, Mouw's tract made a Reformed case for social justice that could appeal to evangelicals otherwise preoccupied by personal salvation. Jesus, he wrote, "came to rescue the entire created order from the pervasive power of sin." Christ's atoning work "offers liberation for people in their cultural endeavours, in their institutions and the making of public policy." *Political Evangelism* came squarely out of the Reformed ethos of Calvin College. Excerpts from the book had been previously published in the *Reformed Journal*, and in the preface Mouw thanked members of Calvin's weekly Reformed colloquium, including philosopher Peter De Vos, historian George Marsden, theologian Henry Stob, and philosopher Nicholas Wolterstorff. Although greatly influenced by these colleagues, it was his fundamentalist background that helped Mouw translate Reformed thought into language that evangelicals could understand.[11]

III

If Mouw's integration of politics and evangelism seemed radical in the mainstream American evangelical context, its challenge was mild indeed compared to that posed by the Institute for Christian Studies. The ICS, which Mouw often visited in the 1970s for scholarly conferences, was a Reformed think tank and graduate school in midtown Toronto. Its founders, who called themselves Reformationalists, sought to do no less than launch a movement that would reshape North American society and politics through the study of theology, philosophy, and political theory. Seeking to flesh out their heritage using Kuyperian logic, ICS adherents castigated what they viewed as the Christian Reformed Church's quaint moralisms that failed to address pressing social issues. For instance, the denomination's periodical explained in the mid-1960s that even if John F. Kennedy's assassination left his agenda incomplete, still Christ could declare, "It is finished." Hendrik Hart, James Olthuis, Bernard Zylstra, and other young turk Reformationalists at the ICS—mostly fiery personalities in their early thirties—denounced such lines as pietistic sophistry. Instead, they envisioned starting new radical, socially active Reformed communities all over North America. From modest beginnings in 1967 as a tiny school with only one instructor and no degree programs, ICS grew steadily. In 1968 alone, Hart gave five series of lectures and taught five courses to 125 students in twelve locations throughout Canada. By 1971 the ICS boasted five teaching and research faculty, 26 full-time students, 100 part-time students, and a master's degree in philosophy. The Free University of Amsterdam, which affirmed ICS's graduate-level ambitions, worked closely with the young school, providing a steady flow of faculty and doctoral students across the Atlantic.[12]

By the early 1970s, the ICS had evolved into an idiosyncratic fusion of Dutch ethnicity and political counterculture. Its constituency came mostly from children of the 185,000 Dutch immigrants who entered Canada between 1947 and 1970 because of a stagnant economy in the Netherlands. Tobacco and marijuana were pervasive at the Toronto school. Baggy jeans and tattered corduroy hung on gaunt frames, and beards proliferated. Communal living in several large houses in Toronto was common. Requiring no assignment deadlines, grades, transcripts, or degrees, ICS nurtured a profoundly anti-establishment ethos that stressed collegiality over hierarchy. Its administrative structure evolved into what faculty member Peter Schouls called "coordinate decentralization," a system in which employees were accountable to boards and committees, not other individuals. An advertisement for ICS in the early 1970s read, "Are you going to grad school? Try the House of Subversion. . . . We are subverting the American university structure. We don't have million dollar buildings. . . . We aren't scholarly imperialists. We've stopped worshipping the Ph.D. We give guerrilla credentials." The ICS also released an "explosive little book" called *Out of Concern for the Church*. One reviewer wrote that "its five essays by as many different Evangelical authors, drag the Evangelical world, kicking and screaming, to the operating room where possibly its life can be saved." Its authors, with close connections to a renegade Reformed congregation called St. Matthew's-in-the-Basement, contended that church structures were teetering toward irrelevance. The Christian Reformed Church could only be saved by closing the denomination's Calvin Theological Seminary, disbanding denominational committees, stripping ministers of their credentials, and letting "ruling elders in the congregations designate as instructors in the Word whosever can bring the Word of Life from the Scriptures."[13]

Out of Concern for the Church also scorned the American church for complicity in the injustices of American culture. Its authors accused Christians of "awhoring after that great American Bitch, the Democratic Way of Life." This criticism reflected the ICS's rigorous critique of mainstream politics, both liberal and conservative. "Our enslavement to technological and economic progress," wrote Bob Goudzwaard in the movement's magazine *Vanguard*, "is leading us down a path to slow death." Noting the limits of nonrenewable energy sources, he argued, "Such consumption cannot go on indefinitely." Paul Marshall, ICS student and founding member of the Evangelical Committee for Social Action, wrote, "Unrestrained agricorporations, armed with government support and approval, the latest technology, tax breaks, and the ideology of economic progress and efficiency, are killing off the family farms of Canada, creating a massive social upheaval with massive social costs that must be paid by us all." This hostility toward both conservative and liberal camps reflected ICS's resonance with New Left critiques of mainstream politics. In 1971 an angry Robert Carvill, the editor of *Vanguard*, called the U.S. government "a friend of the anti-Christ" after guards at the Canadian border held up a batch of *Vanguard* magazines for being "subversive literature."[14]

ICS's suspicion of mainstream political ideologies and its simultaneous desire to engage social structures put it in a bind. Students for a Democratic Society—as well as Dutch political philosopher Herman Dooyeweerd and the Dutch Reformed experience in Holland—modeled a way out. Instead of integrating into mainstream culture, ICS confronted the mainstream with separate structures entirely. It promoted separate Christian school systems and the creation of Christian political parties and other national institutions. John Olthuis, executive director of ICS, imagined this distinctive vision:

> I find myself hurrying along to catch the opening of Parliament in Ottawa. The Christian political party is now the official opposition. . . . In the Parliamentary galleries I meet the head of the *Christian Labor Association of North America,* the international association of Christ-believing workers. I leave the gallery and pick up a copy of *Voice,* the Christian daily newspaper. . . . I bump into one of the members of the *Institute for Christian Curriculum Studies.* I mumble my apologies and

rush on only to be engulfed by a horde of students buzzing excitedly
on their way to the campus of Ottawa's Christian University. . . . I
take a deep, clean breath. My heart is full of joy, for America is a
good place to live, a free place, free for all people to live out of their
convictions.[15]

If Toronto's stark separatism and dismissal of traditional pieties troubled
many in Grand Rapids, a common commitment to universal principles of
Reformed doctrine and worldly engagement unified them. Both sides agreed,
despite their institutional rivalry, that human arrogance could be redeemed
only by "the radical message of the gospel." In the end, Mouw's *Political
Evangelism* fundamentally affirmed a position paper written by ICS students:
"We would want to speak of 'evangelism' as the magnetic Life-Way of a
People who are compellingly attractive because they are engaged as a Shalom-
bringing People in politics, education, economics, the arts . . . engaged in
everything as a distinctive People, drunk on the New Wine of Jesus Christ!"
An intra-Reformed détente was still a decade away, but a commitment to so-
cial transformation characterized both camps from the beginning.[16]

Through the 1960s this Reformed vision was beginning to carry over to
neo-evangelical circles. To be sure, the Reformationalists were working with
a cultural handicap. ICS's use of marijuana, profanity, tobacco, and idiosyncratic Reformed language often alienated this audience. Its countercultural
position, though, appealed to evangelical draft-dodgers who welcomed ICS's
hostility toward capitalism, the Vietnam War, and the establishment. And
there was a much larger potential constituent base in more moderate sectors
of evangelicalism. ICS and Reformed progressives in Grand Rapids thus
tacked to the center. They learned to soften their cultural idiosyncrasies and
imperial rhetoric. By the mid-1970s, most of ICS's new students were non-
Dutch, many of them American evangelicals coming from Young Life chapters in Minneapolis and the Coalition for Christian Outreach in western
Pennsylvania. Reformed progressives from Grand Rapids also nurtured
evangelical ties. Writers in the *Reformed Journal* (a full half of whose readers in 1973 also subscribed to *Christianity Today*) and *Vanguard* began to
invoke Kuyper more sparingly—and when they did, as a way "to start conversations, not to end them." Moreover, they went out of their way to publish
articles from evangelical sources, especially on issues of social and political
concerns. Calvin College and ICS brought in numbers of evangelical guest
lecturers, including Samuel Escobar and René Padilla of the Latin American

Theological Fraternity, Trinity theologian Clark Pinnock, Wheaton philosopher Arthur Holmes, and Post-American Jim Wallis. Some evangelicals—like Mouw, ICS historian Carl McIntire, son of the notorious fundamentalist preacher of the same name; political scientist Paul Henry of Calvin College and son of Carl Henry; and Robert Carvill, a Baptist graduate of the evangelical Gordon College and Trinity College in Deerfield, Illnois—remained in Grand Rapids and Toronto. They integrated more fully into the Reformed world and interpreted the Reformed vision to Billy Graham-style evangelicals. The annual Christianity and Politics conference held at Calvin College in the early 1970s, which many prominent members of the emerging evangelical left attended, was, according to Mouw, "one of the most important instruments for the opening up of Calvin to the larger Christian world."[17]

Reformationalists also traveled to evangelical sites. In 1968, ethicist Lewis Smedes left Calvin for Fuller Theological Seminary in Pasadena. In 1969, ICS representatives spoke at a philosophy conference at Wheaton College. In 1970, 40 students from ICS and several other Christian Reformed colleges attended InterVarsity's Urbana convention, where *Vanguard* got its start. For four straight days, Reformationalists blanketed the convention floor with elaborate four-page spreads decrying the stifling middle-class character of Urbana '70. "We have tried such a vast pantheon of idols," wrote Richard Forbes, "Individualism, Capitalism, Democratism, Militarism. Just how do we escape them all?" By "transforming North American Christianity," answered fellow student John Hultink. The transformation was already "slowly but surely being driven into the spinal cord of complacent North American Christianity." If InterVarsity organizers felt insulted, many young evangelicals responded with "great enthusiasm." ICS faculty Calvin Seerveld and Bernard Zylstra traveled to western Pennsylvania every summer to train new staff members for the Coalition for Christian Outreach, a Presbyterian-oriented student ministry. Based in Pittsburgh and sprawled throughout the Allegheny region on more than 40 college and university campuses, CCO brought in many Reformed speakers in the evangelical left to its annual convention in downtown Pittsburgh. The convention drew tens of thousands of students during the 1970s and 1980s. Several of CCO's staffers maintained close ties with ICS, taking students to Toronto for conferences.[18]

One of those students, Jennie Geisler, an evangelical student from Grove City College, remembers that COO staffers disillusioned with evangelicalism's tepid sense of political mission pounded into her head that "ALL of life is religion." The influences of CCO and ICS took her on a path of social justice that led far from her pietistic upbringing. In the 1970s Geisler refused to pay taxes for several years, read the *Post-American*, moved to Pittsburgh to start an intentional community, joined political campaigns, and protested the nuclear arms race. While this burden to shape all spheres of life was not new, the way in which the Reformationalists melded it with the heady radicalism of the 1960s and 1970s was. And the growing intersection with evangelical ethnics, many of whom transposed an active Dutch Reformed politics to the American context, profoundly shaped many evangelicals such as Geisler who were emerging out of their tradition's passive conservatism.[19]

By 1972 Reformed dissenters boasted impressive numbers and a wide reach. There were 6,000 *Vanguard* subscribers, a small but growing graduate school of 125 students, a publishing house, a prolific stable of writers, and new motivation to reform evangelicalism. Curriculum materials produced by ICS spread through evangelical, Mennonite, Lutheran, and Pentecostal circles. In 1974 InterVarsity printed extended excerpts of Mouw's *Political Evangelism* in its student magazine. Both Mouw, who went on to become the president of Fuller Seminary, and Jim Skillen, president of the Reformed-oriented Association for Public Justice which emerged in the late 1970s, would shape evangelical thought and practice through into the 1980s and beyond. Mouw in particular spoke graciously and inclusively of a common "evangelical self-understanding" as he interacted with InterVarsity, *Christianity Today*, and a multitude of conferences on social action. Other Reformed evangelicals, more critical than Mouw, sought to redeem a flawed and pietistic American evangelicalism. "We evangelicals," wrote George DeVries in the *Reformed Journal*, "have interpreted our responsibilities to our neighbor far too narrowly and limited our neighborhood far too much." "A faith," he continued, "that lacks social concern is a dead faith." DeVries and a host of Reformed thinkers pushed broader evangelicalism to shape all spheres of life for God's Kingdom.[20]

IV

As the 1973 Thanksgiving Workshop approached, progressive neo-evangelicals began to reflect several of the most salient demographic categories and cultural impulses of Reformed evangelicals associated with Calvin and ICS. First, both groups invested heavily in the public and social service sectors. Well over two-thirds of the evangelical left held education, social service, and religious jobs. Second, both esteemed education; 85 percent of *Reformed Journal* readers and 86 percent of *Sojourners* readers held a college degree. The median educational level of *The Other Side* readers was two years of graduate work. Some scholars, noting these characteristics, have classified progressive evangelicals as prototypical members of the "knowledge class," the term used in the 1980s by sociologists to describe the post-industrial proliferation of professional vocations whose workers manipulate symbols rather than produce material goods.[21]

Perhaps most significantly, progressive evangelicals—like Reformationalists in Toronto—typically emerged out of the crucible of urban living. "The frontline of the battle for the gospel," said Jimmy Allen, pastor of an urban Southern Baptist congregation in San Antonio, "is in the cities." Living in the city exposed many in the evangelical left to the structural nature of poverty and often led to dramatic changes in social perspectives. Bill Leslie, for example, bred in his fundamentalist home in rural Ohio and at Bob Jones University to be a political conservative, underwent a political transformation as pastor of the Elm-LaSalle Bible Church, a daughter church of Moody Bible Church in downtown Chicago. Elm-LaSalle moved quickly out of fundamentalism into neo-evangelical circles in the early 1960s under its young pastor. With close ties to InterVarsity, Leslie and the Elm-LaSalle church began to denounce the fundamentalist antipathy toward social programs and political involvement. The church instead called its members to become "corporately involved in human services." By 1964 Leslie had become a political independent "distressed over the agonies of the poor and dispossessed." By 1968 he strenuously opposed the Republican ticket, concerned that Nixon would cut off federally funded programs for the poor. Elm-LaSalle members, most of whom were political conservatives before joining the church, described themselves in the early 1970s as "more politically liberal." By 1973 Elm-LaSalle had opened a coffee house, a tutoring ministry, and a legal aid clinic near the Cabrini-Green and Carl Sandburg housing projects. Leslie soon found himself deeply involved in local politics, heading up the Chicago-Orleans Housing Corporation and the Near North Area council.[22]

Church of the Saviour in Washington, D.C., one of the most prominent urban evangelical churches in the United States, also nurtured a strong sense of social justice. Inner piety and prayer, member Elizabeth O'Connor contended, ought to spark an "outer journey" that addresses a multitude of social issues such as "alcoholism, dope addiction, the aged, the blind, the sick, the broken in mind and spirit; there are slums, with all the problems of housing and education; there are nuclear warfare and the problems of automation and leisure." Church of the Saviour worked with the Welfare Department to restore crumbling homes in the District, befriended youth in the Lily Ponds Housing Development, established a coffee shop and arts center called The Potter's House, and aided alcoholics and mentally handicapped persons in the Renewal Center. Many members practiced intentional poverty. In the 1960s and 1970s Church of the Saviour became a haven for evangelical government bureaucrats, social service workers, and those otherwise disillusioned with the apolitical tendencies of their tradition. The church mentored several important evangelical moderates and left-wingers—Bob McCan, a former Baptist minister who sought to establish "a polycultural college, which would be a miniature world community"; Jim Wallis, founder of the Post-Americans; Wes Michaelson, an aide to Mark Hatfield and future general secretary of the Reformed Church in America; and Richard Barnet, a leftist historian and State Department bureaucrat in the Kennedy administration. The evangelical left in turn often cited Church of the Saviour as a model of spiritual and social engagement.[23]

Hundreds of other evangelical congregations and dozens of urban study programs also bucked the 1950s and 1960s trend of suburban flight.[24] In fact, networks of progressive evangelicals emerged in many major American cities by the early 1970s. Initially coalescing around civil rights action in the 1960s, they began to assist federal government programs related to the War on Poverty. When the Nixon administration cut federal funding, they began to work more closely with local and state initiatives. Many also initiated their own holistic programs. In Des Moines, Iowa, Democratic governor Harold Hughes, an outspoken evangelical, mobilized religious and civic leaders to build medical clinics and start summer jobs programs for youth. The Des Moines program proved so successful that it expanded to six other Iowa cities. In Grand Rapids, Michigan, the Inner City Christian Foundation sought to "bring biblical justice to bear on . . . the inner city" by purchasing, renovating, and selling homes to urban residents. In Denver, a network of congregations called Evangelical Concern of Denver launched programs to promote low-income housing and help for mentally handicapped persons. In St. Louis, the Cornerstone Corporation, spearheaded by Grace and Peace Fellowship, purchased deteriorating buildings, restored them, and rented apartments to poor tenants. In Chicago, the Circle and LaSalle congregations were key participants in "Conversations on the City," one of several organizations, including the Wesleyan Urban Coalition and the Englewood Economic Development, intended to promote social justice. Progressive evangelicals in Texas launched the Texas Baptist Urban Strategy Council. Other initiatives included the Central City Conference of Evangelicals (CCCE) in Detroit, Christians United Serving Everyone in Cincinnati; and the Evangelical Committee for Urban Ministries and Boston Urban Ministries in Massachusetts. Working cooperatively in local politics, soup kitchens, and medical clinics, reformist evangelicals created urban counterparts to the suburban Orange County coffee klatches that historian Lisa McGirr posits were so critical to launching the New Right in California.[25]

Dozens of books, hundreds of conferences, and thousands of articles buttressed these urban programs with provocative analyses of deteriorating cities.[26] For over a decade progressive academicians associated with the *Reformed Journal* had been holding out hope that researchers could solve global hunger, poverty, even militarism. In 1964 Calvin's James Daane wrote, "Because of the advance of science and technology, and particularly with the coming of automation, the potential wealth of the world is for all practical purposes infinite. For the first time in history it is technically possible to eliminate poverty on a world scale." When global famine reached the American consciousness in the 1970s, *Reformed Journal* contributors urged technical solutions. They hoped to develop new technologies to discover and channel new energy sources and to stabilize grain prices and availability. Even those influenced by the New Left, which distrusted technology as the tool of an authoritarian government-university-corporate unholy trinity, began to welcome the contributions of science and technology. The Post-Americans, for example, avidly devoured technical reports on social problems, notably the Kerner Commission's report on riots. "The best means are found by hard-headed analysis and experimentation, not by appeal to revelation," wrote *The Other Side*'s John Alexander about whether to decrease unemployment rates through tax cuts, government spending, or unbridled competition. "This is a very complicated, technical question of economics which the Christian as such has no special competence to judge. That is a question which, like it or not, has to be left to experts." The progressive coalition could in good faith intone the lyrics of a hymn entitled "From Thee All Skill and Science Flow" at the Thanksgiving Workshop in Chicago.[27]

The evangelical left turned to progressive politics to implement technical solutions to structural problems. Calvin's Paul Henry charged that too many

Christians "have shunned politics as a dirty, worldly, and humanistic endeavor alien to the concerns of the gospel." To make a real difference, evangelicals needed to work within the system, to practice a "progressive realism," explained Stephen Monsma, another political scientist at Calvin College and a Democratic member of the Michigan House of Representatives from 1974 to 1978. Relying solely on church aid to tackle poverty, reformist evangelicals advised, might be ideal, but religious organizations lacked expertise and a central organization to address structural injustices. "While private initiative in charity and improvement of conditions is essential," wrote Jack Buckley in *HIS* magazine, "the only way to achieve intensive and long-lasting change is to bring about change in government policy." What evangelical conservatives "have failed to see," wrote Paul Henry, "is that the gospel itself is, among other things, a gospel of political redemption." By 1973, well ahead of the Moral Majority, Richard Mouw's *Political Evangelism* had come to typify the approach of a new guard that saw social work and politics as legitimate, even divinely appointed, vocations.[28]

*   *   *

At the Thanksgiving Workshop in 1973, when progressive evangelicals met in Chicago to disown the passive conservatism of their tradition, at least half a dozen Reformed evangelicals were there. They included Fuller's Lewis Smedes, *Reformed Journal* editor Marlin VanElderen, ICS historian C. T. McIntire, and Calvin's Richard Mouw. Together they insistently articulated the Reformed vision that God is Lord of all, including politics. "We affirm that God lays total claim upon the lives of his people," read the Chicago Declaration. "We cannot, therefore, separate our lives in Christ from the situation in which God has placed us in the United States and the world." Mouw, bridging the ethnic Dutch traditions of Reformed culture and the revivalist ethos of Billy Graham, showed an emerging evangelical left at Calvin, Chicago, and Fuller that Reformed and non-Reformed evangelicals could work together toward a progressive politics.

CHAPTER 8

Ron Sider and the Politics of Simple Living

> If God's Word is true, then all of us who dwell in affluent
> nations are trapped in sin. . . . We have profited from
> systematic injustice. . . . We are guilty of an outrageous
> offense against God and neighbor.
> —Ron Sider in *Rich Christians in an Age of Hunger*

Like the Dutch Reformed, Swiss-German Anabaptists also broadened post-war evangelicalism. With a history reaching to the turbulent sixteenth-century Reformation, most Anabaptists opposed infant baptism, iconography, church-state collusion, the use of violence, and other Catholic and Reformed innovations they saw as extra-biblical. In early modern Europe, persecution and martyrdom had resulted from these contrarian views. Their Amish, Mennonite, and Brethren descendants, many of whom immigrated to the United States, took a lower profile. Known as the "quiet in the land," most worked the soil as farmers in the American Midwest. During the mid-twentieth century, however, many reversed this quietist trajectory, emerging out of ethnic enclaves in the 1950s. Increasingly identifying with evangelicalism, some Anabaptists prodded it toward prophetic social engagement. The evangelical left in fact featured a disproportionate number of Anabaptists. Chicago Declaration signees such as Ron Sider, author of *Rich Christians in an Age of Hunger*; John Howard Yoder, author of the soon-to-be-released *Politics of Jesus*; and Art Gish, a Brethren activist, propounded several Anabaptist themes that resonated with the zeitgeist of the 1960s and 1970s.[1]

Anabaptists' clearest link to the emerging evangelical left was their shared antiwar position. For Post-American Jim Wallis and Senator Mark

Hatfield, both revolting against the Vietnam War, Anabaptism offered a theological and historical precedent for their dissent. But principled non-violence would ultimately prove too radical for many evangelicals. In the end, Ron Sider's emphasis on global injustice ultimately proved far more resonant and influential. His best-selling *Rich Christians* amplified Samuel Escobar's critique of structural inequality in U.S. society and affirmed Reformed evangelical Richard Mouw's stress on Christ as Lord of all creation. It dovetailed nicely with the growing attention to corporate responsibility promoted by Carl Henry and his coterie of non-rightist neo-evangelicals. And it resonated with a broader cultural fascination in the 1970s with natural, simple, relational, and global habits of living. Abandoning traditional quietism at a serendipitous moment in American and evangelical history, Ron Sider and his fellow Anabaptists helped a new evangelical left coalesce around issues of global justice and simple living.

I

Sider grew up in the 1940s on a 275-acre farm in rural southern Ontario. He was firmly ensconced in the close community of the nonconformist Brethren in Christ, a denomination equal parts Anabaptist and evangelical holiness. Growing up in a family in which faith mattered "more than anything else in the world," Sider knelt at the altar at age eight during a revival service and "accepted Jesus Christ." An Anabaptist ethos pervaded this very evangelical experience. His mother wore a prayer veiling. His father rigorously kept the Sabbath. His cousin Roy Sider, an influential bishop in Ontario, preached that it was wrong to vote. Very few of the Brethren played organized sports or pursued higher education. Sider himself struggled with guilt over his "worldly" decision to wear a tie and to part his hair to the side. Sometimes burdened by the perfectionistic theology of his tradition, he was relieved when his father once cussed after a prized cow died. A sense of Anabaptist history also characterized his childhood. One side of his family—with the German last name of Wenger—tried to trace its roots back to the sixteenth-century Reformation in the Alps. Four centuries later the Wengers and Siders still identified with the cultural and political marginalization of the early Anabaptists. Each genealogical line contained ancestors who had been persecuted—sometimes even tortured and executed—by their Reformed and Catholic antagonists.[2]

In his teenage years Sider abandoned many of his tradition's cultural idiosyncrasies. He was a star athlete and an outstanding student in his one-room country school. One of the first in his family to attend college, he headed off to Waterloo Lutheran University in Ontario in 1958. Struggling with doubt over faith and modern science, he specialized in apologetics under John Warwick Montgomery, who was just emerging in the 1960s as an important evangelical opponent of the "death of God" movement. Montgomery, who would go on to debate atheist Madalyn Murray O'Hair and situation ethicist Joseph Fletcher in the late 1960s, taught Sider proofs for the resurrection of Christ and inspired him to pursue a life in academia. When Sider received the news that he had received a full graduate fellowship at Yale University to study early modern European and Reformation history under noted Luther scholar Jaroslav Pelikan, he fell to his knees "breathless with gratitude" for this opportunity to be a faithful witness to Christ in the secular academy. At Yale Sider began his mission to become a college professor and InterVarsity campus advisor.[3]

Sider's research, however, led to an unexpected vocation as social activist. His dissertation subject, Reformation-era theologian Andreas Von Karlstadt, inspired his desire not to "let the doctrine of justification sell out sanctification." Faith, he decided, required right behavior, not merely correct belief. Seeking to understand poverty, racial inequities, and evangelical indifference in the face of urban blight, Sider experimented with urban living. He lived at first on the edge, then in the center, of New Haven's black community. In 1967 he joined the NAACP and sat with his black landlords the night Martin Luther King, Jr. was assassinated. In 1968 he participated in voter registration drives and encouraged the InterVarsity chapter at Yale to do so as well. These experiences, he remembers, "got me so concerned with racial issues that I felt I could not go on doing nothing but reading Latin and German for my dissertation."[4]

Despite his new passions, Sider did in fact finish the dissertation. Subsequently, Messiah College, his denomination's leading institutional of higher education, hired him to teach at an urban satellite campus next to Temple University in Philadelphia. This move completed his shift away from history to social concerns. Instead of teaching classes on Reformation history, he focused on war, poverty, and racism. The Sider family lived in a largely black neighborhood in Germantown, and their sons went to a nearly all-black public school. Sider's wife, Arbutus, organized parents' groups and led marches on city hall. They attended several non-Mennonite churches: a black

Presbyterian congregation and a semi-intentional community called Jubilee Fellowship (where John Alexander of *The Other Side* also attended). But Sider's concern for social injustices, he later explained, emanated largely from his childhood. He had observed his parents, who had never voted, adopt a needy child out of an "Anabaptist concern for peace and justice and for the poor." Sider later explained that "I didn't start out in life seeing the world from the windows of a Cadillac but rather [from] the other side." His childhood—rural, Canadian, Anabaptist—gave him a "distance from the culture that . . . has been a real blessing." These marginal identities and a literalistic Mennonite reading of Jesus' Sermon on the Mount, which stressed radical generosity, animated Sider's vision for simple living.[5]

Sider burst onto the broader evangelical scene in the early 1970s. In a widely read 1972 article he urged Christians to avoid excessive wealth and give very generously to the needy. He proposed that they increase giving beyond the standard ten percent tithe. As income grows, he argued, so should the proportion of giving. Sider's anti-prosperity gospel resonated with evangelicals in the midst of economic recession and oil embargoes. He became a sought-after speaker across the nation, and his "graduated tithe" article swelled into a best-selling book on simple living and global injustice. *Rich Christians in an Age of Hunger*, which represented Anabaptism's most influential contribution to evangelicalism in the postwar era, opened darkly. "Hunger and starvation stalk the land," intoned Sider. "Ten thousand persons died today because of inadequate food. . . . The problem, we know, is that the world's resources are not evenly distributed. North Americans live on an affluent island amid a sea of starving humanity." Perpetuating current American policies, explained Sider, would lead the world toward global economic collapse.[6]

Rich Christians, however, was more of a moral indictment than an appraisal of economic conditions. Evangelicals, he complained, all too often failed to right injustices because of an inadequate conception of sin. "Christians frequently restrict the scope of ethics to a narrow class of 'personal' sins," Sider explained. "But they fail to preach about the sins of institutionalized racism, unjust economic structures and militaristic institutions which destroy people just as much as do alcohol and drugs." White flight from the cities to the suburbs, with the concomitant loss of resources from such a demographic shift, only exacerbated structural injustice embedded in economic and political systems. Even the purchase of bananas, Sider continued, confronted evangelicals with moral questions. Why are bananas from Central

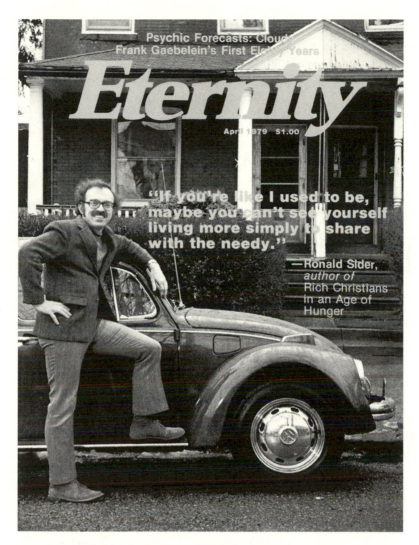

Figure 15. Ron Sider, founder of Evangelicals for McGovern and convener of the Thanksgiving Workshops, was the most prominent supporter of evangelical simple living. After publishing *Rich Christians in an Age of Hunger*, Sider was profiled in numerous evangelical magazines.

America so much less expensive than apples from a neighboring state? Despite shipping costs, they are cheaper, he answered, because U.S. fruit conglomerates pay unfair wages to Latin American workers. "If God's Word is true, then all of us who dwell in affluent nations are trapped in sin," Sider wrote. "We have profited from systematic injustice. . . . We are guilty of an outrageous offense against God and neighbor." Sider's incorporation of the language of sin offered a distinctive evangelical contribution to broader debates on global poverty.[7]

Sider concluded with a call to political engagement. The virtue of individual acts of economic penance, he suggested, would multiply if Christians banded together to transform foreign and domestic policy. "We must demand a foreign policy that unequivocally sides with the poor. If we truly believe that 'all men are created equal,' then our foreign policy must be redesigned to promote the interests of all people and not just the wealthy elites in developing countries or our own multinational corporations." He urged evangelicals to lobby Congress into dropping trade barriers of imports from developing countries and to devoting more money to third-world nations than to the arms race. He also addressed the structure of world trade and the international debt crisis. This detailed attention to economic structure represented significant movement from Carl Henry's posture in *Uneasy Conscience of Fundamentalism*. Sider, in prescribing specific solutions for social problems, was taking Henry to his logical conclusion.[8]

Sider also offered a striking global perspective. In an era when global hunger had not yet captivated the public's attention with televised images of Africans' distended bellies, *Rich Christians* presented an unrelenting international focus. Sider told stories from Africa and cited statistics from the Southern Hemisphere. Elsewhere, he lambasted Richard Nixon for a 1973 speech in which the president declared, "I have made this basic decision: In allocating the products of America's farms between markets abroad and those in the United States, we must put the American consumer first." "Such a statement may be good politics," rebutted Sider, "but it certainly is not good theology." Alongside Samuel Escobar's global witness, Sider's emphasis on American materialism, imperialism, social injustice, and global need set much of the developing evangelical left's agenda.[9]

Rich Christians—in addressing social structures as well as personal sin, in embracing politics as a method of structural correction, in focusing on global realities—was a remarkably innovative work. Predictably, these were the very elements that drew fire from politically conservative evangelicals. A coterie of evangelical economists associated with a think tank called the Institute for Christian Economics (ICE) criticized Sider for embracing a theory of zero-sum markets in which economic exchanges benefit one economic actor at the expense of another economic actor. On the contrary, ICE economists Gary North, David Chilton, and Ronald Nash contended, capitalism offered a positive-sum game in which both parties could win. This economic system, they suggested, was the best possible system in an inherently sinful world. Chilton's book *Productive Christians in an Age of Guilt Manipulators* (1981), a direct rejoinder to *Rich Christians in an Age of Hunger*, stated that third-world poverty could be traced to "cultural, moral, and even religious dimensions" that reveal themselves in a "lack of respect for any private property," "lack of initiative," and a "high leisure preference." In other words, Sider should fault third-world nations for not emulating Western prosperity rather than the wealthy for not alleviating global poverty. A more sophisticated analysis came from University of Michigan philosopher George Mavrodes, who complained that *Rich Christians* did not take into account the dozens of unintended changes that occur when altering only one part of an economic system. "Suppose that we [Americans] voluntarily increased the price that we pay for crude rubber (a recurrent suggestion of Sider's). Then, Sider says, rubber workers would get higher wages. Fine. But wouldn't rubber producers scramble to increase production? And wouldn't land and labor be diverted from other enterprises, such as food production, to cash in on higher rubber prices? Since we don't need more rubber, the increased production would represent a waste of resources. Sider seems not to notice such consequences."[10]

Despite (or perhaps because of) the book's scathing indictment and fiery critics, *Rich Christians* enjoyed astonishing attention. Growing numbers of evangelicals experimented with Sider's "modest proposals toward a simpler lifestyle." Some gave money away according to a graduated tithe. Some lived communally. Some cooked without meat. Sider received glowing reviews from InterVarsity's *HIS* magazine, which rejoiced that it was now not as "socially damaging to question the motives of the government/military/ business complex in the U.S. The time may have arrived for American evangelicals to venture an extension of official belief into riskier economic and social areas." Many InterVarsity chapters, churches, and evangelical colleges assigned the text in classes and seminars. In 1977 Sider even appeared as guest on the 700 Club, before Pat Robertson turned explicitly right-wing. By 1997 the book had gone through four editions and sold over 350,000 copies. Among progressive evangelicals, *Rich Christians* enjoyed status as a cult classic.[11]

II

If Sider's treatment of global injustice was primarily theoretical, a second influential Anabaptist text was eminently practical. On the kitchen counters of many evangelicals in the 1970s lay a cookbook called *More-with-Less*, printed by Mennonite publisher Herald Press. Ron Sider praised author Doris Longacre for providing "good concrete models" for the "astonishing numbers of people" who had responded to *Rich Christians* and the new simplicity movement. Longacre was making theology in the kitchen.[12]

In addition to Anabaptist simple-living beliefs, international experiences profoundly shaped Longacre's effort. After graduating from Goshen College in Indiana, she served with the relief agency Mennonite Central Committee (MCC). She managed a Language Study Center in Vietnam from 1964 to 1967 and worked in Indonesia from 1971 to 1972. When Longacre returned to the United States, she became a frequent lecturer on world hunger and an assistant in the MCC division of Rural Development and Food Production. Her husband Paul Longacre became MCC coordinator for Food and Hunger Concerns. These experiences shaped *More-with-Less*, a thrifty yet exotic cookbook boasting "500 delightful recipes that prove that when we reduce our need for heavily grain-fed meat, the superprocessed, and the sugary, we not only release resources for the hungry, but also protect our health and our pocketbooks." Recipes from Uganda, Mexico, Vietnam, and other corners of the globe filled the pages. Especially popular were "Brazilian Beans and Rice" offered by a contributor from Recife, Brazil, "Middle-Eastern Lentil Soup" from Egypt, and "Zucchini Omelet" from Lancaster County, Pennsylvania. In the first chapter Longacre wrote that the "average North American uses five times as much grain per person yearly as does one of the two billion persons living in poor countries." *More-with-Less* was not vegetarian; Longacre knew that a meatless cookbook, like Frances Lappé's immensely popular and rigidly vegetarian *Diet for a Small Planet* (1971), was not "realistic" for its intended audience of Mennonite farm families. She did, however, drastically cut meat ingredients to an intake level on a par with third-world nations and eliminate

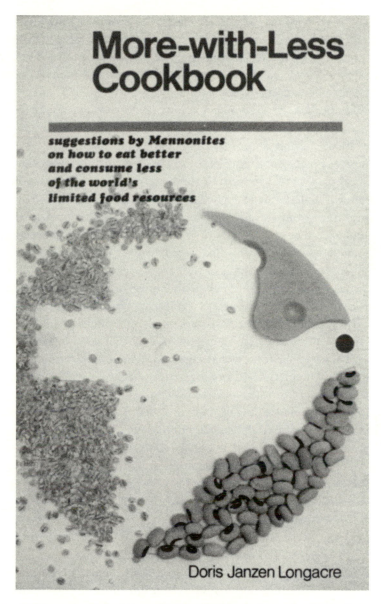

Figure 16. The cover of the *More-with-Less Cookbook* pictured a dinner plate that represented many evangelical Anabaptist themes: a cross, the world, the simplicity of beans and rice, and a peaceful dove. By the year 2000 it had sold over 800,000 copies. Courtesy of Audrey Miller and Herald Press.

instructions on roasting and carving meat. The cookbook's sequel—*Living More with Less*—offered critiques and suggestions from around the world on nearly every page of the lifestyle manual. In a chapter entitled "Learn from the World Community," Christians from around the world admonished American readers to build energy-efficient public transportation networks between towns and cities; to learn to cook simple, nutritious meals; to use fewer kitchen appliances; to recycle; to plant home and community gardens; and to value families and friendships above making money.[13]

Anabaptist in its global egalitarianism, *More-with-Less* also reflected an evangelical piety in its approach to simple living. In a cassette tape devotional entitled "Entertaining Simply," Longacre told listeners, "Jesus frequently used mealtime settings to share and teach important values, build relationships, and celebrate events." The way we prepare and eat food, she suggested, should model spiritual truths. She urged readers to read passages from Scripture and devotional books and to share stories of God's grace with one another before leaving the dinner table. Longacre also affirmed growing evangelical politicization. She urged attention to structural injustices: global hunger caused by too-high tariff barriers imposed by affluent nations against poor nations, lack of involvement by poor nations in international economic agencies, corporate farming, global unemployment, unfair farm policy, and arms sales to dictators. After cooking simple, healthy meals, Longacre instructed her readers, write letters to lawmakers. "The two realms—conserving resources at home and taking on economic and political issues—are as inseparable as the yolk and white of a scrambled egg."[14]

More-with-Less sold remarkably well despite its preachy premise, unconventional recipes, and Mennonite asceticism. Its expressions of evangelical piety and its perfectly timed release in the midst of global hunger awareness resonated with the public. Upon its release in 1976, sales boomed in Mennonite counties throughout Pennsylvania, Ohio, and Indiana. The cookbook, however, soon spread within broader evangelicalism. The Southern Baptist Book Club ordered 2,000 copies. A Methodist order of 2,000 more followed. Within months, the publishers told Longacre that interest in her cookbook was "phenomenal." Sales reached 68,000 within the first year. Many read reviews in hundreds of newspapers, including the *Los Angeles Times* and the *Chicago Tribune*, and in dozens of evangelical journals such as *Eternity*, *National Courier*, *Vanguard*, *Right On*, *Sojourners*, and *The Other Side*. Catholics (who learned about it from Arthur Simon's *Bread for the World*), Christian World Liberation Front members in Berkeley, Covenant church members in

Minnesota, and Christian Reformed congregants in Grand Rapids, Michigan, purchased copies. *More-with-Less* was ubiquitous in the Wheaton College Graduate School apartment complex. Longacre received letters from delighted housewives and prominent evangelicals across the nation. Senator Mark Hatfield praised her "large contribution" toward alleviating world hunger, and World Vision's Stanley Mooneyham wrote that "there is nobody in the country doing more to sensitize the conscience of North Americans." By August 1980, just four years after its release, *More-with-Less* had entered its twenty-fourth printing with 355,000 copies in print.[15]

One of those copies was used by Walter and Ginny Hearn, two evangelical pioneers of the simple living movement. Walter, a professor in biochemistry at Iowa State University, earned tenure at age forty-five and sponsored ISU's InterVarsity chapter. Ginny cared for two children and her elderly mother. But in 1972, burned out by life on the tenure track, they "dropped out of the system." They wanted an egalitarian marriage, one that avoided labor divisions along gender lines. Moreover, after twenty years on the ISU faculty, Walter felt as if he had done all he could to "humanize the bureaucracy." He wanted to make a more direct impact on society as a writer. Not sure at first that they could afford this new venture, the Hearns experimented with a new system of personal finances. Accustomed to fully spending their $20,000 salary, they cut their spending by one-half for two full years. Mostly, they just avoided stores. When they had to shop, they went to day-old bakeries, thrift stores, and flea markets. They frequented co-op bulletin boards and garage sales, and bought furniture from classified advertisements. With a full year's income saved, Walter quit his job, and the family moved to Berkeley to "find a lifework of wholeness."[16]

The Hearns applied lessons learned in Ames to their new home in California. They purchased a large, inexpensive house on an earthquake fault line that had at some point tilted the floors and cracked the foundation. They paid their mortgage with various editing projects and some adjunct teaching at the University of California at Berkeley. They ate primarily from farmers' markets, their garden, and forays into local dumpsters. After three years they reported satisfaction with their new lives. They enjoyed working together as a couple, sharing kitchen responsibilities, and collaboratively editing over fifty Christian books. They held seminars for young writers, collaborated with the Christian World Liberation Front, started a house church, and hosted many guests in their large home. They effused to guests about spending time, if not money, "extravagantly."[17]

The Hearns became minor evangelical celebrities. Dozens of books and magazines featured their story. The *Los Angeles Times* syndicated a 1975 article depicting the Hearns as earthy romantics: "Wandering down an alley behind a grocery store, the bearded man with shoulder-length hair picked up a useful wooden box, an onion and two tomatoes. Of course, admitted Walter Hearn, a little 'glop' would have to be washed off to make them usable. Thus prepared, the tomatoes (minus bruised spots) and the onion (minus a moldy spot) were dropped into an aromatic curry stew he simmered for lunch." Assuming a whimsical unconcern about where they would find their next meal, the Hearns nonetheless spread their cause militantly. Charging that anyone who couldn't make it on $2,500 a year was "locked into the wasteful, spiritually destructive American way of life," the Hearns became exemplars of the nascent evangelical simple living movement.[18]

Living simply, an important impulse of the evangelical left, intensified during the 1970s for several reasons. New technology and foreign travel brought global evangelicals deeper into the web of American evangelicalism. The Latin American Theological Fraternity, for example, deeply shaped the Hearns. South African opponents of apartheid influenced Sider. Experiences in Vietnam and Indonesia inspired Longacre. Sojourns into the earthy sensibilities of global cultures often entranced evangelicals, many of whom expressed new desires to grow corn, bathe less frequently, and buy fewer plastics. Many were repelled by American conspicuous consumption upon their return. Nearly all expressed a desire, redoubled after reading *Rich Christians*, to give generously and live on little.[19]

The integration of Anabaptist champions of simplicity into evangelical circles also catalyzed the simple living movement. Art Gish, a Church of the Brethren pastor, itinerant evangelist, and graduate of Manchester College and Bethany Theological Seminary, wrote frequently on simplicity for evangelical periodicals. His first book, *The New Left and Christian Radicalism* (1970), argued that the New Left was an ideological descendant of Anabaptism in its espousal of participatory democracy, anti-capitalism, and antiestablishmentism. Its sequel, *Beyond the Rat Race* (1973), sought to apply the "radical theology of revolution to life-style." Gish urged readers to get rid of televisions and radios, to quit washing their cars, to encourage men to wash dishes and women to fix cars, and to live in sharing communities in efforts to repudiate the materialistic technocracy. Gish sought this "recovery of the Anabaptist vision" for broader evangelicalism. Reprinted in 1981 and 2002, *Beyond the Rat Race* influenced CWLF, civil rights activist John Alexander, and InterVarsity students. In addition, Sider collaborated with the Hearns, and *Rich Christians* became required reading for students in leadership training classes at Xenos Fellowship, an evangelical congregation in Columbus, Ohio. The Anabaptist sensibilities of Jim Wallis and the *Post-American*, which published a monthly column called "Simplicity" by Etta Worthington, also shaped many younger evangelicals.[20]

The 1974 Lausanne Congress revealed the full potential of these Anabaptist themes in broader evangelical circles. Mennonite scholar John Howard Yoder abetted the wildcat "radical discipleship" caucus out of which Samuel Escobar and hundreds of representatives from the developing world critiqued North American mission strategies. The resulting "Lausanne Covenant" emphasized simple living and generosity toward the poor as an important element of evangelism. "We cannot hope to attain this goal without sacrifice," it stated. "All of us are shocked by the poverty of millions and disturbed by the injustices which cause it. Those of us who live in affluent circumstances accept our duty to develop a simple life-style in order to contribute more generously to both relief and evangelism." The Lausanne movement, very much in the evangelical mainstream and moved along by influential Anabaptists, continued to stress simple living through the 1970s and 1980s. As the movement peaked in the late 1970s, an International Consultation on Simple Lifestyle convened by Ron Sider released "Lausanne Occasional Paper 20: An Evangelical Commitment to Simple Life-Style." A proliferation of simple-living appeals supplemented the official pronouncements of the Lausanne consultations. Dozens of books and hundreds of articles, many of them written by Anabaptists, appeared in evangelical magazines such as *Christianity Today*, Evangelicals for Social Action's *Update*, InterVarsity's *HIS*, the *Post-American*, and *The Other Side*.[21]

The evangelical simple living movement also resonated with a broader cultural concern with environmental degradation and global justice. Sider and Longacre's admonitions to live healthier, less consumer-driven, more authentic lives represented an evangelical adaptation of a long tradition of American anti-materialism from Jeffersonian Republicans and nineteenth-century transcendentalists to social thinkers and arts-and-crafts practitioners of the Progressive Era to contemporaneous small-is-beautiful social critics. In the 1970s, according to historian David Shi, this impulse revealed itself in the form of Americans "who planted organic gardens, experimented with food production and communal living, and emulated romantic versions of Native American tribal culture." During these years, cultural critics released a flurry of simple living how-to manuals. Among the most read were *The Tassajara Bread Book* (1970), *Diet for a Small Planet* (1971), *Living Poor with Style* (1972), *Small Is Beautiful* (1973), *Enough Is Enough* (1977), *No Bigger Than Necessary* (1977), *99 Ways to a Simpler Lifestyle* (1977), and *Muddling Toward Frugality* (1978). Even the conservative *Reader's Digest* printed "The Case for a Simpler Life-Style" by Laurence Rockefeller, a conservationist, venture capitalist, and third-generation member of the Rockefeller dynasty.[22]

Trenchant sociological and economic criticisms, rooted in New Left opposition to liberal culture, added ideological heft to simplicity chic. The postwar economic boom had given Americans hope that poverty could be eliminated altogether through consumer spending. Dwight Eisenhower advised the nation to "Buy anything" during a slight recession in the 1950s. John F. Kennedy argued that "a rising tide lifts all boats," and Lyndon Johnson maintained that the Great Society "rests on abundance for all." But evidence mounted in the 1960s that American prosperity was nowhere close to being distributed equally. Public intellectual Michael Harrington described an isolated underclass suffering from a "culture of poverty" in the wealthiest nation in the world. Poverty, wrote Harrington in *The Other America* (1962), perpetuated itself. The poor, tangled in a web of bad health, poor housing, low levels of ambition, and high levels of mental distress, were unable to break free. Social critics such as Theodore Roszak, C. Wright Mills, Rachel Carson, and Jacques Ellul echoed the conviction that poverty was not always the fault of those suffering from it, and they decried the rancid effects of the "power elite" on the environment and the poor. *More-with-Less* echoed Roszak and Ellul's critiques of modern consumerism and advertising. Longacre instructed the graphic artist to "exclude a lot of lavish color photos . . . of super pretty foods, elegantly garnished and displayed." The final version featured a few simple photographs of international scenes and variations on a theme of measuring spoons. Longacre also modeled *More-with-Less* after *Diet for a Small Planet*, a book which drew attention to the politics of hunger and eventually helped launch the Food and Development Policy think tank and the Center for Living Democracy. That the evangelical simple living movement reflected many of the same themes as its secular analogue revealed some of the dissolving boundaries between evangelicalism and broader culture.[23]

Yet if evangelicals reflected the sensibilities of the 1970s in some ways, they adapted the simple living ethos to their own purposes. They planted organic gardens but used recipes from cookbooks cobbled together by their own churches and missionaries. They lived in communes but organized their

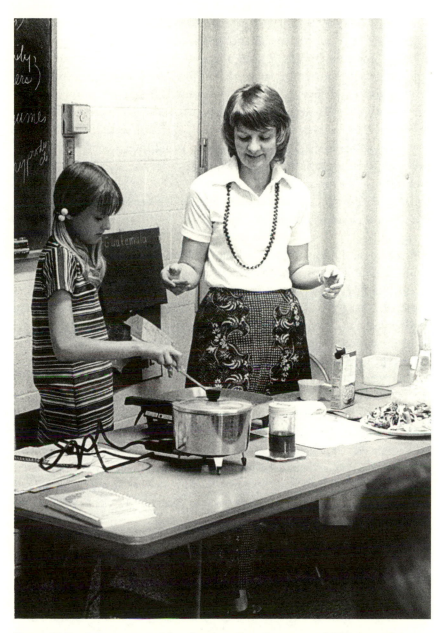

Figure 17. Doris Longacre and her daughter Cara Sue prepared Chinese and Guatemalan recipes from the *More-with-Less Cookbook* at a seminar for home economists in 1976. Courtesy of the Mennonite Church USA Archives, Goshen, Indiana.

schedules around Bible studies, prayer meetings, and antiwar protests, rather than rituals of tribal culture. Sider urged evangelicals to give generously to meet the financial costs of sharing the gospel with two and a half billion non-Christians. Kitchens in Francis Schaeffer's L'Abri wasted nothing out of concern for the environment, yet also affirmed "the Lord's world and creation" through delicious meals, the beauty of candlelight, and fresh flowers. The emerging evangelical left imbued the politics of secular simple living with evangelical piety. The political and spiritual intertwined as evangelicals sought to expiate the sin of materialism in the face of third-world hunger.[24]

This simple living impulse eventually extended to one of the world's most famous evangelicals, President Jimmy Carter. In the throes of the late 1970s energy crisis, Carter retreated to Camp David. He read Schumacher's *Small Is Beautiful* and met with cultural critics. He emerged ten days later with a message about "a crisis of the American spirit." Echoing Sider, Gish, and others, his July 15, 1979, speech featured many elements of an evangelical jeremiad. Carter declared, "In a nation that was proud of hard work, strong families, close-knit communities, and our faith in God, too many of us now worship self-indulgence and consumption." "Human identity is no longer defined by what one does but by what one owns," Carter sermonized, but "owning things and consuming things does not satisfy our longing for meaning." Critics panned the President's politically "naïve" response to the energy crisis. But millions of Americans, among them many evangelicals, identified with Carter's condemnation of materialism. In just one day, his approval rating shot up eleven points. The White House enjoyed messages of support and goodwill, which Carter squandered by firing his cabinet several days later. "Americans might have been able to take a tough speech about the state of their country and the energy crisis," writes historian Kevin Mattson, "but they couldn't take a complete shakedown of the government at the same time." Carter never recovered, unable to compete two years later with Ronald Reagan's promises of limitless optimism and consumption. But during the 1970s, many Americans thirsted for less, not more. The evangelical simple living movement reflected and advanced that spirit.[25]

*   *   *

Half a dozen Anabaptists, including Ron Sider of the Brethren in Christ; Art Gish of the Church of the Brethren; John Howard Yoder, president of

Goshen Biblical Seminary; Dale Brown, former moderator of the Church of the Brethren; and Myron Augsburger, president of Eastern Mennonite College, gathered with an emerging evangelical left to write the Chicago Declaration. Sections of the document could nearly have been lifted from Sider's *Rich Christians*: "We must attack the materialism of our culture and the maldistribution of the nation's wealth and services. We recognize that as a nation we play a crucial role in the imbalance and injustice of international trade and development. Before God and a billion hungry neighbors, we must rethink our values regarding our present standard of living and promote a more just acquisition and distribution of the world's resources." Casting simple living as faithfulness to Jesus—and buttressing the growing evangelical impulse to expand personal responsibility to corporate responsibility—Anabaptists interpreted the seventies in theological and social categories that evangelicals could understand.

CHAPTER 9

The Chicago Declaration and a United Progressive Front

We acknowledge that God requires justice. But we have
not proclaimed or demonstrated his justice to an unjust
American society. Although the Lord calls us to defend
the social and economic rights of the poor and the
oppressed, we have mostly remained silent.

—The Chicago Declaration

In the 1960s politically progressive evangelicals were "scattered, lonely, and frustrated," according to Reformed philosopher-theologian Richard Mouw. They came from diverse traditions, nurtured different impulses, and pursued disparate projects. In the early 1970s, however, they began to find each other. In 1970 African American evangelical Bill Pannell traveled to Costa Rica to tell Latin Americans about the black experience in the United States. In 1972 Mouw helped organize the annual Calvin College Conference on Christianity and Politics, which brought prominent neo-evangelicals to Grand Rapids, Michigan, where they learned about the political implications of Dutch Reformed theology. Anabaptist Ron Sider and Samuel Escobar of the Latin American Theological Fraternity brought their visions of global justice and simple living to InterVarsity circles. John Alexander, who continued to preach racial justice, added contributing editors to *The Other Side*'s masthead. Wheaton College students joined Jim Wallis at rallies against the Vietnam War. Senator Mark Hatfield gained headlines as a contrarian. Sharon Gallagher and the Christian World Liberation Front enjoyed growing prominence as practitioners of a third way of intentional spiritual community. Carl Henry, already well known, continued to repudiate quietism in the pages of *Christianity Today*.

Provoked anew by animus against Richard Nixon, the continuing war in Vietnam, and persistent racial strife, progressive evangelicals of different types began to make common cause. Ron Sider, who had spent the last decade living in poverty-stricken sections of New Haven and Philadelphia, emerged as the driving force for this evangelical left coalition. Holding policy positions in the mainstream of Democratic politics and speaking the language of mainstream evangelicalism, he stood opposed to Nixon's reelection. In 1972, Sider organized Evangelicals for McGovern. In 1973, he brought the growing movement together in Chicago. On Thanksgiving weekend at the downtown YMCA hotel, Henry, Alexander, Wallis, Gallagher, Mouw, Escobar, Sider, and thirty others rallied for social justice. There they drafted the Chicago Declaration, a striking document that condemned social, not just personal, sin. The national press, including the *Washington Post*, began to take note of the evangelical left's growing numbers, proliferating literature, and political activism. *Sojourners* associate editor Jim Stentzel, voicing the feistiness of an evangelical left on the move, declared, "If the connection between the Bible and the nation's alienation is made, things will start popping. Fifty million 'born-again' Christians could be one hell of a political force." Spoken ahead of the Moral Majority, Stentzel's words betrayed not a trace of irony. Up for grabs, evangelical politics looked as if it might take a progressive shape.[1]

I

In August 1972 Messiah College professor Ron Sider opened a letter that asked for donations toward Mark Hatfield's reelection campaign for the U.S. Senate. After sending in some money, Sider asked himself, "Why can't we do the same thing for the Democratic presidential candidate, George McGovern?" In September, Evangelicals for McGovern (EFM) was born among a small circle of evangelical social activists gathered in Sider's Philadelphia home. As the effort turned national in the following months, many in both the press and the evangelical communities took note. Not only was this the first explicitly evangelical organization in postwar American politics officially to support a presidential candidate, EFM was endorsing a liberal Democrat.[2]

Progressive evangelicals found McGovern's political ideology far more congenial to their own reformist impulses than Nixon's. "We like the way McGovern is getting his feet dirty. He's concerned about hunger, war, poverty and ecology," explained Wheaton professor Robert Webber to a *Newsweek* reporter. Jim Wallis, who served as a regional manager for McGovern's campaign, called the candidate "a first ray of hope in the midst of widespread despair." Official EFM documents praised McGovern's evangelical background, his religious rhetoric, and his stances on school busing, poverty, and the war. "A rising tide of younger evangelicals," asserted an early news release, "feels that the time has come to dispel the old stereotype that evangelical theology entails unconcern toward the poor, blacks and other minorities, and the needs of the Third World." But animus against Nixon and conservative politics as much as resonance with McGovern motivated EFM. While some students and professors at Calvin College rallied with considerable enthusiasm for the McGovern candidacy in a student election, it became clear when students heckled and booed Nixon's running mate Spiro Agnew at a nationally televised campaign event that this support was in large part a protest vote against the incumbent. EFM, for example, devoted little effort to parsing the particulars of McGovern's planks. In an article entitled "Seven Reasons Why to Elect George McGovern," most of the reasons centered on how McGovern's policies were not Nixon's. More than supporting McGovern—they could only muster weak superlatives such as "candid and decent"—members of EFM mostly scorned the president.[3]

Nixon troubled progressive evangelicals for reasons domestic and diplomatic. He had failed to maintain civil rights progress, and his southern-strategy campaign was saturated with "law and order" rhetoric. In an EFM fundraising letter Sider decried "policies, however camouflaged, which are designed to slow down or reverse racial progress" and condemned Nixon for profiting from "a white backlash." In addition to criticizing Nixon for race-baiting, EFM charged him with expanding tax loopholes for the rich and with failing to end the Vietnam conflict. Nixon was responsible for the deaths of thousands of American soldiers and even more deaths of Vietnamese innocents. Operation Linebacker, the massive American aerial attack in the summer of 1972 that pushed back the Viet Cong's Easter Offensive, "has bombed just as many Asian men, women and children into eternity." Disregard for non-American casualties smacked of "Western racism." Such policies, EFM maintained, "grieve the one who had his eternal Son become incarnate in the Middle East." Jim Wallis, in a vitriolic diatribe against the president, declared, "A vote for Richard Nixon is a vote for cabinet corruption and I.T.T. payoffs, for government secrecy and deception. A vote for Richard Nixon is a vote for southern strategies, for the manipulations of racial prejudice and patriotic fervor, for the erosion of basic civil rights. A vote for Richard Nixon is a vote for a foreign policy of military interventions, political subversion, and economic blackmail. A vote for Richard Nixon is a vote for a campaign characterized by the politics of fear—fear of blacks, fear of communists, fear of crime, fear of change, fear of not being number one." McGovern was the default choice for progressive evangelicals, who excoriated Nixon throughout the 1972 election season.[4]

As the presidential contest entered its final months, EFM embarked on an offensive. Hoping to sway as many evangelical voters as possible to McGovern's side, Sider sent over 8,000 letters to evangelical leaders. Support for EFM quickly spread. A woman from North Carolina wrote, "You don't know how thrilled I am to get your letter." A graduate student from Ohio University wrote of his disgust with Nixon's "sordid and totally hypocritical tugs at the sentimentality of Americans—especially Christians with his entourage of Billy Grahams, Norman Vincent Peales, and other Pharisees and anti-commies." He declared his intent to "proselytize for McGovern." A Pentecostal man from Chicago declared his support for McGovern and EFM. A 1956 graduate of Wheaton College praised EFM, complaining that a recent commencement address at his alma mater was "concerned entirely with how social justice was bad and contrary to true justice, which was not defined." Supporters of EFM at Gordon-Conwell Seminary, where a mock election yielded a 127–127 tie between Nixon and McGovern, rallied with supporters twenty miles south at Harvard.[5]

Of the hundreds who sent EFM $10 and $20 checks, most fit the profile of the new evangelical left. Many held key leadership positions in flagship neo-evangelical organizations such as Wheaton College, Gordon-Conwell Seminary, Fuller Seminary, *Christianity Today*, and World Vision. Additional support came from other quarters of evangelicalism. Some faculty members from Wesleyan colleges Olivet Nazarene, Asbury, and Taylor sent support and served on EFM's Board of Reference. Members of ethnic and confessional schools, just entering the neo-evangelical orbit, also contributed. Reformed representatives included Stephen Monsma and Richard Mouw of Calvin College and Deane Kemper of Gordon-Conwell Seminary. Supporters from Anabaptist institutions included Mennonite Biblical Seminary, Messiah College, and Mennonite Central Committee. Mennonite voluntary service centers in rural eastern Kentucky prominently displayed EFM letters on their bulletin boards. The core group also included prominent black evangelical activists Columbus Salley and Tom Skinner, who served as vice-chairman of EFM. Most members, however, were white, male, middle-class, and educated. Many had attended Billy Graham crusades and still respected the evangelist's outspoken evangelical faith—but had grown increasingly embarrassed about Graham's close ties with Nixon. EFM's response to Graham's barely veiled support for Nixon was that "our organization is the message that Billy Graham does not speak for all of the nation's evangelicals."[6]

As the campaign wore on, however, it became clear that Graham did speak for most evangelicals. After a month of fundraising, EFM received only $3,500 from about 220 contributors. While the novelty of a northern-based evangelical organization stumping for a Democratic president generated more publicity than actual influence and made for good copy in publications such as *Time*, *Newsweek*, and *Christian Century*, EFM earned less than adulatory praise from the general evangelical constituency. A faculty member at Washington Bible College told EFM board members, "I am amazed, and indeed dismayed that I should be asked by evangelicals to support this movement in the light of the type of campaign which has been conducted by the men whom you are endorsing." Her primary complaint was that McGovern had used an obscenity on the campaign trail in Michigan. (In a charged reply that reflected the emerging dichotomy between those who emphasized structural sin or personal piety, EFM's Richard Pierard responded, "It appears that you and I fundamentally differ as to what comprises moral leadership. I gather that you regard the use of profanity (an action which I do not condone) as the greatest evil. For me, however, the napalming of Vietnamese children, the bugging of Democratic Party headquarters, and the widely publicized corrupt milk and grain deals are far more serious sins." The mainstream evangelical standard *Christianity Today*, at its most conservative in the early 1970s under the leadership of Harold Lindsell and J. Howard Pew, also signaled its preference for Nixon. Lindsell quoted Graham as saying that the incumbent "will probably go down in history as one of the country's greatest presidents."[7]

The fawning support of Nixon by certain notable evangelical elites infuriated progressive leaders. Besides Graham, the most egregious case was Harold Ockenga, a longtime pastor in Boston and founding president of the National Association of Evangelicals. In a newspaper article written just one week before the election, Ockenga effused about the "high moral integrity" of his "personal friend" Nixon. In a letter to EFM, Ockenga wrote, "I for one cannot understand how any of you men of evangelical conviction can back Mr. McGovern." Soon after, the local newspaper, the *Hamilton-Wenham Chronicle*, printed a gossipy report on the Ockengas' attendance at the inaugural. Ockenga and his wife had chatted with the Rockefellers, Billy Graham, and Henry Kissinger at a formal dinner to which Mrs. Ockenga wore "a striking creation" by designer Oscar de LaRenta. It was a "formal, empire-waisted gown of a gold motif," reported the *Chronicle*, "beautiful to behold." Relieved that "the city was extremely calm—I really didn't see any hippies" and pleased by "the number of times God was mentioned in the various events," Mrs. Ockenga reported that attending the inaugural was "the greatest thrill of my life."[8]

Despite these stories about Graham and the Ockengas, some reports left EFM organizers hopeful. They sensed a growing discontent toward Nixon, especially among younger evangelicals. A stormy Campus Crusade meeting in 1972 featured Bright's staff, concerned about politicizing a religious event, voicing opposition to Nixon's presence at Explo, the religious youth rally in Dallas. According to historian John Turner, politically conservative evangelical leaders such as Ockenga, Bill Bright, and Billy Graham—not to mention Nixon himself—had worried that McGovern might "compete effectively for the moderate and conservative Protestant vote." In an effort to make headway among the evangelical middle, EFM began to emphasize McGovern's evangelical credentials. They noted that McGovern's father was a Wesleyan Methodist pastor who graduated from the evangelical Houghton College. EFM leaders similarly stressed their own evangelical theology. An early appeal letter, for example, read, "We continue to assert vigorously that Jesus of Nazareth rose from the tomb, that He is Lord of the Universe and that men can find genuine fulfillment only when the risen Lord Jesus regenerates and transforms selfish hearts." These gestures culminated in an EFM-engineered McGovern appearance at Wheaton College, an impressive coup, given that twelve years before John F. Kennedy had not been permitted to rent the college gymnasium for a rally.[9]

On October 11, 1972, McGovern took his campaign to the stage of Wheaton's Edman Memorial Chapel. After being introduced by Tom Skinner, the candidate spoke fluently in evangelical idiom in front of an overflow crowd of over 2,000 during the Tuesday chapel service. McGovern explained that "in our family, there was no drinking, smoking, dancing or card-playing." He would have attended Wheaton, he said, if his family could have afforded the tuition. He identified with the mid-century evangelical preoccupation

Figure 18. Presidential candidate George McGovern and Tom Skinner spoke at
Wheaton College on October 11, 1972. McGovern's visit, just a month before the
election, provoked a wide range of reactions from the crowd, including boos,
catcalls, and a standing ovation. Courtesy of Archives and Special Collections,
Wheaton College, Wheaton, Illinois.

with individual conversion and change: "As President, I could not resolve all
the problems of this land. No President and no political leader can. For our
deepest problems are within us—not as an entire people—but as individual
persons." Yet McGovern, affirming John Winthrop's declaration on the *Ar-
bella* in 1630 of America as a "city on a hill," also stressed moral and spiritual leadership in the public square. "The wish of our forebears," he
concluded, "was to see the way of God prevail. We have strayed from their
pilgrimage, like lost sheep. But I believe we can begin this ancient journey
anew." Citing evangelical icons such as Jonathan Edwards, John Wesley, and
William Wilberforce, McGovern contended that his presidency would nurture conditions in which spiritual, moral, and social revival could occur.
Faith, he declared in contradistinction to President John F. Kennedy's careful delineation before a gathering of Protestant clergy in Dallas just ten
years earlier, would very much shape his presidency. At the conclusion of his
speech, McGovern received a standing ovation.[10]

Some opposition, however, tempered EFM's delight. Several students booed, jeered, and hung a hostile banner from the chapel balcony. Others at Wheaton, reported journalist Wesley Pippert, seemed "suspicious of McGovern because of his liberal views and perhaps even more because he was once one of them, and in their opinion, he has strayed." The candidate's mixed reception by establishment evangelicals pointed to a much broader lack of success by EFM. By the date of the election on November 7, 1972, the organization had contributed negligible amounts—only $5,762 from only 358 people—to the coffers of a presidential campaign in desperate need of more money and votes. The cause had been taken up too late and by a group that lacked electoral experience and savvy. Moreover, it relied too much on young evangelical educators who could offer their moral support but little money. One New Jersey woman wrote EFM lamenting, "All the Christians we know are for Nixon, except a few young people who have no money." From Athens, Ohio, came a letter that read, "I have no money for you (being a destitute graduate student with a huge obstetrics bill), but that which I have I give to you: a list of people who profess Christianity but are, regrettably, staying in the Nixon camp." Though they did not mobilize as they would in 1976 and 1980, rank-and-file evangelicals helped carry the incumbent to a landslide victory—a 520–17 majority in the Electoral College and a 23 percent margin in the popular vote, the second largest margin in American history.[11]

Despite the disheartening defeat, many in the evangelical left remained upbeat. After all, they had been working on behalf of a hamstrung candidate. Not yet aware of Nixon's patterns of profane speech and corrupt governance, even moderate liberals, by a margin of over two to one, chose Nixon over McGovern as the candidate who best reflected high moral and religious standards. Moreover, members of EFM had experienced the exhilaration of finding like-minded evangelical progressives in their work on behalf of McGovern. Collectively they had challenged the evangelical establishment and earned wide coverage of their political activism in the national press. Their mobilization effort was in some respects respectable, given its late starting date just two months before the election. EFM had succeeded in its hope "that evangelicals as a group can be heard."[12]

Just a year later, as the dark shadow of Watergate eclipsed the Nixon presidency, EFM took on new significance. In a letter to Sider, EFM board chair Walden Howard wrote, "I expect to see such a crisis in confidence as all of these things become public that it will be extremely difficult for

President Nixon to govern. The unredeemed part of me is licking its chops, but the better part of me feels sad for our country. Would to God that Mc-Govern had been elected! We would certainly be in a very different position today." But McGovern had not won, so the nascent evangelical network instead capitalized on growing disillusionment with Nixon. On Thanksgiving weekend of 1973, that disillusionment sparked a surprisingly strident call for a new social conscience—and the birth of an organized evangelical left.[13]

II

Sider, heartened by the modest evangelical support for McGovern, began to think about a more permanent organization to promote progressive politics. "There is a new movement of major proportions within evangelical circles," Sider wrote to fellow EFM member David Moberg in early 1973. "It is still a minority movement, but it is widespread and growing. This emerging group of evangelical social activists . . . needs direction." Sider, Moberg, and several other members of the now-defunct EFM proposed a workshop to be held over Thanksgiving weekend. Hashing out plans in April at Steak and Four Restaurant near Calvin College in Grand Rapids, they sought to infuse symbolic value into what they hoped would be the evangelical left's coming-out party. First, they decided to meet not in suburban Wheaton, the initial suggestion, but instead at the YMCA in downtown Chicago. Just down the street from the historic Pacific Garden Rescue Mission, the YMCA's location pointed to evangelicalism's nineteenth-century legacy of social action and urban concern. Second, organizers, searching for consensus among a broad range of traditions and interest groups from which a movement could be launched, sought diversity. They invited blacks and whites, old and young, evangelists and relief workers, and leaders from a variety of evangelical traditions. Third, they decided conference delegates should release a concise, hard-hitting manifesto that would articulate their social concerns to the evangelical world and the national media.[14]

Fifty evangelical leaders, some of the most influential in the younger generation, felt the weight of history when they finally convened on a chilly, foggy Friday morning in late November for the Thanksgiving Workshop of Evangelical Social Concern. After an opening address in which Sider instructed those gathered to "not hesitate to stop and pray" when they got bogged down in debate, delegates immediately declared their opposition to Watergate, the Vietnam War, Nixon, and fellow evangelicals who blindly supported the president. In a major address Tom Skinner, acknowledging that evangelicals had "missed the Civil Rights movement," stated that it was not too late to "emphasize social sins and institutionalized evils as vigorously as personal sins." Bill Pannell said that "a new breed of evangelicals" had arrived, that the time for "significant breakthroughs was now." Sider concurred, "I don't think it is mere rhetoric to say that we have come together at a moment of historic opportunity." In a prescient forecast, he predicted that "for better or for worse, [American evangelicals] will exercise the dominant religious influence in the next decade."[15]

If the Workshop enjoyed consensus in its criticism of conservative politics, it nonetheless encountered difficulties in trying to draw up its manifesto. The composition of what became the Chicago Declaration, a process begun months before the Workshop itself, was plagued by fits and starts. The drafting committee's first attempt was so strident that Frank Gaebelein, a sympathetic editor at *Christianity Today*, proclaimed it "heretical." John Alexander, no conservative himself, agreed with Gaebelein, calling the initial draft "leftist propaganda." Delegates at the Workshop itself continued to criticize the more moderate revised draft. At four pages, everyone agreed, it was too long. A more cutting critique came from black participants, who perceived hints of "evangelical triumphalism." How could the evangelical left, they asked, use self-congratulatory language after its own tradition had failed to embrace the civil rights movement? After someone blamed fundamentalist doctrine for their failures—"We've been victimized by our own heresy," a white delegate said. "We're still good people"—William Bentley, president of the National Black Evangelical Association, retorted, "What does good mean? If you are part of an oppressing community, your goodness means nothing to me." Very quickly, Sider recalled, "the lid blew off." Black participants sharply attacked the planning committee for including only one black member. Then over a separate lunch of turnip greens and ham hocks prepared "for atmosphere," they drew up an alternative declaration much more radical than the original. Palpable tension permeated the Workshop through the first evening. When after the day's final session delegates entered the dark streets in search of a snack, they traveled in two racial groups that, according to one participant, "vented their frustration in angry separation."[16]

The handful of invited female delegates also demanded that evangelicals "clean up their own houses." Nancy Hardesty, an alumna of Wheaton and graduate student at the University of Chicago, and Sharon Gallagher of the

Christian World Liberation Front in Berkeley discovered that there was no mention of sexism in the first draft of the Declaration. The women caucused and presented their demand for such a statement. As the Workshop progressed, they grew even more offended. Amid high-powered evangelical executives and scholars, one woman felt as if "she had walked into an Eastern men's club. The men tended to be insensitive to women as people." Delegate Ruth Bentley, for example, was listed as "Mrs. William Bentley." And when the section in the Declaration on sexism was discussed, Gallagher reported that the few women present were "commanded to speak and then expected to shut up when the men felt the issue had been covered." Evangelical men, she suggested, regarded women as little more than personal house slaves.[17]

Pacifists added to the ferment. John Howard Yoder, president of Goshen Biblical Seminary, complained, "Blacks have a paragraph they can redo; women have a word they can redo; but there is nothing at all about war. It contains something about the military-industrial complex being bad for the budget, but nothing about it being bad for the Vietnamese." Yoder, supported by fellow Anabaptists Ron Sider, Jim Wallis, Dale Brown, and Myron Augsburger, persuaded the delegates to insert the following into the Declaration: "We must challenge the misplaced trust of the nation in economic and military might—a proud trust that promotes a national pathology of war and violence which victimizes our neighbors at home and abroad."[18]

This agreement on what to say about American militarism led the way to resolution over the controversial questions of gender and race. After the initial shock of unexpected disagreement, all sides rallied and rediscovered their common enemies: racism, Nixon, unchecked capitalism, and theological liberalism. After a coffee break late Saturday afternoon, black delegates decided to "let up," according to attendee Marlin VanElderen. Then Stephen Mott, a professor at Gordon-Conwell, interceded on behalf of Nancy Hardesty, who wrote the following sentences into the Declaration: "We acknowledge that we have encouraged men to prideful domination and women to irresponsible passivity. So we call both men and women to mutual submission and active discipleship." Despite dissent from some, delegates accepted the insertion. Participants began approving section after section of the reworked document and by the final Saturday session had nearly completed their task. On this evening, Sider recalled, "one group of black and white brothers and sisters went out to enjoy soul food together."[19]

The final text of the Chicago Declaration (reprinted in Appendix A) confessed that evangelicals had failed to defend the social and economic rights of the poor, the oppressed, and minorities. It attacked America's materialism, sexism, and "pathology of war." It pledged to acknowledge God's "total claim upon the lives of his people," even in the political arena. "We endorse no political ideology or party," signers maintained, "but call our nation's leaders and people to that righteousness which exalts a nation." This less radical version, written by Jim Wallis but heavily edited by Paul Henry "not to sound too harsh, anti-American," eliminated references to Nixon's "lust for and abuse of power" and alleged United States involvement behind the overthrow of the Allende government in Chile. It instead reflected a new moderate consensus. Final approval was given to the Declaration during a worship service on Sunday morning. When the vote had been tallied, Sider rose to speak of "a deep sense of presence and guidance of the risen Lord." He then invited delegates to sing the Doxology, marking the end of a remarkable weekend of progressive politics and evangelical piety.[20]

The media, fascinated by the idiosyncratic blend of conservative theology and progressive social critiques, reported widely on the weekend. Reporters from United Press International, the *Washington Post*, the *Chicago Tribune*, and others framed their reports in terms of mainline Protestant stagnance and evangelical resurgence. A reporter for the *Chicago Sun-Times* suggested that "some day American church historians may write that the most significant church-related event of 1973 took place last week at the YMCA Hotel on S. Wabash." Upon hearing of Evangelicals for McGovern and the Chicago Declaration, William Sloane Coffin, a prominent civil rights and peace activist who served as a mainline chaplain at Yale, declared, "Now this is the real McCoy, rooted in deep personal experience! . . . I've always suspected that the future was with these Evangelical guys."[21]

Not all reports, however, were positive. John Howard Yoder hesitated to sign the Declaration because it "failed to undercut the 'Christian America' assumptions of many who will read it." Evangelical journalist Wesley Pippert declared, "I thought it was inept. It was weak and it was spineless. It said nothing that should not have been said 15 years ago. I don't know what everybody was shouting hallelujah about." Paul Jewett of Fuller Seminary refused to sign the Declaration because it lacked specificity. "My past experience tempts me to greet this plan to have 'another meeting sometime next year' with a cool smile," he wrote. "But we all live in hope." Bruce Shearer, leader of a rural commune in New Hampshire that housed Korean and Vietnamese war children, affirmed the Declaration's language but worried that few evangelicals understood its implications. "Real discipleship, prophetic witness and resistance, etc.," he wrote, "may very well cost us our wallets, our jobs, our reputations, our citizenship, life insurance, retirement benefits, comforts such as home and friendships, our families, maybe even our lives." The Declaration, in the opinion of these critics, was mere empty words. Did signers realize the hard work and sacrifice it would take to bring about justice?[22]

A very different sort of criticism emanated from more conservative fundamentalist and evangelical circles. Segregationist Bob Jones, Jr., upon hearing of the Thanksgiving Workshop, declared that "no Fundamentalist would be caught dead in this kind of meeting." A "Mrs. Peter R. Vroon" wrote to the *Presbyterian Layman* that "the 52 signers of the above Declaration are strangely silent about pornography, drugs, lawlessness, immorality, and many of the other evils that are ruining our country and invading Christian homes." She also complained about the participation of the "far left *Post American* newspaper." The most prominent absentee, Billy Graham, was far less vitriolic. Though Graham declined to sign the Declaration, he told *Christianity Today*, "We have a social responsibility and I could identify with most of the recent Chicago Declaration of Evangelical Concern. I think we have to identify with the changing of structures in society and try to do our part." Roger Palms, a Billy Graham Evangelistic Association administrator, expressed similar ambivalence. In a June 1974 letter to Sider, Palms explained that he would sign the Declaration. In a postscript, however, Palms recanted. "Just as I was about the sign the statement I took a minute to re-read the article in *Christianity Today* by Jim Wallis, and as a result could not get peace about signing it. Maybe I will in the future. There are questions that I have more about attitude than practical theology and I am not sure if I want to be related to a negative attitude." The vast evangelical middle seemed to agree that evangelicals had a duty to be more socially and politically active, but that the Chicago Declaration seemed a bit radical in tone.[23]

Despite these rebuffs, Sider and other progressive evangelicals remained convinced that evangelicalism was up for grabs. Hundreds of prominent evangelicals, including Mark Hatfield, Wheaton philosopher Arthur Holmes, historian Timothy Smith, and Billy Graham's junior evangelist and brother-in-law Leighton Ford, sent their names to be added to the Declaration. The InterVarsity branch of the University of Texas at Austin expressed its support of the Declaration and its wish to add signatures. Thousands of letters, most written by pastors, seminarians, college students, and professionals, expressed resonance with the Declaration. Many, asking to be added as signatories, expressed hope that their days as lonely evangelical progressives were over. Sider also saw evidence that suggested potential ecumenical collaboration. Mainline bureaucrats associated with the National Council of Churches (NCC) issued a statement that read, "We are moved by the Holy Spirit to express a deep feeling of kinship with that statement and with our fellow-Christians who issued it."[24]

These overtures invigorated Workshop organizers. Sider campaigned for even more generous media coverage, scrambled to add prominent signatures to the Declaration, and invited additional ecumenical support. He also announced plans for a second Workshop to be held at the same Chicago YMCA on Thanksgiving 1974, at which specific social-political proposals could add flesh to the skeletal agenda of 1973. The Declaration, planners hoped, was the opening salvo in a battle to preserve evangelicalism from "big business Republicanism." Whether or not the new evangelical left would succeed in this effort, the Declaration signaled a new day in evangelical politics. In its repudiation of evangelical apoliticism and in its affirmation that "God lays total claim upon the lives of his people," the signers of the Declaration were contending that politics, in addition to prayer, was a spiritual discipline.[25]

*   *   *

The organized evangelical left in the early 1970s was small. But amid the porous boundaries between left, right, and center evangelicalism—and the consequent ferment of a fluid evangelical politics—it held very real potential for growth and political impact. George McGovern, who traveled to Wheaton College to woo evangelicals at a critical moment in his 1972 campaign, recognized this. So did several of the most important newspapers in the country as they covered the Thanksgiving Workshop. Evangelicals for McGovern and the Chicago Declaration were "signs of a new order," as the Post-Americans called the flood of progressive evangelical organizations and literature in the early 1970s. That flood continued unabated after Chicago. Evangelicals released dozens of books urging progressive political action.[26] A set of periodicals—*The Post-American* (55,000 at its highest circulation), *The Other Side* (13,000), *Eternity* (46,000), *Vanguard* (2,000), *Right On* (65,000), *HIS* (90,000), *Wittenburg Door, Inside*, and others—maintained a running commentary on current political developments from a progressive evangelical perspective. Intentional communities flourished. Urban networks of progressive evangelicals grew. Journalist Wesley Pippert spotted progressives in evangelical pews as he spoke in churches throughout Midwest and even the South. "Many evangelicals in the pew are far out front in their social concern of the moment than many of their 'leaders,'" he told *Christianity Today*. "The pitiful thing is that many church people and religionists could have signed the Chicago Declaration ten years ago."[27]

As Sider organized the Thanksgiving Workshop sequel, political events seemed to validate concerns about a corrupted political conservatism. Sordid Watergate details emerged. Nixon resigned in disgrace. Billy Graham penitently confessed to blind faith in Nixon. Many evangelicals questioned their 1972 vote for the president. From the mid-1960s to the mid-1970s, Democratic identification among evangelicals increased from 34.9 percent to 38.7 percent, a remarkable increase given southern conservative Democrats' defection to the Republican Party. Observer Richard Quebedeaux argued that the evangelical left was infiltrating mainstream evangelical organizations such as the Billy Graham Evangelistic Association and the Evangelical Theological Society. The Social Concerns Commission of the National Association of Evangelicals, he asserted, had become a "haven for Democrats, minorities and pacifists." All the while, Sider and other leaders of the Thanksgiving Workshop worked to build the growing progressive coalition, recruited evangelical business leaders, and planned an ambitious agenda that included a massive national congress. They spoke longingly of "Jesus people" and twenty-somethings who were "neither turned on nor turned off to social action—but just uninformed." If recruited, these young evangelicals could "accelerate the movement." For a newly organized evangelical left, the mid-1970s was a time of great expectations.[28]

PART III

Left Behind

CHAPTER 10

Identity Politics and a Fragmenting Coalition

Last year's meeting was focused; we wrote the
Declaration. This year everyone was doing his or her
own thing.

—James Skillen, founding member of the
Center for Public Justice

As Watergate erupted in the hot summer months of 1974, so did evangelical politics. The ferment began when Ron Sider, the Anabaptist organizer of the 1973 pan-evangelical Thanksgiving Workshop, tried to address the complaint most registered by delegates who had been in Chicago: that the Declaration, lacking specificity, resembled the bureaucratic pronouncements of mainline Protestants and so, like them, could be safely ignored. For the much larger second Workshop, held one year later in November 1974, Sider organized six caucuses—on evangelism, evangelical feminism, politics, education, evangelical nonviolence, and race—so that the 134 delegates could produce "action proposals." On the surface, the new approach succeeded. Eight of the nine action proposals passed unanimously, among them initiatives to establish a Center for Biblical Social Concern, inaugurate a forum for dealing with white racism, endorse the Equal Rights Amendment, plan fifteen regional conferences in major cities across the United States, and continue discussions about evangelical nonviolent direct action and global hunger. Caucuses appointed individuals to implement each of the proposals within twelve months. The continued momentum seemed to confirm Sider's confidence that "a new movement of biblical social concern is afoot in this land."[1]

The reality was more complicated. Sider's "buckshot approach," as one observer described the eight action proposals, had "misfired" in unintended ways. The caucus approach divided delegates by interest—blacks to the race caucus, women to the gender caucus, Anabaptists to the economic lifestyles and nonviolence caucuses, Calvinists to the politics and education caucuses. When members of each caucus finally introduced their proposals to the larger Workshop, fireworks resulted over idiosyncratic and inordinately specific suggestions. Moreover, the caucus protocol undercut individual investment in the overall vision. As political philosopher Jim Skillen complained, "Each person had only to vote his or her support of a proposal with the intent that such a project could be one legitimate mode of action for 'someone' to take (not necessarily the voter)." Delegates dutifully ratified most proposals in a process engineered to create consensus. Yet the unanimous votes hid sharp disagreements. One delegate noted, "Last year's meeting was focused; we wrote the Declaration. This year everyone was doing his or her own thing."[2]

If the 1974 Workshop exposed profound disagreements, the 1975 Workshop completely splintered as battles over identity raged. Many black participants continued to bemoan white insensitivity. Many women condemned persistent sexist attitudes and language. Those accused—mostly white men—complained of persecution themselves. "While I am deeply committed to the elimination of prejudice and intolerance, and certainly aware of the need for the elimination of sexism," wrote Ira Gallaway, pastor of a United Methodist congregation in Fort Worth, Texas, "it is not my opinion that unrealistic quotas or groveling guilt supply the answer. . . . I think that we all should participate as equal human beings and not in the role of continued castigation and suspicion of each other." To pacify female and African-American delegates, organizers implemented a quota system to fill the planning committee. White men caucused to select four white men; women chose four women; and black participants added eight to the committee. Despite the emergency measure, the contentious Workshop broke up a day early. Indiana State University history professor Richard Pierard confided to a fellow delegate, "I don't know if the workshops will continue after the way this last one went." Pierard's prediction was correct; the 1975 Workshop was the last. The consensus of 1973, built around anti-Nixon sentiment more than shared language or political philosophy, proved surprisingly ephemeral.[3]

The fragmentation of the Workshop points to the powerful effects of identity politics. Many historians, pointing to the new salience of sexual, racial, gender identities that emerged in the 1960s and 1970s, contend that identity politics stunted the agenda of the larger political left and impoverished political and social discourse. These scholars argue that liberal culture requires some basis of commonality, that the particularism of identity celebrates differences to the point that it distracts from shared social commitments. Others point to the flowering of multiculturalism and gains in civil rights for minorities brought about by the new emphasis on rights and identity. For good or ill, identity politics pervasively shaped the postwar left, touching even evangelicals who shared similar theological convictions, religious cultures, and critiques of conservative politics. The heightened salience of identity, while offering inspiration to women, African Americans, Anabaptists, and Reformed evangelicals, sapped the broader evangelical left of the fragile sense of common purpose that came out of the first Thanksgiving Workshop.[4]

I

Of the identities that emerged with vigor in the early 1970s within the evangelical left, black racial identity was the most developed. The National Black Evangelical Association (NBEA) had been founded in 1963 by a coalition of black congregations within traditionally white fundamentalist and evangelical denominations. Organizers intended to proselytize non-churched blacks and to encourage solidarity among its members isolated in white denominations. By the mid-1960s, however, the NBEA also launched a program of dissent that criticized its host denominations for failing to join the civil rights movement. The allure of black power accelerated this trajectory, ultimately sparking a stronger sense of black consciousness and a separation from progressive white evangelicals.[5]

As late as 1969 most prominent black young evangelicals still expressed ambivalence toward Stokely Carmichael, the Student Nonviolent Coordinating Committee, and other advocates of black power. On one hand, they affirmed the broad critique of American society as structurally racist and the need for some independent black institutions. On the other hand, they criticized what they saw as the corrupt methods and excesses of the movement, specifically the new openness to violence among SNCC members and a more strident black separatism emerging in some quarters. The ultimate goal, they maintained, was to fulfill Martin Luther King, Jr.'s vision of "beloved community."

Their skepticism of black power, however, dissolved. Bitter black evangelical students, incensed by discrimination at evangelical colleges, "poorly accepted" evangelist Tom Skinner's moderate book *Black and Free* at the 1969 Black Christian Literature Conference. Howard Jones, a Billy Graham Evangelistic Association associate who gave the closing address at the conference, came under attack too. Many regarded Jones as "too White in his thinking, on the 'house-nigger' side of things." Similar sentiments surfaced in *Freedom Now*. Eight students posed for the civil rights magazine with a black power salute. In an extended interview, these "black militant evangelicals," as the magazine's editor called them, insisted on the creation of separate black institutions. White institutions were irrelevant, one explained, and white educational institutions created for blacks were inferior and failed to use black symbols to teach children. Another asserted, "What we need is a black, fundamental, Bible-believing, Bible institute and college that will dehonkify our minds and teach us how to communicate Christ to black people." The impulse by early black leaders to create an integrated evangelical community lost momentum as a younger generation embraced racial separatism.[6]

These young activists first introduced notions of black power on an institutional level at NBEA's 1969 convention in Atlanta. Most participants, both black and white, according to association president William Bentley, arrived "totally unprepared" for the "militant emphasis" that broke out among the younger set. In a fiery keynote address, Columbus Salley, author of *Your God Is Too White* (1970), urged NBEA delegates to nurture a blacker identity. Salley's speech drew a clear line between socially conservative blacks who "enjoyed close relationship with the white evangelical establishment" and those who wanted to relegate white leadership within the NBEA "to the periphery." The emerging conflict threatened to tear apart the NBEA. After an equally contentious New York City convention in 1970 in which "radicalism" and "get whitey-ism" flourished, participation by whites (who comprised one-third of the organization in the mid-1960s) dropped. Numbers of whites and blacks charged that NBEA was being overrun by "a bunch of fanatical, white-baiting bigoted Black reverse racists." During the rest of the 1970s, a range of separatist sentiment continued within NBEA— from those, according to Bentley, who were "so Black that they found no time for those less 'Black' than themselves" to those who encouraged white participation. NBEA as a whole, however, turned sharply toward separation.[7]

In the meantime, failed attempts at racial integration in other quarters seemed to confirm black separatist fears of white interference. Conflict over

Figure 19. Attempts by InterVarsity to attract black students drew the Soul Liberation band and nearly 1,000 black students to Urbana '70. Like many on the evangelical left, however, InterVarsity ultimately failed to create the "beloved community" ideal of the civil rights movement. Courtesy of the Archives of the Billy Graham Center, Wheaton, Illinois.

whether whites could participate in a black caucus marred the worship service led by Tom Skinner and the band Soul Liberation at InterVarsity's Urbana '70 convention. Three years later, at an InterVarsity seminar on black theology, participants drafted a bitter statement "from the Afro-American People." They declared that "significant progress" in incorporating the black perspective into convention planning had not been realized. Signers found it "imperative to protest all over again." "These cries of oppression are only scratching the surface of rumblings that are deeply embedded in the black community," they wrote. "If you don't hear these rumblings, ask God to give you a will to hear them before they erupt."[8]

The case of the Post-American community, the evangelical commune in Chicago founded in 1970, also suggested the limits of beloved community. While drawing praise for their deep involvement in the inner city, they failed in their efforts to incorporate more than a few blacks into their group.

Perhaps the most dramatic instance of racial discord took place at Voice of Calvary, an evangelistic and social service ministry in Jackson, Mississippi. Founder John Perkins watched helplessly as his social experiment "Freedom Summer 1971" fell apart. Perkins had brought together members of the black student association at the University of Michigan and white fundamentalist youths from California for a three-month period of intense community-building. The whites came armed with Campus Crusade's "Four Spiritual Laws" booklet; many of the blacks had just read Black Panther Eldridge Cleaver. The summer, said Perkins, turned into "a disaster" as cultural misunderstandings and resentments mounted. Half of the black students, according to Charles Marsh, ended up "bunkered down in the Jackson headquarters of the Republic of New Africa, sparring with local police and the FBI in a gun battle." The fearful white students could hardly bring themselves to step outside the community center. Perkins would later write, "Here were the fragments of what we believed in coming together—the preaching of the gospel, the social action that met people's needs, blacks and whites working together. But they were coming together without any mediation. There was nothing to glue them together. The poles were just too far apart. It seemed there could be no reconciliation."[9]

Hoping that the racial divisions in evangelicalism were rooted in youthful immaturity, a group of moderate black and progressive white evangelicals staged several final efforts in the mid-1970s to model beloved community. At the Thanksgiving Workshops many black participants were at first "deeply encouraged" to find whites of "like precious faith" willing to sign a statement that confessed "the conspicuous responsibility of the evangelical community for perpetuating the personal attitudes and institutional structures that have divided the body of Christ along color lines." Moreover, delegates seemed responsive to a laundry list of proposals from a hastily formed black caucus. But after the unsatisfying 1974 Workshop, at which the caucus requested "substantive" action, that optimism receded. The disastrous 1975 Workshop, which primarily addressed theoretical models of social concern, alienated back delegates who desired immediate and decisive steps. After listening to long presentations on Anabaptist, Lutheran, and Reformed political theory, William Bentley rose to "shatter the calm, analytical atmosphere," declaring, "I question whether you people can even see us blacks."[10]

Events over the next several years exacerbated Bentley's sense of betrayal. A 1975 conference on race and reconciliation, which drew a disappointingly small crowd and only a few top evangelical leaders, suggested that the battle against racism had been overtaken by concerns about Vietnam, Watergate, and poverty. Editors of the *Post-American*, after stressing racial concerns in its first issue, failed to devote much space to racism in succeeding years. The Post-Americans' preoccupation with the war led Wheaton College student Ron Potter to observe that "many New Black Evangelicals see the White Evangelical 'left' as irrelevant to them as neo-evangelicalism was to their predecessors in the fifties. The new Blacks feel that White Evangelicals, as a group, no matter how radical or young, will never come to grips with the demon of racism embedded within them." Bentley concurred, "Evangelicalism's treatment of and dedication to the eradication of racism within Christian and other contexts, falls far short of the time, attention, and commitment it invests in other areas of social concern." A series of confrontational meetings between editors of the *Post-American* and representatives of the NBEA in the mid-1970s only aggravated the rift.[11]

Disillusioned with the white evangelical left and dismayed by the lack of cultural cohesiveness among black youth, Bentley and other black evangelical leaders redoubled their efforts to nurture black identity. Exploring the ways in which white influence had corrupted black evangelicalism, they sought to establish their independence from white theology and culture. "Black Power begins with the realization that blacks have been conditioned by white institutions to hate themselves and to question their basic worth," Columbus Salley wrote in *Your God Is Too White*. Evangelicalism had trained blacks to believe in a "white, blue-eyed Jesus—a Jesus who negates the humanity of their blackness, a Jesus who demands that they whiten their souls in order to save them." Potter called for the "theological decolonization of minds," mourning that black evangelicals still "see through a glass whitely." Bentley, dubbed the "godfather" of militant black evangelicals, proclaimed a "Declaration of Independence from uncritical dependence upon white evangelical theologians who would attempt to tell us what the content of our efforts at liberation should be." He called instead for an authentic black evangelical theology, one that was biblical, grounded in "concrete sociopolitical realities," and that did not "merely blackenize the theologies of E. J. Carnell, Carl F. H. Henry, Francis Schaeffer, and other White Evangelical 'saints.'" While such thinkers could offer some insight, Bentley acknowledged, too many young black evangelicals were "under the academic spell" of white evangelical intellectuals who suffered from "blindness to the specifics of the Black American experience." Rather, Salley insisted, "God must become black." Clarence Hilliard, co-pastor of the interracial Circle

Church in Chicago, echoed, "Jesus stood with and for the poor and oppressed and disinherited. He came for the sick and needy. . . . He came into
the world as the ultimate 'nigger' of the universe." Black evangelical theology, wrote Bentley and Potter, should build on an "ethnic brand" and draw
from black sources such as James Cone and the collective experience of
black evangelicals.[12]

The call for the creation of a black theology grew into a broader push
for black identity and "ethnic self-acceptance." Since black culture "has been
lost, stolen, or destroyed," wrote Walter McCray, noted author and founder
of Black Light Fellowship in Chicago, "syncretism and integration must be
checked. We must, as best we can, isolate what is our own culture." McCray,
who discouraged interracial dating, encouraged black students to "read and
ponder on Blackness. Students must be ever learning about themselves as
Blacks." Wyn Wright Potter, staff member of the Douglass-Tubman Christian Center in the Robert Taylor housing project in Chicago, told white
participants at the second annual conference on politics at Calvin College
in 1974 about how "Jesus Christ the Liberator" heals the wounds of black
America by "fostering black identity and human dignity." In order to heal
their psyches, blacks needed to be part of an all-encompassing black community, and whites needed to stay out of the way. "Whatever role whites play
in a leadership capacity," explained Bentley, "it should be of an indirect nature and complementary to, not in advance of indigenous Black leadership."
Before racial integration could occur within evangelicalism, black leaders
maintained, individuals needed psychological wholeness rooted in ethnic
consciousness.[13]

The stress on black identity exacerbated the already wide cultural divide
and contributed to the deterioration of black-white cooperation on the ground
in the late 1970s. At Circle Church a bitter clash between white lead pastor
David Mains and black associate minister Clarence Hilliard raged. In 1978
Gordon-Conwell Seminary fell under sharp attack by John Perkins and Tom
Skinner, who called the Seminary the "biggest rip-off in evangelical history"
for its failure to fulfill founder A. J. Gordon's original intent of training
urban blacks. Efforts by Workshop organizers to build a center for the study
of racism went nowhere, and the organization's plan to include blacks in
its leadership—reserving four of eight spots on the planning committee—
backfired when it became difficult to find enough blacks to serve. By the late
1970s, white evangelical energy on racism seemed spent, and black evangelicals focused their own energy into dozens of black organizations, such as

National Black Evangelical Students Association, the National Association of Christian Communicators, and the Women's Commission of NBEA. The NBEA itself built local chapters in Portland, Chicago, New York City, Pittsburgh, Dallas, Seattle, Phoenix, Los Angeles, Philadelphia, Cleveland, San Francisco, and Detroit. By 1980, NBEA had a mailing list of five thousand and claimed an "extended constituency" of thirty to forty thousand. These were microscopic numbers compared to the fifteen million Protestant, churchgoing blacks. They were significant, however, within the lily-white neo-evangelical sphere.[14]

Meanwhile, other racial minorities emerged, many dismayed by the sole focus on black-white issues. Ka Tong Gaw, a sociology professor at Wheaton, resigned his position on the Thanksgiving Workshop planning committee in 1975 because of the committee's lack of attention to Asian affairs. When we refer to "minorities," Gaw complained, "We are referring primarily to the blacks." He felt like a "token chink," he told Sider, and suffered from a "blatantly unfair, let alone unchristian, expulsion of my participation in their caucus." "All I have received so far are laughs and more laughs" at "my Third World Action proposal." Gaw and others held an "ABC Conference" of Asian, black, and Chicano participants in Pasadena in February 1976, and InterVarsity Press alone printed nearly 100 books in support of multi-culturalism over the next several decades. But the hoped-for coalition of minority progressive evangelicals never materialized.[15]

White progressive evangelicals in principle affirmed separate racial institutions in the 1970s. But the reality, according to *The Other Side* magazine's John Alexander, left them "hurt, confused, and frustrated." That "letting Christ live through my blackness" would lead black evangelicals to racial separation heightened the white evangelical left's sense that it had forfeited its moral voice. The loss of beloved community, they also recognized, was dissipating much-needed talent and resources. This combination proved to be a devastating blow to the prospects of the evangelical left coalition.[16]

II

Female delegates at the Thanksgiving Workshops also dissented. In the weeks after the 1974 Workshop, many of the nearly thirty frustrated female participants sent Ron Sider letters, one of them a fiery dispatch from Evon Bachaus of Minneapolis. In the letter Bachaus accused men of following precisely the same pattern as the New Left, which "fell apart as a cohesive movement when the men . . . refused to take feminism seriously." Evangelical men at the Workshop, she reported, gave inordinate attention to racial issues at the expense of important gender issues such as the Equal Rights Amendment (ERA) and women's ordination. Bachaus balked at suggestions that highlighting such controversial gender issues might "ruin the credibility of the Workshop" or that "we need to take more time to study this thoroughly." She noted that "'further study needed' has been the Church's standard answer to women for some time now." For the sake of the progressive evangelical coalition, she implored Sider, give women 50 percent representation on the planning committee and 50 percent of the delegate body. As a gesture of good faith, Bachaus offered to distribute 50 copies of the Chicago Declaration to the Minneapolis chapter of the just-formed Evangelical Women's Caucus. Such signs of support for the larger progressive movement, however, would soon fade. After successfully placing their concerns on the agenda of the Thanksgiving Workshops, evangelical feminists largely abandoned the broader movement to build instead an organization focused more directly on women's issues.[17]

The confidence and stridency of Bachaus's letter belied the undeveloped progressive evangelical female consciousness prior to the early 1970s. To be sure, evangelical women had encountered feminist literature at state universities in the 1960s. University of Wisconsin student Mildred Meythaler, for example, remembered being "surprised to see myself, and my mother-in-law and grandmother, in the pages of *The Feminine Mystique*." Anne Eggebroten, who attended the 1974 Workshop, had converted to Christianity in 1964, then to feminism while at Stanford University. She joined the National Organization for Women and went to graduate school at the University of California at Berkeley to study medieval English literature. Sharon Gallagher, editor of CWLF's *Right On*, attended consciousness-raising groups in Berkeley and read feminist literature. As a whole, though, evangelical feminists were isolated and lacked a coherent program of action prior to the Workshops.[18]

The Thanksgiving Workshops gave evangelical feminists both the opportunity to meet and a forum in which to voice their concerns. At the 1973 Workshop the six women present managed to push through a section of the Chicago Declaration urging "mutual submission" between husbands and wives. They also lobbied for more participation by women in upcoming Workshops. Their efforts paid off as Sider fired off letters asking for ideas of women to invite, even suggesting that "men be willing to stay home to give wives a chance to attend conferences." In the end, the planning committee invited over sixty women, each investigated by the caucus to ensure she was sufficiently egalitarian on gender issues, to attend the 1974 Workshop.[19]

Over thirty nearly all white, urban, professional, and highly educated women showed up. They included Bok Lim Kim, assistant professor of social work at the University of Illinois; several Wheaton College professors; Letha Scanzoni, who was working on a book about evangelical feminism; Nancy Hardesty, an alumna of Wheaton and graduate student at the University of Chicago; Pamela Cole, the first female graduate of Gordon-Conwell Seminary to be ordained; Lucille Dayton, historian of women in the holiness tradition; Karen De Vos of the Christian Reformed World Relief Committee; Virginia Mollenkott, English professor at Paterson State College; and Neta Jackson of Reba Place. Together, they comprised nearly one-third of the attendance at the second Workshop. While these women were active participants in the Workshop's plenary sessions, they nonetheless spent much of their time in Chicago organizing themselves. They established a formal organization called the Evangelical Women's Caucus (EWC), which immediately issued demands regarding inclusive language, women's ordination, women's studies programs at evangelical colleges, the ERA, and equal employment opportunities in evangelical organizations.[20]

Of these major planks, the EWC most strongly advocated for gender-inclusive language. Members vehemently insisted that evangelicals cease "subtle discrimination against women in language which emphasizes the masculine to the exclusion of the feminine." University of Saskatchewan sociologist Kathleen Storrie complained to InterVarsity administrator Samuel Escobar about the recently issued Lausanne Covenant, in which she considered 17 of 27 uses of "humanity" to be sexist. Such matters were not "picayune," she maintained. "Language does reflect presuppositions about the relative social status of the members of a given culture or society." Sharon Gallagher complained of receiving letters addressed to "Dear Sir" or "Mr. Sherren Gallagher." Nancy Hardesty asked Sider to "be a bit more careful about sexist language." Sider subsequently penciled in "sisterly" before "brotherly" in describing his plea for a cooperative spirit at the Workshop. As the 1970s progressed, the evangelical left developed a library of nonsexist literature—which included titles such as the songbook *Brothers and Sisters Sing!*—and wrote manuals on using gender-inclusive language.[21]

Evangelical feminists, many of whom felt trapped in motherly and wifely duties, also sought to rearrange traditional gender roles. Jean Milliken, wife of a Young Life representative and mother of one son, complained, "The creativity supposedly inherent in marriage and child rearing has squeezed spontaneity from my life. Why am I cooped up here in this lousy apartment while you go traipsing off across the country preaching freedom?" Workshops sought to address this imbalance. Sider instructed that "husband and wife should come together. . . . The style of child care (with men and women taking turns in caring for the children present) should foster mutuality in child care tasks." But even after most in the evangelical left had come to a consensus on gender equality, many found dilemmas of gender roles difficult to navigate. Among the Post-Americans, who tried to promote mutuality by sharing household duties, gender conflict nonetheless prevailed. According to member Jackie Sabath, the "deep reservoir of conscious and unconscious attitudes and behaviors we had accumulated throughout our twenty-some years of being either male or female" contributed to the collapse of its intentional community in Chicago. Only one woman remained in the reconstituted community in Washington, D.C. For evangelical egalitarians wading through the minefield of fluid gender roles, *The Other Side* printed an advice column entitled "In the Realms of the Sexes."[22]

In addition to promoting gender-inclusive language and mutuality in marriage, EWC sought to institutionalize gender equality through support of the Equal Rights Amendment. EWC urged passage of the ERA at its first meetings in 1974. Sojourners held prayer meetings on behalf of the ERA. Evangelical feminists wrote dozens of articles that salved evangelical fear and misconceptions about the amendment. And many in the evangelical left lobbied politically for the ERA. As the deadline for states' ratification loomed in the early 1980s, Britt Vanden Eykel, national coordinator for EWC, lobbied legislators in Oklahoma. Virginia Mollenkott spoke at a National Organization for Women rally, and leaders urged evangelicals to wear buttons that read "People of Faith for ERA" and to affix pro-ERA bumper stickers on their cars.[23]

If the evangelical feminist movement enjoyed outspoken support from the broader evangelical left on behalf of the ERA and nonsexist language, one proposal faced objections from a vocal minority. When the EWC urged the ordination of women, a significant minority of Workshop delegates, including several women, objected. Rufus Jones, a Workshop planner and a Baptist denominational leader, found the ordination proposal difficult to square with Pauline injunctions in scripture. Under pressure from constituents unhappy with the feminist rhetoric, Jones dismissed the "extreme proposals" and the EWC as "merely a discussion group which had no proper organization and therefore, got out of hand when three or four extremists took advantage of the situation." While delegates defeated a motion from the floor to strike ordination from the proposal list, a reporter noted that "the minority wanted it to be known that they did not feel bound by the majority decision." The dissent over ordination, even as many leaders and participants strained to accommodate much of their agenda, alienated many women from the Workshops. Increasingly, a burgeoning network of discouraged women, simultaneously dispirited and energized by the Workshop experience, began to build their own movement. The EWC distributed a directory of "evangelical feminists," produced study materials for churches, and launched its own publication, *Daughters of Sarah*. The EWC soon more explicitly declared itself autonomous from the Workshops.[24]

The movement gained even more traction with the 1974 release of *All We're Meant to Be*. Composed three years earlier by Workshop participants Letha Scanzoni, a "pious and quiet, but tell-it-like-it-is feminist," and the fiery Nancy Hardesty, the book at first proved difficult to publish. Six evangelical publishers in three years rejected the manuscript. When Word Books, a publisher in Waco, Texas, finally printed the book just prior to the second Thanksgiving Workshop, it got rave reviews. *Vanguard* praised its "scholarship, compassion, and commitment to Christ." *Eternity* named it "Book of the Year" in 1975, based on a survey of 150 evangelical leaders. InterVarsity's *HIS* magazine urged its tens of thousands of subscribers to read the book. Evangelical standard *Christianity Today* published a positive review of the book, written by sympathetic editor Cheryl Forbes. Brisk sales matched the editorial praise. By 1978 it had gone through seven printings.[25]

The book marshaled cutting-edge psychological, biological, and exegetical research. Emphasizing the authority of scripture, Hardesty and Scanzoni nonetheless came out firmly against traditional interpretations of the biblical texts, calling the subordination of women a "misrepresentation of the Word of God." In fact, they argued, not letting women preach was "wasting the church's gifts." This latter argument—that women's liberation was necessary for full service to God and the Church—went a long way in reassuring conservatives that evangelical feminists were not "man-hating, marriage-hating, family-hating females who are selfishly trying to take over the world." Hardesty and Scanzoni also argued for the validation of the unmarried life and a "true egalitarianism" in which wives and husbands could interchange gender roles. Either husband or wife could "fulfill the roles of breadwinner, housekeeper, encourager, career-achiever, child-trainer, and so on." For large numbers of evangelical women, *All We're Meant to Be* successfully translated mainstream feminism into evangelical categories.[26]

In addition to Scanzoni and Hardesty's classic apology for egalitarianism, evangelical feminists constructed a historical genre that uncovered precedents for female spiritual leadership in American evangelicalism. At the 1974 Workshop Lucille Sider Dayton distributed a paper arguing that the nineteenth-century holiness movement encouraged women to preach. Dayton's continuing historical work, distilled in her husband Donald Dayton's 1976 book *Discovering an Evangelical Heritage*, tried to show that next to Quakerism, nineteenth-century evangelicalism gave "the greatest role to women in the life of the church." Free-Will Baptists and faculty at Oberlin College encouraged women to attend school and to preach. The Wesleyan Methodists nurtured close ties with the woman's rights movement launched at Seneca Falls. Nazarene women, Dayton noted, comprised 20 percent of the denomination's total clergy around the turn of the century, a figure that dropped to about 6 percent by 1973. Dayton blamed the corrupting influence of fundamentalism for the precipitous drop, which left women subject to lives of "'total' and 'fascinating' womanhood that completely submerges their own personalities and aspirations." This underlying theme also animated Nancy Hardesty's 1976 doctoral dissertation at the University of Chicago, which maintained that, prior to the influence of fundamentalism, a "biblical feminism" rooted in Finneyite revivalism and the Wesleyan Holiness tradition sparked the women's rights movement. The evangelical feminist movement of the 1970s thus drew much inspiration not only from the contemporary feminist movement, but also from evangelicalism's earlier progressive record on gender and social reform.[27]

Historical and biblical scholarship undergirded a growing popular literature. Evangelical feminists launched magazines called *Green Leaf, freeindeed,* and *EWC Update. Daughters of Sarah,* founded by Lucille Sider Dayton, had over 1,000 subscribers within two years of its first issue in November of 1974. The proliferation of evangelical feminist publications birthed numerous informal local, regional, and ecclesiastical networks. Students, housewives, and professionals with a feminist bent gathered in InterVarsity-sponsored Christian Women's Seminars and Nurses Christian Fellowship, the Women's Commission of the NBEA, and EWC chapters. Especially strong EWC chapters, modeled organizationally on the National Organization for Women, thrived in California, particularly in Los Angeles, which had 400 members, and in the Bay Area, which had 70 members and 320 people on its mailing list. Chapters soon followed in Detroit, Seattle, Albany, New York, Minneapolis, the Central Valley of California, Boston, Oklahoma, Oregon, Indiana, Ohio, Nebraska, Newark, New Jersey, Colorado, Missouri, and Toronto.[28]

These regional networks matured into a national movement in the mid-1970s. Over 350 women (with dozens more turned away at the door for lack of space) attended the first Evangelical Women's Caucus convention in Washington, D.C. Broadly evangelical, the 1975 conference featured progressives such as Hardesty and Scanzoni as well as those with more conservative views on gender issues. Delegates passed two resolutions—one to support the ERA as "consistent with Christian convictions" and a second expressing solidarity with the 2,000 Catholic women meeting simultaneously in Detroit urging the ordination of women. The same year, the 1975 Continental Congress on the Family in St. Louis, an event typically cited for its conservatism, also featured a progressive spirit. At the Congress, which, according to historian John Turner, signified "the arrival of the family as one of the central spiritual and political concerns of evangelicals during the last quarter of the twentieth century," Letha Scanzoni contended that "genuine equality [between men and women] plainly means that there is no 'fixed' or ultimate head; power is shared equally." The diversity of thought at these conferences shows the contested nature of evangelical sexual politics in the 1970s. During a time when it was still unclear how evangelicals might emerge culturally and politically, evangelical feminism showed striking potential.[29]

For evangelical feminists gathered in St. Louis and Washington, D.C., meeting like-minded egalitarians proved psychologically significant. Jackie Sabath and other women in Sojourners met monthly to explore "how we felt about ourselves, including discussion about sexuality, singleness, marriage, roles we play or do not play." The meetings encouraged Sabath. "Exciting to us all," she reported, "is the personal and corporate growth that we sense from being together. We have experienced more freedom and flow of conversation than we do in mixed groups." A woman in Washington told a journalist, "I had no one else to turn to. My church and family told me I was a troublemaker and mentally sick for wanting equality." Another tearfully said, "I thought I was alone and that I was wrong in what I was feeling; and now I find that I am not." As scores of participants told their "coming to feminism" stories at one of EWC's national conventions, *Vanguard*'s Bonnie

Greene felt an "overwhelming sense of love." At the thousand-women-strong 1978 convention, Claire Wolterstorff of Michigan felt "as if she were being carried along a river whose quick currents were hidden while the surface bore me over emotions and issues into which I wanted to dive and swim." Student Sue Horner, served communion by a woman for the first time, knelt with other women at simple wooden tables encircling the sanctuary. White-robed dancers and violists performed in the aisles, and daisies were scattered. "Even now, I am moved," she later recalled, by Letha Scanzoni's assertion in the convention's sermon that "we did not become feminists and then try to fit our Christianity into feminist ideology. We became feminists because we were Christians."[30]

If feminism was rooted in their faith, it was nonetheless their gendered identity that sometimes seemed most salient to conservative critics and evangelical feminists alike. By the late 1970s organizational segregation had hardened as evangelical feminists directed considerable energies toward building their own movement. Anne Eggebroten, newly energized by her place in the all-encompassing "sisterhood," explained that "most of my time has been devoted to sharing with others what I have learned, both in my own church and with Christian women in other churches." Others, too, committed their talents to networking and writing literature in the evangelical feminist sphere. In consequence, they gave less time to the Workshop movement. Building organizations devoted to ending "wasted talent in the evangelical community," an important plank in the evangelical left's platform, ironically deprived the progressive coalition of much of that talent.[31]

III

If heightened racial and gender identities deepened cracks in the progressive front, diverging theological commitments seemed to create an unbridgeable chasm. From the beginning it was clear that the progressive coalition was just that—a coalition of many ecclesiastical bodies and theologies. An attendee at the first Thanksgiving Workshop classified participants into six groups: "old-line evangelicals," "traditional Anabaptists," "neo-Anabaptists," "black evangelicals," "non-aligned denominations," and "Calvinists." Particularly sharp clashes between delegates of Anabaptist and Calvinist (commonly called Reformed) theological orientations frustrated hopes that these groups might coalesce organizationally.[32]

At the first Workshop, Reformed delegates assented to proposals from historic peace church delegates. Together they declared that evangelicals must "challenge the misplaced trust of the nation in economic and military might—a proud trust that promotes a national pathology of war and violence which victimizes our neighbors at home and abroad." But Reformed delegates found stronger Anabaptist repudiations of war and wealth wrongheaded. The Anabaptist-Reformed dispute emerged most visibly in the Workshop caucus on economic lifestyles in 1974. The caucus, dominated by Anabaptists, submitted a constellation of provocative proposals: a graduated tithe that would increase as income increased; an additional one percent tithe meant for evangelical projects that would change "white attitudes and power structures"; a boycott of lawn fertilizer; a national day of fasting; one meatless day per week; and a commitment that a family of four live on an annual income of $8,000. Some members of the caucus wanted to propose that "renunciation of possessions was the ideal they saw in the life and teaching of Jesus."[33]

Non-Anabaptist delegates strenuously objected. One critic accused caucus members of hijacking the Workshop with a "radical/Anabaptist" perspective. Another, noting the moral dilemmas and impracticality of such proposals, wondered, "The question is, does our cutting out meat help hungry people or does it just reduce inflation in America so the comfortable can buy more meat for the same money?" The lawn fertilizer boycott encountered resistance from a delegate who wondered if using fertilizer would be appropriate to grow rice in famine-stricken India. Rufus Jones warned against replacing old evangelical legalisms with "a new set of legalisms." Annoyed by the proposal that "no one should live above $2,000 a year," Jones declared, "I would need to question his hermeneutics if he gets that out of the Bible." Reformed delegates suggested that changing political institutions from within offered more potential than taking vows of poverty that might limit political influence. In the end, Workshop delegates compromised, agreeing to release an open-ended "Commitment of Economic Responsibility" that pledged "solidarity with all people who are hungry, poor and oppressed." Each delegate promised to "share my personal resources with them" and to create a church "less enmeshed in its property and possessions."[34]

Sensing that the pledge was only a temporary bandage hiding a festering wound, organizers dedicated the third Workshop to discussion of theological models for social action. Dale Brown, a Brethren seminary professor, offered the first presentation, entitled "An Anabaptist (or Counter Culture)

Model." Brown argued that true discipleship required distance from temporal structures. As "aliens in a strange land" compelled to imitate Christ in
his suffering, Christians should speak prophetically to political structures
from outside the system, not from within. Brown drew heavily from John
Howard Yoder's magnum opus *The Politics of Jesus* (1972), an exegesis of
several New Testament gospels that sought to refute Reinhold Niebuhr's
Christian realism and just war theory. Critiquing the Constantinian merging of church and state, Yoder argued against the Christian coercion of
society. The state, to which Christians do not owe a reflexive obedience, is
inherently corrupt, he maintained, and entanglement in the state is fraught
with danger and compromise. Jesus' greatest temptation was to wield political power, or as Yoder suggested at a conference at Calvin College, to become a Calvinist.[35]

Instead, Jesus ultimately worked toward the visible restructuring of
social relations within the Church. This example, which ought to be central
to Christian social ethics, suggested that suffering and peace were normative
practices. This was not to say, Yoder was quick to point out in *Politics of Jesus*, that the Church had no social or political responsibilities. Rather, Christians, in forming countercultural communities that fed the hungry, cared
for the sick, and spoke prophetically to positions of power on behalf of the
oppressed, could serve as a social model to the world. Servanthood, grass-
roots action, and persuasion, rather than coercion, ought to characterize
Christian politics. As an example of moral suasion, Yoder cited his involvement with an ecumenical group of Christians who were trying to ameliorate
racial segregation in Evanston, Illinois, during the 1960s. Most in the group
found it self-evident that the ministers in the community ought to persuade
the mayor and city council to adopt open housing policies. This would be
the church discharging her social responsibility. But the conversation fell
into disarray when someone pointed out that most of the real estate dealers
and sellers of houses were members of the very Protestant churches the
ministers led. The problem, reported Yoder, was that the typical minister
seemed "powerless to get his own members to take Christian ethics seriously without the coercion of government." More effort ought to be dedicated to discipleship at the church level, he suggested. Why should Christians
expect other forces in society to be more effective and insightful than the
"body of believers in their structured life together"? The primary social
structure through which the gospel works to change other social structures,
wrote Yoder, "is that of the Christian community."[36]

To mainstream and Reformed evangelicals at the Workshop, Anabaptist politics, falling into Richard Niebuhr's classification of "Christ against culture," seemed naïve, otherworldly, and irresponsible. Gordon-Conwell professor Stephen Mott, troubled by "the most widely read political book in young evangelical circles," (the first edition alone sold over 75,000 copies, an impressive number for a dense theological study) declared that *Politics of Jesus* "provides comfort and motivation for the increasing number of evangelicals who are rejecting legislative change as a method of social action in favor of the creation of Christian community . . . and a participation in forms of direct action." Calvin philosopher Richard Mouw noted that "orthodox Calvinists are afflicted with a 'Menno-phobia' of sorts. We want very much not to sound like Anabaptists." In a rebuttal of Dale Brown at the 1975 Workshop, Calvin theologian Gordon Spykman explained precisely why Reformed thinkers opposed neo-Anabaptist strategies. He asserted that "God so loved the cosmos that he sent his son to save it. If then God has not turned his back on the world that he made, we have no right to do so either." God had charged humanity with a cultural mandate to reverse the effects of sin that "distort, corrupt, and pervert" social structures. "Redemption," Spykman declared, "is the restoration of creation." Consequently, "All of life is religion. . . . No dichotomy between Church and world. No separation of piety and politics." Promoting a principled Christian realism in the tradition of Augustine, Aquinas, Luther, Calvin, and Reinhold Niebuhr could reform American politics.[37]

Some in the evangelical left hoped to integrate these divergent theological identities. In a third presentation at the 1975 Workshop, Robert Webber, a Wheaton College professor, proposed such a consensus. Arguing for the validity of each approach, Webber affirmed the Anabaptist commitment to "live life both personally and communally by a new set of standards" as well as Reformed transformationalism which "affirms the new order in the midst of the old." No one model contains the whole truth, Webber insisted. Each one could be "examined, modified, and used as a unifying framework" that would help the group get beyond words and on to the task of social action. "The separatism principle of the Anabaptists ought to separate us from the gods of our age (imperialism, capitalism, etc.)," he argued, "so that we can then use the transformation principle of the Reformed to go about our Christian social and political task in the world." Moreover, said Webber, if the evangelical left could learn to think and work in specifics, it could overcome theological differences and arrive at a consensus on practical ethics and activism. Both Calvinists and Anabaptists, historian Richard Pierard affirmed, could have participated in British abolitionism of the eighteenth and nineteenth centuries.[38]

Webber's plea failed spectacularly. The focus on theoretical models in the third Workshop, while clarifying the conversation for some bewildered delegates unfamiliar with the intricacies of the debate, only exacerbated theological and methodological differences. Meanwhile, activists condemned the "ponderous think approach," wanting to get on with political action already. Jim Wallis, still inspired by the New Left, quit his leadership position because the Workshop was becoming too structured and institutional. Then William Bentley, angered that the Workshop failed to consider a black model of social action, got into a shouting match with a white delegate. In a poisonous mood, the Workshop broke up a day early. The fragmentation extended to a second conference on politics in 1975 at Calvin College, where one participant likened the gathering to a "tower of Babel" in which delegates spoke different theological languages and held to "a motley array of divergent viewpoints." "Here we are in Grand Rapids, all evangelicals, one in Christ, yet our political bases are miles apart," wrote Sherwood Wirt. "And when we leave this conference we shall probably return home believing what we did when we came, only more so." The brief window during which Swiss-German Mennonites and Dutch Reformed Calvinists had emerged out of cultural isolation to engage evangelicalism seemed to be rapidly closing. Neither group seemed willing to abandon its ecclesial structures and traditions.[39]

Events in subsequent years further entrenched the Anabaptist-Reformed division. Critiques of Reformed and Anabaptist political theory filled evangelical left journals. Jim Wallis and contributors to the *Reformed Journal* exchanged fiery missives. Richard Mouw wrote several books rebutting Yoder's *Politics of Jesus*. In the end, those still interested in dialogue could no longer hope for a constructive integration of the two perspectives; they could only assert that they had an important corrective influence on each other. "The Anabaptists can warn the Reformed against selling out to a corrupt establishment," wrote Gordon-Conwell professor Richard Lovelace, "and the Reformed can warn the Anabaptists to avoid accusatory despair." But Lovelace's tactic of soft affirmation—and pleas to keep "justice-minded evangelicals from squaring off against each other"—rarely won the day between religious traditions that each insisted on their perspective as "the biblical" approach.[40]

The two traditions, in fact, soon led down separate institutional paths. Evangelicals for Social Action (ESA), founded by Ron Sider in 1978, came to house a high proportion of Anabaptists. In keeping with Yoder's approach to politics, ESA sought to address social injustices from the bottom up. "Empowering Christians to work for change in their own communities is what ESA is all about," explained the organization as it announced new emphases on education, grass-roots mobilization, and "peace parishes." By the early 1980s ESA had conducted over 60 two-day "Discipleship Workshops" in which attendees participated in interactive activities—seminars, games, role playing, videos, discussions, prayer, and singing. In 1978, for example, ESA blitzed the campuses of the evangelical Gordon College and Gordon-Conwell Seminary. Sider spoke at a faculty symposium, gave lectures to nine classes, and delivered chapel addresses on "God and the Poor" and "Structural Evil." Other ESA representatives gave lectures on topics such as militarism, civil religion, living simply, nonviolence, and the politics of Jubilee. Students also attended a "biblical feminism" seminar that featured calls for gender-inclusive language and chips and dip made from recipes out of the *More-with-Less Cookbook*. ESA's Boston blitz ended with a meeting of evangelical ministers, including Paul Toms, pastor of the venerable Park St. Church and president of the NAE.[41]

Sojourners, which also featured a significant Anabaptist constituency, extended the grass-roots approach of ESA's Discipleship Workshops. In the early 1980s Sojourners moved into a 7,000-square-foot floor of a Washington, D.C. office building, which housed the magazine, a book service, a peace ministry staff of 17, and a stable of interns and volunteers. From their new digs, Sojourners engaged the political realm through protest and strident manifestos. While they nurtured very few contacts with high-level politicians, they did cultivate relationships with editors of important national newspapers such as the *New York Times, Newsweek*, and the *Washington Post*, which could publicize their protests to the masses. Arrested by police hundreds of times in the 1970s and 1980s, Wallis and his colleagues garnered substantial publicity for protests at high visibility sites such as the White House, the Supreme Court, and Congress.[42]

This symbolic, activist style contrasted starkly with that of Reformed evangelicals, who initiated "something of a withdrawal" from the Workshop movement soon after ESA's founding. "The cause of Christian politics in America is now identified with a new name: The Association for Public Justice," declared the first issue of the *Public Justice Newsletter*. Members of APJ, in keeping with the gradualist inclinations of Reformed evangelicals, were more willing to engage in conventional politicking. The organization recruited bright graduate students to research policy and write briefs. It

Figure 20. In April 1977 Sojourners protested against torture practiced by nations supported by U.S. military aid. One participant, reflecting on the use of the cross in the week-long demonstrations in front of the White House and the Capitol, explained that "Jesus too was tortured for siding with the poor." Courtesy of Archives and Special Collections, Wheaton College, Wheaton, Illinois.

organized conferences for evangelical leaders and scholars at Wheaton, Calvin, and Washington. APJ also organized policy and educational panels with top government officials, diligently cultivating intellectual rigor and decrying strident political rhetoric. Though not splashy, their sudden entrée into the political worlds of Washington and Ottawa in the early 1980s was heady. Several of its members won seats in state legislatures and testified before state Supreme Courts. The national organization released election kits and voter guides, and Iowa chapters vetted candidates in the presidential caucuses. APJ associates testified before the U.S. Senate Finance Committee and the House Committee on Ways and Means. They participated in a UN Special Session on Disarmament and filed briefs with the U.S. Supreme Court. The organization enjoyed slow but steady growth through the 1980s, with ten active regional chapters, well over 2,000 dues-paying members, and an active Washington office.[43]

APJ's politics revolved around the political theory of "principled plural-ism." Affirming the varied cultures and social bonds of the world "crafted by the Creator," APJ argued that the state should not obliterate this diversity in pursuit of a single homogeneous community. The "special, irreducible" character of minority populations—including ethnics, religious people, chil-dren, refugees, conscientious objectors, and prisoners—should be protected in the face of majoritarian tyranny. While acknowledging the role of gov-ernment in ordering a complex and differentiated society, APJ encouraged the vitality of localism and the growth of nongovernmental civil structures such as schools, churches, family, neighborhoods, and small civic organi-zations. Along with Richard John Neuhaus, with whom the organization nurtured friendly ties in the 1980s, APJ advocated tuition tax credits and educational vouchers. Private education could protect minority interests better than public education, which too often flattened diversity. APJ, how-ever, broke with conservatives on issues such as the environment, interna-tional policy, and evaluations of capitalism. APJ's politics of Christian realism thus balanced issues on the left and right, denying both individual-istic and collectivistic visions of government.[44]

APJ's legislative and judicial influence may have been remarkable given its size, but its small constituency and idiosyncratic positions necessarily resulted in limited exposure. Like ESA and Sojourners, it labored into the 1980s with only modest growth and stability. Together, the organizations might have coalesced into a significant non-rightist evangelical alternative. But with its resources divided and its identity fragmented over strategies for political transformation, the evangelical left failed to approach the spectac-ular, if short-lived, mobilization of the Moral Majority. The formation of ESA, and then APJ, in the late 1970s signaled that neither Reformed nor Anabaptist evangelicals would fully consummate their flirtation with a broader coalition of progressive evangelicals. The two organizations' divergent approaches to-ward issues of social justice prevented the evangelical left from speaking out with one voice.

IV

Other identities pervaded the evangelical left. High-church traditions such as the Eastern Orthodox Church and the Anglican Church poached sur-prising numbers of young evangelicals. Loyalties to mainline, Lutheran,

charismatic-Pentecostal, and holiness traditions also destabilized the movement. Foy Valentine, a progressive Southern Baptist from Texas, told a *Newsweek* reporter he did not want to be identified as an evangelical. Irritated by
the northern hegemony of neo-evangelicalism, he declared that "evangelical" was "a Yankee word." "They want to claim us because we are big and
successful and growing every year. But we have our own traditions," Valentine explained. Notwithstanding the sociologist Robert Wuthnow's suggestion of a "restructuring of American religion" along liberal-conservative
lines, old denominational and theological categories still remained salient
within the evangelical left. Even evangelical identity itself hurt the evangelical left. Despite overtures from some mainliners and some ecumenical cooperation, many in the evangelical left remained suspicious of their longtime
Protestant rivals. Bill Pannell, an evangelist with Tom Skinner Associates,
mocked mainline spirituality. Their social declarations were entirely deriva-
tive from secular politics, Pannell noted derisively at the second Workshop,
and the most salient element of their social conferences was the predomi-
nance of "really stylish hairshirts." Another Workshop participant criticized
the "mealy-mouthed pieties of liberal Protestantism," which merely echo "the
false values of Americanism." Cooperative efforts, which seemed promising
at first, did not lead to productive co-belligerency.[45]

Division within these evangelical subgroups further fragmented a deteriorating consensus. In the Reformed camp, the strident anti-establishment
rhetoric of the Institute for Christian Studies offended the reformist sensibilities of the *Reformed Journal*. In addition, black women, while sympathetic to the feminist cause, often found race a more salient category than
gender. "I cannot as a black woman fully participate as an activist in a separatist women's movement," explained Wyn Wright Potter. "The black man
and woman must stand together to fight a common foe: white, racist America." Evangelical progressives also extended the politics of identity to the
elderly, the physically disabled, prisoners, and human fetuses. Preoccupation
with minority rights and identity, while essential to their platform, hurt the
political viability of the evangelical left.[46]

If identity politics fragmented the evangelical left, individual identity,
sparked by the rise of evangelical psychology, disrupted the movement in
more subtle ways. Psychology departments in evangelical colleges thrived,
and radio programs and books dedicated to self-help multiplied. Many in
the evangelical left, eager to establish egalitarian communities, avidly con-
sumed the new genre. The Evangelical Women's Caucus in 1974 encouraged

women to learn "skills of assertiveness, negotiation, creative conflict, and confrontation to resist the forces that have so often made women feel 'victims,' helpless, and passive." Richard Quebedeaux, a close observer of progressive evangelicals in the 1970s, noted the popularity of sensitivity training, "group encounter" weekends, Transactional Analysis, and nonverbal forms of communication such as hand-holding, embracing, and dancing. These habits, he observed, created environments in which "an individual can be honest about who he is, his hopes, aspirations, and hurts." Some progressive evangelicals, like critics in the broader political left, complained that the new therapeutic focus on personal authenticity distracted from the movement's political agenda.[47]

By the late 1970s, it was clear that the politics of identity in all its forms was stunting the promise of the evangelical left. Rifts widened between men and women, black and white, Anabaptist and Calvinist—and in countless other permutations. Women were cordoned off in the Evangelical Women's Caucus, African-Americans in the National Black Evangelical Association, Anabaptist progressives in Evangelicals for Social Action, Anabaptist radicals in Sojourners, Calvinist progressives in the Association for Public Justice, and Calvinist radicals in the Institute for Christian Studies. The failure to construct a common vocabulary and shared political commitments at the Thanksgiving Workshop had pushed minority groups to pursue their own strategies. Identity politics in turn subverted the evangelical left's potency as a collective network and a coherent alternative to the religious right, whose fundamentalist hierarchies could more easily enforce cooperation.

The increased salience of racial, gender, theological, and personal identities led to a sense of crisis not only within the progressive front, but also within evangelicalism more broadly. The rising prominence of evangelicalism, mourned leaders in dozens of jeremiads, merely gilded a deteriorating movement. "The ironic fact," wrote Jim Wallis, "is evangelicalism as we have known it in the past few decades is actually coming apart, just when it has been 'discovered.'" *Christianity Today* editor Harold Lindsell lamented, "It is clear that evangelicalism is now broader and shallower, and is becoming more so. Evangelicalism's children are in the process of forsaking the faith of their fathers." Lindsell's predecessor at *Christianity Today*, Carl Henry, mourned the loss of the great neo-evangelical consensus in his 1976 book *Evangelicals in Search of Identity*. In an interview with Jim Wallis and Wes Michaelson for *Sojourners* magazine, Henry declared, "There is a lack of a sense of body in the evangelical community. It is fragmented."[48]

The secular left may not have shared evangelicals' internal disputes over women's ordination and Anabaptist theology. But it did suffer, like the evangelical left, from the centripetal temper of the 1970s. Intentional communities broke apart. As Latinos, feminists, gays, Asian Americans, and Native Americans applied the critiques of the black civil rights movement to their own circumstances, they abandoned assimilation in favor of separation. The great coalition of the left, anticipated by the white elites of SDS and the Great Society, never materialized. As the left fragmented in the 1970s, it was easy to forget the tenuous nature of the coalition in the first place. The 1960s may have held promise, but the failure of the Great Society revealed the "liberal consensus" to be the diverse and fragile coalition that it was. Alongside the familiar stories of the New Left and the New Right, the evangelical left's debates over racial, sexual, and theological difference added to the era's disruptions.

Similarly, Carl Henry's declension narrative failed to recognize already entrenched diversities within evangelicalism. In the 1950s and 1960s evangelical boosters had very effectively created the illusion of a single evangelical identity. The rise of *Christianity Today* and the National Association of Evangelicals, however, masked the reality that evangelicalism was a coalition of people with some traits in common but also with significant differences. Henry and others so remarkably succeeded in portraying a unified evangelicalism that the secular media in the 1970s fell over themselves to proclaim a "blossoming evangelical movement." A vital evangelical center, however, would fail to emerge. Identity politics within the evangelical left exposed the illusion of evangelical unity and suggested that the progressive evangelical front might not thrive.[49]

CHAPTER 11

―――――

The Limits of Electoral Politics

While many may seem consoled by the tendency of
presidential candidates to keep their religious convictions
separate from their political actions, I, for one, remain
distressed.

        ―Senator Mark Hatfield on presidential
              candidate Jimmy Carter

In the mid-1970s, just a few years removed from the Chicago Declaration, it was not yet clear that identity politics would prove debilitating. If anything, expectations for political success heightened as a most unexpected presidential candidate emerged: an outspoken progressive Southern Baptist from rural Georgia. Conservative and progressive evangelicals alike rallied around Jimmy Carter, the candidate. But Carter, the president, fared less well. By 1980 the devout Carter was surrounded by a cadre of nonreligious staffers, many of whom resented his unwillingness to promote the pro-choice cause. At the same time, Carter battled several prominent national evangelical leaders who resented his unwillingness to promote the pro-life cause. These politically conservative leaders began to advocate the candidacy of Ronald Reagan, a divorced Hollywood actor. Though Carter had enjoyed a crucial bloc of support from fellow evangelicals in 1976, he had now become a polarizing figure among that base. "The Carter Presidency with its emphasis on religion has been a spur to bring these folks together," one of Carter's advisers pointed out. Conservative evangelicals were asking, "If *he* can be political why can't *we*?" For evangelicals, who were only now breaking into the political mainstream, negotiating the unprecedented rise of one of their own to the highest office in the nation had turned into an unexpectedly perplexing dilemma.[1]

Carter's presidency, reviled by both the secular left and the religious right, stands as an important representation of the broader evangelical left and the difficult political choices it faced. Despite extending explicit overtures in the form of Evangelicals for McGovern and the Chicago Declaration, the evangelical left was met with apathy and hostility—when it was recognized at all—by the broader left. The evangelical left's conservative theology troubled the broader left, which failed to make a case for progressive politics in the combination of moral and religious terms that would have appealed to evangelicals. In fact, the liberal coalition seemed to go to great lengths—by giving a prominent voice to activist secularists—to alienate a potentially powerful segment of evangelicals.

On the other end of the political spectrum, an increasingly politicized religious right began to enjoy more success with a rising cadre of televangelists and political operatives. Embraced by a receptive Republican Party, conservative evangelicals rapidly moved toward a more activist politics, a process catalyzed by the issue of abortion. Caught between two hostile major political parties, progressive evangelicals in the late 1970s were left behind by both the left and the right. The evangelical left—weighted down by identity politics and its ill fit in an evolving two-party political system—would ultimately fail to capitalize on the promise of the Chicago Declaration.

I

Jimmy Carter, who would become the nation's best known and most politically successful progressive evangelical, initially appealed to a broad evangelical spectrum. His centrist proposals on energy reform, the environment, the Panama Canal, and Mideast peace talks enhanced his standing among former members of Evangelicals for McGovern and signers of the Chicago Declaration. Calvin philosopher Nicholas Wolterstorff hoped that in Carter "we have evangelical Protestantism coming to progressive political expression." *New York Times* assistant news editor Bob Slosser (himself an evangelical) described Carter in a campaign biography as "sincerely liberal in matters of race, both moderate and conservative in the field of social legislation, and staunchly conservative in fiscal matters." David Kucharsky, a *Christianity Today* editor, portrayed Carter as standing in a long line of Protestant luminaries, including John Stott, Reinhold Niebuhr, and J. Gresham Ma-chen, for whom the Christian faith was rational and respectable. Carter's Christian realism and progressive rhetoric fit the evangelical left. His atten-tion to human rights, a social issue of central concern to progressive evan-gelicals, fit the national mood in the 1970s.[2]

Numerous progressive evangelicals collaborated with Carter's campaign. Robert McCan of Church of the Saviour in Washington, D.C., served as the campaign's director of finance for the southeastern United States. In Geor-gia, former Young Life worker Bill Milliken became a close confidant of Carter and received state funds to combat drug abuse. In Texas, Jimmy Allen, a member of Evangelicals for Social Action, president of the Southern Baptist Convention, and close friend to Carter, supported his campaign and later acted as an unofficial emissary to Tehran to help resolve the Iran hostage crisis. At Wheaton College, the Organization of Collegiate Democrats met each Tuesday evening during the election. Student members worked coop-eratively with the local Democratic Party headquarters to bring to campus Senator Adlai Stevenson, who railed in the college chapel against the "terrible failure of national leadership with Republicans in the White House the past 8 years." Jay Hakes, a Wheaton alumnus, led the Carter campaign in Louisi-ana, attended the Democratic National Convention as an at-large Carter delegate, and then worked as an assistant to secretary of the interior Cecil Andrus.[3]

The bulk of evangelical support, however, came not from the organized evangelical left but rather from those evangelicals delighted that an out-spoken, born-again believer was running for president. In Iowa's Democratic caucuses, for instance, evangelical turnout pushed Carter to the top. The in-surgency stunned Floyd Giliotti, a long-time Des Moines Democratic worker and veteran of 23 caucuses over five decades. At one Carter rally, Giliotti recognized only four out of 160 people, an unusual circumstance for the old-timer; most of the new participants, he explained to the New York Times, were evangelicals. Carter went on to win the Iowa caucuses with 27 percent of the vote, doubling second-place finisher Birch Bayh at 13 percent. In Florida and other southern states, great numbers of Southern Baptists cast their ballots for the progressive Carter.[4]

Paeans to Carter emanated from evangelical magazines and presses. Two days after the Democratic convention closed in mid-July, several full-page, pro-Carter advertisements appeared in Christianity Today. The first urged evangelical readers to purchase a just-released book called The Miracle *of Jimmy Carter.* The ad copy exulted, "The newest book about Jimmy Carter is a chronicle of faith—the spiritual odyssey of a man who rose from farmer to presidential candidate. . . . How did the miracle happen? What makes Jimmy Carter different?" The second advertisement, purchased by an organization called "Citizens for Carter," asked, "Does a Dedicated Evangelical Belong in the White House?" The answer, suggested the advertisement, was a resounding "Yes!" The White House needs its windows "thrown open" to "clear out Washington's smoke-filled rooms." There was no one better than Carter, a man of integrity who realizes that "America's problems are the result of a spiritual crisis." The candidate offered humane, yet efficient government, courageous national leadership, and the hope of moral and spiritual renewal. By voting for Carter, an outsider who could bring heartland values to Washington, "you can help restore the fundamental principles this country was founded on." Boosted by a robust hagiographical literature that spread rapidly through the evangelical world in the last half of 1976, Carter's supporters combined populist rhetoric with the fear of a lost America to great effect among evangelicals, who still felt on the margins of American culture. "I'm an outsider and so are you. I'd like to form an intimate relationship with the people of this country," Carter often said during the campaign. "When I'm president, this country will be ours again." Such moral rhetoric resonated in the wake of the general disillusionment with Richard Nixon and Richard Agnew.[5]

At its most exuberant, the hagiographical material portrayed God and Carter working in concert. "There is a sense of history in the making; a feeling that something mysterious and irresistible is at work behind the scenes," wrote Bob Slosser. God had engineered conditions "which seem to have worked together to bring [Carter] to this moment in history." In fact, Carter and God communed regularly. "Carter often—in the midst of a conference or conversation—closed his eyes, put his fist under his chin, bowed his head slightly, and talked to the Lord for a few seconds while the conversation continued around him." Such spiritual integrity, Slosser explained, gave the candidate special resources which could be used to reshape the nation. Slosser surmised that the election "could bring a spiritual revival to the United States and its government." Bailey Smith, Jimmy Allen's predecessor as president of the Southern Baptist Convention, told a crowd of 15,000 that the nation needs "a born-again man in the White House . . . and his initials are the same as our Lord's." Supporters mass-produced posters and pins that read "J.C.," "J.C. Will Save America," "J.C. Can Save America," and "Born

Figure 21. Evangelical literature supporting Carter in 1976 suggested that the candidate could bring spiritual resources to high office.

Again Christian for Jimmy Carter." One poster depicted Carter with long, flowing hair and dressed in biblical garb with the caption "J.C. Can Save America!"[6]

Carter's born-again credentials drew evangelicals, many of whom had been apolitical, to the polls. Evangelicals who had never voted before voted for Carter. Evangelicals who had never campaigned for a candidate campaigned for Carter. A straw poll taken in the Shiloh intentional community in Oregon, for example, showed that "didn't care" ballots dropped to only 17 percent as the evangelical candidate swamped Episcopalian Gerald Ford with the remaining votes. According to historian John Turner, previously apolitical Campus Crusade staffers were "very excited" about Carter. Michael Gerson, later a speechwriter for George W. Bush in the 2000s, remembers enthusiasm in his St. Louis home and church around the fact that Carter was "forthright about his faith." Gerson championed Carter in his school's debate and rode his bicycle downtown to distribute campaign literature. Jerry Falwell, future founder of the Moral Majority, encouraged evangelicals to vote for Carter in 1976. Pat Robertson, who claimed credit for Carter's win in the Pennsylvania primary, hosted the candidate on his *700 Club* television show. Decades later he would say that "Carter was the one who activated me and a lot of others. We had great hopes. . . . [He was] like our champion." For evangelicals not yet established in the political mainstream, Carter's victory was an assertion of evangelical identity and influence. Finally, noted Jim Wallis in *Time* magazine, evangelicals "see they've got a real, live one all of their own." A key component of the Carter coalition, evangelicals helped deliver a solid victory over Gerald Ford.[7]

Carter's impressive performance in 1976 illuminated the politically fluid nature of evangelicalism at the time. That evangelicals would strongly mobilize on behalf of the Republican Party was anything but assured. Even as late as the mid-1970s, according to Turner, "the relationship between evangelicalism and conservative politics was not yet a marriage but had become a lively, if still awkward and incomplete, courtship." In fact several of the most conspicuous examples in recent decades of political activism carried out by religious actors—in civil rights, for example—had taken place on the left. The majority of Democrats were anti-communist, cultural conservatives with strong ties to labor and traditional religion. New Deal programs, argues political scientist Alan Wolfe, "often assumed a two-parent family and a family wage." Working-class labor unionists and pro-family Catholics alike imbued liberal redistributive programs with this sense of moral traditionalism. Moreover, notes historian John McGreevy, the Democratic Party "arguably stood to the right of the Republicans on issues of sexual morality." Cultural conservatives—Catholics opposed to birth control, abortion, and gay rights; Southern conservatives who had not yet defected to the Republicans; and progressive evangelicals—still comprised the majority of the

Democratic Party. Evangelicals were still up for grabs, and the 1976 election suggested that Democrats had a shot at drawing them into their coalition.[8]

II

Carter's success, however, hid an impulse in the Democratic Party toward secularism and cultural libertinism. Live television from national conventions in the late 1960s and early 1970s colorfully broadcast the most sensational scenes. Images of Mayor Richard Daley directing foul ethnic slurs toward Senator Abraham Ribicoff melted away only to reappear as nude Yippies cavorting in the waters of Lake Michigan. Network cameras also captured working-class police officers and youthful protesters, former allies in the liberal coalition, battling in the streets. The 1972 Democratic National Convention at Miami Beach reinforced the emerging image of Democrats as the party of "acid, amnesty, and abortion." Outside the convention hall in Flamingo Park, crowds ogled provocateurs Jerry Rubin, Abbie Hoffman, and Allen Ginsburg. News reports, from evangelical and secular outlets alike, described activists parading around in full drag, smoking dope under a tree with a sign that read "Pot People's Party," and engaging in open sex. Members of SDS, the Progressive Labor Party, and the Revolutionary Communist Progressive Party picketed the convention. Gay liberationists chanted, "2-4-6-8, we don't overpopulate" and "3-5-7-9, Lesbians are mighty fine." By contrast, a "neat, tidy, punctual" Republican Convention held a month later at the same site seemed to confirm the Democratic Party's moral slide. This contrast troubled not only progressive evangelicals but millions more politically uncertain evangelicals around the nation.[9]

The same electoral reforms that would allow evangelical activists to nominate Carter in 1976 also empowered leftist activists. The McGovern-Fraser Commission, launched after the disastrous 1968 convention, sought to integrate minority constituent groups that had been excluded from the convention floor. In 1971 new rules stripped mid-level state managers and local bosses of their substantial control over state primaries, leaving delegates unable to disregard the wishes of primary voters. Federal law also capped individual financial contributions at $1,000. The reforms cleared the smoke-filled back rooms where veteran politicos ruled and opened the convention floor to African Americans, evangelicals, Chicanos, gay activists, opponents of the Vietnam War, senior citizens, and women.[10]

The most vocal of these marginalized groups sought liberation from religious and sexual norms. Political scientists Louis Bolce and Gerald De Maio argue that self-identified agnostics, atheists, and persons who seldom, if ever, attended religious services became the face of the Democratic Party. In fact, a full 21 percent of Democratic delegates at the 1972 convention could be classified as secular in an American population out of which only five percent considered themselves secular. Equally disturbing to pro-life Democrats, Catholics, and evangelicals were sections of the platform entitled "The Right to Be Different," "Rights of Women," and "Family Planning." These planks implied new legal protection for homosexual and abortion rights. To Bella Abzug, prominent feminist and member of the U.S. House of Representatives, the right to reproductive freedom was "a transcending point of view." "Abortion is one issue you can't duck," echoed Martha McKay, co-chair of the National Women's Political Caucus. "It's so central to a woman's being. It's like the race issue. Politicians are fools to think they can duck these issues. Once it's there, you have to take a stand. We had no choice." Pro-life traditionalist Democrats, believing that abortion was "simply murder, the murder of unborn and helpless children," fought back. In one convention address, a pro-life delegate from Missouri mourned "the slaughter of the most innocent whose right to live is not mentioned in the minority report." The contentious floor fight, according to the *Washington Post*, "divided sister against sister."[11]

Traditionalist Democrats won the abortion fight in 1972, the year before the Supreme Court issued its *Roe v. Wade* decision. The final vote resulted in a defeat of the pro-choice plank by a vote of 1,572 to 1,101. The margin would have been even larger had rank-and-file, nondelegates been polled, for delegates that year were much more progressive on abortion than the broader Democratic constituency. The defeat suggested two realities. First, cultural conservatism still predominated in Democratic ranks. Even McGovern, despite his public pro-choice stance, had a personal resistance toward abortion. Second, it solidified a new resolve among the insurgents. The 1972 abortion battle left feminist Gloria Steinem irate. She called McGovern and his campaign manager Gary Hart "bastards" for not more forthrightly supporting the feminist cause. Germaine Greer, author of *The Female Eunuch* and correspondent for *Harper's*, declared, "Womanlike, they did not want to get tough with their man, and so, womanlike, they got screwed."[12]

As President Carter soon discovered, insurgent resolve launched the party on a new pro-choice trajectory. The Democrats' official 1976 platform still recognized "the legitimacy of both pro-life and pro-choice views," but it came under fierce attack. Pro-choice feminists denounced Carter for saying that *Roe v. Wade* was "one instance where my own beliefs were in conflict with the laws of this country." They condemned his support of the Hyde Amendment, which prohibited most Medicaid payments for abortion. They resented that devout, pro-life Catholic Joseph A. Califano, Carter's secretary of health, education, and welfare, enforced the amendment strictly. Presidential assistant Margaret Costanza fielded an extraordinary number of phone calls from public interest groups, the public, and even other White House staff members "expressing concern and even anger" over Carter's position. Costanza urged Carter to reconsider. The President wrote a stark "no" on her written request, adding that his public statement was "actually more liberal than I feel personally." Costanza, in turn, called a protest meeting of nearly 40 high-level pro-choice female members of the administration in July 1977. Carter did not yield, and Costanza eventually resigned. In 1980 Democrats adopted an explicit pro-choice position and strictly enforced the new orthodoxy. Formerly pro-life, Ted Kennedy had declared to a Massachusetts constituent in 1971 that "wanted or unwanted, I believe that human life, even at its earliest stages, has certain rights which must be recognized—the right to be born, the right to love, the right to grow old." Within a decade, Kennedy reversed course. Other pro-life politicians with evangelical or Catholic backgrounds, such as John Kerry, Dennis Kucinich, Mario Cuomo, Bob Kerrey, Dick Durbin, and Bill Clinton, also became defenders of the right to choose. In fact, five of the leading contenders for the Democratic nomination in 1988—Jesse Jackson, Joe Biden, Paul Simon, Dick Gephardt, and Al Gore—had flipped to a pro-choice position under party pressure.[13]

This "secularist putsch," as Bolce and De Maio put it, poisoned evangelicals' view of the Democratic Party. Even Carter and McGovern, both able to proffer evangelical rhetoric, became guilty of cultural subversion through their association with irreligious activists. Many religious conservatives felt as if they had lost a home. Regularly attending Catholics, a key constituency in the New Deal coalition, gradually but substantially left the party. Richard John Neuhaus, a strongly committed Lutheran civil rights activist and future Catholic, veered rightward in the 1970s. In *The Naked Public Square* (1984) he decried the exclusion of religious language from the civic sphere. Evangelical Richard Lovelace similarly feared a "secular religion" that had "placed a moratorium on God-talk." Under pressure from secularist and pro-choice activists not to speak in moral-religious terms, Democrats hemorrhaged evangelicals and Catholics. According to political scientist Lyman Kellstedt, the Democratic Party outpolled the Republican Party by a margin of 59 to 31 percent among evangelicals in the 1960s. By the mid-1980s, the Republican Party enjoyed a 47 to 41 percent lead. Evangelicalism, a large, remarkably fluid, and potentially helpful Democratic constituency, was left behind by the secular left.[14]

It is noteworthy, as an indication of the breadth of the evangelical political spectrum in 1976, that considerable criticism of Carter and the Democratic Party from the left also came from evangelicals. Their grievances, however, had nothing to do with abortion. Carter's politics, these evangelical detractors argued, were mired in establishment politics and failed to acknowledge a radical gospel. *Sojourners*, charging the President with a weak-kneed liberalism, filled its pages with a litany of astonishingly critical articles. Wes Michaelson's bitter list of his shortcomings stretched for pages—that Carter's first criticism of the Vietnam War on moral grounds came not until late 1975; that Carter supported President Harry Truman's decision to drop an atomic bomb on Hiroshima; that Carter was only a "lunch counter civil rights" politician who failed to address the economic nature of racial inequality; that he was "captive of a generally conservative business ideology." Carter's antiestablishment claims and his public persona as a principled evangelical and down-home Georgian, contended *Sojourners*, were farces. His disingenuous claims of being an outsider belied the fact that he was "intimately connected to corporate wealth and power." As the nation tired of Carter's tactical failures, the evangelical left grew increasingly dismayed. Its spokespersons denounced the president for failing to follow through in his human rights rhetoric; for increasing defense spending; for a passive approach to the energy crisis; for not lobbying hard enough to pass the Equal Rights Amendment; for inadequate educational funding; for increasing the nuclear threat; for failing to help the poor; and for elevating efficiency above compassion.[15]

These failings were rooted in a growing conviction that Carter was kowtowing to his secular advisers. To separate faith from politics, preached Reformed philosopher Henry Stob and others, only castrated the Church and subordinated its cultural mandate. "President Carter is obviously a Christian person, a moral leader in those private areas of life most prized by evangelicals," said InterVarsity administrator Joe Bayly midway through Carter's presidency, "but he is a man without Christian leanings, perhaps even com-

With best wishes to Dr. Ron Sider

Jimmy Carter

1-80

Figure 22. Progressive evangelicals were surprisingly critical of President Jimmy Carter. Ron Sider, pictured here with Carter, said of him, "At crucial points where the Bible shows what justice means, Carter doesn't go far enough." Courtesy of Evangelicals for Social Action, Philadelphia.

mitment, in the great areas of his responsibility as President." "At crucial
points where the Bible shows what justice means," echoed Ron Sider, "Carter
doesn't go far enough." Stob wrote, "I have every reason to believe that President Carter is a committed Christian who allows Christianity to set his
goals, posit his values, and shape his personal life. I can scarcely understand,
therefore, why, according to reports, he has on several occasions assured his
secularist critics that he will not allow his Christian faith to affect his presidency." Carter, another critic suggested, "could undermine our efforts to
discover and implement a normative politics for North American society. In
terms of the coming of the Kingdom, this could be the most unfortunate
legacy of the Carter phenomenon." It boiled down to this: Carter's presidency
was sabotaging the promise of a progressive evangelical politics. Withering
critiques, even from those who preferred Carter over Reagan, continued as
the president campaigned for a second term. Many pined for a Mark Hatfield presidency; others cast ballots for independent candidate John Anderson. By 1980 Carter was fully out of sync with the rising evangelical impulse
to tie faith closely to politics.[16]

                                    III

Left behind by the Democratic Party, the evangelical left suffered the same
fate at the hands of the Republican Party and the religious right. Progressive
evangelicals, negotiating their way through a rapidly shifting electoral map,
anticipated the rise of a national religious right before most others. In 1976,
a full three years before the founding of the Moral Majority, *Sojourners*
published a nine-page investigative article entitled "The Plan to Save America." Jim Wallis and Wes Michaelson alleged that Campus Crusade's Bill
Bright, U.S. representative John Conlan of Arizona, Amway Corporation's
Richard DeVos, the conservative Third Century Publishers, and Howard
Kershner's Christian Freedom Foundation (CFF) were conspiring to rebuff
a growing evangelical progressivism. *Sojourners* quoted DeVos as saying
that one goal of the CFF was to "get rid of those so-called liberal Christians
like Mark Hatfield." DeVos and others sought to mobilize born-again Christians on the right. Wallis and Michaelson described a plan to elect politicians
who would pursue "an ultraconservative political agenda" that would include
scaled-back minimum-wage laws, taxes for public schools, right-to-work laws,
and social service provisions. This campaign, they concluded, "dangerously

distorts the fundamental meaning of the Gospel." Top journalists, following up on the story in *Sojourners*, covered the internecine feud and informed the political mainstream about evangelicalism's intensified role in partisan politics.[17]

That evangelicals would mobilize on the right more than the left, however, was not a foregone conclusion. After all, secular elites dominated the Republican Party, whose oligarchs felt little compulsion to bend to the desires of religious conservatives. But the presidential tenure of a progressive evangelical ironically fueled the growth of a rising religious right. Having enjoyed widespread evangelical support in 1976 without having campaigned for it systematically, Carter failed to cultivate his most obvious religious constituency. Evangelicals noted that the president failed to hold religious services in the White House or to appoint evangelicals to high office. Most of all they resented how captive Carter seemed to a Democratic machine veering toward the cultural left. They saw Carter reassure an increasingly fragile New Deal Democratic coalition suspicious of Carter's background—usually by invoking church-state separation in regard to abortion and school prayer. This pattern of deference to "secular humanists," as Democrats were called, galled conservative evangelicals.[18]

Evangelical outrage over abortion was a new phenomenon. In fact, the full ramifications of *Roe v. Wade*, issued by the Supreme Court in 1973, the same year as the Chicago Declaration, were not immediately clear. Difficult as this is to imagine today after decades of pro-life activism, many Republican leaders were not clearly pro-life until the political advantages became obvious. A White House staffer urged Ford to speak against abortion rights only after the Democrats had "absolutely rejected and insulted the pro-lifers." Nor were evangelicals initially exercised over the abortion decision by the high court. The Southern Baptist Convention, rooted in views of the separation of church and state, initially lauded *Roe v. Wade* for promoting "religious liberty." Many evangelicals dismissed abortion as a Catholic issue.[19]

Not until the late 1970s did evangelicals begin to build a more strongly antiabortion stance. Not until the early 1980s did they begin to ally with Catholic pro-lifers and agitate more forcefully. Future Surgeon General C. Everett Koop and L'Abri's Francis Schaeffer, formerly an influential figure for many in the evangelical left, catalyzed the shift in religious right circles. In *Whatever Happened to the Human Race?* (1979), they suggested that toleration of abortion, the "keystone" of the sanctity of life, would lead to genetic engineering, widespread euthanasia, and abuse of the handicapped. Schaeffer and Koop also took to the road, speaking and screening a film version of *Whatever Happened* in major cities across the nation. Evangelical periodicals also reflected this new preoccupation with abortion. The 405 articles on abortion from 1966 to 1981 in *Christianity Today, Christian Life, Moody Monthly*, and *Decision* magazines easily outpaced the 273 articles on prayer in public schools, 152 articles on pornography, 150 articles on homosexual rights, and 102 articles on the ERA. This was a surprisingly high number, given how few articles on abortion were published before the mid-1970s. Abortion had become "*the* evangelical issue," according to Franky Schaeffer, a producer of several antiabortion films. "The anger we stirred up at the grass roots was not feigned but heartfelt. And at first it was not about partisan politics. It had everything to do with genuine horror at the procedure of abortion." Political scientist Jon Shields, author of *The Democratic Virtues of the Christian Right*, concurs, "If abortion weren't an issue, there would be almost no Christian Right, or it would be such a marginal thing that it wouldn't command that much interest." By the late 1970s and 1980s, abortion lay at the center of evangelical politics.[20]

Those who held this antiabortion conviction increasingly aligned with the Republican Party. If by the end of the decade Democrats had begun to enforce a new pro-choice orthodoxy, Republicans adopted an explicit pro-life position that also more starkly demarcated the parties. The 1980 party platform devoted an entire section to "creating strong families" and to "affirming our support of a constitutional amendment to restore protection of the right to life for unborn children." This marked a striking divergence from 1972, the eve of *Roe v. Wade*, when abortion was not politicized and neither party mentioned the issue in its convention platform. This shift very much hurt Carter's reelection prospects, even though the president personally shared the pro-life stance of Koop, Schaeffer, and millions of evangelicals. Constrained by his party's growing pro-choice sentiments, Carter refused to work toward constitutionally banning abortion and regularly declined to meet with antiabortion groups. Moreover, he hired Sarah Weddington, the attorney who argued in favor of abortion in the *Roe v. Wade* case, and the feisty Margaret Costanza, an outspoken pro-choice advocate, as presidential advisors. In many instances, Carter played to the party's new base, especially as Ted Kennedy emerged as a threat to win the Democratic nomination in 1980. Evangelicals felt betrayed by these actions. They denounced Carter's "personally against, but pro-choice" stance and began to plague his presidency. One protestor carried a sign that declared "Carter is nothing but

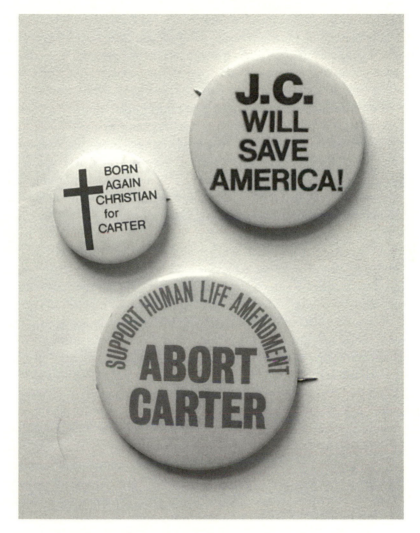

Figure 23. Campaign rhetoric reflected the ambivalent relationship between Carter and evangelicals.

a 621-month fetus." "Abort Carter" pins proliferated. Wheaton College student Michael Gerson turned on the president. As abortion became singularly important, Gerson, who otherwise might have continued voting Democratic, switched his allegiance to Reagan and the Republicans in 1980. "I was typical of evangelicals who'd supported Carter and were dismayed by the hardening of the parties on social issues," he later remembered.[21]

Carter's abortion dilemma illuminates the broad contours of evangelical political mobilization in the 1970s: left-wing concern over Carter's evangelical leanings and evangelical dismay over Carter's secular advisers and application of church-state separation. Applying the principle of church-state separation to abortion made sense constitutionally, even politically. But it did not work amidst overheated rhetoric, a rapidly polarizing party system, and an evangelical religious tradition that increasingly tied faith to politics. Carter found himself impossibly stuck between two diverging constituencies on a long list of issues: not only abortion, but also prayer in school, taxation of private schools, and the Equal Rights Amendment. Many evangelical leaders bitterly rescinded their support of the president. A "high official of the Southern Baptist Convention" who visited Carter in the Oval Office told him, "We are praying, Mr. President, that you will abandon secular humanism as your religion." Rick Scarborough, founder of the conservative organization Vision America, remembers, "The first time I voted was for Carter. The second time was for 'anybody but Carter,' because he had betrayed everything I hold dear." Even the pious Carter, realized evangelicals, could not stanch the secularization of the Democratic Party. The religious right recognized anecdotally the survey data that political scientist Geoffrey Layman would interpret several decades later: "a concomitant growth in secularism and pro-choice sentiments in the Democratic Party" after 1976. The criticisms reached a crescendo during the 1980 election cycle as evangelicals realized their diminished need to use Carter to justify their own political relevance.[22]

Republican Party bosses took advantage by wooing and mobilizing disgruntled evangelicals and Catholics. Party operative Richard Viguerie, according to colleagues Paul Weyrich and Howard Phillips, "spent countless hours with electronic ministers like Jerry Falwell, James Robison, and Pat Robertson, urging them to get involved in conservative politics." The result by the summer of 1979 was the Moral Majority, an organization that mirrored the evangelical left in several important respects. First, the Moral Majority was comprised largely of theological conservatives, some of whom were previously uninvolved in partisan politics. Falwell and Robertson, for example, had preached against getting involved in worldly activities earlier in the decade, and Southern Baptists had appealed to the separation of church and state for over a century. But like the evangelical left, which had urged Christians to address broader structures, they were mobilizing politically. Second, the Moral Majority was ecumenical. Like the evangelical left, which worked with progressive Catholics, secular civil rights leaders, and main-line Protestants, evangelicals in the religious right also allied with political soul mates. The Moral Majority welcomed pro-life Catholics and Mormons, groups previously dismissed as heretical. Together they raised millions of dollars and mobilized in support of Ronald Reagan. The Moral Majority enjoyed stunning growth, from 300,000 members in mid-1980 to over 2 million (though it claimed a membership between 4 and 8 million) by Election Day. Conservative evangelicalism seemed to be merging with the Republican Party.[23]

Carter responded to the evangelical insurgency only late in the campaign, and then only hesitantly. His religious advisor, Robert Maddox, sent a campaign brochure to 250,000 ministers late in the campaign, invited seven conservative evangelical leaders to the White House, and addressed the National Religious Broadcasters convention. These overtures, appreciated by conservative evangelicals who lamented that this was the first time in Carter's presidency they felt welcomed, fell short of the massive campaign launched by his competitor. Reagan, who enticed evangelicals with conservative policy stances on abortion, school prayer, and tuition tax credits, told the National Religious Broadcasters convention, "I know you can't endorse me, but I endorse you," a sentiment that Carter seemed unwilling to articulate during his four years as president. While pockets of support for Carter remained, many evangelicals who voted for him out of evangelical solidarity in 1976 defected to Independent John Anderson and Reagan in 1980. If Carter's candidacy initially added evangelicals to the Democratic ranks, his presidency resulted in an evangelical rejection of the Democratic Party.[24]

When the votes were counted on the night of November 4, 1980, Reagan won a decisive victory, earning 51 percent of the votes to Carter's 41 percent and Anderson's 7 percent. While recession, inflation, the energy crisis, the Iran hostage situation, and an approval rating of only 28 percent contributed to Carter's defeat, many evangelicals agreed with columnist Michael Novak that the incumbent was "inept, incompetent, and amateurish." Even worse, wrote Novak, Carter had brought "piety into disrepute." Scholars estimate that a mobilized evangelicalism registered about two million new voters, of whom 60 percent voted for Reagan. Moreover, the incumbent's percentage of evangelical votes dropped from over half in 1976 to only 34 percent in 1980. This calculated into a shift of five million evangelical voters from Carter to Reagan. Jimmy Carter, who had held so much potential for

Figure 24. Governor Jimmy Carter, pictured here with his wife Rosalynn and evangelist Billy Graham, appeared on stage at the 1973 Atlanta crusade. As a pro-choice president in the late 1970s, Carter failed to retain broader conservative evangelical support in the face of a burgeoning pro-life movement. Courtesy of Billy Graham Evangelistic Association. Used with permission. All rights reserved.

leading the evangelical left into the political mainstream, had been left behind by a burgeoning religious right.[25]

*   *   *

Given Carter's deep unpopularity in the general electorate and the wide margin of Reagan's victory, the 1980 election reveals more about the state of evangelicalism than about its role in the election itself. When Carter again failed adequately to court evangelicals, he did so at his own political peril, not fully recognizing a dramatic shift in the intervening four years. Policy advocacy now trumped religious identification, a development starkly evident in an election in which a divorced Hollywood actor who gave less than one percent of his earnings to charitable causes trounced a born-again Southerner with the help of a theologically diverse coalition. In the 1960s evangelicals dismissed Catholic positions on human reproduction as "antiquated," "intolerable," even "dangerous." By the late 1970s evangelicals, along with Mormons and conservative Jewish rabbis, had joined Catholics in the leadership of the National Right to Life organization. By the early 1980s, they had strongly mobilized behind a party that opposed abortion and bans on prayer. Compared to Carter, Reagan did not offer greater piety. But he did offer greater spoils.[26]

Evangelicals energized by the life-and-death issue of abortion may have resonated more with Reagan than Carter, but they were also indebted to progressive evangelicals. First, it took the provocation of Jimmy Carter himself to launch the religious right on a national scale. Second, along with fundamentalist initiatives against Prohibition and for Goldwater in southern California, the evangelical left offered a model of political mobilization for the many mainstream evangelicals associated with *Moody Monthly*, *Christianity Today*, and the Billy Graham Evangelistic Association who nurtured apolitical habits. For these evangelicals who had not been engaging partisan politics on a national and electoral level, the evangelical left modeled a structural mode of thought, a dualistic application of moralism, a precedent of co-belligerency, and an activist approach to social change. Certainly, without the evangelical left, a religious right would have emerged in an era when the nation was turning southern and conservative—but perhaps not as *the* religious right that forged a tighter and more synergistic bond between white evangelicalism and modern conservatism. During the heyday of the Moral Majority, one former student of Richard Mouw reread *Political*

Evangelism (1973). "In going back through the book," he said, "I was surprised to realize how the Moral Majority types could now read it and tell you they are doing exactly what you asked them to be doing back in the older days of 'otherworldliness.'" Ron Sider similarly quipped that "we called for social and political action, [and] we got eight years of Ronald Reagan." The mechanisms were more complex than Sider's formulation, but the evangelical left hastened the arrival of the religious right and encouraged its intensity.[27]

This, of course, was not the legacy that Carter and the evangelical left had wanted. On one level, progressive evangelicals missed an opportunity, for 1976 was the precise moment when the evangelical left could have more fully influenced electoral politics. But it failed to attach to a resonant politician in the way the religious right did with Reagan four years later. As the prominence and size of the religious right became apparent in the early 1980s, racial activist John Alexander asked, "Did we blow it? The evangelical right mobilized for Reagan, but Carter wasn't good enough for the left; were we crazy?" On a deeper level, however, it was the evangelical left's profound misfortune to emerge in an era of hardening party structures and increased enforcement of cultural orthodoxies. That trend continued into the 1980s. Democratic leaders, under pressure from secular feminists and leftists, turned back the McGovern electoral reforms, which had inadvertently given the evangelical Carter an advantage. In an act that served to marginalize the evangelical populist activists who had upset the Democratic nomination process in 1976, party leaders introduced a complex set of policies that apportioned "superdelegate" votes according to demographic characteristic and political office. In the early 1980s Democratic leaders, having driven evangelicals out, coalesced even further into a party dominated by secular, urban elites and hostile to antiabortion concerns. Evangelicals flocked to "God's party" as the fault lines in the new realignment grew larger. Antagonistic toward the Republican platform and antagonized by Democratic leaders, remaining members of the evangelical left were left without a political home.[28]

CHAPTER 12

====

Sojourning

So, we are on the outside. Pro-lifers don't like us because
we push them to embrace a consistent pro-life ethic.
Our friends in the justice and peace movement don't
like us because we make them uncomfortable with our
anti-abortion talk. The presidential campaign forces
us to focus on this. We have no clear choice. Neither
candidate is genuinely pro-life. Neither comes close.

—*Sojourners*

In 1983 conservative activists repeatedly disrupted a conference on peacemaking at Fuller Theological Seminary. During a workshop on Central
America, one protester shouted his objection to evangelical accommodation
with communist totalitarianism until he was ushered out of the room. Another protester berated the 1,700 delegates from a balcony during a plenary
session. When the disturbance brought the proceedings to a halt, the audience sang the hymn "Amazing Grace" to drown him out. A display table
manned by the Institute for Religion and Democracy urged delegates to
sign a "research report" accusing Senator Mark Hatfield and *Sojourners'*
Jim Wallis of advocating Soviet-style communism.[1]

These scenes and what they represented—an increasingly vocal and activist right-wing coalition of Christians—appalled progressive evangelicals.
Incensed by President Reagan's right-wing extremism, lack of experience,
"one-sentence remedies for complex problems," and the evangelical role in
his victory, the evangelical left battled the religious right. David Chilton's
Productive Christians in an Age of Guilt Manipulators (which attacked the

economic positions of Ron Sider's *Rich Christians in an Age of Hunger*) and
Francis Schaeffer's *The Great Evangelical Disaster* (which condemned Evangelicals for Social Action, Wheaton College, and the Evangelical Women's
Caucus for having succumbed to secular humanism) sparked an epistolary
reaction from many of those it targeted. Even prominent evangelical moderates such as Billy Graham and representatives of the National Association
of Evangelicals felt compelled to explain that they were "not part of the New
Christian Right." These fiery exchanges between evangelical right, center,
and left indicated how profoundly contested the political soul of evangelicalism was. That the religious right felt threatened; that Sider and Wallis
continued to gain a hearing in evangelical circles; that certain titans of evangelicalism such as Graham distanced themselves from the religious right—
all point to a persistent evangelical left. Evangelicals for Social Action, the
Association for Public Justice, Sojourners, and many other organizations in
the 1980s continued to agitate on issues of nuclear defense, global interventionism, and domestic policy.[2]

These campaigns, however, ultimately failed to rival the reach and influence of the religious right. Efforts to resist Reagan's interventions in Central
America by cooperating with mainline Protestants and Catholics sparked
questions about how evangelical the evangelical left really was. Continuing
fragmentation wrought by identity politics also plagued the movement. Unable to build a substantial constituency, the evangelical left remained overshadowed by the Moral Majority, which became identified in the popular
mind as "evangelical." A final effort in the mid-1980s to build a "consistent
pro-life" coalition failed to reconcile competing identities and shifting constituencies within an unforgiving electoral system that fit poorly with the
movement's concerns. The movement did not disappear, and it labored on
under difficult conditions. But the evangelical left enjoyed less political impact than it wanted, and few noticed its work in the 1980s. It was clear that
the movement, while clearly not stillborn in 1973, had nonetheless failed
to thrive.

I

No issue more dramatically underscored the continuing diversity of evangelical politics in the 1980s than the debate over covert U.S. military action
in Nicaragua. Reagan's military actions in Central America, designed to roll

back communist gains, provoked kaleidoscopic reaction among evangelicals. While the religious right steadfastly supported American intervention
in Nicaragua and elsewhere, progressive evangelicals denounced the Reagan Doctrine. Robert Zwier, chair of the Northwest Iowa chapter of the
Association for Public Justice, declared that the U.S. was trying to "throw its
weight around the world like a bully." Both sides sought to sway a large
swath of evangelicals in the middle, most of whom remained uneasy about
Reagan's quick use of the military but hopeful that intervention could promote global justice and install democracy in Central America.[3]

Progressive evangelicals cast their rhetoric against American interventionism in terms that would appeal to mainstream evangelicals. Instead of
raging against American imperialism as evangelical radicals like Jim Wallis
did in the 1970s, the broader evangelical left began to frame its opposition to
conservative politics in terms of religious freedom and human rights. "The
projection of American power to protect American interests," wrote Wallis,
"has completely superseded any concern for human rights in the conduct of
U.S. foreign policy." Periodicals printed story after story on how third-world
dictators, propped up by the United States, were inflicting destruction on
their own citizens. A Sandinista government in Nicaragua, argued *Sojourners*, would result in fewer human rights violations and offered a better
environment for the growth of the evangelical church.[4]

Efforts to appeal to the evangelical middle also led progressive evangelicals to more forthrightly denounce communist regimes. The leftist Sandinistas might be preferable to Nicaraguan Contras, ESA's Ron Sider said, but this
reality should not allow evangelicals' "extremely important condemnation of
past and present injustices committed by Western powers to dull their sensitivity to the ghastly history of Marxist-Leninist totalitarianism in this century." Marxism, progressive evangelicals increasingly pointed out, promoted
atheism, suppressed dissidents, and nurtured an imperialistic drive of its own.
Evangelicals, encouraged Sider, ought to "praise what is good and beautiful in
America; champion the American tradition of democratic process and religious and political liberty; and refuse to allow their valid critique of Western
colonialism and current U.S. policy to blind them to the evils of Marxism."
Prone in the 1970s to criticize the United States almost exclusively, the evangelical left began to censure Marxist totalitarianism more vigorously.[5]

The evangelical left nonetheless refused to ignore Reagan's support of
Contra forces in Nicaragua. In the early 1980s several delegations of evangelicals traveled to Nicaragua at the invitation of the Evangelical Committee

for Aid and Development (CEPAD), a Nicaraguan relief agency formed after a devastating 1972 earthquake. The largest nongovernmental relief agency in the country, with projects in 400 Nicaraguan communities, CEPAD represented 80 percent of the 400,000 Protestants in Nicaragua. Its president Gustavo Parajón, a Baptist with a doctorate in medicine from Harvard, took representatives of the NAE, ESA, Sojourners, InterVarsity, *Christianity Today*, and a dozen professors and administrators of evangelical colleges on tours of territory devastated by Contras. Parajón, seeking to expose "a covert effort by the United States government to destabilize the new government," also showed off areas rejuvenated by Sandinista reform. The majority of Nicaraguan evangelicals, he explained to the delegations, lauded the reforms. Evangelicals enjoyed unfettered religious freedom and better economic prospects under the new government. In fact, Sandinista leaders met with CEPAD each month to listen to evangelical concerns. Parajón suggested that the U.S. resented Sandinista governance only because the new government refused to take "orders from Washington."[6]

With few exceptions the American evangelical observers relayed Parajón's conclusions to their own constituents. Sandinistas may have had some "serious errors in judgment," *Sojourners* reported, but the Contras who served as "mercenary soldiers," the Reagan administration, and the religious right who supported them were the true oppressors. Delegates from InterVarsity chided American evangelicals for looking at Nicaragua "through made-in-U.S.A. glasses" and for believing that "the U.S. is a bunch of good guys who always pursue justice." A Reformed evangelical traveling in Nicaragua with the Christian Medical Society blasted Reagan for trying to destabilize the nation through the CIA and for "lying about the situation there." In the end, he declared, Reagan's hostility was "driving the Sandinistas into the arms of the Cubans and Soviets." The group of evangelical college professors and administrators reported "amazing strides" by Sandinistas in literacy, education, health, religious freedom, and humanitarianism. They "strongly condemned" U.S. efforts to weaken Sandinista autonomy. *Christianity Today's* Tom Minnery, noting the dynamic growth of Nicaraguan evangelicalism, wrote that Nicaragua was "testing some cherished convictions" about Western capitalism. *Sojourners* noted the religious themes that saturated the Sandinista countryside. Signs everywhere read, "Christ lives, and is coming soon!" "We are all the Revolution!—Social Christian Party," "Young Christian Revolutionaries Celebrate the Fourth Anniversary of the Revolution." The Sandinistas, far from limiting religious freedom, according to these evangelical leaders, encouraged evangelical faith.[7]

The visit to Nicaragua provoked an evangelical left campaign of direct action. Sojourners' Jim Wallis and Joyce Hollyday observed that Contra forces did not attack towns where Americans were present, a pattern suggesting not only CIA intelligence aid to the Contras but also a possible avenue of intervention. In cooperation with CEPAD, Baptist church leaders, and Sandinista leaders including Daniel Ortega, American evangelicals began to place themselves strategically in towns under attack by Contra forces with hopes that their presence would prevent more attacks. Sojourners, which led the operation, called it "Witness for Peace." Ron Sider and Vernon Grounds, president emeritus of Denver Conservative Baptist Seminary, both served on the initial advisory committee. Witness for Peace immediately scored a coup when NBC's *Today* show covered one of the first interventions—in Ocotal in December 1983—on live television. Every major national newspaper carried stories of Witness for Peace's "shield of love." The direct action quickly expanded to dozens of towns, often at the request of Nicaraguan evangelicals disturbed by the patrols of Contra forces on the northern mountains near the Honduran border. Volunteers, who attended a one-week training program on nonviolent reactions to mortar attacks, kidnappings, and rapes from Contra insurgents, flooded Sojourners' Washington office with offers to pay their own travel expenses to the Nicaragua-Honduran border. By the early months of 1984, Witness for Peace was maintaining a constant presence in Nicaragua with four rotating teams. In the first six months of 1984, 260 Americans traveled to Nicaragua in 13 delegations. By the end of the 1980s, more than 4,000 activists had participated in Witness for Peace. Positive press reinforced the significant effects of the campaign. The popular song "El Salvador" was written after Noel Paul Stookey read Sojourners' report entitled *Crucible of Hope: A Study Guide for the Churches on Central America*. In 1988 Witness for Peace inspired a *People* magazine article entitled "Agonies of the Innocents" that brought the biggest reader response of any article in the history of the magazine.[8]

North American evangelical cooperation with CEPAD resulted in a second related campaign called the Pledge of Resistance. After the U.S. invasion of nearby Grenada in November 1983, CEPAD's Parajón pleaded, "We are anticipating an invasion at any time now. For God's sake, please try to help us!" Drawn up by Sojourners' Jim Wallis and Jim Rice, the "Pledge" promised action if Nicaragua was invaded: "We will assemble as many North American Christians as we can to join us and go immediately to Nicaragua to stand unarmed as a loving barrier in the path of any attempted invasion." Sojourners organized a network of regional offices prepared to signal activists should such an invasion begin. If activated, thousands would launch nonviolent vigils at every congressional field office in the nation, engage in civil disobedience at the White House, and plant activists in Nicaragua as deterrents to U.S. bombs. Sojourners sent these detailed plans—and lists with over 40,000 signatures—to every member of Congress, the Departments of State and Defense, the CIA, and the White House. At an introductory news conference in front of the State Department, Wallis declared, "Now, if Reagan invades Nicaragua, he's going to have to put thousands of U.S. Christians in jail around the country."[9]

Subsequent events confirmed the seriousness of Wallis's declaration. After the Reagan administration imposed a full trade embargo on Nicaragua and Congress passed $27 million in aid to the Contras in 1985, Pledge signers demonstrated in 200 cities across 42 states. Police arrested more than 1,200 activists for civil disobedience. As Congress debated eight more Contra aid bills in 1986, tens of thousands of Pledge activists occupied congressional offices for days, blocked gates at military bases, staged funeral processions and "die-ins," disrupted traffic in major cities, and rented airplanes that carried "U.S. Out of Nicaragua Now!" banners over sporting events. By mid-1986 organizers had gathered 80,000 signatures. Boston-area organizer Anne Shumway remembered, "In fifteen years of activism, I never saw anything explode the way the Pledge did. It just took off. At public signings, people were just lining up to sign on." The Reagan administration paid close attention. An assistant secretary of state for Inter-American affairs, taken aback by the evangelical-initiated activism, told a *Washington Post* reporter, "We don't normally think of them as political opponents, and we don't know how to handle them." The Pledge of Resistance, one scholar contends, very well may have helped avert a U.S. invasion of Nicaragua.[10]

For all their influence beyond the traditional evangelical community, the Pledge of Resistance and Witness for Peace revealed several weaknesses within the evangelical left. First, a close look at the constituencies of the Pledge and Witness shows how support from evangelicals for these initiatives slipped. Wallis, torn between the political potential of a larger, ecumenical approach and a more narrowly evangelical approach, struggled to carve out a broadly Christian identity. Leaders resolved early debates by describing Witness for Peace as a "prayerful, biblically based community" that accepted people "comfortable" with this approach. "The stronger the religious identity, the stronger will be the Witness," Wallis stressed. Such an approach would keep the press, the government, and critics from writing off the movement as Marxist and un-American. Yvonne Dilling, a Witness for Peace veteran, added, "The last thing you want to be doing when people you love are getting killed is worrying about whether your prayer is going to offend someone." But within a few years, most of the ground troops were being supplied by mainline participants, Catholics, peace denominations, and nonreligious sources. The movement itself bogged down in debates over the roles of non-Christians on trips to Nicaragua. "Hours and hours of conference calls we would have," remembers Witness activist Bob Van Denend, "thirty people on a conference call arguing endlessly about how to be more inclusive." Ecumenical participants in Witness for Peace overwhelmed evangelical participants by the late 1980s.[11]

The much larger Pledge of Resistance, which depended on tens of thousands of grass-roots activists, moved beyond its evangelical roots even more quickly. Initially most protests were "very religious," but as the movement mushroomed and came under coalition authority, Sojourners lost organizational control. Leaders from twenty-one organizations debated whether outspoken, noncelibate gays and lesbians could participate. They wrangled over removing crosses and references to Christ in their literature to avoid offense to Jewish participants. By 1986 activists no longer gathered for worship and prayer before protests, and bitter disputes broke out between secular and religious activists. Evangelicals of all stripes eyed these developments with suspicion when they saw them at all. Even *The Other Side* and ESA, both of which provided cursory affirmation and initial labor, failed to join the Pledge and Witness as readily as Catholics, mainliners, and interfaith groups. Sojourners may have instigated these two ventures, and much of the theoretical weight may have come from evangelical sources, but both campaigns veered sharply in an ecumenical direction.[12]

Sojourners itself even turned in an ecumenical direction. Frustrated by the slow movement of his own evangelical tradition toward progressive politics, Wes Michaelson mourned that "theologically, evangelicals have abandoned the biblical hope that the kingdom of God breaks into our history. . . . Evangelicalism on its own has lacked the resources that are necessary to build and sustain a life of faithful discipleship." In its place, Michaelson said, Sojourners was drawing from ecumenical traditions and engaging social activists of all stripes. A 1981 issue of the *Catholic Reporter* noted that of three pictures hanging over Jim Wallis's desk—St. Francis, Dorothy Day, and Groucho Marx—two were Catholic (the *Reporter* failed to note that the third was Jewish and the only funny one). The Sojourners intentional community began to host nearly as many ecumenical advocates and conferences as evangelical ones. *Sojourners* magazine likewise featured increasing numbers of non-evangelical advertisements and contributors. Mainliners and Catholics reciprocated, expressing identification with the evangelical left. A group of mainline pastors in Milwaukee, for instance, referred to themselves as "Sojourner Christians." Paulist Press, a Catholic publisher, reprinted Ron Sider's *Rich Christians*. "We have broadened beyond our evangelical beginnings," explained one Sojourner, "as those of diverse Christian backgrounds, including mainline Protestants, Anabaptists, and Catholics, have joined us and shaped our community's life." By 1985, national news reporters were calling Sojourners "ecumenical," when five years earlier nearly all descriptions and self-descriptions referred to the community as evangelical.[13]

Second, a debate over methods of dissent exposed continuing diversity within the evangelical left. Sojourners typically unleashed symbolic, activist campaigns of dissent. Jim Rice, a member of the Sojourners intentional community, explained, "Reagan was about to invade Nicaragua and Congress was always about to send millions of dollars to the Contras and El Salvador. So the imperative, the urgency of the moment took over. It had to." This same urgency, however, sometimes led to a collapse of evangelical piety, especially as Witness for Peace and Pledge of Resistance attracted secular activists. Sojourners' Dennis Marker remembers the public relations nightmare that resulted from out-of-control protest: "These hardcore activists showed up saying, 'Straight to civil disobedience! Forget this church, man. We're going to meet at the civic center. And forget the prayer services. We're going to yell and scream and bang pots and dance.' And the church people said, 'Well, that's not really what we intended.'" News reports of Pledge protesters urinating in a plant pot in a congressman's office in Washington and throwing rocks through windows of buildings in Chicago horrified evangelical activists. Marker remembers, "A person of faith would never do that. . . . They were hurting people! They're throwing rocks and I'm telling the press, 'We're totally nonviolent, you know, life?' I had to do serious damage control." Sojourners sought to rein in the violence, turning instead to peaceful symbolism. They presented a "tractor for peace" covered in flowers

Figure 25. Karin Granberg-Michaelson and Wes Granberg-Michaelson, former top aide to senator Mark Hatfield and editor of *Sojourners*, marched alongside members of the Sojourners community in favor of a nuclear freeze in New York City in the late 1970s. Courtesy of the Joint Archives of Holland, Hope College, Holland, Michigan.

and surrounded by bags of flour to Nicaraguan Ambassador Antonio Jar-
quin. Asking for forgiveness, Sojourners activists declared that "Ronald
Reagan and Jeane Kirkpatrick and the CIA are not our representatives in
Central America."[14]

Neo-evangelicals and Reformed evangelicals in the 1980s decried even
these comparatively irenic protests as unhelpful publicity stunts. The Association for Public Justice, like Sojourners, deplored Reagan's foreign policy,
but it took a more measured tone, disinclined toward activism and ritualis-
tic symbolism. Reformed scholars, less convinced than Sojourners of Reagan's diabolical intent and deceit, argued that U.S. policy towards Nicaragua
was one of "aimless confusion." U.S. diplomacy was merely misguided and
could be corrected by paying attention to diplomatic precedent, investing
in local Nicaraguan development, and lobbying (not protesting) the Reagan
administration. Reformed evangelicals sought to develop a long-range plan
that centered on legislative solutions, local development, and education. Calvin College's Center for Christian Scholarship, for instance, gathered ten
scholars to research and write for one year on the topic of "A Reformed Response to the Conflicts in Central America." A second effort involved six-
teen scholars, a two-month trip to Central America, and 170 on-site interviews
that resulted in a 270-page book called *Let My People Live*. These cerebral
efforts implicitly and explicitly indicted Sojourners' activist approach.[15]

ESA forged a middle course. Individual members participated in Witness for Peace and Pledge of Resistance, but the organization itself focused
more on education and prayer than protest. ESA organized "Intercessors
for Peace and Freedom," a prayer network of Christians concerned about
Central America. It also brought eleven Nicaraguan CEPAD members to the
United States to speak at evangelical congregations, the State Department,
Congress, and the White House. In keeping with its focus on education and
dialogue, ESA also planned a fact-finding trip to Nicaragua, even inviting
its right-wing rival Institute for Religion and Democracy (though IRD eventually declined in order to protest Sandinista atrocities). ESA itself quickly
backpedaled from support of the Sandinista government as it learned of
more abuses of power and violations of religious freedom.[16]

These diverging and merging streams of evangelical activism in Nicaragua suggest the instability of the evangelical left in the 1980s. Initially root-
ing their opposition to Reagan in New Left scholarship that framed American
intervention as imperialism, the evangelical left gradually recast their opposition in ways that might appeal to broader evangelicalism. Witness for Peace,

for example, highlighted Sandinista support of evangelical missionary work and the CIA's complicity in human rights abuses. At the same time, Sojourners, collaborating with nonevangelical cobelligerents, continued to indict the United States for bloodlust in its push for global dominance and economic hegemony. By the mid-1980s, it became clear that the evangelical left had misstepped in trying to straddle the evangelical-ecumenical divide. The activist and ecumenical trajectory of Witness for Peace and the Pledge of Resistance vexed Reformed evangelicals, who preferred methods of education and political lobbying. The campaigns also concerned mainstream evangelicals, who wondered if the evangelical left was still evangelical. For their part, ecumenical allies objected to exclusive religious claims. Despite a unified objection to Reagan interventionism, failed attempts to mobilize around Nicaragua highlighted the difficulties in mobilizing a broad swath of progressive and moderate evangelicals. As APJ, ESA, and Sojourners pioneered a new approach to evangelical globalism, the most defining characteristic of that approach was its methodological and ideological diversity. This diversity, also seen in debates over nuclear weapons, housing reform, and environmental justice, exposed the evangelical left's continuing inability to coalesce around a viable identity and to build a substantial constituency.

II

As evangelical activism in Nicaragua faltered, progressive evangelicals sought to bring coherence to a fragmenting movement by appealing to a "consistent pro-life ethic." They linked opposition to U.S. imperialism in Central America to a much larger agenda that also opposed patriarchy, capital punishment, pornography, assisted suicide, nuclear proliferation, poverty, and abortion. *The Other Side* magazine, for instance, mourned the double tragedy of the Pentagon's importing of "45,000 human fetuses from South Korea for testing the effects of the neutron bomb on fresh human tissue." Sojourners likewise grieved that "life has become cheap at the Pentagon and in abortion clinics, at the headquarters of large corporations and in pornographic movie houses, at missile silos and genetic research laboratories, in the ghetto and in homes where families are breaking up." In its unconventional linking of issues from both left and right based upon an overarching concern for "life," progressive groups such as ESA and Sojourners sought to reconcile its competing identities and shifting constituencies.[17]

The idea for a "consistent life ethic" came from American Catholics. "The protection of life," the Catholic pacifist activist Eileen Egan had written in 1971, "is a seamless garment. You can't protect some life and not others." Juli Loesch, founder of Pro-Lifers for Survival, confounded observers by distributing anti-Pentagon tracts at anti-abortion rallies and pro-life tracts at peace demonstrations. Catholics such as Joseph Cardinal Bernardin, Archbishop of Chicago, carried the campaign to a much larger audience. Progressive evangelicals looked on with increasing resonance and sought to imitate the growing Catholic movement. In March 1981, Vicki Sairs, a college student converted at the evangelical Grace Haven Farm community in Mansfield, Ohio, sought out Loesch at an antinuclear power demonstration on Three Mile Island near Harrisburg, Pennsylvania. The meeting led Sairs to establish a Pro-Lifers for Survival chapter at Penn State University that tried to persuade campus leftists toward a pro-life position on abortion and Inter-Varsity students toward a position against nuclear weapons. Sojourners, which came out more explicitly against abortion, launched a more substantial campaign in the early 1980s. In the issue of *Sojourners* magazine that marked the beginning of its consistent life initiative, many of the seventeen articles were written by Catholics or cited significant Catholic influences.[18]

When a flood of supportive letters arrived at *Sojourners'* offices, the broader evangelical left began to sense grassroots potential in concentrating its agenda around the issue of life. "The energy of the pro-life movement must be removed from the ideological agenda of the New Right," warned Jim Wallis in late 1980, as passion grew in conservative evangelical circles against abortion. *Radix*'s Sharon Gallagher, noting that elections were being defined for Christians largely by school prayer and abortion, lamented that "focusing in on those two issues only is a terrible narrowing of the gospel." Instead, Wallis argued, the evangelical left should rally around a broadly defined pro-life campaign as a "threshold issue" that might soften evangelical conservatives and moderates into accepting other progressive causes. Ron Sider argued that such a strategy was feasible, pointing out in a 1981 memo to top evangelical leaders that a recent Gallup Poll showed that 20 percent of evangelicals were "left of center," 37 percent were "right of center," and 30 percent were centrist. If more than half of evangelicals were "non-right," Sider asked, then why was the Moral Majority constructing the terms of evangelical politics? Not only was the Christian right's agenda "not biblical enough," it failed to represent evangelicalism as a whole. A political vacuum existed, he wrote, among evangelicals who hold to the Moral Majority's "basic pro-life and pro-family concerns" but do not resonate with its positions on the nuclear arms race, poverty, wealth, and racism. Sider hoped that "a fairly broadly based centrist movement led by prominent leaders of established evangelical agencies" would emerge.[19]

In May of 1981 Sider and Jay Kesler, president of Youth for Christ International, convened meetings in Washington, D.C., and Wheaton, Illinois, with dozens of evangelical luminaries to organize such a coalition. They talked with Senator Mark Hatfield, Chicago pastor David Mains, World Evangelical Fellowship executive director David Howard, InterVarsity Press editor James Sire, Baptist mission executive Rufus Jones, Wheaton College theologian Robert Webber, and others. They also surveyed nearly 80 evangelical leaders by correspondence. From these efforts they sensed a consensus to launch a consistent pro-life campaign. Soon after, ESA, led by new executive director Bill Kallio, established a nonprofit political organization called the American Coalition for Life. At prominent universities, conferences, and evangelical colleges, Sider gave speeches on "Being Completely Pro-Life." The World Evangelical Fellowship regularly highlighted life issues in its periodical *Transformation*. The Association for Public Justice became more expressively anti-choice, and during a short-lived Anabaptist-Reformed détente in the early 1980s agreed "to seek avenues of closer cooperation" with ESA. ESA also proposed that dozens of progressive evangelical organizations— such as APJ, Voice of Calvary, Sojourners, ESA, the Southern Baptist Christian Life Commission, and *Radix*—should simultaneously issue consistent pro-life declarations, at which point masses of evangelicals could sign them in a reprise of the 1973 Chicago Declaration.[20]

Activism within the evangelical left soon began to reflect the new emphasis. In late 1983 ESA members participated in both the Witness for Peace campaign in Nicaragua and the National Right to Life march from the White House to the Supreme Court. At a Sojourners-organized "Peace Pentecost" demonstration in May 1985, participants touched on all points of the consistent pro-life ethic. Featured speaker Ron Sider, just completing his book *Completely Pro-Life* with InterVarsity Press, rallied participants gathering outside the White House with a rousing speech. Carrying signs that read "Choose Life: All Life is Sacred," protesters prayed against "the twisted priorities of a nation that reverses the biblical wisdom by busily beating plowshares into swords." Next they moved to the State Department to denounce U.S. "promotion of violence and terror in Central America"; then to the Soviet embassy, where they prayed for the people of Afghanistan, who have "been brutally invaded by another arrogant superpower"; then to the South African embassy to pray against apartheid; then to the Supreme Court, where they interceded for the victims of crime and for those on Death Row; and finally to the Department of Health and Human Services, where they "prayed for the unborn and for an agenda of justice and compassion for women and children that will create alternatives to the desperate, painful choice of abortion." The cumulative protests yielded 248 arrests and generated impressive media attention from UPI radio, the *New York Times*, and the *Washington Post*. An indication of the event's success was that Jerry Falwell held a news conference the same day in Washington to denounce the event. He called Sojourners a "pseudo-evangelical group" and stating that "[Jim Wallis] is to evangelicalism what Adolf Hitler was to the Roman Catholic Church." Wallis himself characterized the protest as "a day for the movement of the Spirit, a day when political stereotypes were shattered and ideological labels were swept aside to make room for the new wind of Christian conscience blowing across our land. The selective and inconsistent morality of both the Right and the Left was challenged by a simple message—all life is sacred." The evangelical left hoped that this "fresh vision" would transcend its reputation as an "embittered alternative" to the religious right.[21]

The new emphasis culminated in the formation of JustLife. The evangelical left launched this political action committee after Michigan state senator Steve Monsma lost his bid for a congressional seat in 1984. A pro-life Democrat, Monsma had experienced difficulty raising money for his campaign. The new organization sought to help nontraditional candidates like Monsma who opposed abortion, euthanasia, capital punishment, nuclear weapons, and unequal access to education and health care. ESA's Sider, named JustLife's executive director, immediately announced a campaign to boost its membership and strengthen its alliance with pro-life Catholics. JustLife issued voter guides, contributed to twenty-two life-friendly Senate and House candidates in 1986, conducted petition drives, and publicized its endorsements of candidates in local newspapers across the nation. JustLife also introduced eight pro-life legislative bills with provisions for informed consent, family consent, viability testing for women who were twenty weeks pregnant, no public support for abortions, coordination of services for pregnant women, parental leave from work, Medicaid for unborn children, and adoption subsidies. Many in the evangelical left harbored high hopes for JustLife.[22]

Evidence soon mounted, however, that a grand evangelical coalition would not materialize. The peak of the campaign came in 1988 with 6,000 members and a glossy voter guide called *JustLife '88*. In it, Sider, Billy Graham, and Joseph Cardinal Bernardin urged "aggressive negotiations" with the Soviet Union to end the nuclear arms race, governmental programs that "empower the poor to become self-sufficient," and an end to abortion, except when necessary to save the life of the mother. Despite the participation of these religious luminaries, *JustLife '88* sold only 27,000 copies. Its sequel fared even worse. While endorsing 56 candidates in 1990, the PAC contributed only $22,000 to their political campaigns. In 1993, after mustering only $6,000 in donations to candidates during the 1992 election, JustLife folded, deeply in debt after an unsuccessful emergency fundraising campaign.[23]

The same forces that doomed the evangelical left's campaign against U.S. intervention in Nicaragua also sabotaged the consistent life campaign. First, JustLife failed to overcome long-standing divisions over activist methods. Despite common policy resonance on nearly every issue articulated by JustLife, the Association for Public Justice refused to enter the coalition. Jim Skillen, APJ's director, objected primarily to JustLife's premature jump into electoral politics without a clearly stated public philosophy, biblical rationale, or political constituency. "A PAC without a political philosophy or base of support may only prove one more time that Christians don't know how to take politics seriously," wrote Skillen. He suggested that ESA—and evangelicals in general—instead spend at least a decade formulating a public philosophy, then building a constituency, and finally beginning to elect officials based on that philosophy. Second, the failure of JustLife reflected the evangelical left's inability to finesse its new ecumenical trajectory. Should the evangelical left emphasize the "evangelical" or the "left"? Should boundaries be constructed theologically or politically?[24]

Abortion, the most difficult component for the evangelical left to weave into the seamless garment, offers a telling example of these dilemmas. Progressive evangelicals, like the religious right, came late to the pro-life movement. Eying strident anti-abortion activity with suspicion during the 1970s, many progressive evangelicals voiced concern about women's reproductive rights, rape, safety of the mother, stress on existing family structures, the silence of Scripture on abortion, and the question of when a fetus is infused with a soul. Secular leftists kept these doubts alive and made it clear that friendships and political alliances forged in 1970s antiwar activism would be jeopardized if the evangelical left assumed an activist stance against abortion. "When the subject of abortion comes up, our shared energies and values come to an awkward and embarrassing halt," explained Sojourners'

Bill Weld-Wallis. Cathy Stentzel made a "conversion from pro-abortion to pro-life," but only after she and others in Sojourners blocked pro-life articles from being printed in the magazine in the late 1970s. "We had a highly charged debate but could not reach consensus about abortion itself," she explained. The issue came up twice every year in planning sessions until 1980, when *Sojourners* came out more clearly against abortion. Well into the mid-1980s, the group felt leftward pressure from ecumenical circles. *Sojourners* ultimately declined Sider's invitation to provide a representative on the Just-Life board of directors because "it would give the wrong impression to some feminists."[25]

Other progressive evangelical leaders, if considerably more pro-life on abortion than Sojourners, also articulated a certain measure of ambivalence. The Association for Public Justice periodically discussed the economic and constitutional dilemmas of abortion legislation. After ESA came out more explicitly against abortion in the mid-1980s, a consultant noted that the organization's "position on abortion is seen as very high-profile by people in related organizations" and might be contributing to a low female membership. Hesitant to alienate this key part of their constituency, the evangelical left continued to focus more on other issues such as hunger, economic justice, defense spending, the nuclear arms race, racism, and Central America. Each of these issues rated higher than abortion in an October 1987 survey of ESA members' concerns. Some members were willing to take a position of personally opposed, but legally pro-choice or to restrict abortion without banning it altogether. Others simply wished that the issue would go away.[26]

In the end, the measured tone did not resonate. The evangelical left's consistent pro-life message could not match the immediacy and intensity of the religious right's antiabortion rhetoric. Nothing, contended antiabortion activists on the right, could compare to millions of babies aborted each year in their own backyards. One activist spoke of the "demonic atrocity of abortion." Another, condemning *Sojourners*, wrote, "Amid all these screams for justice [Central American, inner-city, etc.], I have yet to find a single word on behalf of the preborn [and] the potential holocaust going on every day in clinics around the world. . . . Much has gone unreported in four years, including the termination of 4.5 million unwanted pregnancies!" The evangelical left simply lacked the fervor and populist flair of the religious right. Staunch evangelical pro-lifers, many of who saw the debate in dualistic terms, sensed the evangelical left's ambivalence and kept their distance from the consistent pro-life campaign. Some feared that evangelical progressives had engineered a pro-life stance on abortion as a ploy to entice other evangelicals to liberal stands on poverty, the death penalty, and nuclear weapons. The consistent pro-life campaign thus faltered as support from evangelical moderates and conservatives—and then progressives such as Sojourners—failed to materialize.[27]

What little momentum remained in the evangelical left radiated from non-evangelical sources. *Sojourners,* half of whose 60,000 subscriptions in the mid-1980s were purchased by Catholics, worked with Feminists for Life more than National Right to Life. Despite evangelical roots, JustLife folded with a membership that was only 27 percent evangelical. The relief and development agency Bread for the World, whose original board in 1973 included prominent evangelicals such as Mark Hatfield, John Perkins, Myron Augsburger, Frank Gaebelein, and Stanley Mooneyham, by 1984 had a constituency that was only 15 percent evangelical. ESA considered removing "evangelical" from its name, noting that the word's use puts the organization "immediately in a defensive mode." By the late 1980s it was clear that the evangelical left, reticent and tardy in capturing the energy of evangelical animus against abortion, had lost its base constituency to the religious right. ESA's ambition to build a "new Seamless Garment Network," while earning substantial media attention and a diverse membership, failed to gain widespread traction.[28]

The evangelical left thus straddled many worlds—evangelical, mainline, Quaker, Catholic, and leftist. In a 1982 seven-day, five-city tour of the Eastern seaboard, Sojourners' indefatigable Jim Wallis spoke to 500 Franciscan women, to members of the evangelical Jubilee Fellowship in Philadelphia, to mainline ministers at a conference held in New York City's Riverside Church, to members of the evangelical Jubilee Partners in Georgia, to Trappist monks at Conyers Monastery, to members of the evangelical intentional community Open Door in Atlanta, and to Catholic parishioners in Miami Beach at the National Lay Evangelism Conference. On other occasions Sojourners worked closely with Quakers and the Catholic Berrigan brothers on antiwar and anti-nuclear proliferation initiatives. These connections were evidence of significant evangelical left influence on non-evangelicals and the potential for a "politically significant movement" that transcended parochial ecclesiastical boundaries. But the evangelical left's ecumenism also diffused its resources and left it open to attack from all sides. Whenever the movement offered a carrot to political allies on the left, conservative evangelicals shouted heresy.

Whenever it made a move back toward its theologically conservative evangelical roots, ecumenical activists cried betrayal. Unlike the religious right, it
was unable to attract its evangelical constituency deeply. Thorny issues of
ecumenicity and identity politics sabotaged the consistent life campaign, the
final attempt to revive the evangelical left in the 1980s.[29]

III

More than strategic missteps or even the dilemmas of identity, the political
realities of the 1980s doomed the evangelical left's push for viability. As the
case of Stephen Monsma demonstrates, the consistent pro-life campaign simply did not fit the hardening American political party structure. Monsma, a
pro-life Democrat from Michigan, lost two political bids: for the U.S. House
of Representatives in 1984 and the Michigan Senate in 1985. In both cases,
hostility from Democratic colleagues toward his pro-life stance on abortion
(despite his reliable support of welfare measures and a tight race for party
superiority in the State Senate) plagued Monsma's campaign. Aide David
Medema told the *New York Times* that Monsma's opposition to state financing
of abortions alienated colleagues. "We expected tolerance from the Democratic Party but found that tolerance evaporated around the abortion issue.
For pro-life Democrats, money would dry up in election campaigns." Monsma
also encountered opposition from anti-abortion activists despite his pro-life
stance. He had previously secured the endorsement of Michigan's Right to
Life organization, but many insiders loudly objected because it was in the
interest of their cause to retain Republican control of the Senate. The difficult experience prompted Monsma to collaborate with JustLife on behalf of
other marginalized candidates. But JustLife too failed, and soon thereafter a
dispirited Monsma moved to California.[30]

Other pro-life Democrats felt just as isolated. In 1985 U.S. representative
Don Bonker (D-Wash.), told *Christianity Today*, "Regrettably, the Democrats come up short on questions of personal morality." U.S. representative
Bill Nelson (D-Fl.) complained that "activists in the Democratic Party . . .
have formed the image of the party." U.S. representative Tony Hall (D-Oh.),
who embraced a pro-life stance after converting to evangelical faith while in
office, explained that his switch on the issue "caused me a lot of trouble. . . .
You can mention my name [among the Democratic Party leadership] and
they spit . . . [They] even . . . walk across the street not to talk to me because

they hated the fact that I . . . was a Democrat and yet pro-life." In 1992 Democratic leaders prohibited Senator Robert Casey (D-Pa.) from speaking on the subject at the party's national convention.[31]

The evangelical left felt even more out of place in the Republican Party, which likewise failed to offer a consistent pro-life position. Gary Govert, a constituent of Jesse Helms in North Carolina, could not bear to support a party that "when they aren't lobbying for abortion legislation, they are busy being militarists, opposing civil rights legislation, and opposing virtually all nonmilitary foreign aid." Like Democrats, Republicans also began to enforce the new political orthodoxies. Liberal Republicans found it increasingly difficult to dissent from their party's planks on trickle-down economics and national defense. Sojourners felt this acutely and accused the Reagan administration of targeting them in a bungled mid-1980s NSA investigation and IRS audit. In the face of hostility from all sides, wrote Sojourners' Bill Weld-Wallis, what could a consistent pro-life evangelical do except "seek God's Spirit for counsel, and ask for forgiveness for our part in a world that leaves us with choices such as these."[32]

The evangelical left's paucity of electoral options showed itself in the 1984 and 1988 elections. No single establishment candidate won over progressive evangelicalism. Some voted for Reagan in the 1980s based solely on his anti-abortion stance. More endorsed Democrats. Sojourners' Danny Collum, for example, came out in 1984 for Walter Mondale as the "lesser of two evils" (but only after deriding Mondale as being "total establishment"). Others avoided the ballot box entirely, though these nonvoters despaired that their abstinence was "in essence a vote for Reagan and his war on the poor and the Third World." APJ, drawing from its Dutch heritage, looked across the Atlantic to weigh the merits of European party structures.[33]

The evangelical left ultimately found a more resonant tradition by looking back in American history to the turn-of-the-century populist movement. Like southern and western farmers in the 1880s who tried to wrest power from eastern power brokers, many in the evangelical left sought to ensure that disadvantaged citizens participated in decisions affecting their lives. John Alexander of *The Other Side* exegeted Scripture passages as examples of populist rhetoric and affirmed a proposal for a "people-oriented economics" for the 80 percent of the population "consistently excluded from economic decision-making." APJ introduced legislation to protect political minorities from being "smothered by an artificial majority." Sojourners pushed for public control over investments, which would take power away from financial oligarchs. Its members launched letter-writing campaigns, programs of direct action, and alliances with the poor. Establishing a day-care center and the Southern Columbia Heights Tenant Union, they believed, would empower the lower classes to become "shapers of history." ESA workers likewise organized communities in Chicago and Philadelphia and joined Housing Now!, a national coalition of organizations outraged by "a governmental process that allows the rich and powerful to make billions through manipulation of housing programs while the poor lack decent homes." The evangelical left's neo-populist rhetoric and activism sought to stanch the power of any structure—corporate, governmental, or labor—that exerted undue authoritarian control.[34]

Unable to vote for the People's Party (Jim Wallis liked to call himself a nineteenth-century evangelical born in the wrong century), the evangelical left nonetheless expressed admiration for contemporaneous alternative parties and candidates. Sojourners lauded the Green Party. APJ praised John Anderson for running as an independent in 1980. Most of all, the evangelical left commended Jesse Jackson for subverting conventional politics during his runs for the White House in 1984 and 1988. Progressive evangelicals as diverse as APJ and Sojourners liked his "public philosophy," his pro-life position (until he recanted), his clear articulation of faith, and his populist rhetoric. APJ declared that Jackson's neo-populism fit its own impulse to marshal "a people's power . . . in democratic opposition." ESA board member Barbara Skinner served as Special Assistant to the Jackson presidential campaign. For a time, Jackson's candidacy sparked new hope among the evangelical left that their domestic agenda might expand from local community organizing to a "national political strategy on the foundation of local empowerment." In the end, however, both the evangelical left and Jackson's campaign faltered because of their unconventional politics.[35]

Lacking a political home, the evangelical left also suffered from a lack of money. In contrast to a religious right that settled in the Sunbelt and tightly aligned with the burgeoning Republican Party, the evangelical left labored in the rust belt, a region burdened by high oil prices and the failures of the auto industry. Nor did most even want to benefit from the spoils of federal defense contracts. Teachings on the renunciation of wealth and criticisms of unfettered capitalism led progressive evangelicals away from high-paying business and industry jobs, and their strident rhetoric against affluence alienated evangelicals who did take those jobs. Attempts to corporatize the evangelical left were often hesitant and tardy, befitting its anti-technocratic origins. "Whenever I go and meet a wealthy person," complained Fuller Seminary's David Hubbard, "I find that [Campus Crusade CEO] Bill Bright has been there first." Cal Thomas, a disgruntled former lieutenant of Jerry Falwell who in 1984 renounced the religious right, explained, "Since I started living a simple lifestyle, I can't afford all the stamps I once could when I was a captive of the profit motive and working for Falwell!" A small-is-beautiful inclination militated against the development of a well-funded, large movement.[36]

ESA, for example, seemed to be in perpetual danger of insolvency. At the Thanksgiving Workshops, attendance was sporadic for lack of money, despite clear indications of interest and support. After travel allowances of $9,800 disbursed by the Lilly Foundation ran out, some established scholars at major state universities could not afford to attend planning meetings. By 1981 ESA's books were in disarray, and the organization was in debt. Administrator Bill Kallio engineered a remarkable recovery in the early 1980s. Giving increased 30 percent. Kallio attracted 2,500 new members. And the number of ESA chapters grew to thirty-five. Still, that Kallio could exult over a financial turnaround of only $26,000 showed the huge financial distance that separated ESA from the Moral Majority. ESA struggled to survive through the rest of the 1980s, surviving primarily through small donations as well as Sider's numerous speaker fees. Others in the evangelical left also struggled financially. CWLF suffered significant deficits. ICS's *Vanguard* magazine failed to publish an issue for seven straight months in 1978 and begged subscribers for additional funds in order to stay afloat. Although 300 readers sent in $25 each, temporarily keeping the magazine alive, *Vanguard* folded in 1981. JustLife survived on average donations of $30 before folding in 1992. *Sojourners* did better, growing to 55,000 subscriptions in 1983. But the magazine only paid employees "subsistence level salaries." One cover of the *Wittenburg Door* magazine, employing self-deprecating humor over their anemic cash flow, read "Celebrating Five Years of Operating with a Loss."[37]

As the 1980s came to an end, the evangelical left was foundering. *Sojourners*, despite its impressive subscription base and normally upbeat rhetoric, seemed resigned to political obscurity. Wallis, contending that a spiritual awakening was needed before political action could take place, began to talk more explicitly about pastoral work and revivalism. ESA suffered from a stagnant membership and the decline of JustLife. In 1990 a consultant barraged the organization's leadership with a series of questions about its identity: Was its mission to "disciple evangelicals" or to influence politicians about public policy? Was its primary constituency evangelicals or non-evangelicals? Had it lost its evangelistic focus? Was it flitting from one idea to the next without follow-up? Was ESA merely the lengthened shadow of Ron Sider? In a drawn-out discussion at ESA headquarters, board members and administrators clashed over these questions, leaving the group frustrated and confused about how to proceed.[38]

The Reagan era thus ended as it began for the evangelical left: with a confused identity and uncertain vision. While the evangelical left's wide reach across traditions made it broadly influential, that ecumenism came at the cost of a weak evangelical identity. And by failing to conform to hardening political structures, it forfeited its chances for large-scale evangelical mobilization. The religious right, by contrast, had successfully attached itself to a flourishing conservative movement and Republican Party. By 1990 the evangelical left as a coherent organizational movement was exhausted by internal friction. Exiled from American political structures and power, it had indeed been left behind.

Epilogue

The evangelical left also left behind a legacy. Seeds of social justice took root in unnoticed crevices of North American evangelical structures, sometimes sending up shoots in unexpected quarters from thinkers and leaders who had been nourished by progressive evangelicals. Even the voices of individuals who took part in the 1973 Thanksgiving Workshop continued—and continue among those still living—to speak prophetically from the edges, often playing the role of gadfly, public conscience, and counterweight to the rightward postwar direction of the broader movement.

Carl Henry, already a neo-evangelical elder statesman and perhaps the most conservative delegate at the Workshop in Chicago, continued in those roles. He collected honorary degrees and served on the boards of many evangelical organizations. In 1983 he published the final installment of his magisterial six-volume theological work *God, Revelation, and Authority*. Like most establishment evangelicals, Henry viewed both the evangelical left and the religious right with profound ambivalence. He lauded the attention each movement paid to issues of social concern. But he criticized partisan excess and decried political, cultural, and theological fragmentation. His political instincts, however, became more recognizably conservative. He actively participated, along with Michael Novak and Richard John Neuhaus, in the Institute on Religion and Democracy. In addition, he saw the work of his son Paul Henry, a member of the U.S. House of Representatives and a rising star in the Republican Party, as carrying on some of his vision. Paul died tragically of a brain tumor in 1993, and Henry died a decade later at age ninety. Fifty years after Henry's critique of obscurantism in *The Uneasy Conscience of Fundamentalism*, movement leaders lauded him as an indefatigable champion of evangelical respectability. "Few people in the twentieth century," reported *Christianity Today* in its obituary, "have done more to articulate the importance of a coherent Christian world and life view."[1]

John Alexander, evangelical promoter of racial justice, more clearly embodied the sensibilities of the Chicago Declaration. He expanded *The Other Side*'s civil rights platform to include other progressive issues such as global justice, gender equality, communal living, and simplicity. Jubilee Crafts, for instance, was one of the first American nonprofits to sell fairly traded third world goods. The Philadelphia offices of *The Other Side* and Jubilee Crafts became something of an unofficial East Coast regional headquarters for the evangelical left. The magazine rented out office space to socially moderate and leftist organizations such as Evangelicals for Social Action, American Christians for the Abolition of Torture, Clergy and Laity Concerned, the Center on Law and Pacifism, Coalition for a Simple Life-Style, the Nuclear Moratorium Project, and the Central America Organizing Project. The unpretentious Alexander, who for years wore the same cream-colored (originally white, his colleagues thought) sweater with big holes, remained the face of the organization. In the early 1980s *The Other Side* enjoyed an outsized reputation and influence. Alexander's domain, however, rapidly fell apart as the organization fragmented over personality conflicts and the issue of homosexuality. In 1984, Alexander was forced out of the very magazine he had founded two decades earlier. He moved to San Francisco, attended Church of the Sojourners, wore tie-dyed tee shirts, and fell off the evangelical map. On Good Friday 2001, Alexander died of leukemia. In 2004 *The Other Side* ceased publication.[2]

Other civil rights activists remained more securely in the evangelical fold. John Perkins, son of a black Mississippi sharecropper, served on the boards of World Vision and the National Association of Evangelicals. He wrote half a dozen significant books and founded as many influential ministries, including the Christian Community Development Association (now with over 500 institutional members), Mendenhall Ministries, Voice of Calvary, the John Perkins Center at Seattle Pacific University, and the John Perkins Foundation for Reconciliation and Development in Jackson, Mississippi. Perkins, known as "Grandpa John" to his many young colleagues, mentored a burgeoning new generation of urban evangelical activists in the 2000s. Tom Skinner, Harlem gang leader turned civil rights advocate, continued work as an evangelist. In the 1980s Skinner became chaplain of the Washington Redskins and a much sought-after motivational speaker for church groups and corporations. When he died in 1994 at age fifty-two, dozens of celebrities, including politician Jesse Jackson, poet Maya Angelou, and the Nation of Islam's Louis Farrakhan, attended his funeral.[3]

Jim Wallis, former SDS activist, continued to labor on the political margins during the 1980s and 1990s, and the Sojourners intentional community disbanded. The magazine and a partner organization Call to Renewal, however, surged in the 2000s. "I've been 40 years in the wilderness, and now it's time to come out," he told a reporter. Sojourners' new prominence began in 1997 when Wallis met unknown Illinois state legislator Barack Obama at the Saguaro Seminar on civic engagement. Obama would go on to consult with Wallis on faith-based issues from the White House. Catapulted to celebrity by this relationship—and by his 2005 bestselling book *God's Politics: Why the Right Gets It Wrong and the Left Doesn't Get It*—Wallis in the 2000s regularly appeared as a guest on CNN and comic Jon Stewart's *The Daily Show*. He attended World Economic Forum meetings in Davos, Switzerland, each year, and sales from *God's Politics*, which spent fifteen weeks on the *New York Times* bestseller list, infused Sojourners with cash. In 2006, old staffers, along with a new team of political organizers, fundraisers, and communications specialists, moved into gleaming new headquarters in Washington. In 2007 Sojourners sponsored a CNN forum on faith and religious values in which three of the top Democratic presidential candidates—Hillary Clinton, John Edwards, and Barack Obama—participated. According to *Time* editor Amy Sullivan, several years earlier the same forum had attracted only a single congressperson. Thirty-five years after the Chicago Declaration, Wallis had arrived at the center of American politics.[4]

Mark Hatfield, who wrote a supportive telegram to Thanksgiving Workshop delegates in 1973, continued for many years to represent Oregon in the U.S. Senate. He also continued to dissent from the Republican Party on issues of national defense. With Massachusetts senator Ted Kennedy, he sponsored nuclear freeze legislation, opposed Reagan's invasion of Grenada, and was one of only two Republicans to vote against the 1990 invasion of Iraq. Confounding political allies and opponents alike, he also remained an outspoken opponent of abortion and the death penalty. For these and other positions, Hatfield came under relentless attack by the Republican leadership through the 1980s and 1990s. After he cast the decisive (and lone Republican) vote against a balanced budget amendment in 1995, party leaders tried to strip him of the chairmanship of the Senate Appropriations Committee. Weary of bucking his party, Hatfield retired a year later. Hatfield's political courage garnered praise once he was out of office. Recognizing his forty-six years of public service and eleven consecutive election victories, officials in Oregon named dozens of buildings after him. The evangelical George Fox University added him to their faculty. Tom Brokaw featured him in a chapter in *The Greatest Generation*. "Some of the newer Republican Senators, with their strict conservative dogmas, may never understand a man like Mark Hatfield," wrote Brokaw several years before Hatfield's death in 2011.[5]

Sharon Gallagher edited *Right On* (renamed *Radix*) after the Christian World Liberation Front and the Berkeley Christian Coalition disbanded in the late 1970s. Continuing to bridge American culture and evangelicalism, Gallagher taught classes on faith and the media at New College Berkeley, an affiliate of the Graduate Theological Union. Into the 2000s she delivered talks on "Mystery, Morality and Meaning: What Woody Allen and Others are Saying About Our Culture," wrote movie reviews, and interviewed novelists, artists, and other Christian leaders. Forty years after its launch, a reader described *Radix* as "a more worldly magazine than one would expect from its deep commitment to Christ." Comfortable articulating an evangelical vision in chic Berkeley coffeehouses, Gallagher represented the new cosmopolitan path of many twenty-first-century progressive evangelicals.

Samuel Escobar, founder of the Latin American Theological Fraternity and fiery critic of American capitalism at the 1974 Lausanne conference, continued to bridge Latin American and North American evangelical worlds. During the 1980s and 1990s, he worked for the International Fellowship of Evangelical Students. Thereafter he split his time between the United States as a professor of missiology at Palmer Theological Seminary in Philadelphia and Spain as a professor at the Baptist Seminary of Madrid. A prolific missiologist and leading Latin American theologian, Escobar in the 2000s lived in Valencia, Spain, where he cared for his wife, who suffered from Alzheimer's disease.

Richard Mouw, a former SDS member and proponent of a Reformed strain of evangelical politics at the Thanksgiving Workshops, continued to broaden his own evangelical commitments. During the 1970s and 1980s, Mouw taught at Calvin College, the Free University of Amsterdam, and Fuller Theological Seminary. Elected president of Fuller in 1993, Mouw engaged in intensive dialogues with Mormons, Anabaptists, Wesleyans, Catholics, and mainliners. Like Escobar and Ron Sider, he was a contributing editor to *Christianity Today*. Journalists regularly called on him to offer cultural commentary. Mouw has been called, with justification, evangelicalism's "premier public intellectual."

Ron Sider, leader of the Thanksgiving Workshop, continued to preach Anabaptist messages of justice, peace, and simple living to evangelicals. *Rich Christians in an Age of Hunger*, which catapulted Sider to prominence, sold nearly half a million copies by its fifth edition. As president of Evangelicals for Social Action and a professor of theology, holistic ministry, and public policy at Palmer Theological Seminary, he helped launch the Evangelical Environmental Network. In the early 1990s EEN campaigned for and donated $1 million to preserve the Endangered Species Act and in the early 2000s launched a "What Would Jesus Drive?" campaign, which garnered articles in at least 4,000 media outlets over four months. With the exception of his pro-life stance, support for school vouchers, and 2000 vote for George W. Bush's "compassionate conservatism" (which he later said he regretted), Sider, like Sojourners' Jim Wallis, routinely embraced Democratic policies. Yet ESA, characterized by Sider's warm and conciliatory personality, can be distinguished from Sojourners' more partisan style. Into the 2000s Sider and his wife Arbutus, a family therapist, still practiced simple living. They cooked out of the *More-with-Less Cookbook*, by then in its 47th printing. They purchased most of their clothes at thrift stores and maintained a modest home in a mostly black neighborhood in the Germantown section of Philadelphia. The décor, reported a journalist, was comfortably worn, falling "somewhere between Graduate Student and Junior Faculty."[6]

The evangelical left, exemplified by this diverse cast of figures, enjoyed relatively little success in politics strictly defined. It nonetheless did significantly shape the culture of many evangelicals. Having labored for decades with little help on issues of poverty, women's rights, and inequities in the global economy, Ron Sider's concerns became more mainstream among evangelicals associated with megachurch pastors Rick Warren and Bill Hybels, editors at *Christianity Today*, and the many evangelicals who have never closely identified with Jerry Falwell and Pat Robertson. Sider's *Rich Christians in an Age of Hunger*, for example, while not profoundly influencing American economic or foreign policy, guided the giving and consumptive patterns of millions of evangelicals. After attending the 1989 missionary convention Lausanne II in Manila, Philippines, Sider could in good faith declare, "What especially impressed—and delighted—me was the extent to which the ESA vision of holistic concern for both evangelism and social action has now become the prevailing perspective of mainstream evangelicalism worldwide. That was not the case when ESA was launched with the Chicago Declaration in 1973!" These could be interpreted as the self-justifying

words of an evangelical progressive activist at the nadir of his electoral influence, but Sider's judgment was largely correct. Moderate evangelicals in
the 1990s and 2000s, increasingly comfortable with the language of social
justice, had roots in the 1970s evangelical left.[7]

As the twenty-first century began, moderate and progressive sectors of
evangelicalism had somewhat revitalized. This was in part because older
luminaries of the evangelical left, in the context of a growing conservative
movement in America, had tacked toward the center. Ron Sider, for example,
softened his critiques of capitalism. In the twentieth-anniversary revision of
Rich Christians, published in 1997, Sider wrote, "My thinking has changed.
I've learned more about economics." The revised manuscript revealed new
confidence in free markets, an emphasis on generosity over poverty (the new
subtitle read "Moving from Affluence to Generosity"), and fewer statist prescriptions. Jim Wallis, softening from his fiery New Left suspicion of traditional political structures, worked comfortably with political moderates and
the Democratic Party. A virulent critic of the technocratic Jimmy Carter
in the 1970s, Wallis began to appear on event stages with the former president.
By all accounts, the two had become good friends and found common political ground. Wallis now worked with some of the most powerful leaders in
the nation and world. On a single day in March 2009, he testified at a Senate
hearing on the Employee Free Choice Act, participated in a conference call
with President Obama's Advisory Council on Faith-Based and Neighborhood Partnerships, and then enjoyed dinner with United Nations Secretary
General Ban Ki-moon. Observers suggested that this new centrist trajectory
might in the long run offer progressive evangelicalism more political space
and more potential to build an organized movement.[8]

Alongside these still-active veterans of the evangelical left, a vigorous
set of younger progressives began to emerge. Amy Sullivan, an evangelical
Democrat and editor at *Time* magazine, pushed for progressive health care
reform and efforts to stem abortion rates. In *The Party Faithful* (2008), she
chided Democrats for bowing to the secular left and encouraged the party to
"level the praying field." Eric Sapp, an ordained evangelical minister and
former legislative aide for Senator Edward Kennedy on the Health, Education, Labor, and Pensions Committee, worked for the Eleison Group, a con-
sulting group that promotes progressive policy to faith and values voters.
Urban activists such as Shane Claiborne, reversing the suburban flight of
their parents, returned to the city. The Simple Way community, led by Claiborne and located in the Kensington neighborhood of Philadelphia, ad-

dressed issues of homelessness and poverty while trying to nurture intimate Christian community. Cassie and Chris Haw, former members of the evangelical megachurch Willow Creek, started the Camden House across the Delaware River from Philadelphia. These communities and dozens of others, including Rutba House in Raleigh-Durham, North Carolina, and Communality in Lexington, Kentucky, became collectively known as "the new monasticism," a movement squarely in the tradition of John Howard Yoder, Reba Place, and the Christian World Liberation Front. Many of these young groups worked with older progressive organizations, themselves experiencing a youth movement. At the end of the century's first decade, half the *Sojourners'* readership were under age thirty.[9]

Polls seemed to confirm a progressive youth movement. George W. Bush's approval rating among young evangelicals dropped from 87 percent in 2002 to 45 percent by the end of his presidency, a plunge reminiscent of Jimmy Carter's sagging popularity in the late 1970s. A less dramatic, but still highly suggestive, Pew Research Center poll showed that over the course of only a few years, young white evangelicals' identification with the Republican Party dropped by 15 percentage points. Sociologist Michael Lindsay noted, "Fully 70 percent of evangelicals in America do not identify with the religious right." Some Democratic activists, long hostile to the evangelical left, began to encourage these new "young evangelicals." Senator Chris Dodd, a Catholic from Connecticut, said that his party had made "a huge mistake over the years" by not talking about how faith informs public policy. The most prominent contenders for the 2008 presidential nomination sought to avoid repeating that strategic misstep. Hillary Clinton hired Burns Strider, a born-again evangelical from Mississippi and leader of the Democratic Faith Working Group, as senior adviser and director of faith-based outreach. Barack Obama chose Joshua DuBois, a young minister with the Assemblies of God, as his religious affairs adviser. Obama gave an interview to *Christianity Today*, and publicly identified several evangelicals, including Jim Wallis, Joel Hunter, T. D. Jakes, and Kirbyjon Caldwell, as spiritual mentors. Democratic candidates also visited numerous evangelical venues, including Messiah College, Saddleback Church, and the "Presidential Forum on Faith, Values, and Poverty" sponsored by Sojourners and broadcast on CNN. Several evangelical Democratic political action committees emerged, including Democrats for Life, Faithful Democrats, and Common Good Strategies.[10]

Still, significant challenges remained for the evangelical left as it entered the 2010s. First, some progressive sectors remained unmindful of or opposed to key evangelical concerns. Democratic pollsters, for example, repeatedly failed to ask if voters were evangelical or born again, even as a flood of articles about candidates' faith flooded the media. Moreover, Democrats continued to route large amounts of funding and personnel away from faith and values initiatives. A sharp back-hand to the full one-third of evangelicals who have voted Democratic since the 1980s, this failure raised questions about whether the party's new religious fluency was substantive or merely cosmetic. Second, many evangelical voters remained tied to Republicanism through identity politics. It could take half a generation or more for evangelicals to switch parties, even if Democratic outreach succeeds. Third, the rise of the Tea Party and presidential candidates from the religious right reinforced the equation of conservative politics and evangelicalism in the public's eye. Fourth, in order to attract a broader set of evangelicals, the Democratic Party needed to demonstrate more flexibility on abortion. A 2007 survey of evangelical politicians by Michael Lindsay found that the top reason given for their political affiliation was their party's pro-life position. If Democrats opened up to pro-life policies, Lindsay suggested, unexpected new political alignments could take place. If not, abortion would trump any amount of resonance on poverty and faith talk.[11]

Such obstacles suggested that the bulk of evangelicals were probably headed for less partisan identification. The 15 percent drop in Republican identification resulted in a mere 5 percent rise in Democratic affiliation, but a 10 percent jump for independence. Political scientist John Green called these new evangelical non-rightists "freestyle evangelicals." Michael Lindsay called them "cosmopolitan evangelicals." They included Rick Warren, pastor of the 7,000-member Saddleback Church in Orange County, California. Anointed by many as Billy Graham's successor, Warren in the early 2000s added social issues to his agenda of saving souls. During a 2003 trip to South Africa, he visited a small church that worshipped in a tattered tent that also housed 25 children orphaned by AIDS. "I realized they were doing more for the poor than my entire megachurch," he said. "It was like a knife in the heart." Sidestepping electoral politics—he was fond of saying "I'm not right-wing or left-wing. I'm for the whole bird"—Warren used his church's resources and the proceeds of his best-selling spiritual guidebook *The Purpose-Driven Life* (2002) to fund initiatives on poverty and disease. Bill Hybels, pastor of the megachurch Willow Creek outside of Chicago, similarly told the *New York Times* that he considered politics a path to "heartache and disappointment." He envisioned a less political (at least electorally), but no less socially engaged path that, according to the *Times*, "would warm a liberal's heart." "We have just pounded the drum again and again that, for churches to reach their full redemptive potential, they have to do more than hold services—they have to try to transform their communities," Hybels said. "If there is racial injustice in your community, you have to speak to that. If there is educational injustice, you have to do something there. If the poor are being neglected by the government or being oppressed in some way, then you have to stand up for the poor." Progressive social action outside of electoral structures stands as one of the principal legacies of the evangelical left. Its political relevance goes well beyond its marginal influence on the Democrats or Republicans. It has helped to launch engagement around a much broader array of issues—from African poverty to peacemaking to simple living—to which neither party pays much attention.[12]

Initiatives from mainstream evangelical institutions in the early 2000s reflected these social sensibilities. The National Association of Evangelicals articulated a vision for social justice in a 2001 statement called *For the Health of the Nation: An Evangelical Call to Civic Responsibility*. Its centrist call for religious freedom, family life and the protection of children, sanctity of life, caring for the poor and vulnerable, human rights, peacemaking, and creation care drew attention to what the evangelical left had been quietly doing all along. Political scientists Robert Putnam and David Campbell found that slightly more evangelicals than mainline Protestants think that the government bears primary responsibility for the welfare of the poor. In an increasingly fluid and idiosyncratic electorate—in 2007 Americans aged 18 to 30 were the least likely demographic to support "the death penalty," "embryonic stem-cell research," "the separation of church and state," "abortion rights," "physician-assisted suicide," or "affirmative action," but were the most likely to support "gay rights" and "same-sex marriage"—evangelicalism's reprise of the 1970s Chicago Declaration and the 1980s "consistent life" campaign may enjoy more cultural, even political, space.[13]

But this is reading tea leaves. The shifting fortunes of the evangelical left most decisively point to the flexibility and diversity of evangelicalism itself. Structurally fragmented, the National Association of Evangelicals proper consists of 43 member denominations. Scholars consider at least a thousand more of the nearly 4,000 Protestant denominations in the United States to be theologically evangelical. Given the decreasing salience of denominational markers, even these remarkable numbers do not fully convey the high level of evangelical diversity. Many evangelicals now identify primarily with social service agencies, missionary organizations, colleges, individual congregations, or even religious celebrities. Reinforced by the democratizing impulse of the Second Great Awakening in the early nineteenth century and the decentralized "priesthood of all believers" theology that undergirds the modern movement, most sectors of evangelicalism shun hierarchical systems of governance. This bottom-up structure allows the movement to react to market forces, in turn giving it a stunning resilience and a capacity for growth. But evangelical flexibility—layered on top of religious particularism and theological rivalry—hinders political uniformity. Evangelicalism, consisting of and reaching out to different social classes, geographies, and ethnicities with the foremost message of salvation, has been characterized historically by great diversity in both political method and theory.[14]

A long Protestant narrative dating back to the sixteenth century has taught this historical lesson. Anabaptists, sometimes called the left wing of the Reformation, challenged the establishment with populist, democratic, and anti-hierarchical fervor. In the eighteenth century, British abolitionists challenged the slave trade. In the nineteenth century, some American evangelicals dissented from the Whig establishment to establish communitarian utopias. At the turn of the twentieth century, North Carolinian populists for a time challenged Jim Crow. Others worked on social issues such as temperance, abolition, industrialization, suffrage, and civil rights unionism. This unpredictable and strikingly variable politics has persisted globally. In contemporary Brazil, for example, *evangelicós* have participated in all the major political parties. They and others, according to sociologist Paul Freston, have dismantled "facile equations of evangelicalism with conservative stances" and demonstrated "the distance of these actors—indeed, total independence of these actors—from the American evangelical right." Many, like Ruth Padilla De-Borst, the influential daughter of Ecuadorian theologian René Padilla, have combined conservative theological and moral stances with progressive economic and foreign policy views in ways that defy the Western imagination. In a world where 60 percent of the world's Christians now live outside the North Atlantic region and in a nation increasingly opened to nonwhite immigrants since the Immigration Act of 1965, these views—especially if joined with black evangelical and white progressive voices—will only continue to carry more weight.[15]

Attention to historical and global realities suggests, then, that evangelicalism is not inherently conservative, nor universally fixed to individual solutions to social problems. Rather, conditions outside the movement, especially the ideological platforms and cultural sensibilities of political parties, significantly shape the direction of evangelical politics. Thus, the alliance with current forms of contemporary conservatism may be fundamentally unstable. Evangelicals may ultimately question whether small government, lower taxes, and a strong national defense comfortably square with New Testament directives about blessing peacemakers, caring for the poor, and turning the other cheek. Without a robust antipoverty program, Republicans may find it difficult to retain an evangelical constituency that—compared to other Christian traditions—has given generously to the poor. Conversely, it also may be difficult for evangelicals to ally comfortably with secular liberals who insist on a party platform that includes reproductive rights and the redefinition of marriage and family. The many ways evangelicals read the Bible do not fit comfortably within the American electoral system. For instance, researchers found that evangelicals who read the Bible every day are more likely to favor more humane treatment of criminals, to be more concerned about issues of poverty and conservation, and to oppose same-sex marriage and legalized abortion more than evangelicals who do not consistently read Scripture. Evangelicals, anticonfessional and revivalist in sensibility, are more religiously and politically creative than the electoral structures that try to contain them.[16]

The flexible, fragmented nature of evangelicalism itself, then, helps explain the convoluted political history of the movement. For a time in the 1970s, it appeared that the evangelical left had the advantage over politically conservative forms of evangelicalism. The momentum of a conspicuous progressive politics five years before the emergence of the Moral Majority was stopped only by the hardening of the political parties, which exposed the movement's ecclesiastical and social diversities. Evangelicals could have taken a very different trajectory, if in the 1970s there had existed an indifferent Republican Party and a welcoming Democratic Party. Historian Seth Dowland, charting the "unpredictable contingencies" that launched the religious right's political emphasis on the traditional family, implicitly suggests that possibility. That the religious right would successfully devise rhetoric that "made liberal reformers enemies of the family and position 'family values' as mainstream fare" was more contingent than certain. Nor was it inevitable that Democrats would turn pro-choice. Had Democrats, for instance, taken a pro-life stance in the 1970s, or even remained neutral on abortion, more evangelicals might now hold progressive stances on economics and diplomacy. The fluidity of evangelical politics within an inherently fragmented movement means that essentialist notions of evangelicalism, often based on the small sample of rightist partisan politics in the 1980s, will always need revision.[17]

If a unified politics continued to elude evangelicals, political involvement itself did not. Evangelicals agreed by the end of the first decade of the new millennium—in far greater proportion than fifty years before—that the Gospel calls for holistic, not just personal, transformation. Followers of Jesus, evangelicals say almost in unison, must take up cultural, social, even political responsibilities. The evangelical left, representing one of the most serious postwar attempts to mobilize evangelicals for organized political action, hastened this broader shift toward a sense of corporate obligation. It carved out space for the rhetoric and activism of social justice—both on the left and on what became a much larger right. Even if evangelicals did not agree precisely on what the public good looked like, they no longer had to legitimize participation in debate over the public good. Thus the *Washington Post* prediction in 1973 that the evangelical left might help transform political and religious life was realized. By the dawn of the twenty-first century, more evangelicals on more points of the political spectrum were engaging in spirited public debate.[18]

As evangelical Christians committed to the Lord Jesus Christ and the full authority of the Word of God, we affirm that God lays total claim upon the lives of his people. We cannot, therefore, separate our lives from the situation in which God has placed us in the United States and the world.

We confess that we have not acknowledged the complete claim of God on our lives.

We acknowledge that God requires love. But we have not demonstrated the love of God to those suffering social abuses.

We acknowledge that God requires justice. But we have not proclaimed or demonstrated his justice to an unjust American society. Although the Lord calls us to defend the social and economic rights of the poor and oppressed, we have mostly remained silent. We deplore the historic involvement of the church in America with racism and the conspicuous responsibility of the evangelical community for perpetuating the personal attitudes and institutional structures that have divided the body of Christ along color lines. Further, we have failed to condemn the exploitation of racism at home and abroad by our economic system.

We affirm that God abounds in mercy and that he forgives all who repent and turn from their sins. So we call our fellow evangelical Christians to demonstrate repentance in a Christian discipleship that confronts the social and political injustice of our nation.

We must attack the materialism of our culture and the maldistribution of the nation's wealth and services. We recognize that as a nation we play a crucial role in the imbalance and injustice of international trade and development. Before God and a billion hungry neighbors, we must rethink our values regarding our present standard of living and promote a more just acquisition and distribution of the world's resources.

We acknowledge our Christian responsibilities of citizenship. Therefore, we must challenge the misplaced trust of the nation in economic and military might—a proud trust that promotes a national pathology of war and violence which victimizes our neighbors at home and abroad. We must resist the temptation to make the nation and its institutions objects of near-religious loyalty.

We acknowledge that we have encouraged men to prideful domination and women to irresponsible passivity. So we call both men and women to mutual submission and active discipleship.

We proclaim no new gospel, but the Gospel of our Lord Jesus Christ who, through the power of the Holy Spirit, frees people from sin so that they might praise God through works of righteousness.

By this declaration, we endorse no political ideology or party, but call our nation's leaders and people to that righteousness which exalts a nation.

We make this declaration in the biblical hope that Christ is coming to consummate the Kingdom and we accept his claim on our total discipleship until he comes.

November 25, 1973, Chicago, Illinois

Original Signers	James Dunn	Nancy Hardesty
John F. Alexander	Daniel Ebersole	Carl F. H. Henry
Joseph Bayly	Samuel Escobar	Paul Henry
Ruth L. Bentley	Warren C. Falcon	Clarence Hilliard
William Bentley	Frank Gaebelein	Walden Howard
Dale Brown	Sharon Gallagher	Rufus Jones
James C. Cross	Theodore E. Gannon	Robert Tad Lehe
Donald Dayton	Art Gish	William Leslie
Roger Dewey	Vernon Grounds	C. T. McIntire

Wes Michaelson
David O. Moberg
Stephen Mott
Richard Mouw
David Nelson
F. Burton Nelson
William Pannell
John Perkins
William Petersen

Richard Pierard
Wyn Wright Potter
Ron Potter
Bernard Ramm
Paul Rees
Boyd Reese
Joe Roos
James Robert Ross
Eunice Schatz

Ronald J. Sider
Donna Simons
Lewis Smedes
Foy Valentine
Marlin VanElderen
Jim Wallis
Robert Webber
Merold Westphal
John Howard Yoder

ARCHIVES

=====

ACRC: Archives of the Christian Reformed Church, Calvin College, Grand
        Rapids, Michigan
BGCA: Billy Graham Center Archives, Wheaton, Illinois
BL: The Bancroft Library, University of California, Berkeley, California
CCA: Calvin College Archives. Grand Rapids, Michigan
ESAA: Evangelicals for Social Action Archives, Philadelphia, Pennsylvania
FTSA: Fuller Theological Seminary Archives, Pasadena, California
GTUA: Graduate Theological Union Archives, Berkeley, California
HIA: Hoover Institution Archives, Palo Alto, California
MCA: Mennonite Church Archives, Goshen, Indiana.
MCPA: Miller Center of Public Affairs, University of Virginia, Charlottesville,
        Virginia
WCSC: Wheaton College Special Collections, Wheaton, Illinois
WCA: Wheaton College Archives, Wheaton, Illinois

NOTES

Introduction

1. Marjorie Hyer, "Social and Political Activism Is Aim of Evangelical Group," *Washington Post*, November 30, 1973, D17. Also see Hyer, "Evangelicals: Tackling the Gut Issues," *Christian Century* 90, 46 (December 19, 1973): 1244–45; Roy Larson, "Historic Workshop: Evangelicals Do U-Turn Take on Social Problems," *Chicago Sun-Times*, December 1, 1973.

2. Marjorie Hyer, "Evangelical Protestants Turn Political," *Washington Post*, December 28, 1973, C13; Ron Sider, "An Historic Moment," in *The Chicago Declaration*, ed. Ron Sider (Carol Stream, Ill.: Creation House, 1974), 25, 29.

3. Richard Quebedeaux, *The Young Evangelicals: Revolution in Orthodoxy* (New York: Harper and Row, 1974).

4. "Born Again! The Year of the Evangelicals," *Newsweek* (October 25, 1976): 75.

5. On the paucity of helpful data on evangelicals and politics in the twentieth century, see Lyman A. Kellstedt and Mark A. Noll, "Religion, Voting for President, and Party Identification, 1948–1984," in *Religion and American Politics: From the Colonial Period to the 1980s*, ed. Luke Harlow (New York: Oxford University Press, 1990), 255–79. Increasingly, denominational identifiers mean less than other groupings such as "evangelical" or "charismatic."

6. For recent work on the modern conservatism and the religious right, see Lisa McGirr, *Suburban Warriors: The Origins of the New American Right* (Princeton, N.J.: Princeton University Press, 2001); David Farber and Jeff Roche, eds., *The Conservative Sixties* (New York: Peter Lang, 2003); John G. Turner, *Bill Bright and Campus Crusade for Christ: The Renewal of Evangelicalism in Postwar America* (Chapel Hill: University of North Carolina Press, 2008); Steven P. Miller, *Billy Graham and the Rise of the Republican South* (Philadelphia: University of Pennsylvania Press, 2009); Darren Dochuk, *From Bible Belt to Sunbelt: Plain-Folk Religion, Grassroots Politics, and the Rise of Evangelical Conservatism* (New York: Norton, 2010); Daniel K. Williams, *God's Own Party: The Making of the Christian Right* (New York: Oxford University Press, 2010). For several studies of non-evangelical religious progressivism, see David Chappell, *A Stone of Hope: Prophetic Religion and the Death of Jim Crow* (Chapel Hill: University of North Carolina Press, 2004); Susan Curtis: *A Consuming Faith: The Social Gospel and*

Modern American Culture (Baltimore: Johns Hopkins University Press, 1991); Doug Rossinow, *The Politics of Authenticity: Liberalism, Christianity, and the New Left in America* (New York: Columbia University Press, 1998); Jared Roll, *Spirit of Rebellion: Labor and Religion in the New Cotton South* (Urbana: University of Illinois Press, 2010).

For journalistic accounts of the evangelical left, see Quebedeaux, *The Young Evangelicals*; Quebedeaux, *The Worldly Evangelicals* (New York: Harper and Row, 1978); Carol Flake, *Redemptorama: Culture, Politics, and the New Evangelicalism* (Garden City, N.Y.: Anchor, 1984). The few scholarly works include James Davison Hunter, "The New Class and the Young Evangelicals," *Review of Religious Research* 22, 2 (December 1980): 155–69; Robert Booth Fowler, *A New Engagement: Evangelical Political Thought, 1966–1976* (Grand Rapids, Mich.: Eerdmans, 1982); Kyle Cleveland, "The Politics of Jubilee: Ideological Drift and Organizational Schism in a Religious Sect," Ph.D. dissertation, Temple University, 1990; Boyd T. Reese, Jr., "Resistance and Hope: The Interplay of Theological Synthesis, Biblical Interpretation, Political Analysis, and Praxis in the Christian Radicalism of 'Sojourners' Magazine," Ph.D. dissertation, Temple University, 1991; Brantley Gasaway, "An Alternative Soul of Politics: The Rise of Contemporary Progressive Evangelicalism," Ph.D. dissertation, University of North Carolina, 2008.

7. On the Religion and Politics 2000 survey investigated by Robert Wuthnow of Princeton University, see Corwin E. Smidt, "Evangelical and Mainline Protestants at the Turn of the Millennium: Taking Stock and Looking Forward," in *From Pews to Polling Places: Faith and Politics in the American Religious Mosaic*, ed. J. Matthew Wilson (Washington, D.C.: Georgetown University Press, 2007), 43. On the insufficiency of the prevailing liberal-conservative dichotomy, see Douglas Jacobsen and William Vance Trollinger, Jr., eds., *Re-Forming the Center: American Protestantism, 1900 to the Present* (Grand Rapids, Mich.: Eerdmans, 1998). For more on evangelical voting patterns, see Albert J. Menendez, *Evangelicals at the Ballot Box* (Amherst, N.Y.: Prometheus, 1996).

8. Gordon Spykman, "The Tower of Babel Revisited," *Vanguard* (July–August 1975): 24.

9. Curtis J. Evans, "White Evangelical Protestant Responses to the Civil Rights Movement," *Harvard Theological Review* 102, 2 (2009): 261.

10. Sider quoted in Michael Cromartie, "Fixing the World: From Nonplayers to Radicals to New Right Conservatives: The Saga of Evangelicals and Social Action," *Christianity Today* 36, 5 (April 27, 1992): 25.

Chapter 1. Carl Henry and Neo-Evangelical Social Engagement

Epigraph: Carl F. H. Henry, *The Uneasy Conscience of Modern Fundamentalism* (Grand Rapids: Eerdmans, 1947), 35.

1. Breese quoted in Jim Wallis, *The Call to Conversion* (New York: Harper & Row, 1981), 23. Anderson quoted in James C. Hefley and Edward E. Plowman, *Washington: Christians in the Corridors of Power* (Wheaton, Ill.: Tyndale House, 1975), 195.

2. George Marsden, *Fundamentalism and American Culture*, rev. ed. (New York: Oxford University Press, 2006), 120, 231–32.

3. On the political impotence of fundamentalism, see Mark A. Noll, "The Scandal of Evangelical Political Reflection," in *Being Christian Today: An American Conversation*, ed. Richard John Neuhaus and George Weigel (Washington, D.C.: Ethics and Public Policy Center, 1992), 81; Dean C. Curry, "Biblical Politics and Foreign Policy," in *Evangelicals and Foreign Policy: Four Perspectives*, ed. Michael Cromartie (Washington, D.C.: Ethics and Foreign Policy Center, 1989), 44. On rebuilding fundamentalist evangelical organizations, see Joel Carpenter, *Revive Us Again: The Reawakening of American Fundamentalism* (New York: Oxford University Press, 1997). On the marginalization of Hargis and McIntire from the evangelical mainstream, see Robert Booth Fowler, *A New Engagement: Evangelical Political Thought, 1966–1976* (Grand Rapids, Mich.: Eerdmans, 1982), 10–12. On evangelical apoliticism, see Lyman A. Kellstedt, "Religion, Voting for President, and Party Identification," in *Religion and American Politics*, ed. Mark A. Noll (New York: Oxford University Press, 1990), 371.

4. Carl Henry, *Confessions of a Theologian: An Autobiography* (Waco, Tex.: Word, 1986), 15–59.

5. George M. Marsden, *Evangelicalism and Modern America* (Grand Rapids, Mich.: Eerdmans, 1984), xv; Henry, *Confessions*, 69.

6. Paul M. Bechtel, *Wheaton College: A Heritage Remembered, 1860–1984* (Wheaton, Ill.: H. Shaw, 1984), 122, 177–83, 214; Henry, *Confessions*, 64–65.

7. On government aid to evangelical colleges, see Bechtel, *A Heritage Remembered*, 252; Joseph A. Thacker, *Asbury College: Vision and Miracle* (Nappanee, Ind.: Evangel Press, 1990), 184; Michael Hamilton, "The Fundamentalist Harvard: Wheaton College and the Continuing Vitality of American Evangelicalism, 1919–1965," Ph.D. dissertation, University of Notre Dame, 1995, 123, 252–55; Chester E. Finn, Jr., *Scholars, Dollars, and Bureaucrats* (Washington, D.C.: Brookings Institution, 1978), 14; Axel R. Schäfer, "The Cold War State and the Resurgence of Evangelicalism: A Study of the Public Funding of Religion Since 1945," *Radical History Review* 99 (Fall 2007): 29–37; Robert Burkinshaw, "The Funding of Evangelical Higher Education in the United States and Canada in the Postwar Period," 290, and Michael Hamilton, "More Money, More Ministry: The Financing of American Evangelicalism Since 1945," in *More Money, More Ministry: Money and Evangelicals in Recent North American History*, ed. Larry Eskridge and Mark A. Noll (Grand Rapids, Mich.: Eerdmans, 2000), 134.

8. On evangelical rates of college attendance, see John Stephen Hendricks, "Religious and Political Fundamentalism: The Links between Alienation and Ideology," Ph.D. dissertation, University of Michigan, 1977. On government aid and rapid growth at other evangelical schools, see Thacker, *Vision and Miracle*, 185–93, 226; Lyle Charles Hillegas, "A History of Westmont College," Ph.D. dissertation, Dallas Theological Seminary, 1964, 151–60.

9. On Wheaton's improving academic credentials, see Bechtel, *Heritage Remembered*, 133, 235. On Clark's Reformed vision, see Carpenter, *Revive Us Again*, 192. On

Fuller, see George Marsden, *Reforming Fundamentalism: Fuller Seminary and the New Evangelicalism* (Grand Rapids, Mich.: Eerdmans, 1987). Fuller's faculty included Harold Lindsell (Wheaton, UC-Berkeley, Harvard); Burton Goddard (Wheaton, Westminster Seminary, Harvard); Edward John Carnell (Wheaton, Westminster, Harvard); Paul King Jewett (Wheaton, Westminster, Harvard); Charles G. Chaeffele (Wheaton, Westminster, Harvard).

10. On the new image of evangelicalism, see Kathryn Long, "In the Modern World, but Not of It: The 'Auca Martyrs,' Evangelicalism, and Postwar American Culture," in *Foreign Missionary Enterprise at Home*, ed. Daniel Bays and Grant Wacker (Tuscaloosa: University of Alabama Press, 2003), 229.

11. Donald W. Dayton, *Discovering an Evangelical Heritage* (New York: Harper & Row, 1976).

12. On Henry's premillennialism, see David Harrington Watt, "The Private Hopes of American Fundamentalists and Evangelicals, 1925–1975," *Religion and American Culture* 1, 2 (Summer 1991): 162. On the Fuller faculty's views of dispensationalism, see William LaSor, review of *Our Blessed Hope* in *Theology News & Notes* 3, 4 (July 1956): 2; John A. D'Elia, *A Place at the Table: George Eldon Ladd and the Rehabilitation of Evangelical Scholarship in America* (New York: Oxford University Press, 2008). For more on new evangelical repudiation of dispensationalism, see Donald W. Dayton and Robert K. Johnston, *The Variety of American Evangelicalism* (Knoxville: University of Tennessee Press, 1991), 30. On having to defend sympathies for dispensationalism at Fuller, see Daniel P. Fuller, "Report on Visit of President Hubbard and Dean Fuller with Dr. Edward Hayes," June 12, 1967, FTSA.

13. Carl F. H. Henry, "Is Evangelical Theology Changing?" *Christian Life* 17, 11 (March 1956): 16–19; Henry, "Dare We Renew the Controversy?" *Christianity Today* 1, 19 (June 24, 1957): 23–26; Henry, "What Is Fundamentalism?" *United Evangelical Action* (July 16, 1966): 303; Calvin Veltman, "Farewell to Fundamentalism," *Wheaton Record* 85, 16 (January 10, 1963): 2.

14. Henry, *Uneasy Conscience*, 17, 20, 68. On *Uneasy Conscience* as "a bombshell," see Linder, "The Resurgence of Evangelical Social Concern (1925–1975)," 221.

15. Henry, *Uneasy Conscience*, 11, 35, 65.

16. On Henry's ambiguous political orientation, see Henry, *Uneasy Conscience*, 73, 85–86; Louis Smedes, "The Evangelicals and the Social Question," *Reformed Journal* 16 (February 1966): 9–13.

17. Henry, *Uneasy Conscience*, 32, 71; Smedes, "Evangelicals and the Social Question," 32, 71, 73. On the growth of the new evangelicalism, see Carpenter, *Revive Us Again*, 24.

18. For examples of the fundamentalist rejection of *Uneasy Conscience*, see George W. Dollar, *A History of Fundamentalism in America* (Greenville, S.C.: Bob Jones University Press, 1973), 203–11; Robert Lightner, *Neo-Evangelicalism* (Findlay, Ohio: Dunham, 1961), 115–44; Charles Woodbridge, *The New Evangelicalism* (Greenville, S.C.: Bob Jones University Press, 1969). On Henry's inspiration of Hubbard, see David Allan

Hubbard, "An Ecumenical Experiment," lecture delivered at Drew University, October 23, 1979, 15, FTSA.

19. On *Christianity Today*'s early years, see Henry, *Confessions of a Theologian*. On the symbolism of its headquarters, see "Why Christianity Today?" *Christianity Today* 1, 1 (October 15, 1956): 20–21. On its rapid rise in the evangelical consciousness, see "Conservatism Today," *Time* 80, 2 (July 13, 1962). In his autobiography Henry recounts the hundreds of television, radio, and print outlets that regularly quoted the magazine in its early years: *Confessions*, 179–81. For the "triple melting pot," see Will Herberg, *Protestant, Catholic, Jew: An Essay in American Religious Sociology* (Garden City, N.Y.: Doubleday, 1955). On evangelicalism's reputation among the liberal elite, see, for instance, James T. Fisher, "American Religion Since 1945," in *A Companion to Post-1945 America* (Malden, Mass.: Blackwell, 2002), 50. For *Christianity Today* subscription figures see Curtis J. Evans, "White Evangelical Protestant Responses to the Civil Rights Movement," *Harvard Theological Review* 102, 2 (2009): 262.

20. On being apolitical and conservative, see Dayton, *Discovering an Evangelical Heritage*, 2.

21. On civil rights, see Henry, "What Social Structures?" *Reformed Journal* 16 (May–June 1966): 6–7. On social transformation as rooted in spiritual revival, see "The Church and Political Pronouncements," *Christianity Today* 8, 23 (August 28, 1964): 29–30. For Henry's warnings about politics, see "Southern Baptists and Society," *Christianity Today* 11, 14 (April 14, 1967): 46–47; Adon Taft, "The Gospel in a Social Context," *Christianity Today* 11, 19 (June 23, 1967): 33–34; "Christian Social Action," *Christianity Today* 13, 12 (March 14, 1969): 24–25; "Editorial," *Christianity Today* 12, 7 (January 5, 1968): 26–27; "Why *Christianity Today*?" 20–21. On "Bible to the ballot box," see Henry, "What Social Structures?" 6–7.

22. On "the American Way of Death," see Richard Forbes, "Is Urbana Really Lost," *Vanguard* (December 31, 1970), copy in Box 68, Folder 7, "Urbana 1961–1974," InterVarsity Collection, BGCA.

Chapter 2. John Alexander and Racial Justice

Epigraph: John Alexander, "I'm All Fired Up!" *Freedom Now* 1, 2 (October 1965): 3.

1. For "individualistic approach," see Curtis J. Evans, "White Evangelical Protestant Responses to the Civil Rights Movement," *Harvard Theological Review* 102, 2 (2009): 245. For "faith is personal," see Jim Wallis interview by Terry Gross on *Fresh Air*, National Public Radio, January 20, 2005.

2. On coverage of race relations in *Christianity Today*, see Michael O. Emerson and Christian Smith, *Divided by Faith: Evangelical Religion and the Problem of Race in America* (New York: Oxford University Press, 2001), 46. For Graham on King, see "Billy Graham Urges Restraint in Sit-Ins," *New York Times*, April 18, 1963, 21; Steven

P. Miller, *Billy Graham and the Rise of the Republican South* (Philadelphia: University of Pennsylvania Press, 2009), 91–96; Richard V. Pierard, "From Evangelical Exclusivism to Ecumenical Openness: Billy Graham and Sociopolitical Issues," *Journal of Ecumenical Studies* 20, 3 (Summer 1983): 429–32. For Niebuhr's "pietistic individualism," see Evans, "White Evangelical Responses," 254–55.

3. For several exceptions to the absence of evangelical participation in civil rights historiography, see Charles Marsh, *God's Long Summer: Faith and Civil Rights* (Princeton: Princeton University Press, 1999); David L. Chappell, *A Stone of Hope: Prophetic Religion and the Death of Jim Crow* (Chapel Hill: University of North Carolina Press, 2004). On Dayton's civil rights activity, see Donald W. Dayton, *Discovering an Evangelical Heritage* (New York: Harper & Row, 1976), 4; Dayton, "An Autobiographical Response," in *From the Margins: A Celebration of the Theological Work of Donald W. Dayton*, ed. Christian T. Collins Winn (Eugene, Ore.: Pickwick Press, 2007), 399–400. On Lewis and InterVarsity, see Russell Maatman, "Report from Ole Miss," *HIS* 23, 8 (May 1963): 1–3; "Feedback: A Debate on Integration," *HIS* 24, 6 (May 1963): 26–27; Ruth Lewis, "New Face at Alabama," *HIS* 28, 9 (May 1964): 11–13. On civil rights advocacy at Wheaton, see "S.C. Civil Rights Committee Views Local Discrimination," *Wheaton Record* 85, 9 (November 1, 1962): 1; Steve Mott, "Grad Student Replies to Colleague's Letter," *Wheaton Record* 87, 6 (October 29, 1964): 2. Also see Paul Henry, "De Jure," *Wheaton Record* 85, 5 (October 4, 1962): 2; "Midwest Students Critically Discuss Civil Rights Acts," *Wheaton Record* 87, 11 (December 3, 1964): 4. On Calvin, see Robert VanDellen, "Just How, Senator?" *Chimes* 59, 3 (October 2, 1964): 2; Mark Wagenveld, "Neighborhood Association Copes with Area Racial Problems," *Chimes* 59, 3 (October 2, 1964): 1; Marlin VanElderen, "The Anti-Social Gospel," *Chimes* 60, 3 (October 1, 1965): 3; Lois Short, "Students Join March to Protest Civil Rights Death," *Chimes* 59, 20 (March 19, 1965): 3. On the march to Montgomery, see Stoney Cooks, "Memories of the March," 216–17, in Howell Raines, *My Soul Is Rested: Movement Days in the Deep South Remembered* (New York: Penguin, 1983). Cooks later became civil rights leader Andrew Young's administrative assistant. For other evangelical groups who traveled to Selma in 1965, see Elizabeth O'Connor, *Journey Inward, Journey Outward* (New York: Harper & Row, 1968), 138–41. Calling the march a "transcendent" experience in the next week's sermon, Cosby preached "that to be in Selma was to touch a spirit and go away changed. 'What I saw there was a people being wounded for our transgressions, who were being bruised for our iniquities.'" On Elm-LaSalle Bible Church, see James Hefley and Marti Hefley, *The Church That Takes on Trouble: The Story of Chicago's Historic Lasalle Street Church* (Elgin, Ill.: Cook, 1976), 56. On two carloads from Christian Reformed churches in New York City, see Edson Lewis, Jr., "We Went to Alabama," *Reformed Journal* 15 (April 1965): 3–5. On Fuller students, see David Allan Hubbard, "Lecture Two: An Academic Adventure," delivered at Drew University, October 23, 1979, in "Marsden Notes" folder, FTSA. Fuller also sent a faculty and student representative to Martin Luther King, Jr.'s funeral in Memphis in 1968. On Frank Gaebelein, evangelical pastor and future edi-

tor of *Christianity Today* who joined King on marches and voter registration drives in Selma in 1965, see Michael Cromartie, "Fixing the World: From Nonplayers to Radicals to New Right Conservatives: The Saga of Evangelicals and Social Action," *Christianity Today* 36, 5 (April 27, 1992): 24. Inspired by civil rights speeches and shocked by the confrontation with state police at the Alabama River during the day, two Wheaton students were physically assaulted by white segregationists later in the evening. They breathlessly told a *Record* reporter, "The scum who carry out these activities are supported by the system which presently exists—and this system must be smashed by a bold show of Christian love." See "Seniors Travel to Alabama, Engage in Peaceful Protest," *Wheaton Record* 87, 23 (March 18, 1965): 1, 5.

4. On Goldwater and pro-civil rights sentiment at Wheaton, see Dan Kuhn, "Kuhn Explains Convictions Behind Civil Rights Picketing," *Wheaton Record* 87, 3 (October 8, 1964): 4; Paul Henry, "De Jure," *Wheaton Record* 85, 5 (October 4, 1962): 2; "Mississippi Profs Leave University as a Result of Integration Dispute," *Wheaton Record* 85, 19 (February 7, 1963): 5; and "Midwest Students Critically Discuss Civil Rights Acts," *Wheaton Record* 87, 11 (December 3, 1964): 4; "Johnson for President," *Wheaton Record* 87, 5 (October 23, 1964): 12; Dan Kuhn, "Kuhn Explains Convictions Behind Civil Rights Picketing," *Wheaton Record* 87, 3 (October 8, 1964): 4.

5. Fred Alexander, "White Pastor, Black Church," *Freedom Now* 5, 6 (November–December 1969): 21–23; Kyle Cleveland, "The Politics of Jubilee: Ideological Drift and Organizational Schism in a Religious Sect," Ph.D. dissertation, Temple University, 1990, 47–51.

6. John Alexander, "Stages in the Journey," *The Other Side* (March–April 1990): 50; Alexander, "Taking Jesus Seriously," *The Other Side* 21, 7 (October 1985): 10–15; Alexander, "White Pastor, Black Church," 21–23.

7. On the early years of *Freedom Now*, see Mark Olson, "Beyond the Horizon," *The Other Side* 21, 7 (October 1985): 16–17; "Past Epistles," *The Other Side* 21, 7 (October 1985): 22–23; Cleveland, "Politics of Jubilee," 124.

8. On *Freedom Now*'s new evangelical constituency, see Alexander, "Taking Jesus Seriously," 10–11; Fred Alexander, "Integration Now," *Freedom Now* 1, 3 (December 1965): 3; "Social Concern," *Freedom Now* 3, 3 (May–June 1967): 3.

9. On Wheaton students and faculty who supported and wrote for *Freedom Now*, see "Alexander Edits Civil Rights Magazine, 'Freedom Now!'" *Wheaton Record* 91, 10 (November 22, 1968): 4; "About the Writers" and "In This Issue," *The Other Side* 7, 1 (January–February 1971): 2, 33; Mark Olson interview by author, South Bend, Indiana, May 21, 2009. For examples of anti-segregation rhetoric at Wheaton, see Bill Larkin, "Racial Progress in Suburbia," *Wheaton Record* 88, 13 (December 16, 1965): 2; James O. Buswell, III, *Slavery, Segregation, and Scripture* (Grand Rapids, Mich.: Eerdmans, 1964).

10. Other key black evangelical voices included Michael Haynes, minister of a Baptist church in Boston and representative in the Massachusetts legislature; James Earl Massey, campus pastor and professor at Anderson College; Samuel Hines, son of a Jamaican fundamentalist preacher; theologian William Bentley; Ruth Lewis Bentley,

a sociologist who taught at Trinity College and the University of Illinois Medical Center; Columbus Salley, author with Ronald Behm of *Your God Is Too White* (Downers Grove, Ill.: InterVarsity, 1970); Ron Potter, a leader in Voice of Calvary Ministries in Jackson, Mississippi; and Clarence Hilliard of Chicago's interracial Circle Church. Many were personal friends of King. On black evangelicals and King, see Emerson and Smith, *Divided by Faith*, 54.

11. For biographical details on Perkins, see Will Norton, Jr., "I Wouldn't Expect Humans to Believe This," *The Other Side* 7, 5 (September–October 1971): 8–12, 38–40; Charles Marsh, *Beloved Community: How Faith Shapes Social Justice* (New York: Basic Books, 2005), 5, 170–72, 183–84; John Perkins, *Let Justice Roll Down: John Perkins Tells His Own Story* (Glendale, Calif.: G/L Regal Books, 1976), 160–79; Perkins interview by Paul Ericksen, June 1991, transcript in John M. Perkins Collection, BGCA. On Perkins's beating, see "Hotheads and Professionals," *Time* 96, 6 (August 10, 1970), 42–43.

12. On Skinner, see McCandlish Phillips, "Evangelist Finds Harlem Vineyard," *New York Times* August 16, 1964, 78; "Religion: Preachers of an Active Gospel," *Time*, September 19, 1969; Tom Skinner, *How Black Is the Gospel?* (Philadelphia: Lippincott, 1970), 69, 90; Edward Gilbreath, "A Prophet out of Harlem: Willing to Tell the Hard Truth, Evangelist Tom Skinner Inspired a Generation of Leaders," *Christianity Today* 40, 16 (September 16, 1996): 36–43; Fred Alexander, "The Ultimate Insult," *Freedom Now* 3, 1 (January–February 1967): 8–9, 16; "NAE and NNEA," *Freedom Now* 4, 4 (July–August 1968): 22; "Books by Black Evangelicals," *Freedom Now* 5, 5 (September–October 1969): 30; "Tom Skinner Too Radical for WMBI," *The Other Side* 7, 3 (Summer 1971): 32–33; Tom Skinner, "Black Power," *The Other Side* 8, 1 (January–February 1972): 6–11.

13. For Pannell's contributions to *Freedom Now*, see William Pannell, "Memorial to Martin Luther King, Jr." *Freedom Now* 4, 3 (May–June 1968): 4–5; "Books by Black Evangelicals," *Freedom Now* 5, 5 (September–October 1969); "Conference on Faith and History," *The Other Side* 6, 2 (March–April 1970): 25; Pannell, "How Blacks Must Change," *The Other Side* 7, 1 (January–February 1971): 16–20; Pannell, "Maybe," *The Other Side* 7, 3 (Summer 1971): 29–31. For criticism of evangelical political conservatism, see William Pannell, *My Friend, the Enemy* (Waco, Tex.: Word, 1968), 1–53, 62; "Books by Black Evangelicals," *Freedom Now*.

14. On the new focus on race after Urbana '67, see "Student Resolution, African Students," December 30, 1967, Box 52, Folder 3, "Pannell, William: 1967–1970," InterVarsity Collection, BGCA; Keith Hunt and Gladys M. Hunt, *For Christ and the University: The Story of InterVarsity Christian Fellowship of the U.S.A., 1940–1990* (Downers Grove, Ill.: InterVarsity Press, 1991), 252–53; John F. Alexander, "Thinking White," *HIS* 30, 4 (January 1970): 9; Columbus Salley and Ronald Behm, "The Bible and Black Theology," *HIS* 30, 6 (March 1970): 1. On "impatience toward racism," see Marvin Mayers, "An Anthropologist Looks at Urbana," *HIS* 28, 9 (June 1968): 8. On Ellis and InterVarsity, see Gilbreath, "Prophet out of Harlem," 36; Ken Ripley, "I-V 'Umbrella' for Blacks?" *The Branch* 1, 9 (May 21, 1973): 6.

15. Copy of audio tape in author's possession; Richard Hauser, "Missionary Convention Bids for New Concept," *Los Angeles Times*, January 2, 1971, 27. On Pannell's reaction, see Gilbreath, "A Prophet out of Harlem," 42.

16. On Skinner's criticism of the black church, see Tom Skinner, *Black and Free* (Grand Rapids, Mich.: Zondervan, 1968), 39. For similar statements, see Howard O. Jones, *Shall We Overcome* (New York: Fleming Revell, 1966); John Perkins, "Black Religion," *The Other Side* 8, 1 (January–February 1972): 24–29. On the emerging Black Power movement, see Harold Cruse, *The Crisis of the Negro Intellectual* (New York: William Morrow, 1967); W. L. Van Deburg, *New Day in Babylon: The Black Culture Movement and American Culture, 1965-1975* (Chicago: University of Chicago Press, 1992). On Jesus and Barabbas, see Skinner, *How Black Is the Gospel?* 95–96. For Potter's evaluation of Skinner, see Gilbreath, "A Prophet out of Harlem," 40.

17. On King's rebuff of Black Power, see Martin Luther King, Jr., *Where Do We Go from Here: Chaos or Community?* (New York: Harper & Row, 1967), 52. On black evangelical statements in favor of racial reconciliation, see Skinner, *How Black Is the Gospel?*, 97; Salley and Behm, *Your God Is Too White*, 98. On Skinner at Wheaton, see Gilbreath, "A Prophet out of Harlem," 40. On Skinner at Urbana '70, see Ron Mitchell, *Organic Faith: A Call to Authentic Christianity* (Chicago: Cornerstone Press, 1997), 112.

18. On race as overblown, see Dave Rockness and Bill Dyrness, "Hurt Minority Means Missed Goal?" *Wheaton Record* 87, 32 (May 27, 1965): 2. On the lack of support for the NAACP chapter, see Paul M. Bechtel, *Wheaton College: A Heritage Remembered, 1860-1984* (Wheaton, Ill.: H. Shaw, 1984), 285; "Campus NAACP Wins Charter Approval," *Wheaton Record* 87, 23 (March 18, 1965): 4. On black students' complaints about discrimination and discomfort on Wheaton's lily-white campus, see Ted Ryan, "Schoenherr Denies Charges of Discriminatory Practices," *Wheaton Record* 87, 11 (December 3, 1964): 4; So Yan Pul, "Senior Deprecates Racial Attitudes," *Wheaton Record* 88, 18 (February 10, 1966): 4; Steve Aulie, "Worse Riots This Summer, Civil Rights Leader Predicts," *Wheaton Record* 90, 20 (March 22, 1968): 4; Ron Thomas, "We Discuss Racism as a Problem, Ignore Blatant Practice," *Wheaton Record* 92, 17 (February 13, 1970): 4; Ron Potter, "The 'Black Problem' Is Your Problem," *Wheaton Record* 82, 19 (February 27, 1970): 3. See especially the weekly 1972 *Record* column called "Black Light." On the failure of a minority recruitment program designed to bring in black and Puerto Rican students from Chicago and New York City, see Bechtel, *A Heritage Remembered,* 286. On conflict between black youths and Wheaton students at LaSalle Church in Chicago, see Hefley, *Church That Takes on Trouble*, 83. On banning *Freedom Now* in the bookstore, see Philip Harnden, "Remembering John," *The Other Side* 37, 5 (September 2001): 9.

19. On Potter, see Paul Potter, *A Name for Ourselves: Feelings About Authentic Identity, Love, Intuitive Politics, Us* (Boston: Little, Brown, 1971).

20. On the "personal view" of the gospel, see Jim Wallis, *Revive Us Again: A Sojourner's Story* (Nashville: Abingdon Press, 1983), 24. For subscription numbers, see Cleveland, "The Politics of Jubilee," 124.

21. For examples of the repudiation of black inferiority and segregation, see John Alexander, "Ham and the Curse, or the Biblical Inferiority of the Negro?" *Freedom Now* 1, 2 (October 1965); W. B. Wallis, "The Bounds of their Habituation," *Freedom Now* 2, 4 (August–September 1966). On the *Freedom Now* campaign to support interracial couples, see Dan Orme, "The Bible and Interracial Marriage," *Freedom Now* 3, 2 (March–April 1967): 10–13; Fred Alexander, "Moody, Intermarriage, and the Bible," *The Other Side* 6, 3 (May–June 1970): 24–26. On *Freedom Now's* initial suspicion of civil rights activism, see "Books in Review," *Freedom Now* 3, 5 (September–October 1967): 19; Pannell, "Memorial to Martin Luther King, Jr.," 4–5; "The Social Gospel and the Black Preacher," *The Other Side* 8, 2 (March–April 1972): 41; C. Herbert Oliver, *No Flesh Shall Glory* (Philadelphia: Presbyterian and Reformed Publishing, 1959).

22. On young evangelical criticism of their parents' failure to support civil rights, see Fred Smith and Jay Hakes, "Evangelical Pulpits Silent on Civil Rights," *Wheaton Record* 88, 12 (January 6, 1966): 2; Dayton, *Discovering an Evangelical Heritage*, 3. On "Negro evangelism," see Dan Orme, "Black Power and the Church of Jesus Christ," *Freedom Now* 4, 3 (May–June 1968): 16–17, 21. On black rage against white evangelicals, see Joseph Grabill, "Black and Jesus: A Personal Reflection," *Freedom Now* 5, 4 (July–August 1969): 22–25. Grabill of Normal, Illinois, wrote, "A year ago I did not quite understand when a black person with whom I had spent a lot of time said to me right after Martin Luther King, Jr.'s, death. 'I hate all white people.' There was an embarrassing silence. Finally I hazarded a painful question, 'Even me?' 'Yes, you.'" On "Whitey's religion," see an undated, untitled document that begins "Dear Brothers and Sisters," in Box 2, "Jill Shook, Jack Sparks' letters," CWLF Collection, GTUA. On the "door to Negro evangelism," see "Statement of Purpose," *Freedom Now* 4, 3 (May–June 1968): 28. For criticism of "old style evangelism," see John F. Alexander, "Communications Conference," *Freedom Now* 4, 3 (May–June 1968): 11.

23. On progress in integration, see Jim Wallis, "America's Original Sin: The Legacy of White Racism," *Sojourners* 16, 10 (November 1987): 14–17. On the integration of Wheaton's barbershops, see "S.C. Civil Rights Committee Views Local Discrimination," *Wheaton Record* 85, 9 (November 1, 1962): 1. On King's assassination, see Alexander, "Communications Conference," 12; Alexander, "Taking Jesus Seriously," 10–15; Alexander, "A Time to Act," *Freedom Now* 4, 3 (May–June 1968): 3.

24. On Potter, see Charles Troutman to John Alexander, May 4, 1965, Box 41, Folder 13, "Association for the Coordination of University Religious Affairs, 1965–1975," Inter-Varsity Christian Fellowship Collection, BGCA. On Abernathy, see "Abernathy Urges Brotherhood; Graham Criticized," *Jet* 36, 26 (October 2, 1969): 50; Hayes Minnick, "Billy Graham: Champion of Compromise and Confusion." On Skinner, see "The Gospel with Candor," *Christianity Today* 11, 1 (October 14, 1966): 53. For Gaebelein, see Albert R. Beck, "All Truth Is God's Truth: The Life and Ideas of Frank E. Gaebelein," Ph.D. dissertation, Baylor University, 2008, 335.

25. On the lack of attention to domestic issues, see William Bentley, "The Other America," *The Other Side* 6, 1 (January–February 1970): 30–33. For "white Christ," see

Skinner, *How Black Is the Gospel?* 13, 69, 108–9, 120; Skinner, untitled article, *The Other Side* 6, 4 (July–August 1970): 34; Tom Skinner, "Jesus or Barabbas?" *Right On* 2, 21 (February 3, 1971): 1–2. For Perkins's "Demands," see Marsh, *Beloved Community*, 153–54.

26. For a sample of the vocations of *Freedom Now* contributors, see "The Writers," *The Other Side* 5, 3 (May–June 1969): 30. On the growing social sciences, see "Sociology Forum Questions Church Role, Pastorate as Highest Christian Vocation," *Wheaton Record* 88, 18 (February 10, 1966): 5; Mark Olson, "Radical Social Activists Blame Chicago Machine," *Wheaton Record* 90, 11 (December 8, 1967): 5; Alan Keith-Lucas, *Integrating Faith and Practice: A History of the North American Association of Christians in Social Work* (St. Davids, Pa.: North American Association of Christians in Social Work, 1994); David Moberg, *Inasmuch: Christian Social Responsibility in the Twentieth Century* (Grand Rapids, Mich.: Eerdmans, 1965): 154–57; Phil Harnden email interview by author, March 11, 2009.

27. On the Kerner Report and other examples of social scientific literature, see Wallis, *Revive Us Again*, 49; Post-American bibliography in Box VII7, Folder "People's Christian Coalition, Trinity," Sojourners Collection, WCSC; Don and Madelyn Powell, "We Stayed in the Inner City," *HIS* 30, 2 (November 1969): 18–19; William Bentley, "The Other America," *The Other Side* 6, 1 (January–February 1970): 30–33. On the black dialect, see Charles R. Taber, "Black Dialects," *The Other Side* 8, 1 (January–February 1972): 30–35. On sin as black, see Neta Jackson, "You've Read in Black and White," *Freedom Now* 5, 3 (May–June 1969): 16–22; Alison Short, "Sin Is Not Black" *Freedom Now* 5, 5 (September–October 1969): 26–27. On placing blacks in positions of power, see James O. Buswell III, "Sambo and Jim Crow," *The Other Side* 8, 1 (January–February 1972): 36–42.

28. On the magazine's new name, see Judy Alexander, "The Other Side," *The Other Side* 8, 4 (July–August 1972): 46–47. On the Poor People's Campaign, see Donald Oden, "On the Bus Back to Akron," *The Other Side* 4, 6 (November–December 1968): 21–22. On busing, see Loy, "Busing: The Real Issue," *The Other Side* 8, 4 (July–August 1972): 14; Steve Mott, "Busing and Racism in Boston," *Right On* 8, 2 (September–October 1976): 13.

29. On continued structural discrimination, see William Stringfellow, *My People Is the Enemy* (New York: Holt, Rinehart, 1964), 7–22, 111; Ka Tong Gaw, "Wheaton No Utopia," *Wheaton Record* 92, 19 (February 27, 1970): 4; Charles Furness, *The Christian and Social Action* (Old Tappan, N.J.: Fleming H. Revell Company, 1972), 35–44; David Gill, "More on School Busing," *Right On* 8, 4 (January–February 1977): 16; Ron Mitchell, "Christianity and American Racism, *Right On* 5, 9 (March 1974): 9–10; "Notes from the Catacomb," *Right On* 8, 2 (September–October 1976): 2; "The Church and Economics," *Right On* 8, 2 (September–October 1976): 6–7; David O. Moberg, *The Great Reversal: Evangelism Versus Social Concern* (Philadelphia: Lippincott, 1972), 120–49; Ron Sider, "Mischief by Statute: How We Oppress the Poor," *Christianity Today* 20, 21 (July 16, 1976): 14.

30. On ambivalence toward Black Power, see William H. Bentley, "Our Engagement with Black Power," paper read at national Negro Evangelical Association convention, Chicago, April 1968, cited in Ronald C. Potter, "Race, Theological Discourse & the Continuing American Dilemma," in *The Gospel in Black and White: Theological Resources for Racial Reconciliation*, ed. Dennis Ockholm (Downers Grove, Ill.: InterVarsity Press, 1997), 33. On the new ecumenical impulse and cooperation with government agencies and mainline denominations, see Hefley, *Church That Takes on Trouble*, 60, 85–86, 159; Elizabeth O'Connor, *Call to Commitment: The Story of the Church of the Saviour* (New York: Harper & Row, 1963), 18. Bill Leslie of Elm-LaSalle Church, for example, headed the Chicago-Orleans Housing Corporation and the Near North Area Council. Church of the Saviour in Washington, D.C., worked with the National and World Council of Churches. On Alexander's stress on salvation, see John Alexander, "Letters," *The Other Side* 8, 2 (March–April 1972): 6.

31. For "the other side of the world's affluence," see John Alexander, "A Politics of Love," *The Other Side* 8, 4 (July–August 1972): 2–3, 42–44; Robert D. Linder, "Politics: Spectators or Participants?" *The Other Side* 8, 4 (July–August 1972): 18–22. For "sitting comfortably," see John F. Alexander and Fred A. Alexander, "Repent and Revolt," *HIS* 29, 3 (December 1968): 1–2. On King and civil rights as a continuing inspiration for the evangelical left, see Danny Collum, "A Day for Beginnings," *Sojourners* 12, 8 (September 1983): 4–6; Danny Collum, "What Kind of Country?" *Sojourners* 12, 1 (January 1983): 3–4; Vincent Harding, "Struggle and Transformation: The Challenge of Martin Luther King, Jr.," *Sojourners* 13, 9 (October 1984): 18–21; the entire January 1986 issue of *Sojourners*; John F. Alexander, "The Authority of Scripture," *The Other Side* 9, 1 (January-February 1973): 45; Gerald Postema, "Why We Can't Wait," *Chimes* 63, 6 (October 25, 1968): 2; Marlin VanElderen, "Anyone Here for Sit-Ins?" *Chimes* 60, 6 (October 22, 1965): 2; Jay Hakes, "It's About Time Christians Joined War Protests," *Wheaton Record* 82, 3 (May 11, 1967): 3; Bill Pannell, Fred Alexander, and Vern Miller, "Memorial to Dr. Martin Luther King, Jr.," *Freedom Now* 4, 3 (May–June 1968): 4–7; Wesley Pippert, *Memo for 1976: Some Political Options* (Downers Grove, Ill.: InterVarsity Press, 1974), 28; Bill Pannell interview by author, July 13, 2006, Pasadena, California.

Chapter 3. Jim Wallis and Vietnam

Epigraph: Jim Wallis, *Revive Us Again* (Nashville: Abingdon Press, 1983), 53.

1. "Taking Jesus Seriously," *The Other Side* 20, 10 (October 1985): 11; Letter to the editor, *The Other Side* 7, 5 (September–October 1971): 6–7.

2. On the mainline response, see Anne C. Loveland, *American Evangelicals and the U.S. Military, 1942-1993* (Baton Rouge: Louisiana State Press, 1996), 119–20. On the new evangelical response, see Carl F. H. Henry, "Ignorance Often Has a Loud Voice," *Christianity Today* 9, 10 (February 12, 1965): 511; David Breese, "Highway to Viet Nam," *United Evangelical Action* 24, 10 (December 1965): 12–15.

3. On antiwar sentiment in InterVarsity, see John Howard Yoder, "Vietnam: A Just War?" *HIS* 28, 7 (April 1968): 1–3; "Vietnam: Another Option" *HIS* 28, 8 (May 1968): 8–11; Ancil K. Nance, Letter to the Editor, *HIS* 29, 6 (February 1965): 31. Also see other antiwar letters to the editor in the December 1964, February 1965, April 1968, and January–December 1969 issues of *HIS*. On Vietnam and just war theory, see Lewis Smedes, "On Picking and Choosing Wars," *Reformed Journal* 17, 2 (February 1967): 3–4. On the Post-American response, see notes from a diary of on a discussion on peacemaking led by Jim Wallis, April 12, 1979, Box VI8, Folder 6, "Elders' Group, 1971–1979," Sojourners Collection, WCSC.

4. On Vietnam and alienation, see Jim Wallis, *Revive Us Again* (Nashville: Abingdon Press, 1983), 51, 53, 62. Such narratives of quests for authenticity fill the historiography of modern industrial America. On the existential crises of turn-of-the-century American intellectuals and the alienation of mainline Protestant students in Austin, Texas, see T. J. Jackson Lears, *No Place of Grace: Antimodernism and the Transformation of American Culture, 1880–1920* (New York: Pantheon, 1981); Douglas C. Rossinow, *The Politics of Authenticity: Liberalism, Christianity, and the New Left in America* (New York: Columbia University Press, 1998). Scholars, however, have not examined young evangelicals who displayed much of the same kind of social and spiritual angst found in both Austin and the New Left's Port Huron Statement.

5. Jim Wallis, *The Call to Conversion* (New York: Harper & Row, 1981), 40; Wallis, *Revive Us Again*; Wallis, *Faith Works: How Faith-Based Organizations Are Changing Lives, Neighborhoods, and America* (Berkeley: PageMill Press, 2000), 7–10. On race, housing, and economics in postwar Detroit, see Thomas Sugrue, *The Origins of the Urban Crisis: Race and Inequality in Postwar Detroit* (Princeton: Princeton University Press, 1996).

6. On Wallis at Michigan State University, see Carol Langston, "Campus Rebel Finds New 'Revolt,'" *Tulsa Tribune*, March 26, 1971, 5B; "Crucible of Community," *Sojourners* 6, 1 (January 1977): 14; Student government candidate platform of Jim Wallis, Jim Moore, Bob Sabath, and Tom Morris, Box VII8, Folder 6, "Jim Wallis at Trinity," Sojourners Collection, WCSC; Wallis, *Call to Conversion*, xv. On "humanistic platitudes," see James H. Bowman, "They Oppose 'Personal Salvation in a Vacuum,'" *Chicago Daily News*, June 16–17, 1972, 37. On the self-immolation of the New Left, see Todd Gitlin, *The Sixties: Years of Hope, Days of Rage* (New York: Bantam, 1987), 285–438. For more evangelical critiques of SDS's spiritual vacuity, betrayal of participatory democracy, and descent into violence, see Richard Mouw interview by author, July 12, 2006, Pasadena, California; Wallis, *Faith Works*, 11–13; Jim Wallis, "The Movemental Church," *Post-American* 1, 2 (Winter 1972): 2–3; Os Guinness, *The Dust of Death: A Critique of the Establishment and the Counter Culture and the Proposal for a Third Way* (Downers Grove, Ill.: InterVarsity Press, 1973); "A Brief History of the Revolution," Box 2, "CWLF and Redeemer King Church," CWLF Collection, GTUA; Bill Kallio, "An American Tragedy: The Generation of Cynics," *Wheaton Record* 93, 6 (November 1970): 4; Bill Milliken, *So Long, Sweet Jesus: A Street Worker's*

Spiritual Odyssey (New York: Prometheus Press, 1973), 100; Schaeffer, *How Should We Then Live?* (Old Tappan, N.J.: Revell, 1976), 210; Pinnock, "Christian Revolution," *Post-American* 1, 1 (Fall 1971); Vernon Grounds, *Revolution and the Christian Faith* (Philadelphia: Lippincott, 1971), 160–79.

7. John Blake, "Progressive Preacher: As an Activist, Evangelical Christian, Jim Wallis Challenges Religious Right," *Atlanta Journal-Constitution*, May 21, 2005. For a clear statement by Wallis on spiritual conversion and how "oppression and death are swallowed up in Christ's victory," see Wallis, *Call to Conversion*, 160–69.

8. Jonathan Bonk phone interview by author, January 12, 2006.

9. Ibid.; "At Trinity—Students Are Niggers," circa May 1971, Box VII8, Folder 6, "Jim Wallis at Trinity," Sojourners Collection, WCSC; Wallis, *Revive Us Again*, 80; Kenneth S. Kantzer to students, June 3, 1971, Box VII8, Folder 6, "Jim Wallis at Trinity," Sojourners Collection, WCSC.

10. For Sabath, see "Magazine Helped Publish Church's Activism," *Milwaukee Journal*, April 11, 1979, copy in Box IV3, Folder 2, "News Releases," Sojourners Collections, WCSC. For the Deerfield Manifesto, see Boyd T. Reese, Jr., "Resistance and Hope: The Interplay of Theological Synthesis, Biblical Interpretation, Political Analysis, and Praxis in the Christian Radicalism of 'Sojourners' Magazine," Ph.D. dissertation, Temple University, 1991, 47. On the beginnings of the People's Christian Coalition, see "An Open Letter to Students and Trinity Evangelical Divinity School," circa Fall 1972, Box VII8, Folder 6, "Jim Wallis at Trinity," Sojourners Collection, WCSC; Wallis, *Revive Us Again*, 81; "Crucible of Community," 17; Kenneth S. Kantzer to Jim Wallis, April 10, 1973, Box VII8, Folder 6, "Jim Wallis at Trinity," Sojourners Collection, WCSC. On financial contributions to Trinity lost because of the notoriety of the Post-Americans, see Wallis, "The Business of Seminaries," *Sojourners* 6, 8 (August 1977): 6–7.

11. On the "American captivity of the church," see "A Joint Treaty of Peace between the People of the United States South Vietnam and North Vietnam," *Post-American* 1, 1 (Fall 1971): 15. On the first printing of the *Post-American*, see Wallis, *Revive Us Again*, 15–16.

12. On the growth of the *Post-American*, see "Crucible of Community," 16; Wallis, *Revive Us Again*, 87–89; "Newsletter 4," May 1972, and Minutes of the Peoples Christian Coalition, September 26, 1971, and "Newsletter 3," Box VII7, Folder 6, "Peoples Christian Coalition Trinity," Sojourners Collection, WCSC; Ed Spivey, Jr., email interview by author, June 22, 2005; John Stott, "Impressions of American Christianity," copy in Box VII8, Folder 6, "Jim Wallis at Trinity," Sojourners Collection, WCSC.

13. For a critique of conservative evangelical politics, see John Oliver, "A Failure of Evangelical Conscience," *Post-American* 4, 4 (May 1975): 26–30. For critiques of mainline liberalism, see Dale Suderman, "A Failure of Liberalism," *Post-American* 4, 8 (October–November 1975): 24; "What Is the People's Christian Coalition?" *Post-American* 1, 2 (Spring 1972): 14. For more on evangelical disillusionment with Protestant liberalism, see Leonard J. Sweet, "The 1960s: The Crises of Liberal Christianity

and the Public Emergence of Evangelicalism," in George Marsden, ed., *Evangelicalism and Modern America* (Grand Rapids, Mich.: Eerdmans, 1984), 29–45; Jason Bivins, *The Fracture of Good Order: Christian Antiliberalism and the Challenge to American Politics* (Chapel Hill: University of North Carolina Press, 2003).

14. On the liberal embrace of unlimited growth in the postwar era, see John Maynard Keynes, *The General Theory of Employment, Interest and Money* (London: Macmillan, 1936); Alan Brinkley, *The End of Reform: New Deal Liberalism in Recession and War* (New York: Vintage, 1995), 66. On the Post-Americans' critique of unlimited growth, see "People's Christian Coalition—Newsletter 1," July 1971, Box VII7, Folder "Peoples Christian Coalition—Trinity," Sojourners Collection, WCSC; Herb McMullan, "Man and Technocracy," *Post-American* 1, 2 (Winter 1971): 4–5. Also see Arthur G. Gish, "Simplicity," *Post-American* 1, 2 (Winter 1972): 10. On the number of anti-corporate articles in radical evangelical literature, see James Davison Hunter, "The New Class and the Young Evangelicals," *Review of Religious Research* 22, 2 (December 1980): 163; Michael Foley, "The Poverty of Enough," *Sojourners* 12, 8 (September 1983): 20–22.

15. On technology, see Jacques Ellul, *The Technological Society* (New York: Knopf, 1964), 25; Ellul, *Perspectives on Our Age* (New York: Seabury, 1981). For citations of Ellul in evangelical radical literature, see Lane Dennis, quoted in "A Conversation with Young Evangelicals," *Post-American* 4, 1 (January 1975): 8; Bonnie M. Greene, "Standing in Front of the Wrong Mirror," *Vanguard* (November 1972): 6; Egbert Schuurman, *Reflections on the Technological Society* (Toronto: Wedge Publishing Foundation, 1977). For criticism of infant formula, see James Huber, "The Deadly Formula: The Marketing of Baby Formula in the Third World," *Sojourners* 7, 9 (September 1978): 27–29. On the managerial implications of new technology, see Boyd Reese, "Structure of Power," *Post-American* 3, 1 (January 1974): 8.

16. Jim Wallis, "Invisible Empire," *Post-American* 2, 5 (November–December 1973): 1; William Appleman Williams, *The Tragedy of American Diplomacy* (Cleveland: World, 1959); Gabriel Kolko, *The Roots of American Foreign Policy* (Boston: Beacon Press, 1969); Merlo J. Pusey, *The U.S.A. Astride the Globe* (Boston: Houghton Mifflin, 1971). For Post-American citations of Williams, see "Bibliography: People's Christian Coalition, November 1971," Box VII7, Folder "Peoples Christian Coalition Trinity," in Sojourners Collection, WCSC; James R. Moore, "Mission as Subversion," *Post-American* 2, 5 (December 1973): 6; Reese, "Structure of Power," 8–9. On Barnet's close ties with evangelical institutions such as Church of the Saviour and InterVarsity, see B.B., "Before You Vote," *HIS* 43, 1 (October 1984): 4; Jim Wallis, "The Issue of 1972," *Post-American* 1, 5 (Fall 1972): 2–3. On Barnet's continuing critiques of American foreign policy and his influence on evangelical radicals, see Richard J. Barnet, *Roots of War* (New York: Atheneum, 1972), 3–23; Barnet, *Intervention and Revolution: The United States in the Third World* (New York: World, 1968); Wallis, "Invisible Empire," 1; William Stringfellow, "Open Letter to Jimmy Carter," *Sojourners* 5, 8 (October

1976): 7–8; Barnet, "Losing Moral Ground: The Foundations of U.S. Foreign Policy," *Sojourners* 14, 3 (March 1985): 24–28; issue entitled "Empire: The Religion of America," *Sojourners* 15, 5 (May 1986). On Vietnam as the "current example of a long and bloody record," see Wallis, *Revive Us Again*, 52–53.

17. Arthur G. Gish, *The New Left and Christian Radicalism* (Grand Rapids, Mich.: Eerdmans, 1970), 27, 49, 57, 66, 67, 71, 119. The *Post-American*, *The Other Side*, and several InterVarsity chapter newsletters reprinted excerpts of Gish's tome. On the use of "Amerika," see Richard Quebedeaux, *The Young Evangelicals: Revolution in Orthodoxy* (New York: Harper & Row, 1974), 120; Joe Roos, "American Civil Religion," *Post-American* 1, 3 (Spring 1972): 8; Michael Walton, "Dedicated to all International Students at Urbana '70," *Vanguard* (December 31, 1970), copy in Box 68, Folder 7, "Urbana 1961–1974," InterVarsity Christian Fellowship Collection, BGCA. For America as a modern Rome, see notes from a Post-American Bible study entitled "Political Interpretations of John's Apocalypse," Box XI1, Folder "Post-American Letters/Memos/ Info from the Office," Sojourners Collection, WCSC; Jim Wallis, "Evangelism in Babylon," *Post-American* 1, 4 (Summer 1972): 8; Bert Witvoet, "Jubilee 1979—Visited and Enjoyed," *Vanguard* 9, 3 (May–June 1979): 27; John Perkins, "Bicentennial in the Other America," *Sojourners* 5, 1 (January 1976): 20–23.

18. On picketing, see Carl F. H. Henry, "Equality by Boycott," *Christianity Today* 11, 12 (March 17, 1967): 27. On the demonstrative methods of Wallis and the Post-Americans, see Wallis, *Revive Us Again*, 54–58. On Jesus the contentious prophet and revolutionary, see John Alexander, "Madison Avenue Jesus," *Post-American* 1, 1 (Fall 1971): 14; Milliken, *So Long, Sweet Jesus*, 51, 109; and Joseph Webb, "Gospel as Public Drama," *Post-American* 4, 3 (March 1975): 24; Jim Moore, "Will the Real Jesus Please Stand Up?" *Post-American* 1, 2 (Winter 1972): 13.

19. Gallagher quoted in Edward B. Fiske, "A 'Religious Woodstock' Draws 75,000," *New York Times*, June 16, 1972, 19; "People's Christian Coalition—Newsletter 4," May 1972, Box VII7, Folder "Peoples Christian Coalition Trinity," Sojourners Collection, WCSC; Fiske, "A 'Religious Woodstock' Draws 75,000," 19; Richard K. Taylor, "Hopeful Stirrings among Evangelicals," *The Witness*, copy in Box IV3, Folder "News Releases and Post-American," Sojourners Collection, WCSC; Peter Ediger, "Explo '72," *Post-American* 1, 5 (Fall 1972): 13; Marlin VanElderen, "Explo '72 and Campus Crusade," *Reformed Journal* 22, 6 (July–August 1972): 18.

20. On the group's name change, see Wesley Granberg-Michaelson, *Unexpected Destinations: An Evangelical Pilgrimage to World Christianity* (Grand Rapids, Mich.: Eerdmans, 2011), 113. On *The Organizer's Manual*, see "Bibliography: People's Christian Coalition," November 1971, Box VII7, Folder 6, "Peoples Christian Coalition Trinity," Sojourners Collection, WCSC; O. M. Collective, *The Organizer's Manual* (New York: Bantam, 1971); "Community Statement," Box VI, Folder 1, "Sojourners Community," Sojourners Collection, WCSC. On nuclear weapons protests, see Sojourners newsletter, Summer 1978, Folder "Sojo Community," Boxes VI1–VI3, Sojourners Collection, WCSC. For more on Rocky Flats, see "Flowers at Rocky Flats," *Radix* 8, 3

(September–October 1976): 17. On war taxes, see Joe Roos, " 'Let Your Nay Be Nay,' " *Sojourners* 8, 2 (February 1979): 5; Delton Franz, "Channeling War Taxes to Peace," *Sojourners* 6, 3 (March 1977): 21–23; Donald Kaufman, "Paying for War," *Sojourners* 6, 3 (March 1977): 16–19. On housing protests, see Patricia Camp, "Group Occupies Apartments in Housing Protest," *Washington Post*, September 16, 1978, C1. On other Sojourners protests, see Robert K. Johnston, *Evangelicals at an Impasse: Biblical Authority in Practice* (Atlanta: John Knox Press, 1979), 107; Jim Wallis, *Agenda for Biblical People: Gospel for a New Order* (New York: Harper & Row, 1976), 102; Wes Michaelson, "Theater at the Capitol," *Sojourners* 9, 1 (January 1980): 20–21; "Eight Staff Members of *Sojourners* Magazine, Including Jim Wallis Were Arrested," *Christianity Today* 25, 19 (November 6, 1981): 73; Wallis, *Revive Us Again*, 120–34.

21. "Report of the Task Force on Evangelical Nonviolence," Box 2, Folder 12, "Center for Biblical Social Concern proposal; correspondence September 1974–Sept. 1976," ESA Collection, BGCA; Ronald J. Sider, "Reconciling our Enemies: A Biblical Study on Nonviolence," *Sojourners* 8, 1 (January 1979): 14–17. On InterVarsity, see "Inter-Varsity Christian Fellowship—UMSL Chapter Position on Campus Disorders," Box 21, Folder 2, "Student unrest/dissent (1960s)," InterVarsity Christian Fellowship Collection, BGCA. On boycotting, see "Boycotting Gallo," *Right On* 6, 4 (November 1974): 4; Carolyn Hudson, "March on Gallo," *Right On* 6, 8 (April 1975): 9; Kenneth Winter letter, *Right On* 10, 2 (September–October 1978): 2. On strategies of protest, see Richard K. Taylor, "Manual for Nonviolent Direct Action," *Post-American* 3, 8 (November 1974): 24–29; Richard K. Taylor, "The Peacemakers: Faith and Obedience through Nonviolent Direct Action," *Post-American* 3, 8 (October–November 1975): 16–21. On the importance of personal morality among protesters, see Charles Fager, "Ethics, Principalities, and Nonviolence," *Post-American* 3, 8 (November 1974): 18–20.

22. On Sheats, see "Door Reports," 22; Wes Michaelson and Jim Wallis, "Ladon Sheats: Pilgrimage of a Peacemaker," *Sojourners* 5, 3 (March 1976): 11–19. On Calvin, see "Peace Service, Seminars, City Rally Highlight Calvin Moratorium Activity," *Chimes* 64, 11 (October 17, 1969): 1; "The Dean Burns in Effigy During Ad Hoc Demonstration," *Calvin Chimes* 63 (April 25, 1969): 3. On Wheaton, see "Funeral March Highlights Moratorium Observance," *Wheaton Record* 92, 10 (November 21, 1969): 1; "ROTC Protest Goes Smoothly; Dr. Armerding Holds Front Campus Talk," *Wheaton Record* 93, 27 (May 14, 1971): 2. On Taylor, see Taylor, "The Peacemakers," 16–21; Taylor, "Manual for Nonviolent Direct Action," 29.

23. Ronald J. Sider, "Blockade: A Guide to Non-Violent Intervention," *Christianity Today* 22, 9 (February 10, 1978): 45–46; Joseph Webb, "Gospel as Public Drama," *Post-American* 4, 3 (March 1975): 24. For more on the rise in evangelical activism and dualistic rhetoric, see "CADA to Penetrate Campus Groups to Promote Reforms," *Wheaton Record* 91, 16 (February 14, 1969): 2; Carol Anne Galvin, "Students Peacefully Protest Wheaton College ROTC Image," *Wheaton Daily Journal* (May 14, 1971); "There Will Be a Peaceful Demonstration," both in vertical file "ROTC," WCA; William Stringfellow, *Christians and Other Aliens in a Strange Land* (Waco, Tex.: Word, 1976), 154–55;

"The Dean Burns in Effigy During Ad Hoc Demonstration," *Calvin Chimes* 63 (April 25, 1969): 3. On the Christian World Liberation Front's demonstrations, see folder "Berkeley Liberation Program," Box 21, Folder 41, Social Protests Collection, BL; Box 38, Folder "Christian World Liberation Front," New Left Collection, HIA.

24. C. Wright Mills, "A Pagan Sermon to the Christian Clergy," *Post-American* 3, 9 (December 1974): 12–15. This was a reprint of Mills's speech text originally published in the March 8, 1958, issue of *The Nation*.

25. On the Manichean worldview of fundamentalists, see George Marsden, *Fundamentalism and American Culture*, 2nd Ed. (New York: Oxford University Press, 2006), 211. On leftist radicals as "today's Christians," see Paul Fromer, "The Berkeley Affair Brush Fire," *HIS* 25, 9 (June 1965): 38–40, 44–45. On "apocalyptic sureness," see Seerveld, "Christian Faith for Today," *Vanguard* (January–February 1972): 9. On pessimistic rhetoric within SNCC and the New Left, see David L. Chappell, *A Stone of Hope: Prophetic Religion and the Death of Jim Crow* (Chapel Hill: University of North Carolina Press, 2004). On SNCC as the soul of the New Left, see Gitlin, *The Sixties*, 129. On the religious ethos of the civil rights movement, see Charles Marsh, *The Beloved Community: How Faith Shapes Social Justice* (New York: Basic Books, 2005), 2–3; Chappell, *Stone of Hope*, 87–104.

26. On Barnet and Kennedy, see Wes Michaelson, "Richard Barnet on Multinational Corporations," *Sojourners* 5, 2 (February 1976): 17. On evil residing in the military-industrial complex, see Wallis and Bob Sabath, "In Quest of Discipleship," *Post-American* 2, 3 (May-June 1973): 3. On the war as a "crime and sin," see Allan C. Carlson, "Radical Evangelicals and Their Anticapitalist Crusade," *Gazette Telegraph*, November 8, 1981, 11AA. For other examples, see Arthur G. Gish, *The New Left and Christian Radicalism* (Grand Rapids, Mich.: Eerdmans, 1970), 27, 49, 57, 66, 67, 71, 119; Jim Wallis, "Pilgrimage of a Peacemaker," *Post-American* 5, 3 (March 1976): 5. On "principalities and powers," see Robert A. Sabath, "Paul's View of the State," *Post-American* 3, 3 (April 1974): 8–11; Wallis, *Agenda for Biblical People*, 60–80.

27. For "principalities and powers," see Lee A. Wyatt, "Discipleship Workshops Newsletter," April 15, 1981, Folder "Discipleship Workshops," ESAA; Dale W. Brown, "The Powers: A Bible Study," *Post-American* 3, 1 (January 1974): 3. On Nixon and corporations as "principalities of death," see "Political Interpretations of John's Apocalypse," Box XII, Folder, "Post-American—Internal," Sojourners Collection, WCSC. On "the prince of this world," see Joe Roos, "The Arrogance of Power," *Post-American* 4, 2 (February 1975): 6–7. On the embattlement of the Post-Americans, see Julia Duin, "A Most Unusual Magazine," *Washington Post*, December 25, 1976, copy in Box IV3, Folder "News Releases and Post-American," Sojourners Collection, WCSC. For the metaphor of good and evil, see Wallis, *Agenda for Biblical People*, 132.

28. On Jesus as a boy scout, see Langston, "Campus Rebel Finds New 'Revolt'." On Christian prayer and protests, see Peoples Christian Coalition newsletter 4, May

1972, in Box IV3, Folder "News Releases and Post-American," Sojourners Collection, WCSC.

29. Ron Sider, "Resist but Don't Rebel: Sometimes We Must Disobey the Government to Obey God," *Light and Life* (February 1983): 9–10, copy in Folder "1983," ESAA. On how the religious right achieved New Left goals such as participatory democracy, see Jon Shields, *The Democratic Virtues of the Religious Right* (Princeton: Princeton University Press, 2009).

30. Histories of radicalism at elite American universities dominated early New Left historiography. See Max Heirich, *Spiral of Conflict: Berkeley, 1964* (New York: Columbia University Press, 1971); Irwin Unger, *The Movement: A History of the American New Left, 1959–1972* (New York: Harper & Row, 1974); W. J. Rorabaugh, *Berkeley at War: The 1960s* (New York: Oxford University Press, 1989); George R. Vickers, *The Formation of the New Left: The Early Years* (Lexington, Mass.: D.C. Heath, 1975); Gitlin, *The Sixties*; James Miller, *Democracy Is in the Streets: From Port Huron to the Siege of Chicago* (New York: Simon and Schuster, 1987). A second wave, to which I seek to contribute, explores New Left impulses on nonelite campuses, see Kenneth J. Heineman, *Campus Wars: The Peace Movement at American State Universities in the Vietnam Era* (New York: NYU Press, 1993); Rossinow, *Politics of Authenticity*; Michael Kazin, *American Dreamers: How the Left Changed a Nation* (New York: Knopf, 2011). In a particularly influential article, Wini Breines pointed out the organizational affinities of authors of the first wave, arguing that their former affiliations with SDS shaped their narratives in a necessarily partisan manner. See Breines, "Whose New Left?" *Journal of American History* 75, 2 (September 1988): 528–45.

31. Kirkpatrick Sale, *SDS* (New York: Random House, 1973); Van Gosse, "A Movement of Movements: The Definition and Periodization of the New Left," in *A Companion to Post-1945 America*, ed. Jean-Christophe Agnew and Roy Rosenzweig (Oxford: Blackwell, 2002), 277–302. On evangelical radicals as the *real* New Left, see Jim Wallis, "Reflections," in *The Chicago Declaration*, ed. Ronald J. Sider (Carol Stream, Ill.: Creation House, 1974), 142.

32. For "nigger and napalm," see Jim Wallis, "The Movemental Church," *Post-American* 1, 2 (Winter 1972): 2–3. For "red, white, and blue," see Robert Lehnhart, "Urbana 70: We Can't Afford to Ignore It," *Missionary Aviation* 27, 2 (March–April 1971): 4. On evangelical fears of a totalitarian state, see Les Drayer, Letters to the Editor, *HIS* 29, 5 (February 1969): 14; Joseph Bayly, "Thoughts on the Election," *HIS* 30, 2 (November 1969): 5. For several examples of New Left thought within evangelicalism, see "The Revolutionary Catechism," *Right On* 1, 17 (October 27, 1970): 2; Bill Kallio, "Price of Progress Too High; No Need for SST," *Wheaton Record* 93, 14 (January 29, 1971): 4; John Hesselink, "The Church in a Technological Society," *Reformed Journal* 23, 1 (January 1973): 10; Bonnie M. Greene, "On Leaving It to the Technocrats," *Vanguard* (September–October 1975): 27; Vernard Eller, "A Look at Jacques Ellul," *Wittenburg Door* 22 (December–January 1974–1975): 8–12; Vernon Grounds, "Undercover," *HIS* 33, 4

(January 1973): 22–23; "Echo from a Politico," *Right On* 1, 14 (May 1, 1970): 2; Jill Shook, "Vietnam Today," *Right On* 6, 1 (July–August 1974): 7.

Chapter 4. Mark Hatfield and Electoral Politics

Epigraph: Mark Hatfield, *Between a Rock and a Hard Place* (Waco: Word, 1976), 212.

1. On Hatfield's telephone call to Wallis and invitation to Washington, see Zach Kincaid, "Salting the Seen," *Trinity Magazine* (Summer 2002): 12–13, and "Minutes of the Peoples Christian Coalition," October 17, 1971, Box VII7, Folder 6, "Peoples Christian Coalition Trinity," Sojourners Collection, WCSC. On their lunch in the Senate Dining Room, see Jim Wallis, "Foreword," in Lon Fendall, *Stand Alone or Come Home* (Newberg, Ore.: Barclay Press, 2008); James C. Hefley and Edward E. Plowman, *Washington: Christians in the Corridor of Power* (Wheaton, Ill.: Tyndale House, 1975), 110. For Hatfield's letter to Wallis's landlord, see Mark Hatfield to Greenhoot, Inc., October 20, 1975, Box IV3, Folder 6, "Post-American: Other Papers and Letters," Sojourners Collection, WCSC. On Wallis's father, see James E. Wallis to "Ralph," December 4, 1973, in Box IV3, Folder 6, "Post American: Other Papers and Letters," Sojourners Collection, WCSC. Connections deepened later in the decade when Wes Michaelson, chief of staff for Hatfield, joined the staff of *Sojourners*.

2. Mark O. Hatfield, *Against the Grain: Reflections of a Rebel Republican* (Ashland, Ore.: White Cloud Press, 2001), 1–32; Fendall, *Stand Alone*, 23–25.

3. Hatfield, *Against the Grain*, 37–47; Hatfield, *Not Quite So Simple* (New York: Harper & Row, 1968), 153–54.

4. Hatfield, *Against the Grain*, 51–61; Fendall, *Stand Alone*, 4.

5. James Bassett, "A Comer on the GOP Horizon: Gov. Hatfield," *Los Angeles Times*, September 19, 1962, A4; Zan Stark, "Storybook Politician Gets GOP Keynote Job," *Los Angeles Times*, June 7, 1964, E3; Ray J. Schrick, "Hurry-Up Hatfield: Oregon's 'Liberal' Young GOP Governor Gains Renown; Rockefeller Ticket Mate?" *Wall Street Journal*, May 8, 1959, 10.

6. On self-determination, see Hatfield, *Against the Grain*, 54. On Hatfield and Eisenhower, see Edward T. Folliard, "'Ike' Appears Sure to Win Oregon Race," *Washington Post*, January 23, 1952, 1; Lawrence E. Davies, "Two-Way Oregon Boom on for Eisenhower," *New York Times*, August 12, 1951, 63. On Oregonian politics, see Hatfield, *Against the Grain*, 8; "Regional Barrier Stymies Hatfield," *Los Angeles Times*, February 15, 1963, 2; Robert K. Johnston, *The Radical Middle Class: Populist Democracy and the Question of Capitalism in Progressive-Era Portland, Oregon* (Princeton: Princeton University Press, 2003). On the Young Republican platform and civil rights, see Fendall, *Stand Alone*, 26–30; Hatfield, *Not Quite So Simple*, 13–15.

7. Holmes Alexander, "A Young Patriot," *Los Angeles Times*, November 11, 1955, A5; *Portland Oregonian*, July 5, 1974, quoted in Robert Eells and Bartell Nyberg, *Lonely Walk: The Life of Senator Mark Hatfield* (Portland, Ore.: Multnomah Press,

1979), 16; Megan Rosenfeld, "Born Again Political Forces Not Singing the Same Hymn," *Washington Post*, August 24, 1980, H1.

8. On Hatfield and Rockefeller, see Richard Bergholz, "Gov. Hatfield Calls for Positive GOP Program," *Los Angeles Times*, August 21, 1963, A4. On Hatfield's continued attacks on Goldwater, see "Oregon Gov. Hatfield Answers Critics of Extremist Stand," *Los Angeles Times*, May 26, 1963, L3; "Mud Slinging at Goldwater Prophesied," *Los Angeles Times*, May 17, 1964.

9. On Hatfield at the 1964 Republican convention, see Eells, *Lonely Walk*, 49–51; Hatfield, *Against the Grain*, 94–95; Richard Reston, "Hatfield Hits Extremism in GOP Keynote Address," *Los Angeles Times*, July 14, 1964, 1; "Rousselot Hits Hatfield Blast at Birch Group," *Los Angeles Times*, July 15, 1964, 11. On liberal Republicanism, see Russell Kirk, "The End of Liberal Republicanism Is Here," *Los Angeles Times*, July 26, 1964, J7. On the conservative revival of the 1950s and early 1960s, see Lisa McGirr, *Suburban Warriors: The Origins of the New American Right* (Princeton: Princeton University Press, 2002, and David Farber and Jeff Roche, eds., *The Conservative Sixties* (New York: Peter Lang, 2003).

10. On Hatfield's early antiwar statements, see Hatfield, *Hard Place*, 113. On his antiwar stance as rooted spiritually, see Hatfield, *Hard Place*, 23–24; Mark O. Hatfield, "American Democracy and American Evangelicalism—New Perspectives," *Theology, News and Notes* (November 1970), 8. On the 1965 National Governors Conference, see Hatfield, *Against the Grain*, 99–100; Robert J. Donovan, "2 Governors Balk at Viet Policy Stand," *Los Angeles Times*, July 29, 1965, 2.

11. Rowland Evans and Robert Novak, "Hatfield's Albatross," *Washington Post*, October 2, 1966, E7.

12. On Hatfield's Ivy League appearances, see Megan Rosenfeld, "Born Again Political Forces Not Singing the Same Hymn," *Washington Post*, August 24, 1980, H5.

13. On Hatfield's endorsement of Nixon, see Hatfield, "Nixon for President," *Christianity and Crisis* 28, 13 (July 22, 1968): 165–66; George Lardner, Jr., "Hatfield Endorses Nixon: Senator Says He 'Can Lead Us Out of Vietnam,'" *Washington Post*, June 21, 1968, A1; Fendall, *Stand Alone*, 34. On Nixon's consideration of Hatfield for the vice-presidency, see Kenneth Briggs, "Hatfield's Arms Stand: Evangelical Influence," *New York Times*, April 1, 1982, B10; Rick Perlstein, *Nixonland: The Rise of a President and the Fracturing of America* (New York: Scribner, 2008), 301–2; Hatfield, *Against the Grain*, 127–31; Lowell D. Streiker and Gerald S. Strober, *Religion and the New Majority: Billy Graham, Middle America, and the Politics of the 70s* (New York: Association Press, 1972), 66–67; Eells, *Lonely Walk*, 59–60.

14. On Hatfield's continuing rejection of the war, see T. E. Koshy interview of Hatfield, "Can a Christian Be a Politician?" *HIS* 28, 1 (October 1967): 1–5; Hatfield, *Not Quite So Simple*, 185, 217; Hatfield, "The Lessons of Indochina," *Church & Society* 66, 1 (September–October 1975): 75–77. On Hatfield's relationship with McCarthy, see Eells, *Lonely Walk*, 55–56. On student support for Hatfield and the Amendment, see Hatfield, *Against the Grain*, 141–42; Mark Hatfield, William A. Rusher, and Arlie

Schardt, *Amnesty: The Unsettled Question of Vietnam* (Croton-on-Hudson, N.Y.: Sun River Press, 1973), 114, 123.

15. On Hatfield's opposition to Nixon's domestic agenda, see Warren Unnai, "Frustrated GOP Liberals Challenge Dirksen," *Washington Post*, July 10, 1969, A1; Spencer Rich, "Liberals Challenge Tower on GOP Aid," *Washington Post*, October 1, 1970, A1; Fendall, *Stand Alone*, 89. On Hatfield and Nixon's Supreme Court nominees, see Spencer Rich, "Key Senators Back Restudy of Carswell," *Washington Post*, March 27, 1970, A1; Haynes, Johnson, "2nd Mitchell 'Mess' Hit by Senators," *Washington Post*, April 5, 1970, 1.

16. On Hatfield's Republican credentials, see Spencer Rich, "2nd Colleague Opposes Carswell Nomination," *Washington Post*, March 19, 1970, A1; Fendall, *Stand Alone*, 38; Hatfield, *Against the Grain*, 148. On Hatfield's concern over Nixon's renomination, see George Lardner, Jr., "Hatfield Says Nixon Could Be Dumped," *Washington Post*, June 29, 1970, A1. On Hatfield and McGovern, see Hefley and Plowman, *Corridors of Power*, 113. On the political alignment of Hatfield's aides, see Fendall, *Stand Alone*, 65. On Hatfield and support from Oregon Republicans, see Fendall, *Stand Alone*, 38–40.

17. On Hatfield's prominence in evangelical circles, see Hefley, *Corridors of Power*, 113; C. A. Mortenson, "Return to Christian Principles Urged at Sunrise Services in Rose Bowl," *Los Angeles Times*, April 11, 1955, 4; Hatfield, "Can a Christian Be a Politician?" *HIS* 28, 1 (October 1967): 1–5; Hatfield, "Peace: Within You and Without You," *HIS* 30, 5 (February 1970): 1–3; Joseph A. Thacker, *Vision and Miracle* (Nappanee, Ind.: Evangelical Press, 1990), 210. On re-election efforts, see Ron Sider, "Scholar, Popularizer and Activist: Personal Reflections on My Journey," paper given at Calvin College conference "Christian Scholarship . . . For What?" September 28, 2001, 1, ESAA.

18. On Hatfield's appeal to Wheaton progressives, see "Blanchard Association Plans Moratorium Action," *Wheaton Record* 92, 4 (October 10, 1969): 1. On Young Life, see Hatfield, *Hard Place*, 31–34; James Skillen, ed., *Confessing Christ and Doing Politics* (Washington, D.C.: APJ Education Fund, 1982), 73. For interview with Robert Linder, see Mary A. Wilson, "Evangelical Voices: Attitudes Toward the Vietnam War," M.A. thesis, California State University- Dominguez Hills, 1997, 32. On criticism of Hatfield from conservatives, see Eells, *Lonely Walk*, 73; John Turner, *Bill Bright and Campus Crusade for Christ: The Renewal of Evangelicalism in Postwar America* (Chapel Hill: University of North Carolina Press, 2008), 164. On Hatfield's crisis, see Hatfield, *Hard Place*, 13–17; Hatfield quoted in Skillen, ed., *Confessing Christ*, 25.

19. On the Hatfield-Post-American alliance, see Hatfield, "Repentance, Politics, and Power," *Post-American* 3 (1974): 6–7; Hatfield, "Vietnam: A Sobering Postscript," *Post-American* 4 (1975): 6–7. On "bland optimism," see Hatfield, *Hard Place*, 153–66. On the National Prayer Breakfast, see Wallis, "Foreword," *Stand Alone*, xiv; Eells, *Lonely Walk*, 82–83. For the text of the remarks, see Hatfield, "The Sin That Scarred Our National Soul," *Christian Century* 40, 8 (February 21, 1973): 221.

20. On Hatfield's reception at Fuller, see Hatfield, *Hard Place*, 23–25. For complete text of Hatfield's address, see "American Democracy and American Evangelicalism— New Perspectives," 8.

21. On Hatfield's response to Fuller, see Hatfield, *Hard Place*, 23–25; David Hubbard, "Destined to Boldness: A Biography of an Evangelical Institution—Lecture Two: An Academic Adventure," October 23, 1979, Folder "Marsden Notes," FTSA. "More than once," wrote Hubbard, "Hatfield has told me that that episode thwarted his temptation to retire from politics." On the Fuller debate over Vietnam, see Thomas Johnson, "Hawks, Doves, and Ostriches," *The Opinion* 7, 4 (January 1968): 8; Ralph Winter, "On Not Being a One-Eyed Eagle," *The Opinion* 7, 8 (May 1968); Robert Johnston interview by author, July 14, 2006, and September 12, 2006, Pasadena, Cal.

22. On Hatfield at Wheaton, see Paul M. Bechtel, *Wheaton College: A Heritage Remembered, 1860–1984* (Wheaton, Ill.: Shaw Publishers, 1984), 323; Hefley, *The Church That Takes on Trouble*, 144–45; Bill Kallio, "Christian Must Take Place as Peacemaker," *Wheaton Record* 93, 2 (October 2, 1970): 5; Oral interview of Dan Good, tape 7657, WCA; Jim Bourgoine, "He Came, He Spoke, and We Were Conquered," *Wheaton Record* 96, 15 (February 22, 1974): 3; Wesley Granberg-Michaelson, *Unexpected Destinations: An Evangelical Pilgrimage to World Christianity* (Grand Rapids, Mich.: Eerdmans, 2011), 75–76.

23. On calls by antiwar evangelicals for Graham to condemn the war, see David Poling, *Why Billy Graham?* (Grand Rapids, Mich.: Zondervan, 1977), 81; Peter Ediger, "Explo '72," *Post American* 1, 5 (Fall 1972): 13; Joe Roos, "American Civil Religion," *Post-American* 1, 3 (Spring 1972): 9; Ben Patterson, "Editorial," *Wittenburg Door* 12 (April–May 1973): 4–5; Lewis B. Smedes, "An Appeal to Billy Graham," *Reformed Journal* 22, 7 (September 1972): 3. For the White House tape, see Tape 043, February 21, 1973, "White House Tapes, Presidential Recordings Program," MCPA.

24. On admiration within InterVarsity for Hatfield's stand on Vietnam, see Hatfield, "The Gray Areas of Faith and Politics," *HIS* 39, 2 (November 1978): 17; John A. Bernbaum and Steve Moore, "Should the U.S. Boycott Ugandan Coffee," *HIS* 39, 2 (November 1978): 10. Stephen Board, "Making a Social Difference," *HIS* 32, 8 (May 1972): 27; Wes Pippert, "Christ and Crisis in Washington," *HIS* 34, 7 (April 1974): 1–4. On Graham and Nixon's criticism of Hatfield, see Tape 043-161, "White House Tapes, Presidential Recordings Program," MCPA. On "the Hatfields who fought alone," see David T. Steen, "Epitaph for Viet Nam," *Vanguard* (April–May 1973): 23.

25. Hatfield, "Civil Religion," *Evangelical Visitor* 86, 15 (August 10, 1973): 4–5, 104; "Seeds," *Sojourners* 5, 8 (October 1976): 26; Hatfield, *Hard Place*, 75–109; Hatfield, *Amnesty*, 114, 123; Hatfield, "Judgment and Repentance," *Vanguard* (October 1973): 9–11; "Piety and Patriotism," *Post-American* 2, 3 (May–June 1973): 1–2; "Law, Order, and Justice: An Interview with Senator Hatfield," *Freedom Now* 4, 5 (November–December 1968): 23–29.

26. On Bellah and civil religion, see Robert N. Bellah, "Civil Religion in America," *Daedalus* 96, 1 (Winter 1967): 1–21; Will Herberg, *Protestant, Catholic, Jew: A Study in American Religious Sociology* (Garden City, N.Y.: Doubleday, 1955); Sharon Gallagher, "Emergence of the American 70s: An Interview with Robert Bellah," *Right On* 7, 4 (November 1975): 5, 12, 15; Robert D. Linder and Richard V. Pierard, *Twilight of the Saints:*

Biblical Christianity and Civil Religion in America (Downers Grove, Ill.: InterVarsity Press, 1978), 21; Joe Roos, "American Civil Religion," *Post-American* 1, 3 (Spring 1972): 8–10. For "real issues," see Jack Rogers, "Confessions of a Post-Conservative Evangelical," *Reformed Journal* 21, 2 (February 1971): 11. For "the pernicious nature of this civil religion," see Richard Pierard, "The Golden Image of Nebuchandezzar," *Post-American* 2, 1 (January–February 1973): 10–11.

For criticisms of Graham and Nixon, see Hatfield, *Hard Place*, 100–102; David Kucharsky, "Billy Graham and 'Civil Religion,'" *Christianity Today* 15, 3 (November 6, 1970): 56–58; "News on Watergate," *Christianity Today* 17, 17 (May 25, 1973): 46; Hatfield, *Conflict and Conscience* (Waco, Tex.: Word, 1971), 110, 112, 120. For a fuller text and discussion of Graham's sermon, see Streiker and Strober, *Religion and the New Majority*, 77. On "honoring America and God," see Linder and Pierard, *Twilight of the Saints*, 170–71. For a small sample of the large evangelical left oeuvre on civil religion, see Robert G. Clouse, Robert D. Linder, and Richard V. Pierard, *Protest and Politics: Christianity and Contemporary Affairs* (Greenwood, S.C.: Attic Press, 1968); Richard V. Pierard, *Unequal Yoke: Evangelical Christianity and Political Conservatism* (Philadelphia: Lippincott, 1970); Robert G. Clouse, Robert D. Linder, and Richard V. Pierard, eds., *The Cross & the Flag* (Carol Stream, Ill.: Creation House, 1972); Robert Jewett, *The Captain America Complex: The Dilemma of Zealous Nationalism* (Philadelphia: Westminster Press, 1973); Craig Watts," Identity and Idolatry?" *The Other Side* 20, 7 (July 1984): 10; Review of *Politics, Americanism, and Christianity*, by Perry Cotham, in *Eternity* 27 (September 1976): 48; John F. Alexander, "Land of the Free?" *The Other Side* 14, 8 (August 1978): 12–16. Robert D. Linder and Richard V. Pierard, *Twilight of the Saints*, 21; Joe Roos, "American Civil Religion," *Post-American* 1, 3 (Spring 1972): 8–10.

27. For a discussion of the evangelical Conference on Faith and History in October 1974 that centered on the dilemmas of civil religion, see George Marsden, "Christian Historians and Civil Religion," *Reformed Journal* 24, 9 (November 1974): 26–28. On "Christian jingoism," see section entitled "The Problem of America as a 'Christian Nation,'" in Linder and Pierard, *Twilight of the Saints*, 145, 163–64. On independence celebrations, see David Gill, "Easter and Independence," *Right On* 7, 7 (April 1976): 10; Campolo, "Door Interview," *Wittenburg Door* 32 (August–September 1976): 19, 22; Wes Michaelson, "No King but Caesar," *Sojourners* 5, 1 (January 1976): 4–6; David Gill, "198 Years Old," *Right On* 6, 1 (July–August 1974): 6.

28. Kenneth Woodward, "The New Evangelicals," *Newsweek*, May 6, 1974, 86; Hefley and Plowman, *Corridors of Power*, 114.

29. On politics as a Christian vocation, see Fendall, *Stand Alone*, 44; Hatfield, "Can a Christian be a Politician?" *HIS* 28, 1 (October 1967): 1–5.

30. On Haynes, see "Back to That Old Time Religion: Gaudy and Vital U.S. Evangelicalism Is Booming," *Time* 110, 26 (December 26, 1977): 52. On Harold Hughes, see Hughes, *The Man from Ida Grove: A Senator's Story* (Waco, Tex.: Word, 1979), 214, 234, 256–57, 307; Fendall, *Stand Alone*, 18; Wes Pippert, "Christ and Crisis in Washing-

ton," *HIS* 34, 7 (April 1974): 1–4. On Paul Henry, see Doug Koopman, ed., *Serving the Claims of Justice: The Thoughts of Paul B. Henry* (Grand Rapids, Mich.: Calvin College, 2001). On Monsma, see "Profile/Senators," *Grand Rapids Accent* (January–February 1980), 38, copy in Box 1, Folder 1, "Bibliographic Data, 1976–1980," Paul Henry Collection, CCA; Stephen Monsma, *The Unraveling of America* (Downers Grove, Ill.: Inter-Varsity Press, 1974). On Anderson, see John B. Anderson, *Between Two Worlds: A Congressman's Choice* (Grand Rapids, Mich.: Zondervan, 1970); Anderson, *Vision and Betrayal in America* (Waco, Tex.: Word, 1975), 90, 121. For more vignettes of evangelical politicians in this era, see "God on Capitol Hill," *Christianity Today* 14, 1 (October 10, 1969): 48–50.

31. Mark O. Hatfield to Ron Sider, Western Union telegram sent June 22, 1973, Folder "Chicago Declaration Planning," ESAA.

Chapter 5. Sharon Gallagher and the Politics of Spiritual Community

Epigraph: "The People of Berkeley Passionately Desire Personal Fulfillment, Vital Interpersonal Relationships, and Inner Peace," *Right On* 1, 1 (July 1, 1969): 3.

1. Tom Skinner in Bill Milliken, *So Long, Sweet Jesus* (Buffalo, N.Y.: Prometheus, 1973), 12–13.

2. On evangelicals and southern California politics, see Lisa McGirr, *Suburban Warriors: The Origins of the New American Right* (Princeton: Princeton University Press, 2001); Darren Dochuk, *From Bible Belt to Sunbelt: Plain-Folk Religion, Grassroots Politics, and the Rise of Evangelical Conservatism* (New York: Norton, 2010). On "hackneyed categories," see "Radical Christian," *Right On* 4, 5 (November 1972): 10.

3. Sharon Gallagher in *Our Struggle to Serve: The Stories of 15 Evangelical Women*, ed. Virginia Hearn (Waco, Tex.: Word, 1979), 93–100; Donald A. Heinz, "Jesus in Berkeley," Ph.D. dissertation, Graduate Theological Union, 1976, 240–41; David Gill email interview by author, March 2, 2006; "Sharon Gallagher," Council of Ministries brochure, Box 2, CWLF Collection, GTUA. On the number of sports cars on Westmont campus, see Enroth, "The Westmont Urban Mission," in *The Urban Mission*, ed. Craig W. Ellison (Grand Rapids, Mich.: Eerdmans, 1974), 110.

4. David Gill, "The Messiah(s) of Miami Beach," *Right On* 4, 1 (July 1972): 3; Arnie Bernstein, "Captured by the King," *Right On* 4, 5 (November 1972): 1; "Reach Me," *Right On* 1, 15 (April 24, 1970): 2; Gia Chester, "The Paraphrased Testimony of a Young Evangelical," *Right On* 9, 2 (September–October 1977): 17; Donald Heinz, "The Christian World Liberation Front," in *The New Religious Consciousness*, ed. Charles Y. Glock and Robert N. Bellah (Berkeley: University of California Press, 1976), 154.

5. On Campus Crusade's ministry to the "straight, sorority-fraternity crowd," see John Dart, "Crusade for Christ Opens Hearts and Doors on Campus," *Los Angeles Times*, August 8, 1971, B1. CWLF enjoyed generous publicity from books on the Jesus Movement, *Christianity Today*, and other evangelical periodicals, especially those

identifying with the young evangelical movement. See, for example, Edward Plowman, *The Jesus Movement in America: Accounts of Christian Revolutionaries in Action* (New York: Pyramid, 1971). CWLF also received coverage from the *Los Angeles Times* feature articles that were picked up off the wire by other American newspapers. See, for example, Daryl Lembke, "Christian Front in Berkeley: Religious Group Turns 'Hippie' to Win Youth," *Los Angeles Times*, February 8, 1970, 20; Russell Chandler, "Jesus Movement Still Going Strong," *Los Angeles Times*, December 13, 1975, 34–35; Edward B. Fiske, "A Religious 'Woodstock' Draws 75,000," *New York Times*, June 16, 1972, 1, 19.

6. On Sparks's new countercultural look, see "How to Start Something," *Newsletter of the American Scientific Affiliation* 17, 1 (February 1975). On social problems as rooted in spiritual oppression, see "Moratorium on Internal Wars," October 27, 1969, copy of flyer Box 23, Folder 30, CWLF Collection, BL.

7. On CWLF's various names, see "People's Medical Handbook," Box 2 "CWLF and Redeemer King Church Notes," CWLF Collection, GTUA; "How to Start Something"; Androcles, "Graham Crusade Freak-Out," *Right On* 3, 3 (September 1971): 8; Folder, "Christian World Liberation Front," Box 38, New Left Collection, HIA. For the first issue of *Right On*, see "The People of Berkeley Passionately Desire Personal Fulfillment, Vital Interpersonal Relationships, and Inner Peace," *Right On* 1, 1 (July 1, 1969): 3. On CWLF's tracts, see Jack Sparks, *God's Forever Family* (Grand Rapids, Mich.: Zondervan, 1974), 112. On the Mobilization Parade, see Daryl Lembke, "Christian Front in Berkeley," *Los Angeles Times,* February 8, 1970, 20B; Plowman, *Jesus Movement*, 74. On BLP, see Folder 21, "Berkeley Liberation Program," June 1969, in Social Protest Collection, BL. On CWLF's version of the BLP, see "New Berkeley Liberation Program"; ". . . And After This War?" and "Proposed Social and Economic Foundations for a Christian Society," Box 21, Folder 41, Social Protest Collection, BL.

8. Lembke, "Christian Front in Berkeley," 20; Stephen A. Kent, *From Slogans to Mantras: Social Protest and Religious Conversion in the Late Vietnam Era* (Syracuse, N.Y.: Syracuse University Press, 2001), 180–89.

9. On the *Right On-Berkeley Barb* exchanges, see "Barb Bared," *Right On* 1, 1 (August 1, 1969): 1; "Congratulations, Max," *Right On* 1, 9 (January 15, 1970): 4; Heinz, "Jesus in Berkeley," 296. On the Sproul Hall confrontation, see Edward Plowman, "Battle for Berkeley," *Christianity Today* 14, 16 (May 8, 1970): 40. On the fierce confrontation between SDS and CWLF at the 1969 SDS regional conference in Berkeley, see Plowman, *Jesus Movement*, 70–71. On the 1970 confrontation, see Bill Squires phone interview by author, September 5, 2006; Plowman, *Jesus Movement*, 70–73; "SDS Confronted at West Coast Conference," *Free Water* (October 1970): 1; "How to Start Something" *NASA*; undated, untitled CWLF newsletter, Box 38, New Left Collection, HIA. On the Ramparts-CWLF dispute, see James Nolan, "Jesus Now: Hogwash and Holy Water," *Ramparts* 10, 2 (August 1971): 20–26; "A Brief History of the Revolution," Box 2, "CWLF and Redeemer King Church," CWLF Collection, GTUA; Donald A. Heinz, "Jesus in Berkeley," Ph.D. dissertation, Graduate Theological Union, 1976, 59–60, 289; "An Open Letter to Ramparts," *Right On* 3, 3 (September 1971): 2.

10. On "new brothers and sisters," see "Prayer and Praise," CWLF Newsletter, Box 2, Jill Shook Papers, CWLF Collection, GTUA. On baptisms, see "Ludwig's Fountain Becomes Pool for Christians' Baptism Rituals," *Daily Californian* (November 26, 1973); Heinz, "Jesus in Berkeley," 42. On Fetcho, see "Meet the Staff: David Fetcho," *Spiritual Counterfeits Project Newsletter* 2, 1 (January 1976): 3, copy in CWLF Collection, BL. On former SDSers Randy Berdahl, Jim Fox, and Susan Starkey, see Heinz, "Jesus in Berkeley," 56–65; Berdahl, "Randy Turns On," *Right On* 2, 18 (November 19, 1970): 1; Susan Starkey, "Like Banging Your Head Against the Wall, *Right On* 3, 7 (January 1972): 3; Jim Fox, "I See Nothing But Futility in the World," *Right On* 2, 18 (November 19, 1970): 2. On CWLF's growth, see "Notes from the Catacombs," *Right On* 4, 2 (August 1972): 2; Lembke, "Christian Front in Berkeley," 20.

11. On leftist protest flyers, see Box 21, Folder 41, Social Protest Collection, BL. On Santa Claus, see Heinz, "Jesus in Berkeley," 42. On street theater, see "Street Theater" newsletter, circa 1974, Folder "CWLF—Street Theater," Box 2, Jill Shook Papers, GTUA. On protesting Nixon, see Sparks, *God's Forever Family*, 115–17. On the high number of protests, see Sharon Gallagher interview by author, July 7, 2006, Berkeley, California. For examples of leftist activism in CWLF, see "Echo from a Politico," *Right On* 1, 14 (May 1, 1970): 2; Jill Shook to "Hedie and Fred," circa February 1974, Box 2, Jill Shook Papers, CWLF Collection, GTUA; David Gill, "Radical Christian," *Right On* 4, 7 (February 1973): 15; Jill Shook, "My Story," *Right On* 5, 12 (June 1974): 7; Jill Shook, "Vietnam Today," *Right On* 6, 1 (July–August 1974): 7; "Reach Me," *Right On* 1, 13 (April 24, 1970): 2; Clancy Dunigan, "Do We Need the B-1 Bomber?" *Right On*, 6, 10 (June 1975): 3, 6; "Boycotting Gallo," *Right On* 6, 4 (November 1974): 4; Carolyn Hudson, "March on Gallo," *Right On* 6, 8 (April 1975): 9.

12. On CWLF's pickets, see Sparks, *God's Forever Family*, 115–21. For the text of "Why Your Landlord Makes Money," see "Why Your Landlord Makes Money" Box 21, Folder 41, "Christian World Liberation Front 1969–1971," Social Protests Collection, BL. On CWLF's participation in the Mobilization Parade, see Lembke, "Christian Front in Berkeley," 20.

13. On the distancing of CWLF and Campus Crusade, see Sharon Gallagher interview by author, July 7, 2006, Berkeley, Cal.; Walter and Virginia Hearn interview by author, July 9, 2006, Berkeley, Cal.; David Gill email interview by author, March 2, 2006; Turner, *Bill Bright and Campus Crusade*, 129.

14. On CWLF worship style, see Heinz, "Jesus in Berkeley," 83, 226–28. On CWLF and the arts, see advertisements for Pacific Film Archive, Berkeley Repertory Theatre, and Oakland Symphony in "The Billboard," *Right On* 5, 10 (April 1974): A1–A4. On "repetitious absurdity," see David R. Mains, *Full Circle: The Creative Church for Today's Society* (Waco, Tex.: Word, 1971), 20. On Jesus People music, see David Stowe, *No Sympathy for the Devil: Christian Pop Music and the Transformation of American Evangelicalism* (Chapel Hill: University of North Carolina Press, 2011).

15. For examples of profanity, see "Reach Me," *Right On* 1, 14 (April 24, 1970): 3. On the "hippie Bible," see Jack Sparks and Paul Raudenbush, *Letters to Street Christians*

(Grand Rapids, Mich.: Zondervan Publishing, 1971); flyer advertisement for *Letters to Street Christians*, Box 2, Jill Shook Papers, Folder "Jack Sparks's Letters," CWLF Collection, GTUA. On sales, see Larry Eskridge, "God's Forever Family: The Jesus People Movement in America, 1966–1977," Ph.D. dissertation, University of Stirling, 2005, 196.

16. On "empty bourgeois apathy" and the visits of countercultural celebrities to L'Abri, see Frank Schaeffer, *Crazy for God* (New York: Carroll & Graf, 2007), 211–12. On transforming culture, see Sharon Gallagher interview by author, July 7, 2006, Berkeley, Cal. On CWLF's connections with countercultural figures, see David Gill, "The Messiah in Miami Beach," *Right On* 4, 2 (August 1972): 5–6; Steve Turner, "John and Yoko Interviewed," *Right On* 4, 5 (November 1972): 4; "Just Plain Noel Stookey," *Right On* 4, 8 (March 1973): 5, 11; "An Interview with Eldridge Cleaver," *Right On* 8, 3 (November–December 1976): 3–6.

17. Francis Schaeffer, *The God Who Is There* (Downers Grove, Ill.: InterVarsity Press, 1968), 20–22, 143–47; "Schaeffer Stresses Rational Christianity," *Wheaton Record* 88, 2 (September 30, 1965): 3. On "reasoned comprehension," see Francis Schaeffer, "Letters," *Right On* 3, 5 (November 1971): 2. On Schaeffer's influence on CWLF, see "Letters to the Editor," *Right On* 2, 24 (May 1, 1971): 2; "A Conversation with Francis Schaeffer," *Right On* 5, 10 (April 1974): 1, 10. On the collaboration of CWLF and Os Guinness, "a long-time favorite lecturer of ours," see "Notes from the Catacombs," *Right On* 4, 9 (April 1973): 2.

18. For a series of critiques by evangelical scholars, see Ronald W. Ruegsegger, ed., *Reflections on Francis Schaeffer* (Grand Rapids, Mich.: Zondervan, 1986). On Schaeffer's influence on evangelicalism, see Michael Hamilton, "The Dissatisfaction of Francis Schaeffer," *Christianity Today* 41, 3 (March 3, 1997): 22–30. On evangelical students who visited L'Abri, see "A Conversation with Francis Schaeffer," *Right On* 5, 10 (April 1974): 1, 10.

19. On CWLF's critique and protests of Eastern religions, see "Up from Zen," *Right On* 3, 27 (August 4, 1971): 2, 7; "The Christian Student Coalition of UC Disavows Sun Myung Moon as a Representative of the Christian Faith in any Sense of the Term"; "An Open Letter to the Unified Family of Sun Myung Moon"; and "Prophet? A Challenge to Sun Myung Moon"; and "Open Letter to the Devotees of Guru Maharaj Ji" in Box 2, Jill Shook Papers, CWLF Collection, GTUA. On the Spiritual Counterfeits Project, see carton 22, reel 83, folder 43 in Series "Counterculture, Community, and Alternative Religion, 1963–1981," Social Protest Collection, BL. On CWLF and TM, see "SCP Wins TM Lawsuit: "Victory at Last!! TM Ruled to be Religious in Nature!!" Berkeley Christian Coalition newsletter (November 1977), 1, in Box 2, Jill Shook Papers, CWLF Collection, GTUA; CWLF newsletter, circa 1975, Box 2, Jill Shook Papers, CWLF Collection, GTUA. On the evangelical left and Christian apologetics, see Clark Pinnock, *Set Forth Your Case: Studies in Christian Apologetics* (Nutley, N.J.: Craig Press, 1968); Jim Moore, "In Defense of the Christian Faith," *Post-American* 1, 1 (Fall 1971): 12–13; Ron Sider, "A Case for Easter," *HIS* 32, 7 (April 1972): 26–31.

20. On the Democratic National Convention, see David Gill, "The Messiah in Miami Beach," *Right On* 4, 2 (August 1972): 5. On CWLF's tour, see Jack N. Sparks to

"Brothers and Sisters," Box 2, Jill Shook Papers, CWLF Collection, GTUA; Heinz, "Jesus in Berkeley," 359. On the Merry Pranksters, see Tom Wolfe, *The Electric Kool-Aid Acid Test* (New York: Bantam, 1968).

21. On "the inevitability of Christ's victory," see Dennis MacDonald, "Christian Transcendence: Dope or Hope," *Post-American* 1, 2 (Winter 1972): 8–9. On knowing Jesus existentially, see "Have You Seen Jesus My Lord," *Right On* 4, 1 (July 1972): 6. On a revolutionary politics rooted in faith, see Os Guinness, *The Dust of Death: A Critique of the Establishment and the Counter Culture, and the Proposal for a Third Way* (Downers Grove, Ill.: InterVarsity Press, 1973), 368–69. On *Christianity Today* and Harold Lindsell's preoccupation with the "battle for the Bible," see Lindsell, *Battle for the Bible* (Grand Rapids, Mich.: Zondervan, 1976).

22. On Dennis's vision of spiritual community, see Lane T. Dennis, *A Reason for Hope* (Old Tappan, N.J.: Revell, 1976), 13–50; Dennis, "Living in a Technological World," *The Other Side* 9, 3 (May–June 1973): 36–41; Tom Skinner, "Jesus or Barabbas?" *Right On* 2, 21 (February 3, 1971): 1–2; Charles Reich, *The Greening of America* (New York: Random House, 1970), 376. On the third way and the larger cooperative living movement, see the dozen evangelical communities listed in the "1975 Community Directory," in *Communities: A Journal of Cooperative Living* 12 (1975), copy in Box VI10, Folder "News Articles and Papers," Sojourners Collection, WCSC. On the revolutionary nature of community and its challenge to the establishment, see Jack Sparks, review of *The American Condition*, by Richard Goodwin, peach-colored leaflet in Box 2, Jill Shook Papers, CWLF Collection, GTUA; "Proposed Social and Economic Foundations for a Christian Society," Box 21, Folder 41, Social Protests Collection, BL.

23. On small-scale culture, see Dennis, "Technological World," 38. On fears of modern technology, see Gallagher, "Notes from the Catacombs," *Right On* 4, 11 (June 1973): 2; Brendan Furnish, "The Big Brother Syndrome" *Right On* 4, 11 (June 1973): 1. On a disintegrating world, see "Reach Me" and "Heal the Earth," *Right On* 1, 14 (May 1, 1970): 1, 3. For "The Revolutionary Catechism," see *Right On* 1, 17 (October 27, 1970): 2. On ecological collapse, see "Last Days Boogie," *Right On* 2, 25 (June 3, 1971): 3; Herman Neudiks, "The Ecology of Eden," *Right On* 3, 5 (November 1971): 3.

24. For Roszak's influence, see *Where the Wasteland Ends* (Garden City, N.Y.: Doubleday, 1973), 348; Interview with Roszak, "Counterculture," *Right On* 5, 12 (June 1974): 1, 6. On living communally see undated CWLF newsletters and "Community Farms" brochure in Box 2, Jill Shook Papers, CWLF Collection, GTUA. On Rising Son Ranch, see Eddi Kaliss, "Meanwhile Back at the Ranch," *Right On* 3, 12 (June 1972): 7–8; Walter and Ginny Hearn interview by author, July 9, 2006, Berkeley, Cal. On CWLF's enthusiasm for F. F. Schumacher's *Small Is Beautiful*, see Jack Sparks, *Right On* 6, 1 (July–August 1974): 4.

25. On resocializing new converts into a "forever family," see Heinz, "Jesus in Berkeley," 196, 344–51. For the story of Pedro Ramos, a drug user CWLF picked up in New York City on its nationwide tour, see Walter and Ginny Hearn interview by author, July 11, 2006, Berkeley, Cal.; Pedro Ramos, "Jonah in America," *Right On* 6, 4

(November 1974): 9. On CWLF's resonance with Reba Place's Dave and Neta Jackson's *Living Together in a World Falling Apart* and Dietrich Bonhoeffer's *Life Together,* see *Right On* 6, 1 (July–August 1974): 4. On discipleship, see David Gill, "The Meaning of Conversion: Discipleship and Life," *Right On* 6, 6 (February 1975): 8; Gill, "The Meaning of Conversion: Communities in the World," *Right On* 6, 7 (March 1975): 9; "In Quest of Discipleship: A Post-American Education-Action Seminar in Chicago," Summer 1973, Box IV3, Folder "News Releases and Post-American," Sojourners Collection, WCSC; Wes Michaelson, "Evangelicalism and Radical Discipleship," in *Evangelicalism and Anabaptism,* ed. C. Norman Krauss (Scottdale, Pa.: Herald Press, 1979), 63–82; Bob Sabath and Jim Wallis, "In Quest of Discipleship," *Post-American* 2, 3 (May–June 1973): 3. A key text on discipleship read by young evangelicals was Dietrich Bonhoeffer, *The Cost of Discipleship* (New York: Macmillan, 1959).

26. On community discipline and excommunication, see Heinz, "Jesus in Berkeley," 472–74; Art Gish, *Living in Christian Community* (Scottdale, Pa.: Herald Press, 1979), 133–79; Gish, "Love as Church Discipline," *The Other Side* 9, 2 (March–April 1973): 133–79; Ron Sider, "Spare the Rod and Spoil the Church: Would Your Church Excommunicate Anyone? Why Not?" *Eternity* (July 1976): 18–20, 46. On the intensity of emotions, self-analysis, accountability, and confrontations of fellow members, see Box 2 (1/H/1: 94-9-03), Folder "Redeemer King Church Notes," BL; "Community: The Closeness We Need," *Right On* 6, 8 (April 1975): 4–5. On the formalization of CWLF's structure, see Heinz, "Jesus in Berkeley," 482–85; Jack Sparks, "The Christian Ecclesia: A Community Governed by God" and "Where We Are Going," December 1973, and a set of flow charts regarding organizational clarity and accountability, in Box 2, Jill Shook Papers, CWLF Collection, GTUA.

27. On CWLF's attempt to integrate blacks into their community, see Sharon Gallagher et al., "A Dream We Had," Box 2, Jill Shook Papers, CWLF Collection, GTUA. On titles of distinction, see Walter and Ginny Hearn interview by author, July 9, 2006, Berkeley, Cal.; Arthur G. Gish, "Simplicity," *Post-American* 1, 2 (Winter 1972): 10; Gish, *Beyond the Rat Race* (Scottsdale, Pa.: Herald Press, 1973), 51; Gish, *The New Left and Christian Radicalism* (Grand Rapids, Mich.: Eerdmans, 1970). On Daddy Sparks and "Servant" armbands, see Heinz, "Jesus in Berkeley," 260, 369.

28. On CWLF's "cult of improvisation" and fluid organizational structure, see Heinz, "Jesus in Berkeley," 3, 163–67. On the initial hostility toward feminism by CWLF, see Mary Phillips, "My Experiences with Feminine Oppression," *Green Leaf* 7, 1 (Spring 1983): 4–6; "Donna Quixote and the Impossible Dream," *Right On* 1, 3 (August 1969): 3. On increasing resonance with feminism, see "Women's Lib" by "a liberated sister," *Right On* 2, 21 (February 3, 1971): 3; Sharon Gallagher chapter in *Our Struggle to Serve,* 94–99; Heinz, "Jesus in Berkeley," 238–42; Gish, *Beyond the Rat Race,* 53, 166; "Equality of the Sexes" and "Radical Street Christianity Workshop" in undated CWLF newsletter, Box 2, Jill Shook Papers, CWLF Collection, GTUA; Sharon Gallagher, "Women vs. Politics in Mexico City," *Right On* 7, 2 (September 1975): 5, 10.

29. On Hearst and the SLA, see "Kidnapped: An Open Statement to the Hearsts and the SLA," *Right On* 5, 9 (March 1974): 3. See the next issue for Wallis's statement. On the Crucible, see "The Crucible," *Right On* 4, 3 (September 1972): 5; CWLF newsletter, November 1, 1973, copy in CWLF Collection, GTUA; Heinz, "Jesus in Berkeley," 323.

30. On the Post-Americans' free university, see "Minutes of the People's Christian Coalition," October 3, 1971, Box VII7, Folder "People's Christian Coalition, Trinity," Sojourners Collection, WCSC. On the food cooperative, see Jackie Sabath, *Sojourners' Newsletter* (Spring 1978): 2; "When Religion Blends with Social Activism," *U.S. News and World Report* (December 31, 1979): 81–82; Joyce Hollyday, "The Euclid Food Club," *Euclid Street Journal* (circa 1983): 1, copy in Box X1, Folder "Local Ministries, Sojourners Collection, WCSC. On tenant organizing, see Joyce Hollyday, *Sojourners' Newsletter* (Spring 1977): 1, copy in Box VII1, Folder "Sojo Community," Sojourners Collection, WCSC; "Repair and Deduct Is Stuck," flyer of Southern Columbia Heights Tenant Union, Box VII1, Folder "Sojo Community," Sojourners Collection, WCSC; "The Third Era," Folder "Articles About Community," Sojourners Collection, WCSC. On social justice at the local level, see Dick Taylor, "Discovering Your Neighborhood's Needs: A Practical Guide for Beginning a Local Ministry," *Sojourners* 8, 6 (June 1979): 22–24.

31. See, for example, Jubilee Fellowship of Germantown in Philadelphia; Post-American Community in Chicago/Sojourners Fellowship in Washington, D.C.; Koinonia Farm in Americus, Georgia; Worden Street Community and Christ's Community in Grand Rapids, Michigan; CWLF in Berkeley; Church of the Saviour in Washington; Menominee River Fellowship in Wallace, Michigan; Grace and Peace Fellowship in St. Louis; Patchwork Central in Evansville, Indiana; Bartimaeus Community in Berkeley; Community Covenant in Missoula, Montana; New Covenant Fellowship of Urbana-Champaign, Illinois. For more of the substantial third-way literature, see Dave Jackson and Neta Jackson, *Living Together in a World Falling Apart* (Carol Stream, Ill.: Creation House, 1974); "Even Bibles Are Mass Produced," *Manna* 1, 5 (circa Fall 1970): 1; Joan Wulff, "Searching for Community in an Individualistic Age," *HIS* 42, 6 (March 1982): 5; Jim Wallis, "The New Community," *Post-American* 2, 4 (September–October 1973): 1; David H. Janzen, "The Empire of Mammon and the Joyous Fellowship," *Post-American* 2, 4 (September–October 1973): 2, 15; Elizabeth O'Connor, *The New Community* (New York: Harper & Row, 1976); O'Connor, "Common Life," *Sojourners* 5, 4 (April 1976): 35–37. Also see numerous articles throughout the 1970s in *HIS* on "small groups." On the popularity of the Jacksons' *Living Together* and Dietrich Bonhoeffer's *Life Together*, see Bill Ellis, "Books for Young Evangelicals," *Christian Bookseller Magazine* (January 1975): 25.

32. Sojourners kept a card file with a list of more than 130 U.S.-based communities, house churches, resistance groups, and emerging fellowships with which they had personal contact. They also kept a list of more than 200 additional communities that they had heard about. See Bob Sabath, "A Community of Communities: The

Growing Ecumenical Network," *Sojourners* 9, 1 (January 1980): 17–19. Examples of Anabaptist-oriented communities include Reba Place Fellowship in Evanston, Ill; Plow Creek Fellowship of central Illinois; Grain of Wheat Fellowship in Winnipeg, Manitoba. Examples of charismatic communities include Church of the Redeemer in Houston, Tex.; Church of the Messiah in Detroit; Community of Celebration in Woodland Park, Col.; Community of Celebration in Scotland; New Jerusalem Community in Cincinnati; Son of God in Cleveland. Examples of Jesus People communities include Bethlehem Covenant Community (seven households) in Lake Oswego, Oregon; Highway Missionary Society near Grants Pass, Oregon; House of Elijah in Yakima, Washington; Shiloh Youth Revival Center, which established over 180 communal houses across the nation (70 in Oregon alone) between 1968 and 1978. See Joe V. Peterson, "Jesus People: Christ, Communes and the Counterculture of the Late Twentieth Century in the Pacific Northwest," Master's thesis, Northwest Christian College, 1980, 32, 40. The Brunswick Christian Community, renamed North Coast Christian Community in Ohio, included Silver Spring Christian Community and Akron Christian Community, among others. On groups with a contemplative emphasis, see Jubilee Community, Winnipeg, Manitoba.

33. On Carter's "malaise speech," see Richard V. Pierard and Robert D. Linder, *Civil Religion and the Presidency* (Grand Rapids, Mich.: Zondervan, 1988), 251–55; "President Carter and the Energy War," *Public Justice Newsletter* 2, 10 (August–September 1979): 1–3. On the influence of Christopher Lasch, Catholic intellectuals, and Carter's own evangelical faith on the development of the speech, see Kenneth Morris, *Jimmy Carter, American Moralist* (Athens: University of Georgia Press, 1996), 1–7; Daniel Horowitz, *The Anxieties of Affluence: Critiques of American Consumer Culture, 1939–1979* (Amherst: University of Massachusetts Press, 2004), 225–44.

34. On Hatfield and CWLF, see "Hatfield on Vietnam," *Right On* 6, 10 (June 1975): 9; Hatfield, "On Hunger," *Right On* 6, 7 (March 1975): 1, 3–4. On Carter's "malaise speech," see Hedrick Smith, "Reshaping of Carter's Presidency," *New York Times*, July 22, 1979, 1. On the Thanksgiving Workshop, see "From the Political-Social-Economic Involvement Group," Folder "1973 Chicago Declaration," ESAA. On the counterculture's exodus from the cities, see Douglas C. Rossinow, *The Politics of Authenticiy: Liberalism, Christianity, and the New Left in America* (New York: Columbia University Press, 1998), 249.

35. For an example of criticism of the third way, see Paul B. Henry, "Love, Power and Justice," *Christian Century* 94, 37 (November 23, 1977): 1088–92. For Wallis on spirituality "as the new front," see Jim McManus, "Sojourners: Magazine, Community—And More," *National Catholic Reporter*, copy in Box IV3, Folder "News Releases and More," Sojourners Collection, WCSC.

36. For "socio-economic conditions," see "Notes from the Catacombs," *Right On* 3, 12 (June 1972): 2. On declining to vote, see Jim and Glenda VandenBosch, "Nixon, McGovern and the Only Choice in '72," *Vanguard* (October 1972): 12–17; Jack Buckley, "Enough Is Enough," *Right On* 9, 2 (September–October 1977): 12; Jim Wallis,

"Election Reflections," *Post-American* 2, 1 (January–February 1973): 3; David Gill, "Radical Politics," *Right On* 8, 2 (September–October 1976): 5. On Michaelson's vote, see Walter and Ginny Hearn interview by author, July 9, 2006, Berkeley, Cal. On the Post-Americans' new name, see "Minutes of Post-American Staff Meeting," October 20, 1975, Box IV3, Folder "News Releases and Post-American," Sojourners Collection, WCSC. On the name change, see Wallis, "Sojourners," *Post-American* 4, 8 (1975): 3–4. On worship as politics, see Robert Sabath, "The Politics of Worship," *Post-American* 1, 5 (Fall 1972): 8–9. On dropping out, see David Gill, "Time to Drop Out?" *Right On* 5, 3 (September 1973): 3; Gill, "Radical Christian," *Right On* 8, 2 (September–October 1976): 5.

37. For "close allegiance," see Gallagher, "Notes from the Catacombs," *Right On* 6, 2 (September 1974): 2.

38. On forging "solidarity with those who suffer," see Guinness, *Dust of Death*, 375. On "working in community," see Gallagher, "Notes from the Catacombs," *Right On* 5, 5 (November 1973): 2. On politics as a spiritual quest, see Dennis MacDonald, "The Order of the Shovel," *Post-American* 1, 1 (Fall 1971): 6; Michaelson, "Politics and Spirituality," *Post-American* 3, 3 (April 1974): 26–29.

39. For arguments that the outward-focused 1960s evolved to an inward-focused 1970s, see Charles Morris, *A Time of Passion: America, 1960–1980* (New York: Penguin, 1984); Todd Gitlin, *The Sixties: Years of Hope, Days of Rage* (New York: Bantam, 1987); Erland Jorstad, *Evangelicals in the White House: The Cultural Maturation of Born-Again Christianity* (New York: Mellen, 1981), 40–49; Maurice Isserman and Michael Kazin, "The Failure and Success of the New Radicalism," in *The Rise and Fall of the New Deal Order, 1930–1980*, ed. Steve Fraser and Gary Gerstle (Princeton, N.J.: Princeton University Press, 1989). On the pet rock, see Schulman, *The Seventies*, xii. For a similar attempt to de-center the 1960s by looking for persistence of political activity into the 1970s, see Jama Lazerow, "1960–1974," in *A Companion to 20th-Century America*, ed. Stephen J. Whitfield (New York: Blackwell, 2004), 87–101. On the church as "an inexhaustible revolutionary force," see Jim Wallis, "Biblical Politics," *Post-American* 3, 3 (April 1974): 3–4.

Chapter 6. Samuel Escobar and the Global Reflex

Epigraph: Samuel Escobar, "Evangelism and Man's Search for Freedom, Justice and Fulfillment," in *Let the Earth Hear His Voice*, ed. J. D. Douglas (Minneapolis: World Wide Publications, 1975), 316.

1. Barbara Kingsolver, *The Poisonwood Bible* (New York: Harper, 1998); Bethany Moreton, "The Soul of Neoliberalism," *Social Text* 92, 3 (Fall 2007): 103–23.

2. One of the first scholarly treatments of this "missions reflex" came out of a conference at Wheaton College. The papers were published in Joel A. Carpenter and Wilbert R. Shenk, *Earthen Vessels: American Evangelicals and Foreign Missions, 1880–1980*

(Grand Rapids, Mich.: Eerdmans, 1990). On SDS and third world influence, see Todd Gitlin, *The Sixties: Years of Hope, Days of Rage* (Toronto: Bantam, 1987). On social change as "a top-priority issue," see C. Peter Wagner, "Evangelism and Social Action in Latin America," *Christianity Today* 10, 7 (January 7, 1966): 338. On the rapid growth of Latin American evangelicalism, see Valdir Steuernagel, "The Theology of Mission in Its Relation to Social Responsibility within the Lausanne Movement," Th.D. dissertation, Lutheran School of Theology, 1988, 125; Virgil Gerber, "Latin America's Protestant 'Silent Majority,'" *Evangelical Missions Quarterly* 6, 3 (1970): 166.

3. On Escobar's childhood church, see Escobar, "Los evangelicos y la politica," *Certeza* 8 (1967): 230–32; C. René Padilla, "Latin American Evangelicals Enter the Public Square," *Transformation* 9, 3 (1995): 2–7; Escobar, "Heredero de la Reforma radical," in *Hacia una teología evangélica latinoamericana*, ed. C. René Padilla (San José: Editorial Caribe, 1984), 52–53. On evangelical marginalization, see Escobar, "Conflict of Interpretations of Popular Protestantism," in *New Face of the Church in Latin America: Between Tradition and Change*, ed. Guillermo Cook (Maryknoll, N.Y.: Orbis), 117–19; Escobar, "Heredero," 52.

4. On Peruvian and evangelical social action, see Escobar, "Heredero," 53–55; for "different, more authentic Christianity," see page 53. On liberation theology, see Sharon E. Heaney, *Contextual Theology for Latin America: Liberation Themes in Evangelical Perspective* (Colorado Springs: Paternoster, 2008), 27, 34.

5. Escobar, "Heredero," 53–58; Escobar in *The Chicago Declaration*, ed. Ronald Sider (Carol Stream, Ill.: Creation House, 1974), 119.

6. Escobar, "Heredero," 57–63; "Dr. Escobar Reflects on a Life in Mission," *In Ministry* (Fall 2005): 12–14; René Padilla interview, Carlos René Padilla Collection, BGCA. For Escobar on social and political instability, see Daniel Salinas, "The Beginnings of the Fraternidad Teológica Latinoamericana," *Latin American Theology* 2, 1 (2007): 114–15. On "latinization," see David Stoll, *Is Latin America Turning Protestant?: The Politics of Evangelical Growth* (Berkeley: University of California Press, 1990), 131.

7. Clyde W. Taylor to Billy Graham, July 1, 1968. Box 2, Folder 3, Primer Congreso Latinoamericano de Evangelización Collection, BGCA, quoted in Salinas, "Beginnings," 41; "Evangelism in Latin America," *Christianity Today* 14, 6 (December 19, 1969): 22.

8. On "indignation," see Escobar, quoted in Salinas, "Beginnings," 46. For an English translation of Escobar's speech, see "The Social Responsibility of the Church in Latin America," *Evangelical Missions Quarterly* 6, 3 (1970): 129–52. Núñez quoted in Salinas, "Beginnings," 40.

9. On "thunderous applause," see C. René Padilla, "Evangelism and Social Responsibility: From Wheaton '66 to Wheaton '83," *Transformation* 2, 3 (1985): 27–33. On "contextualized reflection," see Anthony Christopher Smith, "The Essentials of Missiology from the Evangelical Perspective of the Fraternidad Teológica Latinoamericana," Ph.D. dissertation, Southern Baptist Theological Seminary, 1983, 16–17. On "gleefully discovering each other," see Escobar, "La Fundacion de la Fraternidad,"

17. On being "tired of evangelical centers of power," see Escobar, "Heredero," 64. On the "Evangelical Declaration of Bogotá," see Salinas, "Beginnings," 39–40. For "without a theology," see Padilla, "A Church Without Theology," *Christianity Today* 18, 9 (February 1, 1974): 49. On not feeling represented by North Americans, see Escobar, "La Fundacion de la Fraternidad," 17. For "grownups," see Escobar, "Heredero," 64.

10. On the meeting in Cochabamba, see Salinas, "Beginnings," 51–58; Escobar, "La Fundación de la Fraternidad," 7–25. On liberation theology, see Gustavo Gutierrez, *A Theology of Liberation: History, Politics, and Salvation* (Maryknoll, N.Y.: Orbis, 1971). On FTL's concerns about liberation theology, see Padilla, "A Steep Climb Ahead for Evangelical Theology in Latin America," *Evangelical Missions Quarterly* 7, 2 (1971): 99–106; Núñez, *Liberation Theology*, 80; Samuel Escobar, "Divided Protestantism Struggles with Latin American Problems," *World Vision Magazine* 13, 10 (November 1969): 32–35; "Latin American Protestants: Which Way Will They Go?" *Christianity Today* 14, 1 (October 10, 1969): 14–16; Terrell Frank Coy, "Incarnation and the Kingdom of God: The Political Theologies of Orlando Costas, C. René Padilla, and Samuel Escobar," Ph.D. dissertation, Southwestern Baptist Theological Seminary, 1999, 58–60, 204.

11. On liberation theology, see Gustavo Gutiérrez, *A Theology of Liberation: History, Politics and Salvation* (Maryknoll, N.Y.: Orbis, 1988); Christian Smith, *The Emergence of Liberation Theology: Radical Religion and the Social Movement Theory* (Chicago: University of Chicago Press, 1991). On North American views of liberation theology as simplistic, see Escobar, "Heredero," 63. On the rise of contextualization in FTL, see Antonio Carlos Barro, "Orlando Enrique Costas: Mission Theologian on the Way and at the Crossroads," Ph.D. dissertation, Fuller Theological Seminary, 1993, 8–40. On FTL's view of dispensationalism as an eschatology to be repudiated, see Coy, "Incarnation and the Kingdom of God," 69. On FTL as an "evangelical variant," see Orlando E. Costas, *Christ Outside the Gate: Mission Beyond Christendom* (Maryknoll, N.Y.: Orbis, 1982), xii. For "theology of holistic mission," see Samuel Escobar email interview by author, April 19, 2010.

12. On early FTL funding, see Stoll, *Is Latin America Turning Protestant?* 131. On Wagner's constitution, see Salinas, "Beginnings," 57. For Wagner's report on Cochabamba and continued battles between FTL and Wagner, see Salinas 62–63; Wagner, "High Theology in the Andes," *Christianity Today* 15, 8 (January 15, 1971): 29; Salinas, "Beginnings," 60–67; Costas, *The Church and Its Mission: A Shattering Critique from the Third World* (Wheaton, Ill.: Tyndale, 1974), 214. For "foreign intervention," see Escobar interview, quoted in Smith, "Essentials of Missiology," 23.

13. On FTL's invitation to Bonino, see Salinas, "Beginnings," 65; Clyde W. Taylor to Peter Savage, January 6, 1972; Peter Savage to Clyde Taylor, January 27, 1972, in Folder 2, Box 8, Charles Peter Wagner Collection, BGCA. On the diversification of FTL's funding, see Smith, "Essentials of Missiology," 29–30. On FTL's rapid growth, see Salinas, "Beginnings," 67.

14. René Padilla interview, February 22, 2001, audio tape in Carlos René Padilla Collection, BGCA.

15. For biographical material on Costas, see A. Barro, "Orlando Enrique Costas: Mission Theologian on the Way and at the Crossroads," Ph.D. dissertation, Fuller Theological Seminary, 1993, 9–44; Elizabeth Conde-Frazier, "Orlando E. Costas," Biola University website, September 3, 2009. On Costas's role in indigenization, see Stoll, *Is Latin America Turning Protestant?* 131. For significant books by Costas, see *The Church and Its Mission*; *Christ Outside the Gate*; and *La Iglesia y su misión evangelizadora* (Buenos Aires: La Aurora, 1971).

16. On Escobar's involvement in Urbana '70, see "Escobar Brings Prophetic Word," *Vanguard* (December 29, 1970), copy in Box 68, Folder 7, "Urbana 1961–1974," InterVarsity Christian Fellowship Collection, BGCA; Richard Hauser, "Missionary Convention Bids for New Concept: Student Group Attempts to Redefine Evangelism Need in Revolutionary Age," *Los Angeles Times*, January 2, 1971, 23. For more on Escobar's influence on InterVarsity, see Grace Roberts, "Witness from the Ground Up," *HIS* 30, 7 (May 1970): 32; Samuel Escobar, "What's Happening to the Fastest Growing Church in the World?" *HIS* 34, 1 (October 1973): 8–11; "Report from Urbana 73," *HIS* 34, 6 (March 1974): 25–26; Linda Sellevaag, "Urbana in Portuguese? Third World Students face the Great Commission," *HIS* 36, 8 (June 1976): 24. For Escobar's writings in other evangelical publications, see "A Look Ahead," *World Vision Magazine* 15, 5 (May 1971): 11–13; "Good News to the Poor," *Post-American* 3, 9 (December 1974): 10; "Interview," *Sojourners* 5, 7 (September 1976): 17.

17. "A Challenge from Evangelicals," *Time* 104, 6 (August 5, 1974): 48–50; Orlando E. Costas, "In-Depth Evangelism in Latin America," 212; René Padilla, "Evangelism and the World" and Samuel Escobar, "Evangelism and Man's Search for Freedom, Justice and Fulfillment," in *Let the Earth Hear His Voice*, ed. J. D. Douglas (Minneapolis: World Wide Publications, 1975), 125–26, 132–40, 303–04, 317; Escobar, "The Return of Christ," in René Padilla, ed., *The New Face of Evangelicalism* (Downers Grove, Ill.: InterVarsity Press, 1976), 262. For more on these themes, see Escobar, *Diálogo entre Cristo y Marx y otros ensayos* (Lima: AGEUP, 1967), 13–27; Escobar, *Decadencia de la religión* (Buenos Aires: Cuadernos de Certeza, 1972), 64–65; Escobar, "The Social Impact of the Gospel," in *Is Revolution Change?* ed. Brian Griffiths (Downers Grove, Ill.: InterVarsity Press, 1972), 89; Escobar, "Jesus Christ: Lord of the Universe," in *Jesus Christ: Lord of the Universe*, ed. David M. Howard (Downers Grove: Ill.: InterVarsity Press, 1974), 23.

18. On the heavy response, positive and negative, to Escobar, see Salinas, "Beginnings," 76, 84. On the two camps, see Carl Henry, *Confessions of a Theologian* (Waco, Tex.: Word, 1986), 350. On negative reaction from North Americans, see Padilla interview, quoted in Salinas, "Beginnings," 80–83. For "disproportionate emphasis," see C. Peter Wagner, "Lausanne Twelve Months Later," *Christianity Today* 19, 20 (July 4, 1975): 7–9. On "the big picture," see McGavran, "The Dimensions of World Evangelization," in *Let the Earth Hear His Voice*, 108. For the best description of the Lausanne dispute between Escobar and Wagner, see Steuernagel, "Theology of Mission," 132–69. On critiques of Padilla and Escobar from conservative third-world delegates,

see J. Ramsey Michaels, "Lausanne: A Show of Strength," *Reformed Journal* 26 (September 1974): 12.

19. On Padilla's warm reception, see Padilla interview, quoted in Salinas, "Beginnings," 80–83; Heaney, *Contextual Theology*, 58. For the text of "Response to Lausanne," see "Theology Implications of Radical Discipleship," in *Let the Earth Hear His Voice*, 1294–96. On the distribution of and reaction to "Response to Lausanne," see Salinas, "Beginnings," 86–87; René Padilla and Chris Sugden, eds., *How Evangelicals Endorsed Social Responsibility* (Nottingham: Grove Books, 1985), 29. On revisions to the Lausanne Statement, see Athol Gill, "Christian Social Responsibility," in *The New Face of Evangelicalism*, 91–92; Heaney, *Contextual Theology*, 58. For audio recordings of the meeting on radical discipleship, see Tapes 180–84, International Congress of World Evangelization Collection, BGCA. On the agonies of the planning committee, see Dain, quoted in John Pollock, *Billy Graham: Evangelist to the World* (San Francisco: Harper & Row, 1979), 209.

20. On John Stott's changing views on the mission of the Church, see Stott, *Christian Mission in the Modern World* (Downers Grove, Ill.: InterVarsity Press, 1975), 23. On Lausanne as a "death blow," see Padilla, "Introduction," *New Face of Evangelicalism*, 12. For "biblical truth," see Escobar, "The Return of Christ," *New Face of Evangelicalism*, 257.

21. On Athyal and FTL, see Salinas, "Beginnings," 67. On FTL, India, Britain, and the Philippines, see Chris Wright, "Social Ethics," *Third Way* 4, 10 (November 1980): 25–26; Chris Sugden, *Radical Discipleship* (London: Marshalls, 1981), 192–95. For more on the spread of FTL influence, see Steuernagel, "Theology of Mission"; Athol Gill, "Christian Social Responsibility, in *New Face of Evangelicalism*, 87–102. On South Africa, see David Prior, "The Church in South Africa," *Right On* 10, 1 (July–August 1978): 15–18.

22. On "syncretic confusion," see Richard Pierard, *"Pax Americana* and the Evangelical Missionary Advance," in *Earthen Vessels: American Evangelicals and Foreign Missions, 1880–1980* (Grand Rapids, Mich.: Eerdmans, 1990), 155–79. For InterVarsity concerns about imperialism, see John Goodwin, "A Man to Reckon With," *HIS* 23, 3 (December 1962): 3; C. Peter Wagner, "Forced to Choose," *HIS* 26, 6 (March 1966): 23–24. For critiques from Costas, see "The Mission of an Affluent Church," *Reformed Journal* 23, 7 (September 1973); "A Sign of Hope: A Latin American Appraisal of Lausanne 1974," *Latin America Evangelist* 54, 6 (November–December 1974): 2.

23. On Escobar, see Smith, "Essentials of Missiology," 47. On the "western model of ministry," see Jonathan T'ien-en Chao, "Education and Leadership," in *The New Face of Evangelicalism*, 191–204. On the West's paternalism, see Pius Wakatama, "Cultural and Social Qualifications for Overseas Service," speech delivered at Urbana '73, written text in *Jesus Christ: Lord of the Universe*. Wakatama wanted only evangelical missionaries trained in anthropology and meeting certain spiritual criteria to work in Africa. See Pius Wakatama, *Independence for the Third World Church: An African's Perspective on Missionary Work* (Downers Grove, Ill.: InterVarsity Press,

1978). For a similar critique from a Cameroonian pastor, see Samuel Akono, "Sit Down," *The Other Side* 8, 3 (May–June 1972): 10–11, 38.

24. On mission work as irrelevant, see letter to John Alexander, Box 72, Folder 6, "Problems for Solving, 1973," InterVarsity Collection, BGCA. On "anti-missionary feeling," see David Howard to Peter Northrup, April 17, 1973, Box 52, Folder 2, "Brooks report [Western staff]; 1968–1973," InterVarsity Collection, BGCA. For Bill Conard, see "Letter to the Editor," *HIS* 32, 7 (April 1972): 18. For other examples, see Kathryn A. Lindskoog, "Dark Continents of Men's Minds," *The Other Side* 8, 3 (May–June 1972): 28–29, 38; James W. Skillen, "Failing to Love our American Neighbors," *Vanguard* (May–June 1972): 23–25.

25. Ayub Waitara, "Perspective," *Wheaton Record* 87, 20 (February 25, 1965): 2; Núñez, "Personal and Eternal Salvation and Human Redemption," in *Let the Earth Hear His Voice*, 155–79; Núñez and William David Taylor, *Crisis in Latin America* (Chicago: Moody Press, 1989), 102; René Padilla, "The Church and the Third World," *Right On* 7, 3 (October 1975): 6; Padilla, "Spiritual Conflict," in *New Face of Evangelicalism*, 208–11.

26. Fred Smith, "Needed: Reappraisal of U.S. Attitudes," *Wheaton Record* 87, 15 (January 14, 1965): 3; Steve Brobeck, "Communist Unity Broken," *Wheaton Record* 87, 18 (February 11, 1965): 2; David Adeney, "Beyond the Bamboo Curtain," *HIS* 38, 6 (March 1978): 1–6; Charles Troutman to Jim McLeish, May 23, 1976, Box 20, Folder 3, "Campus Crusade: Correspondence and Materials, 1960–1976," InterVarsity Collection, BGCA; Barbara Benjamin, "Immigrant Love: Embracing Our New Neighbors," *HIS* 42, 2 (November 1981): 13.

27. "An Open Letter to North American Christians," *Vanguard* (January–February 1977): 4–5; Paul Leggett, "Panama Canal: Three Myths" *Sojourners* 5, 8 (October 1976): 12–13; Clelia Buastavino, "Letters to the Editor," *HIS* 39, 6 (March 1979): 2; "Letter from Central America," *Sojourners* 6, 10 (November 1977): 9; Plutarcho Bonilla, Saul Trinidad, et al., "A Letter of Tears to North American Christians," Folder "Discipleship Workshops," ESAA.

28. Russell Straayer, "Draft Alternatives Explained by Student Booth and Forum," *Chimes* 62, 10 (December 1, 1967): 4; Joyce K. Ribbens, "The C.I.A. Capers: Keeping the World Safe," *Vanguard* (January–February 1976): 22–23; Delton Franz, "On Why the Hungry Aren't Being Fed," *Vanguard* (June 1976): 11; March–April 1977 issue of *Vanguard* on imperialism in Uganda; Boyd Reese, "America's Empire," *Post-American* 2, 5 (November–December 1973): 10–11, 14; Eqbal Ahmad, "How We Look to the Third World," *Post-American* 2, 5 (November–December 1973): 8–9, reprinted from *The Nation*, March 3, 1969; "Door Interview: Dr. Anthony Campolo," *Wittenburg Door* 32 (August–September 1976): 12–13; "Valuable Sources: Missionaries and the CIA," *Sojourners* 5, 1 (January 1976): 8–9; "Hatfield Urges Ban on CIA Use of Missionaries," *Eternity* 27, 3 (March 1976): 9.

29. Victor Landero, *Victor: The Victor Landero Story* (Old Tappan, N.J.: Revell, 1979), 128–43; Gregorio Landero, "Evangelism and Social Concern," December 28, 1973, speech at Urbana '73, written text in *Jesus Christ: Lord of the Universe*.

30. "Warren and Shirley Webster, "Segregation and World Missions"; Bernard Bancroft, "Color and Missions"; Dave and Anna Gay Newell, "Letters," *Freedom Now* 3, 1 (January–February 1967): 11–13, 17–18. On international pressure at Wheaton, see "International Student Addresses Claphams," *Wheaton Record* 85, 20 (February 14, 1963): 1; "Okite Relates African Strides to U.S. Civil Rights Movement," *Wheaton Record* 88, 19 (February 17, 1966): 4; So Yan Pul, "Senior Deprecates Racial Attitudes," *Wheaton Record* 88, 18 (February 10, 1966): 4. At Calvin, see John LaGrand, "Christian Political Action?" *Chimes* 59, 7 (October 30, 1964): 3. For Howard Jones, see "Missions Prejudice," *HIS* 25, 4 (January 1965): 1, 3.

31. René Padilla interview, Carlos René Padilla Collection, BGCA; Peter Rucro, "Materialism Blights American Sensitivity," *Wheaton Record* 88, 12 (December 9, 1965): 2; "Foreign Students Speak," *HIS* 22, 5 (February 1961): 17; Dennis Pape, "Big Bucks, Big Preachers," *HIS* 43, 4 (January 1983): 31.

32. On CWLF, see flyer from "Christian Information Committee," Carton 23, Reel 86, Folder 30, "Religion, 1966–82," Social Protest Collection, BL; Ronald G. Mitchell, "Christianity and Oppressed Peoples," *Right On* 5, 11 (May 1974): 3, 10. On "exploitive robbery," see Herb McMullan, "Man and Technocracy," *Post-American* 1, 2 (Winter 1972): 4–5. On the World Food Conference, see Mark Hatfield, "An Economics for Sustaining Humanity," *Post-American* 4, 3 (March 1975): 16–21; Robert Eells and Bartell Nyberg, *Lonely Walk: The Life of Senator Mark Hatfield* (Portland, Ore.: Multnomah Press, 1979): 131–43. For other statements against evangelical materialism and its role in economic oppression, see John White, *The Golden Cow: Materialism in the Twentieth-Century Church* (Downers Grove, Ill.: InterVarsity Press, 1979); Delton Franz, "There's Many a Slip Twixt Hand and Lip: On Why the Hungry Aren't Being Fed," *Vanguard* (June 1976): 10–13; Thomas Hanks, *God So Loved the Third World: The Biblical Vocabulary of Oppression* (Maryknoll, NY: Orbis Books, 1983); Elsa Tamez, *Bible of the Oppressed* (Maryknoll, N.Y.: Orbis, 1982).

33. On evangelical global relief, see Linda Diane Smith, "An Awakening of Conscience: The Changing Response of American Evangelicals Toward World Poverty," Ph.D. dissertation, American University, 1986, ii. Bread for the World, with a membership of 43,000, cast its appeals in evangelical terms. The organization, led by Arthur Simon, brother of U.S. senator Paul Simon of Illinois, formed educational and political lobbying arms with over 250 local chapters. See Arthur Simon, *Christian Faith and Public Policy: No Grounds for Divorce* (Grand Rapids, Mich.: Eerdmans, 1976); *A Report on the State of World Hunger* (Washington, D.C.: Bread for the World Institute, 1990); Dennis R. Hoover, "The Political Mobilization of the Evangelical Left," M.Phil thesis, Oxford University, 1992, 97–99. On long-term, political, and scholarly approaches to economics and justice, see Emilio Castro, "Strategies for Confronting Unjust Social Structures," *Reformed Journal* 25, 4 (April 1975): 17; *Reforming Economics: A Christian Perspective on Economic Theory and Practice* (Grand Rapids, Mich.: Calvin College Center for Christian Scholarship, 1986); Alan Nichols, "An Evangelical Commitment to Simple Life-Style," Lausanne Occasional Paper 20, March

1980; Jack Nelson, *Hunger for Justice: The Politics of Food and Faith* (Maryknoll, N.Y.: Orbis Books, 1980); Miriam Adeney, *God's Foreign Policy* (Grand Rapids, Mich.: Eerdmans, 1984), 71–73; Tony Campolo, "The Greening of Gulf and Western," *Eternity* (January 1981): 30–32; George Fuller, "Making Business Behave," *Eternity* (May 1980): 17–22; Smith, "Awakening of Conscience," 111–22.

34. "Third World Participants," Folder "1974 Chicago Workshop," ESA Collection, BGCA; "Workshops," Box 4, Folder 15, "Evangelical Women's Caucus; records; November 1974–May 1976, n.d.," ESA Collection, BGCA.

35. For "real joy," see Samuel Escobar in Ron Sider, ed., *The Chicago Declaration* (Carol Stream, Ill.: Creation House, 1974), 119.

36. Pinnock quoted in Brian Walsh, "The Evangelical Theological Society," *Vanguard* (June 1976): 24–25.

Chapter 7. Richard Mouw and the Reforming of Evangelical Politics

Epigraph: Richard Mouw, *Political Evangelism* (Grand Rapids, Mich.: Eerdmans, 1973), 15–16.

1. Richard Mouw, *The Smell of Sawdust* (Grand Rapids, Mich.: Zondervan, 2000), 29–31.

2. Mouw, *Smell of Sawdust*, 30–32, 101, 153; Mouw, "A Moment in Madison Square Garden," *Washingtonpost.com*, January 8, 2007; Mouw interview by Krista Tippett, "The Power of Fundamentalism," *Speaking of Faith*, August 19, 2004.

3. Mouw, *Smell of Sawdust*, 38–39, 47–49, 54; Mouw interview by Joshua Friedman, "Ultimately Everything Holds Together," *Atlantic Online* (October 2000).

4. Mouw interview by author, July 12, 2006, Pasadena, Cal.; Mouw, *Smell of Sawdust*, 29, 39–40; Alan Rifkin, "Jesus with a Genius Grant," *Los Angeles Times Magazine* (November 23, 2003): 22–40; Mouw, "Weaving a Coherent Pattern of Discipleship," *Christian Century* 92, 27 (August 20–27, 1975): 729; Mouw, "Fool-osophy," *Christian Century* 126, 6 (March 24, 2009): 35.

5. Mouw, *Smell of Sawdust*, 40–43; Mouw interview by Krista Tippett, August 19, 2004.

6. Mouw, "Weaving a Coherent Pattern of Discipleship," 728–31.

7. Abraham Kuyper, *Lectures on Calvinism* (1898; Grand Rapids, Mich.: Eerdmans, 1961), 171; James Bratt, *Dutch Calvinism in Modern America* (Grand Rapids, Mich.: Eerdmans, 1984), 16; Richard Mouw, *Abraham Kuyper: A Short and Personal Introduction* (Grand Rapids, Mich.: Eerdmans, 2011).

8. Martin LaMaire, "All-Out Christianity," *The Other Side* 7, 2 (March–April 1971): 28–31.

9. For the "faith of our fathers," see John Lagerwey, "The Great Gap," *Chimes* 60, 25 (April 22, 1966): 3. On the move to the suburban Knollcrest campus, see Roger Helder, "Suburban Segregation," *Chimes* 63, 7 (November 1, 1968): 2. On campus agitators, see

John J. Timmerman, *Promises to Keep: A Centennial History of Calvin College* (Grand Rapids, Mich.: Eerdmans, 1975), 102, 151. In the late 1960s, students rallied against a Board of Trustees decision that banned black comedian and social activist Dick Gregory from speaking on campus with signs that read "Get the Dead Wood off the Board"; "Bored of Procrustees"; and "No More Hip-Pocket Sanhedrins." In another incident students burned dean of students Philip Lucasse in effigy in protest about student residence policies. See "Demonstration Precedes Board Rationale on Gregory Decision," *Chimes* 62, 12 (January 12, 1968): 1; "The Dean Burns in Effigy During Ad Hoc Demonstration," *Chimes* 63 (April 25, 1969): 3. For the "Youth Manifesto," see *The Other Side* 7, 3 (Summer 1971): 8–11, 34.

10. On "I Am Not One of Us," see Richard J. Mouw, "A Bit of a Gadfly," in *Serving the Claims of Justice: The Thoughts of Paul B. Henry*, ed. Douglas L. Koopman (Grand Rapids, Mich.: Calvin College, 2001), 115. On civil rights activity, see Lester DeKoster in *Reformed Journal* 13, 1 (January 1963): 3. On the March on Washington, see "'The Answer Is Blowing in the Wind," *Reformed Journal* 13, 7 (September 1963): 3–4; Peter Huiner, "Shall We March?" *Reformed Journal* 15, 4 (April 1965): 6–9. On urban work in Grand Rapids, see "Smedes, Urban League Sparks Integration Drive," *Calvin Chimes* 57, 1 (September 12, 1962): 1. On antiwar activity among Calvin's faculty, see "Forty-Seven Calvin Professors Place Anti-War Ad in GR 'Press'," *Chimes* 62, 20 (March 15, 1968): 1; "Report to the President," September 30, 1969, in William Spoelhof Collection, CCA; Mouw interview by author, July 12, 2006, Pasadena, Cal.

11. Richard Mouw, *Political Evangelism* (Grand Rapids, Mich.: Eerdmans, 1973), 7, 13–16.

12. On the growth of ICS, see advertisement from "A Community of Christian Scholars Shaking the Foundations," *Vanguard* (January 1971): 23. On the irrelevant moralisms of CRC, see Bratt, *Dutch Calvinism*, 208. On Hart's itinerant work, see Robert E. VanderVennen, *A University for the People: A History of the Institute for Christian Studies* (Sioux Center, Iowa: Dordt College Press, 2008), 48–49.

13. On ICS's Dutch ethnicity, see VanderVennen, *University for the People*, 1. On the countercultural ethos, see Mouw interview by author, July 12, 2006, Pasadena, Cal.; Morris Greidanus interview by author, January 20, 2008, South Bend, Ind. On Reformed intentional communities, see Gene Beerens, "Christ's Community in Grand Rapids, Mich.: Intentional Community and the Local Church," *Coming Together* 1, 2 (April 1983): 16–18; Joyce K. Ribbens, "Innstead: A Cooperative Way to Homestead," *Vanguard* 9, 1 (January–February 1979): 18–19. On "coordinate decentralization" and the repudiation of academic norms, see VanderVennen, *University for the People*, 62, 97, 169–73. The principle of "coordinate decentralization" was articulated in Peter Schouls, *Insight, Authority, and Power* (Toronto: Wedge, 1972). On *Out of Concern for the Church*, see Thomas Kennalt, "Out of Concern for the Concerned," *Vanguard* (January 1971): 12–15; "Where Are All the Christians Hiding?" *Vanguard* (November 1971): 8–11, 20. On criticisms of the parent denomination, see Calvin G. Seerveld, "A Modest Proposal for Reforming the Christian Reformed Church in North America" in *Out of Concern for*

the Church: Five Essays, ed. John Olthuis (Toronto: Wedge, 1970), 47; VanderVennen, *University for the People*, 63.

14. Hendrick Hart, "The Gospel Is Radical," in *Out of Concern for the Church*, 40. A second, less critical volume—*Will All the King's Men*—was released several years later. On ICS's critique of the technocracy and unlimited economic growth, see Bob Goudzwaard, "From Death to Shalom," *Vanguard* (November–December 1974): 15. For a fuller development of these themes, see Bob Goudzwaard, *Idols of our Time* (Downers Grove, Ill.: InterVarsity Press, 1981); Paul Marshall, "In the Economic Tower of Babel: The Rise of Vertical Integration and the Fall of the Canadian Family Farm," *Vanguard* (February 1972): 23–26; Alan Lewis, "The Oil Companies Have Us over a Barrel," *Right On* 5, 11 (May 1974): A1, A4. For "subversive literature," see Robert Carvill, "Counterpoint," *Vanguard* (January 1971): 22. For more on the Reformationalist "us-versus-them" mentality, see Theodore Plantinga, "The Reformational Movement: Does It Need a History? *Myodicy* 24 (September 2005).

15. John Olthuis, "The Wages of Change," in *Out of Concern for the Church*, 20–21.

16. On the rivalry between Calvin/*Reformed Journal* and ICS, see VanderVennen, *University for the People*, 22–23. For ICS's description of the *Reformed Journal* as a liberal sell-out, see "Where Are the Christians Hiding?" *Vanguard* (January 1971): 8–11, 20. *Reformed Journal* contributors, in turn, described *Vanguard's* fiery rhetoric as juvenile, and its "sweeping" methodology of Christian political action "repugnant." Dale Vree suggested their perspective be called "Theocracy Revisited." See Dale Vree review of Bob Goudzwaard's *A Christian Political Option*, *Reformed Journal* 23, 7 (September 1973): 25. For more exchanges between the *Reformed Journal* and *Vanguard*, see Nicholas Wolterstorff, "The AACS in the CRC," *Reformed Journal* 24, 10 (December 1974): 9–16; Hendrik Hart, "The AACS in the CRC—A Response," *Reformed Journal* 25, 3 (March 1975): 25–28. On evangelism, see *Out of Concern for the Church*, 10–14; "Where Are All the Christians Hiding?" 11.

17. On evangelical draft-dodgers, see Morris and Alice Greidanus interview by author, January 20, 2008, South Bend, Ind. On ICS ties to Young Life and CCO, see VanderVennen, *University for the People*, 117. On growing efforts to engage evangelicals, see Bratt, *Dutch Calvinism*, 216–17; "About You . . . About Us," *Reformed Journal* 24, 3 (March 1974): 3–4; Henry Stob, "The Years of the Journal," *Reformed Journal* 26, 3 (March 1976): 10–18; Mouw, "A Bit of a Gadfly," 118. In the early 1960s the *Reformed Journal* printed articles by Southern Baptist Foy Valentine, historian Richard Pierard, Wesleyan scholar Donald Dayton, *Christianity Today's* Carl Henry, sociologist David Moberg, World Vision's Paul Rees, and Trinity professor Virginia Mollenkott. On neo-evangelical visitors to ICS, see VanderVennen, *University for the People*, 115. On Carvill's politics and ecumenical tendencies, see Bernard Zylstra, "Robert Lee Carvill, 1943–1974," *Vanguard* (September–October 1974): 9–11. On Calvin's Christianity and Politics conference, see Mouw, "A Bit of a Gadfly," 118.

18. On ICS representatives at Wheaton College, see "Philosophy Conference Concludes Tonight with Seminar on 'New Left,'" *Wheaton Record* 92, 8 (November 7,

1969): 1. On ICS at Urbana, see Richard Forbes, "Is Urbana Really Lost?" *Vanguard* (December 31, 1970), copy in Box 68, Folder 7, "Urbana 1961–1974," InterVarsity Christian Fellowship Collection, BGCA. The disruption prompted a Christian Reformed Church executive to write a letter of apology to InterVarsity executives. CRC's recruitment secretary wrote, "While we recognize the magnificence of their quest, we regret that they feel it necessary to so rankle and disorder to achieve their goals. Believe me we shall do all that we can toward reconciliation and a productive integration of their energies into Christ's mission." See Eugene Rubingh to David Howard, March 2, 1971, Box 68, Folder 7, "Urbana 1961–1974," InterVarsity Christian Fellowship Collection, BGCA. On "transforming North American Christianity," see John Hultink, "Wedge and Its Vision for the Seventies," Folder "Wedgewood Foundation Financial Records, 1970–1981," Vanguard Publishing Foundation Collection, CCA. For "great enthusiasm," see VanderVennen, *University for the People*, 144. On ICS ties with CCO, see VanderVennen, *University for the People*, 155–56.

19. Jennie Geisler phone interview by author, March 19, 2008.

20. On the spread of ICS curriculum materials, see VanderVennen, *University for the People*, 163. For an extended excerpt of Mouw's *Political Evangelism*, see *HIS* 34, 4 (January 1974): 22–24. On "evangelical self-understanding," see Mouw, "Evangelical 'Liberals' and 'Religious Language,'" *Reformed Journal* 24, 6 (July–August 1974): 4–5. On the failure of evangelicals to nurture social concern, see George DeVries, Jr., "A Plea for Social Responsibility," *Reformed Journal* 24, 1 (January 1974): 22–25; Lewis Smedes, "Evangelicals, What Next?" *Reformed Journal* 19 (November 1969): 4–5.

21. For demographic information, see "Readership Survey, 1979," 3–4, Box IV3, Folder "News Releases and Post-American," Sojourners Collection, WCSC; "About You . . . About Us," *Reformed Journal* 24, 3 (March 1974): 3–4; "The Truth About All of You," *The Other Side* 14, 4 (April 1978): 6–7; "Reader Survey—A Preliminary Report," *Vanguard* (May–June 1975): 4–5. The merits of applying New Class theory to progressive evangelicals emerged as a hotly contested debate in the 1980s and 1990s. While many, particularly Boyd Reese, have criticized it as too reductionistic, the discussion over New Class theory does highlight the demographic makeup of the young evangelicals who mobilized progressive evangelical politics. See James Davison Hunter, "The New Class and the Young Evangelicals," *Review of Religious Research* 22, 2 (December 1980): 155–59; Peter Berger, "The Class Struggle in American Religion," *Christian Century* 98 (February 25, 1981): 194–99. Critiques followed by John Schmalzbauer, "Evangelicals in the New Class: Class Versus Subcultural Predictors of Ideology," *Journal for the Scientific Study of Religion* 32, 4 (December 1993): 330–42; Boyd Reese, "The New Class and the Young Evangelicals: Second Thoughts," *Review of Religious Research* 24, 3 (March 1983): 261–67; Kyle Cleveland, "The Neoconservative Critique of Liberal Evangelicals: A Response to Berger and Hunter," *Review of Religious Research* 31, 3 (March 1990): 280–90; and Boyd T. Reese, Jr., "Resistance and Hope: The Interplay of Theological Synthesis, Biblical Interpretation, Political Analysis, and Praxis in the Christian Radicalism of 'Sojourners' Magazine," Ph.D. dissertation, Temple University, 1991.

22. For early evangelical literature on the city, see David McKenna, ed., *The Urban Crisis* (Grand Rapids, Mich.: Zondervan, 1969); George Torney, ed., *Toward Creative Urban Strategy* (Waco, Tex.: Word, 1970); Craig Ellison, ed., *The Urban Mission* (Grand Rapids, Mich.: Eerdmans, 1974); and Ronald Vander Kooi, "Can the Church Help Save Cities?" *Reformed Journal* 27, 3 (March 1977): 24–26. Vander Kooi taught sociology at Calvin College and specialized in urban concerns. Also see Allen, "Dr. Jimmy Allen, Evangelical Conference, Chicago," 1, copy in "1974 Thanksgiving Workshop," ESAA; Furness, *Christian and Social Action*, 50; Rip Hodson, "God Is No Respecter of Persons," *The Other Side* 9, 1 (January–February 1973): 16–17; David O. Moberg, *The Great Reversal: Evangelism Versus Social Concern* (Philadelphia: Lippincott, 1972), 92. On Bill Leslie, see James Hefley and Marti Hefley, *The Church That Takes on Trouble* (Elgin, Ill.: Cook, 1976), 43–47, 60, 85–86, 137, 159, 166. The case of Bill and his wife Adrienne Leslie casts the variable of living in the city in sharp relief. During the early years of his pastorate at Elm-LaSalle, the family lived in the far west suburbs of Wheaton. Bill commuted into the city each day. As Bill turned more progressive politically, Adrienne "fretted over welfare cheats with Wheaton neighbors."

23. Elizabeth O'Connor, *Journey Inward, Journey Outward* (New York: Harper & Row, 1968), 31, 34–35, 41–42, 142–47, 159; Elizabeth O'Connor, *Call to Commitment* (Washington, D.C.: Servant Leadership Press, 1994), 21, 167.

24. Other prominent urban centers of progressive evangelicalism included the First Baptist Church of Pensacola, Florida; Nazarene Community of Hope in Washington, D.C.; 12th Baptist Church in Roxbury, Massachusetts; Church of the Nazarene in midtown Manhattan; St. Paul Community Baptist Church and St. John the Evangelist in Brooklyn; Goodwill Home and Rescue Mission of Newark, New Jersey; Mission Waco in Waco, Texas; First Baptist Church, Trinity Baptist Church, and Temple Baptist Church in San Antonio; First Baptist Church in Arlington, Texas; Friendship West Baptist Church in Dallas; South Main Baptist Church in Houston; First Baptist Church in Decatur, Georgia; Wieuca Road Baptist Church in Atlanta; Central City Church in Los Angeles; Salem Evangelical Free Church, Lawndale Community Church, and Immanuel Lutheran Church in Chicago; Cross Lutheran in Milwaukee; Calvary Presbyterian Church in Cleveland; Church of the Redeemer in St. Paul, Minnesota; University Church in Athens, Georgia; Voice of Calvary Ministries in Jackson, Mississippi; and Strathmoor Judson Baptist Church and Central Alliance Church in Detroit. Urban study programs included those launched by Messiah College in Philadelphia, Seattle Pacific in Seattle, the Urban Life Center in Chicago, Biola College in Los Angeles, and Westmont College and Simpson College in San Francisco. Between 1962 and 1976, 27 such educational programs, most evangelical, were launched in cities across the nation. See Harvie Conn, *The American City and the Evangelical Church: A Historical Overview* (Grand Rapids, Mich.: Baker, 1994), 101.

25. For the War on Poverty, see Smedes, "The Evangelicals and the Social Question," *Reformed Journal* (February 1966): 9–13; Smedes, "Where Do We Differ?" *Reformed Journal* 16, 4 (May–June 1966): 10. For local and state initiatives, see "Sidelines,"

The Other Side 14, 4 (April 1978): 11. On the close cooperation between Sojourners and the Department of Human Resources in Washington to set up homeless shelters, see Perry Perkins, "Community Efforts Change Government Policy," *Sojourners* 7, 5 (May 1978): 28–29. On urban networks, see Harold Hughes, *The Man from Ida Grove: A Senator's Personal Story* (Waco, Tex.: Word, 1979), 230–33; "The Other Other People," *The Other Side* 14, 1 (January 1978): 51; David Moberg, *The Great Reversal: Evangelism and Social Concern*, 2nd ed. (Philadelphia: Lippincott, 1977), 111–12, 179; "Evangelical Concern of Denver," *Public Justice Newsletter* 3, 3 (December 1979): 9–10; "Sidelines," *The Other Side* 14, 7 (July 1978): 10; "Leaders Search for Identity of Church in the City," *Chicago Tribune*, May 3, 1975, A25; Robert D. Linder, "Resurgence of Evangelical Social Concern (1925–1975)," in *The Evangelicals*, ed. David Wells and John Woodbridge (Nashville: Abingdon Press, 1975), 203; Pat Mastin, Letter to the Editor, *The Other Side* 8, 6 (November–December 1972): 6; Craig W. Ellison, "Third World in America," *The Other Side* 8, 3 (May–June 1972): 42–43; Ted Moran, "ECUMB," *The Other Side* 7, 2 (March–April 1971): 12–15. On suburban coffee klatches, see Lisa McGirr, *Suburban Warriors: The Origins of the New American Right* (Princeton: Princeton University Press, 2001), 3.

26. In March 1973, for example, Covenant College in Lookout Mountain, Tennessee, held a Conference on the Inner City. In May 1977, Covenant Theological Seminary in St. Louis offered an Urban Ministries Institute. InterVarsity hired a regional specialist in Urban and Cross-Cultural Ministries. All these efforts culminated in April 1980 with a Congress on Urban Ministry held in Chicago. The Congress, sponsored by the Seminary Consortium for Urban Pastoral Education, offered over 60 seminars and workshops. See back cover of *The Other Side* 9, 1 (January–February 1973): 52. Randy Nabons, director of Inner-City Missions Inc. and pastor of New City Fellowship in Chattanooga, Tennessee, organized the conference. See "Personal Identification—A. Randy Nabons," Folder "1977," ESAA. Following the lead of ECUMB, CCCE, and other urban grassroots efforts, the National Association of Evangelicals held its first conference on the inner city in 1969. See Craig Ellison, "Toward Evangelical Urban Alliances," in *The Urban Mission* (Grand Rapids, Mich.: Eerdmans, 1974), 210–14; Roger L. Dewey, "A Comprehensive Model for Evangelical Urban Involvement," in *The Urban Mission* (Grand Rapids, Mich.: Eerdmans, 1974), 215–28; George A. Torney, *Toward Creative Urban Strategy* (Waco, Tex.: Word, 1970). Also see "The Church in the City: A Dialogue with Seven Chicago Christians," *Post-American* 4, 4 (April 1975): 6–13; Michael R. Gordon, "Third World, American Style: Introducing an Urban Tragedy," *The Other Side* 14, 7 (July 1978): 35–37; Perk Perkins, "Concrete Theology: A Response to the Urban Crisis," 11–14, and Stan Hallett, "To Build a City," *Sojourners* 9, 9 (September 1980): 15–18. On the Urban Training Institute offered by the Trinity Christian Community in inner-city New Orleans, see "Seeds," *Sojourners* 9, 1 (January 1980): 30. Speakers included John Perkins, Bill Pannell, and Dave Frechak. On the Urban Institute for Christian Leadership launched by Manuel Ortiz, pastor of an evangelical free congregation in Chicago, see "Personal Identification—Manuel Ortiz,"

Folder "1977," ESAA. The Urban Ministries Institute offered seminars on "The Worship, Theology, and Leadership of the Urban Church" and "Case Studies of Churches in Urban Settings," led in part by Manuel Ortiz of an Evangelical Free church in Chicago. See advertisement in *Sojourners* 6, 5 (May 1977): 36.

27. On the importance of specialization in solving social problems, reaching target audiences, and addressing theoretical concerns, see Roger L. Dewey, "Editorial," *Inside* (November 1973). On the advance of science and technology, see James Daane, "The War on Poverty Can be Won," *Reformed Journal* 14, 4 (April 1964): 3. On energy and hunger, see R. H. Bube, "Tomorrow's Energy Sources: A Summary for Laymen," *Reformed Journal* 24, 6 (July–August 1974): 21–25; George DeVries, Jr., "Systems and Hunger," *Reformed Journal* 25, 4 (April 1975): 4–6; and Orval Friedrich, "What Can We Do for a Hungry World," *The Other Side* 6, 1 (January–February 1970): 26–29. On the Kerner Commission, see "Communications Conference," *The Other Side* 4, 3 (May–June 1968): 11. On "hard-headed analysis," see John Alexander, "A Politics of Love," *The Other Side* 8, 4 (July–August 1972): 3; Gary Collins, ed., *Our Society in Turmoil* (Carol Stream, Ill.: Creation House, 1970). For the Thanksgiving Workshop worship program, see Folder "1974 Thanksgiving Workshop," ESAA.

28. Stephen Monsma, *The Unraveling of America* (Downers Grove, Ill.: Inter-Varsity Press, 1974); Ronald Michaelson, "Positive Politics," *HIS* 32, 8 (May 1972): 13; Emilio Castro, "Strategies for Confronting Unjust Social Structures," 1, speech at 1974 Thanksgiving Workshop, Chicago, copy in Folder "1974 Thanksgiving Workshop," ESAA; Jack Buckley, review of Arthur Simon's *Bread for the World*, *HIS* 36, 9 (June 1976): 19; Paul Henry, *Politics for Evangelicals* (Valley Forge, Pa.: Judson Press, 1974), 22. Also see James M. Dunn, "Lobbying Isn't a Dirty Word," *Eternity* 26, 7 (July 1975): 12–14, 29–30; Moberg, *Great Reversal*, 210; Moberg, *Inasmuch*, 21; David Sullivan, "Lean to the Left, Lean to the Right," *The Other Side* 8, 5 (September–October 1972): 30–34; John B. Anderson, *Vision and Betrayal in America* (Waco, Tex.: Word, 1975), 121; Edward A. Loucks, "Deciding How to Vote," *The Other Side* 8, 5 (September–October 1972): 25.

Chapter 8. Ron Sider and the Politics of Simple Living

Epigraph: Ron Sider, *Rich Christians in an Age of Hunger: A Biblical Study* (Downers Grove, Ill.: InterVarsity Press, 1977), 166.

1. On the trajectory of American Mennonites into the new evangelical orbit, see Perry Bush, "Anabaptism Born Again: Mennonites, New Evangelicals, and the Search for a Usable Past, 1950–1980," *Fides et Historia* 25, 1 (Winter–Spring 1993): 26–47; Paul Toews, *Mennonites in American Society, 1930–1970: Modernity and the Persistence of Religious Community* (Scottdale, Pa.: Herald Press, 1996), 222–23; Calvin Redekop, *Leaving Anabaptism: From Evangelical Mennonite Brethren to Fellowship of Evangelical Bible Churches* (Scottdale, Pa.: Herald Press, 1998). As background to the narrative of

this chapter, particularly the Mennonite "Concern movement" of the 1950s and its new emphasis on social engagement, see Toews, *Mennonites in American Society*, 232–37, 261–66; Keith Graber Miller, *Wise as Serpents, Innocent as Doves: American Mennonites Engage Washington* (Knoxville: University of Tennessee Press, 1996).

2. Tim Stafford, "Ron Sider's Unsettling Crusade," *Christianity Today* 36, 5 (April 27, 1992): 18–22; Jeffrey McClain Jones, "Ronald Sider and Radical Evangelical Political Theology," Ph.D. dissertation, Northwestern University, 1990, 405–9; Sider, *Evangelism and Social Action* (Grand Rapids, Mich.: Zondervan, 1993), 16.

3. For an example of Sider's interest in apologetics, see "A Case for Easter," *HIS* 32, 7 (April 1972): 26–31. On Sider's university years, see Ron Sider interview by author, August 9, 2005, Philadelphia, Pa.; Jones, "Ron Sider and Radical Evangelical Political Theology," 406.

4. On his sociopolitical awakening, see Joel Fetzer and Gretchen S. Carnes, "Dr. Ron Sider: Mennonite Environmentalist on the Evangelical Left," in *Religious Leaders and Faith-Based Politics: Ten Profiles*, ed. Jo Renée Formicola and Hubert Morken (Lanham, Md.: Rowman & Littlefield, 2001), 160.

5. Fetzer and Carnes, "Dr. Ron Sider: Mennonite Environmentalist," 159–60.

6. Ron Sider, "The Ministry of Affluence: A Graduated Tithe," *HIS* 32, 3 (December 1972): 6–8; Ronald J. Sider, *Rich Christians in an Age of Hunger: A Biblical Study* (Downers Grove, Ill.: InterVarsity Press, 1977), 1, 172.

7. Sider, *Rich Christians*, 163–65. On the language of sin, see Tim Stafford, "Ron Sider's Unsettling Crusade," *Christianity Today* 36, 27 (March 17, 1992): 18–22.

8. Sider at Southern Baptist Convocation on World Hunger, quoted in Norman Jameson, "Rich Must Live Simply So the Poor May Simply Live," *Baptist Press*, November 22, 1978, 6.

9. Sider, *Rich Christians*, 172.

10. For Nash on "cultural, moral, and even religious dimensions," see Greg Grandin, "Good Christ, Bad Christ," *Counterpunch* (September 9–10, 2006); David Chilton, *Productive Christians in an Age of Guilt Manipulators: A Biblical Response to Ronald Sider* (Tyler, Tex.: Institute for Christian Economics, 1981). Mavrodes quoted in James P. Gills and Ronald H. Nash, *A Biblical Economics Manifesto: Economics and the Christian World View* (Lake Mary, Fla.: Creation House, 2002), 8–9. Sider himself acknowledged his lack of training and sophistication in economics. Twenty years after *Rich Christians* was published, he said he "didn't know a great deal of economics when I wrote the first edition of *Rich Christians*." See Kevin D. Miller interview with Ron Sider, *Christianity Today* 41, 5 (April 28, 1997): 68–69.

11. For InterVarsity's review of Sider, see Kem Luther, "Undercover," *HIS* 38, 1 (October 1977): 20–21. On Sider's appearance on the 700 Club, see Ron Sider to Everett Larreynaga, August 31, 1977, in Folder "Rich Christians," ESAA. For a sampling of praise for Sider, see Jim Wallis, "The Invisible Empire," *Post-American* 2, 5 (November–December 1973): 1; Chris Sugden, *Radical Discipleship* (Basingstoke: Marshalls, 1981), vii, 7.

12. Doris Janzen Longacre, *More with Less* (Scottdale, Pa.: Herald Press, 1976). For praise of Longacre, see Sider, *Rich Christians*, 182; Sider, "Introduction," in Longacre, *Living More with Less* (Scottdale, Pa.: Herald Press, 1980), 6–7.

13. File "IX-6-3 More with Less Cookbook, 1979–80" in Mennonite Central Committee Collection, MCA; Longacre, *Living More with Less*, 30–36.

14. On Longacre's evangelical language, see "Seeds," *Sojourners* 7, 6 (June 1978): 30. On the structural aspects of global hunger, see Longacre, *Living More with Less*, 26; Sider, *Living More Simply*, 14–15; W. Stanley Mooneyham, *What Do You Say to a Hungry World?* (Waco, Tex.: Word, 1975); Ronald J. Sider, *Cry Justice! The Bible on Hunger and Poverty* (Downers Grove, Ill.: InterVarsity Press, 1980); Arthur R. Simon, *Bread for the World* (New York: Paulist Press, 1975); Richard J. Barnet, *The Lean Years: Politics in the Age of Scarcity* (New York: Simon & Schuster, 1980). Dozens of feature articles on hunger also appeared in all of the mainstream evangelical publications including *Eternity*, *Wittenburg Door*, *Vanguard*, *HIS*, *The Other Side*, and *Post-American*. The issue soon entered the pages of more mainstream evangelical publications. See "Why Are People Starving?" *Christianity Today* 19, 2 (October 25, 1974): 35; "Where Is Tomorrow's Food?" *Christianity Today* 18, 24 (September 13, 1974): 53; "Full Hearts and Empty Stomachs," *Christianity Today* 20, 3 (November 7, 1975): 47–48. See an entire issue of *Christianity Today* devoted to global hunger: J. D. Douglas, "The Bible on Hunger—A Source of Discomfort?" Stanley C. Baldwin, "A Case Against Waste and Other Excesses," Ron Sider, "Mischief by Statute: How We Oppress the Poor," and Arthur Simon, "Hunger: Twenty Easy Questions, No Easy Answers," *Christianity Today* 20, 21 (July 16, 1976): 8–22. In the same issue, see advertisements for evangelical organizations devoted to hunger relief such as Compassion, Inc., Food for the Hungry, World Relief, MAP International, and World Vision. For Southern Baptist interaction with Sider and other action to address global hunger in the late 1970s, see Boxes 36 and 51 in the "Christian Life Commission Resource Files" of the Southern Baptist Historical Library and Archives.

15. Barbara Hansen, "From the Mennonites: A Cookbook That's Critical of Our Eating Habits," *Los Angeles Times*, May 6, 1976, G6. On Baptist and Methodist sales, see Paul Schrock to Doris Longacre, November 18, 1976, Folder IX-6-3, MCC Collection, MCA. On first-year sales and positive reviews, see Herald Press to Longacre, April 8, 1976; Herald Press to Longacre, November 18, 1976, Folder IX-6-3, MCC Collection, MCA. On the diverse readership of *More with Less*, see LaVerne Triezenberg to Herald Press, December 4, 1980, copy in author's possession, sent by mail from Herald Press archives in Scottdale, Pa., in February 2006. Also see Virginia Hearn email interview by author, March 1, 2006; Sharon Gallagher interview by author, July 7, 2006, Berkeley, Cal. On evangelical praise of *More with Less*, see Doris Longacre to Jack Scott, May 19, 1976; Mark O. Hatfield to Doris Longacre, March 4, 1976; W. Stanley Mooneyham, March 22, 1976, copy in author's possession, received from Herald Press archives in February 2006. Longacre spoke at a Wednesday evening meeting of Sojourners in the fall of 1978. See Box VI1–VI3, Folder "Community Newsletters, Fall

1978," Sojourners Collection, WCSC. On the cookbook's popularity at Gordon-Conwell Seminary, see Sider, "A Brief Report," March 1, 1978, in Folder "Discipleship Workshops," ESAA. On the spread of *More with Less* and "hunger awareness" dinners in Christian Reformed circles, see Dan Treizenburg interview by author, April 19, 2007, South Bend, Ind.; Morris and Alice Greidanus interview by author, January 20, 2008, South Bend, Ind. For spin-offs of *More with Less*, see Longacre, *Living More with Less*; Aileen Van Beilen, *Hunger Awareness Dinners: A Planning Manual* (Scottdale, Pa.: Herald Press, 1978); Susan Godshall and Doris Longacre, *Living More with Less: Workshop Outlines* (Akron, Pa.: MCC Hunger Concerns Office, 1980); Delores Histand Friesen, *Living More with Less: Study/Action Guide* (Scottdale, Pa.: Herald Press, 1981); Meredith Sommers Dregni, *Experiencing More with Less: Intergenerational Curriculum for Camps, Retreats, and Other Educational Settings* (Scottdale, Pa.: Herald Press, 1983). For sales figures, see Paul Schrock to Reg Toews, June 15, 1983, in Folder IX-6-3, MCC Collection, MCA.

16. For a short autobiography of Walter Hearn, see Ronald J. Sider, ed., *Living More Simply: Biblical Principles & Practical Models* (Downers Grove, Ill.: InterVarsity Press, 1980), 73–96.

17. Walter and Ginny Hearn interview by author, July 9, 2006, Berkeley, Cal. During my interview with them, thirty years after their move to Berkeley, the Hearns animatedly told me about their first trip to a Safeway, where they uncovered four cases of asparagus. After the interview, Walter took me dumpster diving at a meat shop. We found a slab of pork ribs, which he hosed off at an outside spigot.

18. Walter Hearn and Ginny Hearn, "Poverty," *Right On* 8, 5 (May 1973): 1; "Voluntary Poverty," *Post-American* 3, 2 (February–March 1974): 11, 14; Russell Chandler, "Ph.D. Scrounges for a Living," *Los Angeles Times*, December 1, 1975, 3; Hearn, "Journey to Simplicity," *Radix* 8, 5 (March–April 1977): 10–11, 16–17.

19. On the influence of apartheid, see Jones, "Radical Evangelical Political Theology," 406; Gordon Aeschliman, *Apartheid: Tragedy in Black and White* (Ventura, Cal.: Regal Books, 1986). On the Latin American Theological Fraternity, see Walter and Ginny Hearn interview by author, July 9, 2006, Berkeley, Cal.

20. On Xenos, see Dennis H. McCallum to Ron Sider, October 12, 1989, in Folder "1989," ESAA. On "theology of revolution," see Arthur G. Gish, *Beyond the Rat Race* (Scottdale, Pa.: Herald Press, 1973), 9, 37, 112–32. On connections between the New Left and Anabaptism, see Gish, *The New Left and Christian Radicalism* (Grand Rapids, Mich.: Eerdmans, 1970), 27, 49, 57, 66, 67, 71, 119. Also see Dale W. Brown to Ron Sider, February 21, 1974, Folder "Chicago Declaration," ESAA. For Gish's influence on CWLF and Alexander, see Walter and Ginny Hearn interview by author, July 9, 2006, Berkeley, Cal.; Mark Olson interview by author, May 21, 2009, South Bend, Ind.; Gish, "Simplicity," *The Other Side* 9, 3 (May–June 1973): 14–16. On simplicity in InterVarsity, see Etta Worthington, "'Tis a Gift to Be Simple," *HIS* 35, 8 (May 1975): 4.

21. On the international consultation, see Alan Nichols, "An Evangelical Commitment to Simple Life-Style," copy in Box 36, Folder 9, Lausanne Committee for

World Evangelization Collection, BGCA. For copies of the *Simple Lifestyle Newsletter,* see Box 36, Folder 15. Also see Vernard Eller, *The Simple Life* (Grand Rapids, Mich.: Eerdmans, 1983); Arnold D. Weigel, "The Simple Life," *Lutheran Quarterly* 26, 1 (February 1974): 87–88; David W. Gill, "The Simple Life," *Christianity Today* 18, 21 (July 26, 1974): 29–31; Larry L. Rasmussen, "The Simple Life," *Religion in Life* 43, 3 (Autumn 1974): 381–83; Frank E. Gaebelein, "Challenging Christians to the Simple Life," *Christianity Today* 23, 22 (September 21, 1979): 22–26; Leon Morris, "Thinking Things Through: The Witness of the Church Is Adulterated by the Affluent Lifestyles of Its Members," *Christianity Today* 23, 22 (September 21, 1979): 60; Ronald J. Sider, "Does God Live in Glass Houses? Cautions Against Ecclesiastical Elegance," *Christianity Today* 23, 20 (August 17, 1979): 14–19; Ronald J. Sider, *Living More Simply: Biblical Principles and Practical Models* (Downers Grove, Ill.: InterVarsity Press, 1981); Richard J. Foster, *Freedom of Simplicity* (New York: Harper & Row, 1981); Ronald J. Sider, *Lifestyle in the Eighties: An Evangelical Commitment to Simple Lifestyle* (Philadelphia: Westminster Press, 1982). The ideal extended to radical Calvinists. See John A. Olthuis, "Can Less Be More? Remarks About the Idea of Progress," in *Christian Politics: False Hope or Biblical Demand?,* ed. James Skillen (Indiana, Pa.: Jubilee Enterprises, 1976), 39–50.

22. On the broad sweep of anti-materialism in American history, see David E. Shi, *The Simple Life: Plain Living and High Thinking in American Culture* (New York: Oxford University Press, 1985). For secular simple living titles, see Edward Espe Brown, *The Tasasjara Bread Book* (Boston: Shambala, 1970); Ernest Callenbach, *Living Poor with Style* (New York: Bantam, 1972); E. F. Schumacher, *Small Is Beautiful* (New York: Harper & Row, 1973); John Taylor, *Enough Is Enough* (Minneapolis: Augsburg Press, 1977); Andrew Greeley, *No Bigger Than Necessary: An Alternative to Socialism, Capitalism, and Anarchism* (New York: New American Library, 1977); Albert J. Fritsch, *99 Ways to a Simple Lifestyle* (Washington, D.C.: Center for Science in the Public Interest, 1977); Warren A. Johnson, *Muddling toward Frugality* (San Francisco: Sierra Club Books, 1978); Laurance S. Rockefeller, "The Case for a Simpler Life-Style," *Reader's Digest* 108, 51 (February 1976): 61–65.

23. Michael Harrington, *The Other America: Poverty in the United States* (New York: Macmillan, 1962). For evangelical citations of Harrington, Roszak, and Carson, see Arthur G. Gish, "Simplicity," *Post-American* 1, 2 (Winter 1972): 10; Hendrik Hart, "On Simplicity: A Meditation before Christmas," *Vanguard* (November–December 1974): 27–28; Sider, "The Ministry of Affluence," 6–8; Rick and Cindy Westman, "The Liberated Christian Home," *Post-American* 2, 3 (May–June 1973): 11; Robert Prud'homme, "Undercover," *HIS* 38, 1 (October 1977): 21; Stephen Board, "Ronald Sider: Prophet to a Rich Church," 18–23, and "Can You Live Simply in North America? A Cross Section of Readers Tell How They Cut Back," *Eternity* 30, 4 (April 1979): 18–23; Frank Gaebelein, "Challenging Christians to the Simple Life," *Christianity Today* 22, 22 (September 21, 1979): 22–23; Jim Wallis, "Offensive Simplicity," *Sojourners* 9, 2 (February 1980): 6; Karin Granberg-Michaelson, "Journey Toward Simple Living: How a Middle-Class Couple Struggles to Lower Their Economic Expectations," *The*

Other Side 16, 11 (November 1980): 39–41; Mary L. Kownacki, "Knots in My Stomach: Why Must Those Who Practice Simple Living So Often Fall Toward the Extremes?" *The Other Side* 17, 11 (November 1981): 30–32; Virginia Hostetler, "Riding in Style and Missing the Boat: Some Recent Temptations Bring Us Face-to-Face with Questions of Simple Life-Style," *The Other Side* 19, 10 (October 1983): 54–55; Katherine Cook, "St. Francis, You've Got to Be Crazy!" *The Other Side* 20, 8 (August 1984): 23–24. For influences on *More with Less*, see Frances Moore Lappe, *Diet for a Small Planet* (New York: Ballantine, 1971); Doris Longacre to Marie K. Wiens, March 2, 1976, Folder IX-6-3, MCC Collection, MCA.

24. On "drastically simplifying lifestyles" in order to fulfill the mandate of world evangelization, see Sider, *Living More Simply*, 14–15. On L'Abri, see Sharon Gallagher, "How Should We Then Live?" *Radix* 8, 5 (March–April 1977): 13.

25. Carter quoted in Shi, *The Simple Life*, 270–72; Kevin Mattson, *"What the Heck Are You Up To, Mr. President?": Jimmy Carter, America's "Malaise," and the Speech That Should Have Changed the Country* (New York: Bloomsbury, 2009).

Chapter 9. The Chicago Declaration and a United Progressive Front

Epigraph: Full text in Ronald J. Sider, ed., *The Chicago Declaration* (Carol Stream, Ill.: Creation House, 1974), 1–2.

1. On Sider as a centrist, see interview in Jeffrey McClain Jones, "Ron Sider and Radical Evangelical Political Theology," Ph.D. dissertation, Northwestern University, 1990, 420–21. For "a religious movement that could shake," see Marjorie Hyer, "Social and Political Activism Is Aim of Evangelical Group," *Washington Post*, November 30, 1973, D17. For "one hell of a political force," quoted in John Junkerman, "Voice of the Evangelical Left," *Madison Press Connection*, Box IV3, Folder 2, "News Releases and Post-American," Sojourners Collection, WCSC.

2. Ronald J. Sider, "A Short Unscientific Sketch of ESA's History," manuscript of a speech given at thirtieth ESA anniversary celebration, August 24, 2003, 1, copy in ESAA.

3. For Webber quote, see "The Evangelical Vote," *Newsweek* 80, 18 (October 30, 1972): 93. For "ray of hope," see Jim Wallis, "The Issue of 1972," *Post-American* 1, 5 (Fall 1972): 2–3. For "a rising tide," see Ron Sider, EFM news release, October 6, 1972, Folder "Evangelicals for McGovern," ESAA. For Agnew's appearance at Calvin, see Carl Strickwerda, "Politics: Fall 1972," 1973 *Prism* yearbook, CCA. For more anti-Nixon statements, see Rosemary, "Last Monday the President Went Mad," *The Other Side* 7, 3 (July–August 1971): 16–17; Bill Pannell, "Lawlessness Administration Style," *The Other Side* 7, 5 (September–October 1971): 32–35; Gerald Vandezande, "Blazing the Trail Toward the New Prosperity," *Vanguard* (December 1971): 6; Jim and Glenda Vanden-Bosch, "Nixon, McGovern and the Only Choice in '72," *Vanguard* (October 1972): 12–17; Dwight P. Baker, "Elect George McGovern: Seven Reasons Why," *The Other Side*

(September–October 1972): 26–29; James Daane, "Richard Nixon, Church Member," *Reformed Journal* 24, 3 (March 1974): 5–6; George N. Monsma, Jr., "The Need for Tax Reform: The Lessons of Nixon's 1040," *Reformed Journal* 24, 3 (March 1974): 12–15; Ben Patterson, "Mere Forgiveness," *Wittenburg Door* 24 (October–November 1974): 4–5; Wesley G. Pippert, *Memo for 1976: Some Political Options* (Downers Grove, Ill.: Inter-Varsity Press, 1974), 15.

4. On Nixon and race, see Clark Pinnock, "Election Reflections," *Post-American* 2, 1 (January–February 1973): 2–3; Ron Sider to "Friend," September 20, 1972, ESAA. On EFM's views of Vietnam, see Ron Sider, EFM news release, October 6, 1972, Evangelicals for McGovern folder, ESAA. For some in EFM, even McGovern was "too hawkish" on the Middle East. See Bob Stoner to Sider, September 27, 1972, Evangelicals for McGovern folder, ESAA. On "Western racism" and imperialism, see Ron Sider, EFM news release, October 6, 1972, Folder "Evangelicals for McGovern," ESAA; "Despair Eats at Students," *Manna* 1, 1 (September 14, 1970), copy in Box 342, Folder 2, "Manna," InterVarsity Christian Fellowship Collection, BGCA. For "a vote for Nixon," see Wallis, "The Issue of 1972," 2.

5. For "thrilled," see Daphine Earl to EFM, October 12, 1972, Folder "Evangelicals for McGovern," ESAA. On "proselytizing" for McGovern, see Reinder H. Van Til to EFM, October 20, 1972, Folder "Evangelicals for McGovern," ESAA. On Pentecostal support, see Mary Lyons to EFM, October 30, 1972, Folder "Evangelicals for McGovern," ESAA. On Wheaton alumni support, see Karl Hess to Sider, November 11, 1972, Folder "Evangelicals for McGovern," ESAA. On Gordon-Conwell support, see Jeri Drum to Walden Howard, October 22, 1972, Folder "Evangelicals for McGovern," ESAA; "Religion in Transit," *Christianity Today* 17, 4 (November 24, 1972): 48. Nearly the entire editorial staff of the *Post-American*, for example, worked for the McGovern campaign in 1972. Wallis headed up the Evanston, Illinois, McGovern campaign. See Boyd T. Reese, Jr., "Resistance and Hope: The Interplay of Theological Synthesis, Biblical Interpretation, Political Analysis, and Praxis in the Christian Radicalism of 'Sojourners' Magazine," Ph.D. dissertation, Temple University, 1991, 193. On evangelical support for McGovern in Berkeley, see Walter and Ginny Hearn interview with author, July 9, 2006, Berkeley, Cal. On *The Other Side* support for McGovern, see letter from Ed Drury, *The Other Side* 9, 1 (January–February 1973): 5. On support by some Jesus People groups for McGovern, see Joe V. Peterson, "Jesus People: Christ, Communes and the Counterculture of the Late Twentieth Century in the Pacific Northwest," Master's thesis, Northwest Christian College, 1980, 110–13. Among Shiloh members, McGovern outpolled Nixon by a two-to-one margin, though 59 percent said they "didn't care" or didn't respond to the question. Among members of the House of Elijah in Yakima, Washington, 60 percent voted for McGovern. On support for McGovern at Fuller, where "sentiment for McGovern runs pretty strong," see Ed Reitz to Sider, September 30, 1972, Folder "Evangelicals for McGovern," ESAA. Many on Fuller's faculty were active in EFM, and Lewis Smedes, a theologian and ethicist from Fuller, served on the EFM board.

6. On Mennonite support, see Paul Leatherman, to Ron Sider, October 23, 1972, Folder "Evangelicals for McGovern," ESAA. Walden Howard quoted in "The Evangelical Vote," *Newsweek* 80, 18 (October 30, 1972): 93. On a *Christianity Today* editor's support for McGovern, see Richard Pierard to Ron Sider, June 12, 1973, Folder "Chicago Declaration Planning," ESAA.

7. For criticism of EFM, see W.T. Miller to "Dear Friend," November 8, 1972, Box 1, Folder 4, "Evangelicals for McGovern: Correspondence, Evangelicals for Social Action Collection," ESA Collection, BGCA; David A. Noebel, "The Emerging Evangelical 'Left,'" *Christian Crusade Weekly* 13, 8 (December 24, 1972): 8. On Richard Pierard's response, see Pierard to W. T. Miller, November 15, 1972, Box, 1, Folder 4: Evangelicals for McGovern: Correspondence, ESA Collection, BGCA. On *Christianity Today*'s support for Nixon, see Barrie Doyle, "The Religious Campaign: Backing Their Man," *Christianity Today* 17, 2 (October 27, 1972): 38–39.

8. Harold J. Ockenga, "McGovern vs. Nixon," *Hamilton-Wenham Chronicle*, November 2, 1972, 3b; Robert Waite, "The Inaugural," *Hamilton-Wenham Chronicle*, January 25, 1973, 1B; Harold J. Ockenga to Walden Howard, October 13, 1972, Folder "Evangelicals for McGovern," ESAA.

9. On Bright and Campus Crusade, see John Turner, *Bill Bright and Campus Crusade for Christ: The Renewal of Evangelicalism in Postwar America* (Chapel Hill: University of North Carolina Press, 2008), 141. On McGovern's evangelical credentials, see Ron Sider, EFM news release, October 6, 1972, Folder "Evangelicals for McGovern," ESAA; Stephen Charles Mott, "An Evangelical McGovern at Wheaton," *Qoheleth* 6 (October 25, 1972): 1, 7–8, quoted in James Alan Patterson, "Evangelicals and Presidential Elections of 1972, 1976, and 1980," *Fides et Historia* 18, 2 (June 1986): 44–62.

10. Text of McGovern speech at Wheaton, October 11, 1972, copy in Folder "Evangelicals for McGovern," ESAA; Michael McIntyre, "Religionists on the Campaign Trail," *Christian Century* 89, 47 (December 27, 1972): 1319–22.

11. Tim Rumberger, "Reagan Accepts Offer to Appear on Campus," *Wheaton Record* 105, 3 (October 3, 1980): 2; Mott, "An Evangelical McGovern at Wheaton," 1, 7–8; Wesley G. Pippert, UPI story, October 12, 1972, copy in Evangelicals for McGovern Collection, ESAA; Sider to Stephen Charles Mott, November 14, 1972, Box 1, Folder 4, "Evangelicals for McGovern: Correspondence," ESA Collection, BGCA; Margaret Greydanus to EFM, n.d., Folder "Evangelicals for McGovern," ESAA; Reinder H. Van Til to EFM, October 20, 1972, Folder "Evangelicals for McGovern," ESAA.

12. On "evangelicals as a group" being heard, see Walden Howard letter, circa October 1972, Folder "Evangelicals for McGovern," ESAA.

13. On the "crisis in confidence," see Walden Howard to Ron Sider, April 24, 1973, Folder "Chicago Declaration Planning," ESAA.

14. Sider to David O. Moberg, March 19, 1973, Box 1, Folder 11, "Thanksgiving Workshop, Evangelicals and Social Concern (1973): Correspondence: March 1973–March 1974," ESA Collection, BGCA. The Thanksgiving Workshop planning

committee included David Moberg, Richard Pierard, Ron Sider, Paul Henry, Stephen Mott, William Pannell, and Jim Wallis.

15. Ronald J. Sider, "Evangelicals Sign Social Concerns Document," *The Mennonite* 89 (January 1, 1974): 10; Sider, "On Behalf of the Planning Committee," Folder "Thanksgiving Workshop," ESAA.

16. John Alexander to Ron Sider, n.d., circa summer 1972, Folder "Thanksgiving Workshop Planning," ESAA. For the text of initial drafts, see Box 2, Folder 9, "Proposed Drafts of Chicago Declaration, July–Nov. 1973," ESA Collection, BGCA. On "evangelical triumphalism," see speech by M. VanElderen at Calvin Theological Seminary on December 5, 1974, Box 3, Folder 13, "Thanksgiving Workshop, Evangelicals for Social Action (1974): Reportage; December 1974–January 1975," ESA Collection, BGCA. On the "oppressing community," see James H. Bowman, "Evangelicals Face Social Issues," *Chicago Daily News*, November 24, 1973, 40. For "angry separation," see Sider, "An Historic Moment," in *The Chicago Declaration*, ed. Ron Sider (Carol Stream, Ill.: Creation House, 1974), 26–27.

17. On "cleaning up their own houses," see Nancy Hardesty to Ronald J. Sider, August 29, 1973, Box 1, Folder 11, "Thanksgiving Workshop, Evangelicals and Social Concern (1973): Correspondence: March 1973–March 1974," ESA Collection, BGCA. On "Mrs. William Bentley," see Hardesty, "Reflections," in Ron Sider, ed., *The Chicago Declaration* (Carol Stream, Ill.: Creation House, 1974), 123. Also see Sharon Gallagher, "Radical Evangelicalism: A Conference Report," 64, in Folder "Chicago Declaration Press," ESAA.

18. On "being bad for the Vietnamese," see Sider, "An Historic Moment," 27.

19. On finding "a solid foundation of agreement," see Sider, "An Historic Moment," 28. On black delegates letting up, see Marlin VanElderen speech at Calvin Theological Seminary, December 5, 1974, Box 3, Folder 13, "Thanksgiving Workshop, Evangelicals for Social Action (1974): Reportage; December 1974–January 1975," ESA Collection, BGCA. On the new sexism plank, see Nancy A. Hardesty, "Blessed the Waters That Rise and Fall to Rise Again," *EEWC Update* 28, 2 (Summer 2004). On enjoying soul food together, see Sider, "An Historic Moment," 28.

20. On the softening of the statement, see Paul Henry to Ron Sider, October 8, 1973; Henry to Sider, November 13, 1973, Folder "Chicago Declaration Planning," ESAA. On evangelical piety during the Workshop, see Beth Burbank to Ron Sider, n.d., Folder "Chicago Declaration Planning," ESAA; "Minutes of the Planning Committee," September 19, 1973, in "Chicago Workshop Planning," ESAA; Paul Rees, "Prayer and Social Concern," *The Chicago Declaration*, 78–87; Frank E. Gaebelein, Statement on Chicago Declaration, Folder "1973 Chicago Declaration," ESAA.

21. Alma Kaufman, "Evangelicals Get Cue on Social Concerns," *Cleveland Plain Dealer*, December 1, 1973; "Evangelicals Restate Goals," *Milwaukee Sentinel*, May 19, 1979, 8; Roy Larson, "Evangelicals Do U-Turn, Take on Social Problems," *Chicago Sun-Times*, December 1, 1973. Coffin quoted in *New York Times Magazine*, June 27, 1976, 6, copy Folder "1976," ESAA.

22. Yoder to "To Whom It May Concern," January 28, 1974, in Folder "Thanksgiving Workshop 1974," ESAA; "Door Interview: Wesley Pippert," *Wittenburg Door* 21 (October–November 1974): 22; Paul Jewett, "Why I Won't Sign," *Reformed Journal* 24, 5 (May–June 1974): 8–10; letter from Bruce Shearer, "Put Flesh on Words," *Post-American* 3, 3 (April 1974): 5.

23. Mrs. Peter Vroon, "Letters," *Presbyterian Layman* (June 1974): 6; Roger C. Palms to Ron Sider, June 21, 1974, Folder "Thanksgiving Workshop 1974," ESAA. On Thanksgiving Workshop planners' recruitment of Billy Graham despite their critique of his politics, see David Moberg to Ron Sider, December 28, 1972; Ron Sider to David Moberg, February 19, 1973; Merold Westphal to Ron Sider, August 31, 1973, in Folder "Chicago Declaration Planning," ESAA. For Billy Graham's response, see Graham, "Watergate," *Christianity Today* 18, 7 (January 4, 1974): 9–19. According to Mark Hatfield, Graham refused to sign the Declaration because of its feminist tenor. See Wesley Granberg-Michaelson, *Unexpected Destinations: An Evangelical Pilgrimage to World Christianity* (Grand Rapids, Mich.: Eerdmans, 2011), 77.

24. On InterVarsity support, see Mike Shepherd to Ron Sider, February 1, 1974, Folder "1973 Chicago Declaration Aftermath," ESAA. For hundreds of other letters, see files marked "1973" and "1974." On mainline resonance with the Chicago Declaration, see George Telford, "Evangelical Social Action: A Report," *Presbyterian Survey* (July 1975): 64–65, copy in Folder "1974 Chicago Workshop Media," ESAA; "A Response to 'A Declaration of Evangelical Social Concern,'" October 11, 1974; Box 3, Folder 6, "Thanksgiving Workshop: Evangelical for Social Action: Miscellaneous Materials, November 1974," ESA Collection, BGCA. On evangelical-ecumenical cooperation at the local level, see James Hefley and Marti Hefley, *The Church That Takes on Trouble* (Elgin, Ill.: Cook, 1976), 85–86, 159; Elizabeth O'Connor, *Call to Commitment: The Story of Church of the Saviour* (New York: Harper & Row, 1963), 18.

25. On "big business Republicanism," see Arthur O. Roberts, professor at George Fox University, to Ron Sider, October 17, 1972, Folder "Evangelicals for McGovern," ESAA.

26. C. René Padilla and Chris Sugden, eds., *How Evangelicals Endorsed Social Responsibility: Texts on Evangelical Social Ethics, 1974–83—A Commentary* (Nottingham: Grove Books, 1985). For a printed program of the Calvin conference, see Folder "1973 Chicago Declaration Planning," ESAA. For the extensive oeuvre of evangelical left literature, see William Stringfellow, *A Private and Public Faith* (Grand Rapids, Mich.: Eerdmans, 1962); David O. Moberg, *Inasmuch: Christian Social Responsibility in Twentieth-Century America* (Grand Rapids, Mich.: Eerdmans, 1965); Foy Valentine, *The Cross in the Marketplace* (Waco, Tex.: Word, 1966); Robert G. Clouse, Robert D. Linder, and Richard V. Pierard, *Protest and Politics: Christianity and Contemporary Affairs* (Greenwood, S.C.: Attic Press, 1968); Sherwood Wirt, *The Social Conscience of the Evangelical* (New York: Harper & Row, 1968); Vernon Grounds, *Evangelicalism and Social Responsibility* (Scottdale, Pa.: Herald Press, 1969); Leighton Ford, *One Way to Change the World* (New York: Harper & Row, 1970); Gary R. Collins, ed., *Our Society*

in Turmoil (Carol Stream, Ill.: Creation House, 1970); Carl F. H. Henry, *A Plea for Evangelical Demonstration* (Grand Rapids, Mich.: Baker Book House, 1971); David O. Moberg, *The Great Reversal: Evangelism Versus Social Concern* (Philadelphia: Lippincott, 1972); Bob Goudzwaard, *A Christian Political Option* (Toronto: Wedge Publishing, 1972); Charles Y. Furness, *The Christian and Social Action* (Old Tappan, N.J.: Fleming H. Revell, 1972); Robert G. Clouse, Robert D. Linder, and Richard V. Pierard, eds. *The Cross and the Flag* (Carol Stream, Ill.: Creation House, 1972); Wesley G. Pippert, *Faith at the Top* (Elgin, Ill.: Cook, 1973); Robert D. Linder and Richard V. Pierard, *Politics: A Case for Christian Action* (Downers Grove, Ill.: InterVarsity Press, 1973); Paul B. Henry, *Politics for Evangelicals* (Valley Forge, Pa.: Judson Press, 1974); Stephen V. Monsma, *The Unraveling of America* (Downers Grove, Ill.: InterVarsity Press, 1974); Wesley G. Pippert, *Memo for 1976: Some Political Options* (Downers Grove, Ill.: InterVarsity Press, 1974); William R. Coats, *God in Public: Political Theology beyond Niebuhr* (Grand Rapids, Mich.: Eerdmans, 1974); Richard J. Mouw, *Political Evangelism* (Grand Rapids, Mich.: Eerdmans, 1974); Sider, ed., *The Chicago Declaration*; Johannes Verkuyl and H. G. Schulte Nordholt, *Responsible Revolution: Means and Ends for Transforming Society* (Grand Rapids, Mich.: Eerdmans, 1974); James Skillen, ed., *Christian Politics: False Hope or Biblical Demand?* (Beaver Falls, Pa.: Radix Books, 1974); John B. Anderson, *Vision and Betrayal in America* (Waco, Tex.: Word, 1975); Jim Wallis, *Agenda for Biblical People: Gospel for a New Order* (New York: Harper & Row, 1976); Richard Pierard, "Social Concern in Christian Missions," *Christianity Today* 20, 19 (June 18, 1976): 7–10; Arthur Simon, *Christian Faith and Public Policy: No Grounds for Divorce* (Grand Rapids, Mich.: Eerdmans, 1976); Robert E. Webber, *The Secular Saint: A Case for Evangelical Social Responsibility* (Grand Rapids, Mich.: Zondervan, 1979); Richard J. Mouw, *Called to Holy Worldliness* (Philadelphia: Fortress Press, 1980); John Perkins, *With Justice for All* (Ventura, Cal.: Regal Books, 1982); Stephen Charles Mott, *Biblical Ethics and Social Change* (New York: Oxford University Press, 1982). On "evangelical agonies," see Richard Mouw, "Weaving a Coherent Pattern of Discipleship," *Christian Century* (August 20, 1975): 728–31.

27. On evangelicals in the pew, see Wesley Pippert's letter to the editor, *Christianity Today* 18, 8 (January 18, 1974): 25. On *Eternity*, see K. B. Kraakevik, "The Political Mobilization of White Evangelical Populists in the 1970s and Early 1980s," Ph.D. dissertation, University of Chicago Divinity School, 2004, 304. On the *National Courier*, see John D. Keeler, J. Douglas Tarpley, and Michael R. Smith, "The *National Courier*, News, and Religious Ideology," in *Media and Religion in American History* (Northport, Ala.: Vision Press, 2000), 275–90.

28. On Watergate and young evangelical outrage at Nixon's abuse of power, see David Gill, "The Abuse of Power," *Right On* 6, 2 (September 1974): 5; Jill Shook to Edie Black, May 11, Box 2, Jill Shook Papers, CWLF Collection, GTUA; Wesley Pippert, "Christ and Crisis in Washington," *HIS* 34, 7 (April 1974): 1–3; Henry Stob, "Watergate: Judgment, Healing, and Renewal," *Reformed Journal* 23, 6 (July–August 1973); Richard Pierard, "Can Billy Graham Survive Richard Nixon," *Reformed Journal* 24

(April 1974): 7–13; Henry, *Politics for Evangelicals*, 8; Donald E. King, Jr., "Perspective on the News," *Vanguard* (September–October 1974): 31; Lane T. Dennis, *A Reason for Hope* (Old Tappan, N.J.: Revell, 1976), 57. On Democratic affiliation, see Lyman A. Kellstedt and Mark A. Noll, "Religion, Voting for President, and Party Identification, 1948–1984," in *Religion and American Politics: From the Colonial Period to the 1980s*, ed. Mark A. Noll (New York: Oxford University Press, 1990), 372, 374. On the NAE as a haven for Democrats, see Richard Quebedeaux, "The Evangelicals: New Trends and New Tensions," *Christianity and Crisis* (September 20, 1976): 197–202. On the Workshop's ambitious agenda, see "Sider to Planning Committee," Folder "1974 Workshop Planning," ESAA. On "accelerating the movement," see Steve Knapp to Ron Sider, July 1, 1974, Folder "1974 Chicago Workshop Planning," ESAA; C. T. McIntire, "Some Thoughts on the Chicago Declaration of Evangelical Social Concern," January 1974, Folder "1973 Chicago Declaration," ESAA.

Chapter 10. Identity Politics and a Fragmenting Coalition

Epigraph: Skillen quoted in Cheryl Forbes, "Doing the Declaration," *Christianity Today* 19, 6 (December 20, 1974): 28–29.

1. Ron Sider, manuscript of opening address, Folder "1974 Thanksgiving Workshop," ESAA.

2. On the "buckshot approach," see Robert T. Coote, "Evangelicals for Social Action Miss Target with Buckshot Approach," *Evangelical Newsletter* 2, 4 (December 20, 1974): 4. On the action proposals, see Arthur Simon to Ron Sider, December 4, 1974, Folder "1974 TW Aftermath," ESAA; Stephen Mott and Wesley Roberts, "A Report on the Second Thanksgiving Workshop," December 20, 1974, Box 3, Folder 13, "Thanksgiving Workshop, Evangelicals for Social Action (1974): Reportage; December 1974–January 1975," ESA Collection, BGCA; James Skillen to Ron Sider, circa December 1974, Folder "1974 TW Aftermath," ESAA. On "doing his or her own thing," see Cheryl Forbes, "Doing the Declaration," *Christianity Today* 19, 6 (December 20, 1974): 28–29.

3. Ira Gallaway to Richard Pierard, December 17, 1976, Box 4, Folder 15, "Evangelical Women's Caucus; records; November 1974–May 1976"; Richard Pierard to Rufus Jones, September 16, 1975, Box 3, Folder 15, "ESA and Third Workshop (1975): Correspondence; March 1975–February 1976," ESA Collection, BGCA.

4. For critical assessments of identity politics, see Mary Ann Glendon, *Rights Talk: The Impoverishment of Political Discourse* (New York: Free Press, 1991), x; Arthur Schlesinger, Jr., *The Disuniting of America* (New York: Norton, 1993); Todd Gitlin, *The Twilight of Common Dreams: Why America Is Wracked by Culture Wars* (New York: Metropolitan Books, 1995); Richard Rorty, *Achieving Our Country* (Cambridge: Harvard University Press, 1998). On the flowering of multiculturalism and civil rights, see L. A. Kauffman, "The Anti-Politics of Identity," *Socialist Review* 20, 1 (January–March 1990): 67–80. On the feminist left, see Sara Evans, *Personal Politics:*

The Origins of Women's Liberation in the Civil Rights Movement and the New Left (New York: Knopf, 1979); Alice Echols, *Daring to Be Bad: Radical Feminism in America, 1967–1975* (Minneapolis: University of Minnesota Press, 1989). On the gay awakening, see Paul Berman, *A Tale of Two Utopias: The Political Journey of the Generation of 1968* (New York: Norton, 1996), 123–94; Dudley Clendinen and Adam Nagourney, *Out for Good: The Struggle to Build a Gay Rights Movement in America* (New York: Simon & Schuster, 1999); and Steve Valocchi, "Individual Identities, Collective Identities, and Organizational Structure: The Relationship of the Political Left and Gay Liberation in the United States," *Sociological Perspectives* 44, 4 (Winter 2001): 445–67.

5. On the NBEA, see Albert G. Miller, "The Rise of African-American Evangelicalism in American Culture," in *Perspectives on American Religion and Culture*, ed. Peter W. Williams (Malden, Mass.: Blackwell, 1999), 259–69; William H. Bentley, *The National Black Evangelical Association: Reflections on the Evolution of a Concept of Ministry* (Chicago: self-published, 1979); Mary Sawyer, *Black Ecumenism: Implementing the Demands of Justice* (Valley Forge, Pa.: Trinity Press, 1994), 113–33. The NBEA's white fundamentalist and evangelical roots contrast with the heritage of most black evangelicals, who come out of historic American black denominations such as the African Methodist Episcopal Church and many independent Baptist groups. I use the term "black evangelical" because they self-identified as such. On NBEA criticism of white denominations, see Tom Skinner, *Black and Free* (Grand Rapids, Mich.: Zondervan, 1968); Bill Pannell, *My Friend, the Enemy* (Waco, Tex.: Word, 1968); Columbus Salley and Ronald Behm, *Your God Is Too White* (Downers Grove, Ill.: InterVarsity Press, 1970); Tom Skinner, *How Black Is the Gospel?* (Philadelphia: Lippincott, 1970).

6. On being "too White in our thinking," see Gladys Hunt to IVCF Cabinet, May 13, 1969, Box 52, Folder 3, "Pannell, William; 1967–1970," InterVarsity Christian Fellowship Collection, BGCA. For "dehonkify our minds," see Dan Orme, "Black Militant Evangelicals: An Interview," *The Other Side* 5, 5 (September–October 1969): 20–25.

7. Bentley, *NBEA*, 19–20; Ronald C. Potter, "The New Black Evangelicals," in *Black Theology: A Documentary History, 1966–1979*, ed. Gayraud S. Wilmore and James H. Cone (Maryknoll, N.Y.: Orbis, 1979), 304.

8. On Urbana, see Potter, "The New Black Evangelicals," 304; "Statement From: The Afro-American People," December 30, 1973, Folder, "1974 TW Aftermath," ESAA.

9. On Voice of Calvary, see Charles Marsh, *The Beloved Community: How Faith Shapes Social Justice* (New York: Basic, 2005), 176–78; John Perkins, *Let Justice Roll Down* (Glendale, Cal.: Regal Books, 1976), 178; Perkins, *A Quiet Revolution: The Christian Response to Human Need* (Pasadena, Cal.: Urban Family Publications, 1976), 167; John Perkins interview by Paul Ericksen, June 19, 1987, transcript in John Perkins Collection, BGCA.

10. Joel A. Carpenter, "Compassionate Evangelicalism," *Christianity Today* 47, 12 (December 2003): 40; "A Proposal on Action to Combat Racism," Folder "1973 TW," ESAA; James Robert Ross, "A Proposal for an Evangelical Center for the Study and Eradication of Racism," Folder "1973 TW," ESAA; "The Black Caucus," 3–4, Folder

"1974 Thanksgiving Workshop," ESAA. For Bentley, see Bonnie M. Greene, "Confrontation in Black and White: Evangelicals for Social Action, Third Annual Workshop," *Vanguard* (September–October 1975): 25–26.

11. John K. Stoner, "National Workshop on Race and Reconciliation, Atlanta, June 13–15, 1975," June 24, 1975, Folder "1975 Atlanta Race Workshop," ESAA. On the "demon of racism," see Potter, "The New Black Evangelicals," 306; Bentley, *NBEA*, 128. On evangelicalism's failure to address racism, see Bentley, *NBEA*, 129. On the *Post-American*-NBEA rift, see Reese, "Resistance and Hope," 112–13.

12. Salley, *Too White*, 65, 73. For "theological decolonizaton," see Potter, "New Black Evangelicals," 307. For "Declaration of Independence," see Bentley, "Origin and Focus of the National Black Evangelical Association," 313–14. For "merely blackenize," see Potter, "New Black Evangelicals," 307. For "ultimate nigger," see Clarence Hilliard, "Down with the Honky Christ, Up with the Funky Jesus," *Christianity Today* 20, 9 (January 30, 1976): 6–8.

13. For "ethnic self-acceptance," see Bentley, *NBEA*, 11; Ronald Potter, "The Black Christian Student and Interracial Male-Female Relationships," in *Handbook for Black Christian Students, or How to Remain Sane and Grow in a White College Setting* (Chicago: National Black Christian Students Conference, 1974), 39–43; Ertie Hilliard Nevels, "Interracial Dating: A Brief Word from a Black Sister," in *Handbook*, 44. For "read and ponder on blackness," see Walter Arthur McCray, *Toward a Holistic Liberation of Black People: Its Meaning as Expressed in the Objectives of the National Black Christian Students Conference* (Chicago: National Black Christian Students Conference, 1977), 29. Potter quoted in Jim Wallis, "'New Evangelicals' and the Demands of Discipleship," *Christian Century* 91, 20 (May 29, 1974): 581–82. For "indigenous Black leadership," see Bentley, *NBEA*, 109.

14. On Circle Church, see Glen Kehrein and Raleigh Washington, *Breaking Down Walls* (Chicago: Moody Press, 1993), 75–81; Manuel Ortiz, "Circle Church: A Case Study in Contextualization," *Urban Mission* 8, 3 (January 1991): 6–18; Hilliard, "Down with the Honky Christ," 6. On Gordon-Conwell, see Titus Presler, "Perkins' Visit Impetus for Criticism," *The Paper* 4, 6 (April 17, 1978): 1. On the growth of NBEA, see John Maust, "The NBEA: Striving to Be Both Black and Biblical," *Christianity Today* 24, 12 (June 27, 1980): 58–59.

15. Ka Tong Gaw to Ron Sider, March 14, 1975, Folder "1975 TW Planning," ESAA. See April 1, 1976, issue of *The Branch* in Box 124, Folder, 12, "The Branch," InterVarsity Christian Fellowship Collection, BGCA. For other expressions of Asian evangelical identity, see magazine *The Asianamerican Journey* published by Agape Fellowship in Los Angeles.

16. John F. Alexander, "Counting the Cost," *The Other Side* 7, 2 (March–April 1971): 3; Carl Ellis, "Black Militant Evangelicals," *The Other Side* 5, 5 (September–October 1969): 20–25.

17. Evon Bachaus to Ron Sider, December 31, 1974, Folder "1974 Chicago Aftermath," ESAA.

18. On the significant influence of secular feminism, see Sharon Gallagher interview by author, July 7, 2006, Berkeley, California; "Women's Lib," *Right On* 2, 23 (February 3, 1971): 3; Donald A. Heinz, "Jesus in Berkeley," Ph.D. dissertation, Graduate Theological Union, 1976, 238–42; Pamela Cochran, *Evangelical Feminism: A History* (New York: New York University Press, 2005), 35–36; contributions by Meythaler and Gallagher in *Our Struggle to Serve: The Stories of 15 Evangelical Women*, ed. Virginia Hearn (Waco, Tex.: Word, 1979), 50–61, 93–100.

19. For early complaints of sexism, see letter from Nancy Goodwin, *HIS* 25, 8 (May 1965): 23; Letha Scanzoni, "The Feminists and the Bible," *Christianity Today* 17, 9 (February 2, 1973): 10–15. On action at the Thanksgiving Workshops, see "Proposals from the Women's Caucus," November 1974, Box 2, Folder 15, "Thanksgiving Workshop, Evangelicals for Social Action (1974): Action Proposals n.d.," ESA Collection, BGCA.

20. "Proposals from the Women's Caucus," November 1974, Box 2, Folder 15, "Thanksgiving Workshop, Evangelicals for Social Action (1974): Action Proposals n.d.," ESA Collection, BGCA.

21. Kathleen Storrie to Samuel Escobar, October 26, 1974, Folder, "1974 Chicago Workshop planning," ESAA; Gallagher in *Our Struggle to Serve*, 97; Hardesty to Sider, October 25, 1974, Folder "1974 Chicago Workshop Planning," ESAA. For nonsexist literature, see Sharon Neufer Emswiler and Thomas Neufer Emswiler, *Sisters and Brothers Sing!* (Normal, Ill.: Wesley Foundation Campus Ministry, 1975); "Sidelines," *The Other Side* 14, 3 (March 1978): 9; Rey O'Day Mawson, "Why All the Fuss About Language?" *Post-American* 3, 6 (August–September 1974): 16–17; David Gill, "Prolegomena to the Male/Female Discussion," *Right On* 7, 8 (May 1976): 12; Virginia Hearn, in *Our Struggle to Serve*, 19.

22. Jean Milliken quoted in Bill Milliken, *So Long, Sweet Jesus* (Waco, Tex.: Prometheus, 1973), 171. For mutuality in childcare tasks, see Ron Sider, "Discipleship Workshops: Focus on Justice" proposal, January 7, 1976, Folder "Discipleship Workshops," ESAA. On conflict within the *Post-American* community, see Jackie Sabath, "Principles to Partnership: A History of Male-Female Relationships at Sojourners," *Sojourners* 9, 7 (July 1980): 19–21. For examples of *The Other Side* advice column, see "Liberated, but . . ." *The Other Side* 14, 3 (March 1978): 52–53. Letha Scanzoni and John Scanzoni, "Help! My Wife's in Tears!" *The Other Side* 14, 7 (July 1978): 48–49.

23. On the ERA, see Betsy Rossen, "ERA: Three Short Sentences You Should Know About," *HIS* 38, 4 (January 1978): 1, 4–5, 26; Carolynn Hudson, Letter to the Editor, *Right On* 9, 3 (November–December 1977): 2; Cochran, *Evangelical Feminism*, 40–41.

24. On women's ordination, see "The Action Proposals Accepted at the Second Thanksgiving Workshop Evangelicals for Social Action Chicago, 1974," 5–9, copy in Folder "1974 Chicago Workshop," ESAA; Rufus Jones to Jay Wells, February 10, 1975, Box 3, Folder 16, "ESA Third Workshop (1975): Correspondence; January–December 1975," ESA Collection, BGCA; Roy Larson, "Evangelism God's 'Truth' in Action," *Chicago Sun-Times*, December 7, 1974, 60.

25. Letha Scanzoni and Nancy Hardesty, *All We're Meant to Be: A Biblical Approach to Women's Liberation* (Waco, Tex.: Word, 1974); Quebedeaux, "We're on our Way, Lord!" 136; Bonnie Greene, review of *All We're Meant to Be* in *Vanguard* (March–April 1975): 16; Barbara Sroka, "Undercover," *HIS* 35, 4 (January 1975): 18–19; Ina J. Kau, "Feminists in the American Evangelical Movement," M.A. thesis, Pacific School of Religion, 1977, 57.

26. Nancy A. Hardesty and Letha Scanzoni, "All We're Meant to Be: A *Vanguard* Interview with Letha Scanzoni and Nancy Hardesty," *Vanguard* (March–April 1975): 14, 145–81. A flood of books and articles on biblical interpretation soon added to *All We're Meant to Be*, most asserting a "developing egalitarianism" view, which acknowledged that Old Testament texts were heavily patriarchal but that the New Testament had launched a trajectory toward gender egalitarianism. See Paul King Jewett, *Man as Male and Female: A Study in Sexual Relationships from a Theological Point of View* (Grand Rapids, Mich.: Eerdmans, 1975); Richard Boldrey and Joyce Boldrey, *Chauvinist or Feminist? Paul's View of Women* (Grand Rapids, Mich.: Baker, 1976); Virginia R. Mollenkott, *Women, Men, and the Bible* (Nashville: Abingdon Press, 1977); George W. Knight, III, *The New Testament Teaching on the Role Relationship of Men and Women* (Grand Rapids, Mich.: Baker, 1976); Patricia Gundry, *Woman, Be Free!* (Grand Rapids, Mich.: Zondervan, 1977); Patricia Gundry, *Heirs Together* (Grand Rapids, Mich.: Zondervan, 1980); Paul Jewett, *The Ordination of Women: An Essay on the Office of Christian Ministry* (Grand Rapids, Mich.: Eerdmans, 1980); Gundry, *The Complete Woman* (Garden City, N.Y.: Doubleday, 1981); Alvera Mickelsen, *Women, Authority & the Bible* (Downers Grove, Ill.: InterVarsity Press, 1986).

27. Lucille Sider Dayton, "Women in the Holiness Movement," Convention of the Christian Holiness Association, Louisville, Kentucky, April 17–19, 1974, copy distributed at 1974 Thanksgiving Workshop, Folder, "1974 Chicago Workshop," ESAA; Donald W. Dayton, *Discovering an Evangelical Heritage* (New York: Harper & Row, 1976), 85–98; Nancy Hardesty, "Your Daughters Shall Prophesy: Revivalism and Feminism in the Age of Finney," Ph.D. dissertation, University of Chicago, 1976; Janette Hassey, *No Time for Silence: Evangelical Women in Public Ministry Around the Turn of the Century* (Grand Rapids, Mich.: Zondervan, 1986).

28. On *Daughters of Sarah* (which grew to 3,000 subscribers by 1983), see Cochran, *Evangelical Feminism*, 33; Quebedeaux, "We're On Our Way, Lord," 138. On the growth of feminist-oriented chapters within evangelical organizations, see Bentley, *NBEA*, 59; Frank Barker to James McLeish, September 24, 1984, Box 345, Folder 25, "Brave New People; 1984-1985," InterVarsity Christian Fellowship Collection, BGCA; Kau, "Feminists in the American Evangelical Movement," 94–95; Cochran, *Evangelical Feminism*, 36–38, 41.

29. On the 1975 EWC convention, see Bonnie Greene, "We're On Our Way! The Evangelical Women's Caucus in Washington," *Vanguard* (January–February 1976): 18–19; "Remembering Washington '75," *EWC Update* 9, 4 (Winter 1985): 4–5. On the

Congress on the Family, see John Turner, *Bill Bright and Campus Crusade for Christ* (Chapel Hill: University of North Carolina Press, 2008), 154.

30. Jackie Sabath, "Principles to Partnership: A History of Male-Female Relationships at Sojourners," *Sojourners* 9, 7 (July 1980): 19–21; "Evangelical Women's Caucus Says 'Jesus is a Feminist,'" *Greeley Tribune*, February 13, 1976, 23, copy in Box 4, Folder 15, "Evangelical Women's Caucus; records; November 1974–May 1976," ESA Collection, BGCA; Greene, "The Evangelical Women's Caucus in Washington," 18–19; Virginia Hearn, *Our Struggle to Serve*; Claire K. Wolterstorff, "Encouragement and Unanswered Questions: Evangelicals Discuss Women's Issues," *Reformed Journal* 28, 8 (August 1978): 16–19; S. Sue Horner, "Remembering: Writing EEWC's Herstory" *EEWC Update* 25, 2 (Summer 2001); Phyllis E. Alsdurf, "Evangelical Feminists: Ministry Is the Issue," Folder "Evangelical Women's Caucus Conference," FTSA.

31. Anne Eggebroten in *Our Struggle to Serve*, 118. On how biblical feminism "undermines Western values and institutions," see John Alexander, "Feminism as a Subversive Activity," *The Other Side* 18, 7 (July 1982): 8–9. On an EWC advertisement in *Ms.* magazine that drew over fifty responses from readers, see "*Ms.* Readers Meet EWC," *EWC Update* 6, 1 (March–May 1982): 3.

32. Text of Marlin Van Elderen speech at Calvin Theological Seminary, December 5, 1974, in Box 3, Folder 13, "Thanksgiving Workshop, Evangelicals for Social Action (1974): Reportage; December 1974–January 1975," ESA Collection, BGCA.

33. Robert T. Coote, "The Second Thanksgiving Workshop: Evangelicals for Social Action Miss Target with Buckshot Approach," *Evangelical Newsletter* 2, 4 (December 20, 1974), 4, copy in Folder "1974 Chicago Workshop Media," ESAA.

34. On the economic lifestyle caucus, see Steve Knapp, "Background and Preliminary Proposal: 'An Evangelical Dialogue on Strategies of Social Change,'" January 17, 1975, Folder "1974 TW Aftermath," ESAA; "Other 1974 Proposals," Box 2, Folder 15, "Thanksgiving Workshop, Evangelicals for Social Action (1974): Action Proposals," ESA Collection, BGCA; Wally Kroeker, "Another Step for Social Concern," *Moody Monthly* 75 (February 1975): 8–10; Cheryl Forbes, "Doing the Declaration," *Christianity Today* 19, 6 (December 20, 1974): 28–29; Rufus Jones to Paul Henry, January 14, 1975, Box 3, Folder 16, "ESA Third Workshop (1975): Correspondence; January–December 1975," ESA Collection, BGCA; "Commitment of Economic Responsibility," November 1974, ESAA.

35. This Anabaptist approach fit well with the New Left, which feared that working from within the system would compromise its ideals. In fact, evangelicals sympathetic to the New Left—including Jim Wallis, Dale Brown, Art Gish, Boyd Reese, John Alexander, and Joe Roos—and Anabaptist participants in the Thanksgiving Workshops of the mid-1970s were often one and the same. Also see John Howard Yoder, *The Politics of Jesus* (Grand Rapids, Mich.: Eerdmans, 1972); Yoder in *The Chicago Declaration*, 86–114; Yoder, *Nevertheless: A Meditation on the Varieties and Shortcomings of Religious Pacifism* (Scottdale, Pa.: Herald Press, 1971); Yoder, "The Persistence of the Constantinian Heresy," *Radix* 10, 4 (January–February 1974): 4–5. On Jesus's greatest

temptation, see Marlin J. Van Elderen, "Evangelicals and Liberals: Is There a Common Ground?" *Christianity and Crisis* 34, 12 (July 8, 1974): 151–55.

36. John Howard Yoder, "The Biblical Mandate," *Post-American* 3, 3 (April 1974): 21–25; Yoder, *Politics of Jesus*, 157.

37. For the Christ-culture typology, see H. Richard Niebuhr, *Christ and Culture* (New York: Harper, 1951). Mott quoted in Perry Bush, "Anabaptism Born Again: Mennonites, New Evangelicals, and the Search for a Usable Past, 1950–1980," *Fides et Historia* 25, 1 (Winter–Spring 1993): 44. On the popularity and sales of *The Politics of Jesus*, see Mark Thiessen Nation, *John Howard Yoder: Mennonite Patience, Evangelical Witness, Catholic Convictions* (Grand Rapids, Mich.: Eerdmans, 2006): 25. For "Menno-phobia," see Richard J. Mouw, "Why I Support Nuclear Disarmament," *Vanguard* (March–April 1979): 17–18. For Spykman's address at Chicago, see "Christian Societal Responsibility: A Reformed Model," Folder "1974 Chicago Workshop Planning," ESAA.

38. Robert E. Webber, "Historic Models of Social Responsibility," November 1975, Folder "1975 Chicago Workshop," ESAA; Bonnie Greene, "Confrontation in Black and White: Evangelicals for Social Action, Third Annual Workshop," *Vanguard* (September–October 1975): 25–26; Webber, "Division in Evangelicalism," *The Other Side* 7, 3 (July–August 1971): 27–28, 36; Richard Pierard, "The Eighteenth-Century Model of British Evangelicals," Folder "1975 Chicago Workshop," ESAA.

39. Bert Witvoet, "A Sojourner Came to Town," *Vanguard* (September–October 1979): 5–7; Greene, "Confrontation in Black and White," 26; "Chicago Crisis," *Christianity Today* 20, 1 (October 10, 1975): 69. For "albatross," see Richard V. Pierard, "Chicago Declaration: Barely Audible," *Christianity Today* 21, 17 (June 3, 1976): 33. For "tower of Babel," see Gordon Spykman, "The Tower of Babel Revisited: The Calvin Conference on Christianity and Politics," *Vanguard* (July–August 1975): 23–25. Wirt quoted in James Davison Hunter, "Shaping American Foreign Policy," in Michael Cromartie, ed., *Evangelicals and Foreign Policy: Four Perspectives* (Lanham, Md.: University Press of America, 1989), 77.

40. For mid-1970s exchanges between Reformed and Anabaptist evangelicals, see Steve Mott, "The Politics of Jesus and Our Responsibilities," *Reformed Journal* 26, 2 (February 1976): 7–10; Isaac Rottenberg, "The Shape of the Church's Social-Economic Witness," *Reformed Journal* 27 (May 1977): 16–21; Jim Wallis, "What Does Washington Have to Say to Grand Rapids?" *Sojourners* 6, 7 (July 1977): 3–4; Isaac Rottenberg, "Continuing the Dialogue," *Sojourners* 6, 10 (September 1977): 38; Nicholas P. Wolterstorff, "How Does Grand Rapids Reply to Washington?" *Reformed Journal* 27 (October 1977): 10–14; Isaac Rottenberg, "Dimensions of the Kingdom: A Dialogue with Sojourners," *Reformed Journal* 27 (November 1977): 17–21. Representatives from *Sojourners* and the *Reformed Journal* met for a two-day conversation in April 1978. For an account of the meeting, see Marlin VanElderen, "Setting Aside Common Stereotypes," *Sojourners* 7, 6 (June 1978): 32.

For Mouw's rebuttal of Yoder, see Richard Mouw, *Political Evangelism* (Grand Rapids, Mich.: Eerdmans, 1974); Mouw, *Politics and the Biblical Drama* (Grand Rapids,

Mich.: Eerdmans, 1976). On corrective influences, see Richard Lovelace, *Dynamics of Spiritual Life: An Evangelical Theology of Renewal* (Downers Grove, Ill.: InterVarsity Press, 1979), 387. On "squaring off against each other," see Judy Brown Hull, "In Praise of Holding Together," *Sojourners* 7, 2 (February 1977): 35.

41. On "peace parishes," see "ESA Sets Goals for 1985," *ESA Update* 6, 6 (November–December 1984): 1. On Discipleship Workshops, see "15 Discipleship Workshops on Evangelism and Justice," Folder "Discipleship Workshops," ESAA. On events at Gordon, see Ron Sider, "A Brief Report on the Discipleship Workshop at Gordon-Conwell," March 1, 1978; Elaine Amerson, "A Sensitivity to Language"; Amerson, "Report on Discipleship Workshop, Gordon College," December 3, 1977; Amerson, "Wow! What Serendipity!" in Folder "Discipleship Workshops," ESAA.

42. Jim Stentzel, "The Good News with the Bad: Covering Religion in the Secular Press," *Sojourners* 8, 4 (April 1979): 19–24.

43. On the Reformed withdrawal, see Richard Mouw interview by author, July 12, 2006, Pasadena, Cal.; "Same Cause, New Name," *Public Justice Newsletter* (October 1977): 1. On the recruitment of evangelical graduate students, see *Public Justice Report* 11, 4 (January 1988). On APJ's engagement of electoral politics, see "McCarthy Testifies Before Senate Finance Committee," *Public Justice Newsletter* (February 1978): 1–3; "U.N. Special Session on Disarmament," *Public Justice Newsletter* (June–July 1978): 1–4; "APJ Joins in Supreme Court Plea," *Public Justice Report* 6, 5 (February 1983): 1–2; "APJ Joins in Brief to Supreme Court on Education Brief," *Public Justice Report* 8, 4 (January 1985): 1, 5; "Transcript of Oral Arguments Before Court on Abortion Case," *New York Times*, April 27, 1989, A1; "APJ Opens Washington Office," *Public Justice Report* 7, 1 (October 1983): 7; "Skillen Meets Reagan," *Public Justice Report* 7, 2 (November 1983): 1–2; "Plasier Will Go to Iowa Legislature," *Public Justice Report* 9, 10 (August–September 1986): 7; *Preparing to Vote* (Washington, D.C.: APJ Education Fund, 1984); James W. Skillen, ed., *1988 Candidate Profiles: A Look at the Leading Presidential Contenders* (Grand Rapids, Mich.: Zondervan, 1988). On the Public Justice Voters' Club, see "McWhertor to Join APJ Staff in Washington," *Public Justice Report* 9, 7 (April 1986): 4. On APJ's hosting of five presidential candidates in forums, which drew up to 2,000 people, see "Will the Iowa Caucuses Name That President?" *Public Justice Report* 11, 6 (March 1988): 6.

44. On "principled pluralism," see Stephen Monmsa quoted in Spykman, "The Tower of Babel Revisited," 24; "Public Justice and Cultural Freedom," *Public Justice Newsletter* (March 1978): 7; "Political Representation: What Are the Problems?" *Public Justice Newsletter* (November 1978): 4–6; James W. Skillen, *Justice for Representation: A Proposal for Revitalizing our System of Political Participation* (Washington, D.C.: Association for Public Justice, 1979). On connections between APJ and a predecessor organization, the National Association for Christian Political Action, see Jim Skillen, "APJ's Vision Continues to Unfold," *Public Justice Report* 9, 6 (March 1986): 3–5; Morris and Alice Greidanus interview by author, January 20, 2008, South Bend, Ind. On education, see Morris and Alice Greidanus interview by author, January 20,

2008, South Bend, Ind.; William A. Harper, Rockne M. McCarthy, and James W. Skillen, *Disestablishment a Second Time: Genuine Pluralism for American Schools* (Grand Rapids, Mich.: Christian University Press, 1982); Rockne McCarthy, Oppewal, Walfred Peterson, and Gordon Spykman, *Society, State, and Schools: A Case for Structural and Confessional Pluralism* (Grand Rapids, Mich.: Eerdmans, 1981); Richard John Neuhaus, ed., *Democracy and the Renewal of Public Education* (Grand Rapids, Mich.: Eerdmans, 1987). On balancing issues of left and right, see "Public Justice and the State," *Public Justice Newsletter* 1, 3 (December 1977): 4–5. Republican Paul Henry, for example, took heat for voting for income tax increases, wetlands protection legislation, and aid to the city of Detroit as a state senator. In Congress he spoke out against a constitutional amendment punishing flag burning, deployment of the MX missile system, and U.S. aid to the Nicaraguan contras. See Paul C. Hillegonds, "Servant Leader in a Political World," in *Serving the Claims of Justice*, ed. Douglas Koopman (Grand Rapids, Mich.: Calvin College, 2001), 228.

45. Larry Christenson, *A Charismatic Approach to Social Action* (Minneapolis: Bethany Fellowship, 1974). For a progressive holiness approach, see Donald W. Dayton, "The Holiness and Pentecostal Churches: Emerging from Cultural Isolation," *Christian Century* 96 (August 15, 1979): 786; issues of *The Epworth Pulpit* and *The Listening Post* in the late 1970s. For Foy Valentine, see "Born Again! The Year of the Evangelicals," *Newsweek* 88 (October 25, 1976): 68–70. On rising interest in Orthodoxy, see Robert Webber and Donald Bloesch, eds., *The Orthodox Evangelicals: Who They Are and What They Are Saying* (Nashville: Thomas Nelson, 1978); Robert E. Webber, *Evangelicals on the Canterbury Trail* (Harrisburg, Pa.: Morehouse, 1985); Peter E. Gillquist, *Becoming Orthodox: A Journey to the Ancient Christian Faith* (Ben Lomond, Cal.: Conciliar Press, 1989). On the changing shape of religion, see Robert Wuthnow, *The Restructuring of American Religion* (Princeton: Princeton University Press, 1988). On the continuing evangelical-mainline rivalry, see speech by Marlin VanElderen at Calvin Theological Seminary, December 5, 1974, Folder 13, Box 3, "Thanksgiving Workshop, Evangelicals for Social Action (1974): Reportage; December 1974–January 1975," ESA Collection, BGCA; Martin Marty, "Needed: Revised Social Gospel," *Context* (March 15, 1974): 1–6; Sider notes on Pannell address, Folder "1973 Chicago Declaration," ESAA.

46. Robert E. VanderVennen, *A University for the People: A History of the Institute for Christian Studies* (Sioux Center, Iowa: Dordt College Press, 2008), 144–45; Wyn Wright Potter, "A Black Woman's Perspective," *The Other Side* 9, 4 (July–August 1973): 28–29. Also see "Report from Women's Meeting," *Update* (April 19, 1982): 1, copy in Box VII, Folder "Sojourners Community," Sojourners Collection, WCSC. On elderly identity, see "Door Interview: Maggie Kuhn," *Wittenburg Door* (December 1976–January 1977): 6–16, 25; Bonnie Greene, "Plight of the Aged," *Vanguard* (March 1973): 14–15, 29; Jim Stentzel, "Gray Panthers," *Sojourners* 6, 10 (October 1977): 16; David O. Moberg, "Numbering our Days: Aging and Christian Stewardship," *Right On* 9, 4 (January–February 1978): 4–7; Sharon Gallagher, "An Interview with Maggie Kuhn," *Right On* 9, 4 (January–February 1978): 8–9.

47. On the rise of evangelical therapy, see Gary R. Collins, *Effective Counseling* (Carol Stream, Ill.: Creation House, 1972); Jay E. Adams, *Christian Counselor's Manual* (Phillipsburg, N.J.: Presbyterian & Reformed, 1973); James Dobson, *Hide or Seek: Building Self-Esteem in Your Child* (Old Tappan, N.J.: Revell, 1974); Gary R. Collins, *The Rebuilding of Psychology: An Integration of Psychology and Christianity* (Wheaton, Ill.: Tyndale, 1977); Bruce Narramore, *You're Someone Special* (Grand Rapids, Mich.: Zondervan, 1978); "Proposals from the Women's Caucus," November 1975, Box 2, Folder 15, "Thanksgiving Workshop, Evangelicals for Social Action (1974): Action Proposals n.d.," ESA Collection, BGCA; Quebedeaux, *Worldly Evangelicals*, 111.

48. Jim Wallis, "Conversion," *Sojourners* 7, 5 (May 1978): 10–14; Robert K. Johnston, *Evangelicals at an Impasse: Biblical Authority in Practice* (Atlanta: John Knox, 1979), 77–112; Harold Lindsell, "Evangelicalism's Golden Age," *Moody Monthly* 86, 4 (December 1985): 114; Carl F. H. Henry, *Evangelicals in Search of Identity* (Waco, Tex.: Word, 1976), 13; "Interview: Carl Henry on Evangelical Identity," *Sojourners* 5, 4 (April 1976): 27–32; Henry, "Footnotes: Strife over Social Concerns," *Christianity Today* 20, 18 (June 4, 1976): 944–45; "The House Divided: An Interview with Carl Henry" *Eternity* 27, 10 (October 1976): 36–39.

49. Garry Wills, "Born-Again Politics," *New York Times Magazine*, August 1, 1976, 8–9; Michael Novak, "The Hidden Religious Majority," *Washington Post*, April 4, 1976, 29; "Born Again!" *Newsweek* (October 25, 1976): 68–70.

Chapter 11. The Limits of Electoral Politics

Epigraph: Mark Hatfield, "Schizophrenia on the Campaign Trail," *Sojourners* 5, 8 (October 1976): 23–25.

1. For "If *he* can be political," see Andrew R. Flint and Joy Porter, "Jimmy Carter: The Re-Emergence of Faith-Based Politics and the Abortion Rights Issue," *Presidential Studies Quarterly* 35, 1 (March 2005): 35, 42–47.

2. For a list of Carter's progressive policy positions, see David Kucharsky, *The Man from Plains: The Mind and Spirit of Jimmy Carter* (New York: Harper & Row, 1976), 115–22; 43; Howard Norton and Bob Slosser, *The Miracle of Jimmy Carter* (Plainfield, N.J.: Logos International, 1976), 6, 71–81. For a sense of what progressive evangelicals liked about Carter's policies, see David Young, "Secret Successes," *Wheaton Record* 105, 4 (October 17, 1980): 5; Nicholas Wolterstorff, "Carter's Religion," *Reformed Journal* 26, 7 (September 1976): 4–5; Robert Christgau, "An Ex-Believer Defends Carter's Religion," *Village Voice*, August 16, 1976; Robert Eels, *Lonely Walk: The Life of Senator Mark Hatfield* (Portland, Ore.: Multnomah Press, 1979), 159. On human rights, see Wes Michaelson, "Human Rights: A Surer Standard," *Sojourners* 6, 4 (April 1977): 3–5.

3. On progressive evangelical support for Carter, see Norton and Slosser, *Miracle of Jimmy Carter*, 53; Ron Mitchell, *Organic Faith: A Call to Authentic Christianity* (Chicago: Cornerstone Press, 1998), 141–43; Robert L. Maddox, *Preacher at the White House*

(Nashville: Broadman, 1984), 161; William Martin, *With God on Our Side: The Rise of the Religious Right in America*, rev. ed. (New York: Broadway Books, 1996), 157, 243; James Hefley and Marti Hefley, *The Church That Produced a President: The Remarkable Spiritual Roots of Jimmy Carter* (New York: Wyden, 1977), 242; Ruth McLatchie, "OCD Gets Democrats Involved," *Wheaton Record* 101, 21 (April 15, 1977): 2; Steve Ray, "Stevenson Campaigns for Jimmy," *Wheaton Record* 101, 7 (October 29, 1976): 1; Charles D. Hadley, "News and Notes," *Journal of Politics* 38, 4 (November 1976): 1099; Ed Griffin-Nolan, *Witness for Peace: A Story of Resistance* (Louisville: John Knox Press, 1991), 46.

4. On Carter in Iowa, see R. W. Apple, Jr., "Carter and Bayh Favored in Iowa: 2 Seem Ahead in Today's Democratic Caucuses for Selection of Delegates," *New York Times*, January 19, 1976, 1, 47; K. B. Kraakevik, "The Political Mobilization of White Evangelical Populists in the 1970s and Early 1980s," Ph.D. dissertation, University of Chicago Divinity School, 2004, 219–29. On Carter's "southern strategy," see Bruce Nesmith, *The New Republican Coalition: The Reagan Campaigns and White Evangelicals* (New York: Peter Lang, 1994), 59–61. On Carter's appeal to Southern Baptists, see Robert Fowler, *A New Engagement: Evangelical Political Thought* (Grand Rapids, Mich.: Eerdmans, 1982), 237; Victor Lasky, *Jimmy Carter: The Man and the Myth* (New York: Richard Marek, 1979), 210–11.

5. *Miracle of Jimmy Carter* advertisement, *Christianity Today* 20, 21 (July 16, 1976): 50; "Does a Dedicated Evangelical Belong in the White House?" *Christianity Today* 20, 21 (July 16, 1976): 43. For other advertisements and hagiographies of Carter, see *Eternity* 27, 8 (August 1976): 5; *Eternity* 27, 6 (June 1976): 8; *Eternity* 27, 10 (October 1976): 73; Norton and Slosser, *Miracle of Jimmy Carter*, 109; Norton, *Rosalynn: A Portrait* (Plainfield: Logos International, 1977). On being an outsider, see Peter Meyer, *James Earl Carter: The Man and the Myth* (Kansas City: Sheed Andrews McMeel, 1978), 111; Kucharsky, *The Man from Plains*, 97–102.

6. Norton and Slosser, *Miracle*, xi–xii, 9; Martin, *With God on Our Side*, 157.

7. On Shiloh, see Joe V. Peterson, "Jesus People: Christ, Communes, and the Counterculture of the Late Twentieth Century in the Pacific Northwest," M.A. thesis, Northwest Christian College, 1990, 110. On Gerson, see Carl M. Cannon, "Soul of a Conservative," *National Journal* 37, 20 (May 14, 2005): 1452–61. On Robertson, see David E. Harrell, *Pat Robertson: A Personal, Religious, and Political Portrait* (San Francisco: Harper & Row, 1987), 176; D. Michael Lindsay, *Faith in the Halls of Power: How Evangelicals Joined the American Elite* (New York: Oxford University Press, 2007), 17; Flint and Porter, "Jimmy Carter," 32. For "real, live one," see "Battling for the Blocs," *Time* 108, 11 (September 13, 1976): 24–25.

Beyond a mass of anecdotal evidence, it is difficult to chart precisely evangelicals' influence on the 1976 election, especially given pollsters' imprecision in categorization. On the difficulty of lumping evangelicals under the broader category of "Protestant," see John C. Green, Corwin E. Smidt, Lyman A. Kellstedt, and James L. Guth, "Bringing in the Sheaves: The Christian Right and White Protestants, 1976–1996," in *Sojourners in the Wilderness: The Christian Right in Comparative Perspective*, ed.

Smidt and James M. Penning (Lanham, Md.: Rowman & Littlefield, 1997), 79–81. For evidence of evangelical significance in Carter's win, see Nesmith, *New Republican Co-alition*, 65; Albert J. Menendez, *Religion at the Polls* (Philadelphia: Westminster Press, 1977), 197–98; Menendez, *Evangelicals at the Ballot Box* (Amherst, N.Y.: Prometheus Books, 1996), 128–29. For a revisionist argument against evangelicals' influence, see Stuart Rothenberg and Frank Newport, *The Evangelical Voter: Religion and Politics in America* (Washington, D.C.: Institute for Government and Politics, 1984), 4.

8. For "incomplete courtship," see John Turner, *Bill Bright and Campus Crusade for Christ* (Chapel Hill: University of North Carolina Press, 2008), 171. On the tradition-alism of the New Deal, see Alan Wolfe, "Whose Body Politic?" *American Prospect* (Winter 1993). On pro-life Catholics, see John McGreevy, *Catholicism and American Freedom* (New York: Norton, 2003), 278–80, 284; James Risen and Judy L. Thomas, *Wrath of Angels: The American Abortion War* (New York: Basic Books, 1998), 18–19, 143.

9. On the 1968 and 1972 Democratic Conventions, see Theodore White, *America in Search of Itself: The Making of the President, 1956–1980* (New York: Harper & Row, 1982), 168, 180–85; David Gill, "The Messiah in Miami Beach," *Right On* 4, 2 (August 1972): 5. On "neat, tidy, punctual," see White, *The Making of the President, 1972* (New York: Bantam Books, 1973), 319. For examples of evangelical disgust toward the cultural libertinism of the Left, see Harold O. J. Brown, *The Protest of a Troubled Protestant* (New Rochelle, N.Y.: Arlington, 1969), 209, 216; Graham, *World Aflame* (Garden City, N.Y.: Doubleday, 1965), 15; J. Edgar Hoover, "An Analysis of the New Left: A Gospel of Nihil-ism," *Christianity Today* 11, 22 (August 18, 1967): 3–6; Robert B. Fowler, *A New Engage-ment: Evangelical Political Thought, 1966–1976* (Grand Rapids, Mich.: Eerdmans, 1982), 27–28; William Sanford LaSor, "Law and Order," *Christianity Today* 14, 9 (January 30, 1970): 13–14; "The Ugly Spirit of Mobbism," *Christianity Today* 12, 17 (May 24, 1968): 26–27; "Editorial," *Christianity Today* 16, 15 (April 28, 1972): 24–25; "The Violent New Breed," *Christianity Today* 12, 4 (November 24, 1967): 25–26; "Vandalism in the Name of Peace," *Christianity Today* 13, 14 (April 11, 1969): 29; "Panthers and 'Pigs'" *Christian-ity Today* 14, 8 (January 16, 1970): 25.

10. Geoffrey Layman, *The Great Divide: Religious and Cultural Conflict in Ameri-can Party Politics* (New York: Columbia University Press, 2001), 294. For more on the Commission on Party Structure and Delegate Selection, commonly known as the McGovern-Fraser Commission, which also tried to increase participation by African-Americans, women, and youth, see William J. Crotty, *Decision for the Democrats: Re-forming the Party Structure* (Baltimore: Johns Hopkins University Press, 1978); Bryon E. Shafer, *Quiet Revolution: The Struggle for the Democratic Party and the Shaping of Post-Reform Politics* (New York: Russell Sage, 1983).

11. Louis Bolce and Gerald De Maio, "Our Secularist Democratic Party," *Public Interest* 149 (Fall 2002): 3–20; Jeane Kirkpatrick, *The New Presidential Elite: Men and Women in National Politics* (New York: Russell Sage, 1976), 53, 138, 208, 255, 264, 275; White, *Making of the President*, 96; Warren E. Miller and Teresa E. Levitin, *Leadership and Change: The New Politics and the American Electorate* (Cambridge: Winthrop,

1976), 6. For the new Democratic planks, see Layman, *Great Divide*, 42, 114. For reproductive freedom as "a transcending point of view," see Susan Tolchin and Martin Tolchin, *Clout: Womanpower and Politics* (New York: Coward, McCann & Geoghegan, 1974), 44. For the right to abortion as "central to a woman's freedom," see Tolchin, *Clout*, 47. For "sister against sister," see Kirkpatrick, *New Presidential Elite*, 448.

12. On the abortion vote, see Tolchin, *Clout*, 48-49; Kirkpatrick, *New Presidential Elite*, 320, 328, 441-49. Steinem quoted in Tolchin, *Clout*, 45-46. On women getting "screwed," see Germaine Greer, "McGovern, The Big Tease," *Harper's* (October 1972): 56-71.

13. On the Democrats' ambivalence toward abortion in the early 1970s, see Layman, *Great Divide*, 115-16. On Carter's animus against abortion, see Flint and Porter, "Jimmy Carter," 38; Susan M. Hartmann, "Feminism, Public Policy, and the Carter Administration," in *The Carter Presidency: Policy Choices in the Post-New Deal Era*, ed. Gary M. Fink and Hugh Davis Graham (Lawrence: University Press of Kansas, 1998), 235. On the Carter-Costanza controversy, see Flint and Porter, "Jimmy Carter," 39-40. On former pro-life Democrats, see Russ Douthat, "A Different Kind of Liberal," *New York Times*, August 31, 2009, A19. On the 1980 Democratic platform, see Layman, *Great Divide*, 117.

14. For "secularist putsch," see Bolce and De Maio, "Secularist Democratic Party." On the voting patterns and "pervasive secularism" of Democrats, see Layman, *Great Divide*, 96, 129. On evangelical criticism of McGovern's perceived lack of integrity, see Fowler, *New Engagement*, 33; "Let Your Yes Be Yes" *Christianity Today* 16, 23 (August 25, 1972): 29; "Objective: 1600 Pennsylvania Avenue," *Christianity Today* 16, 21 (July 28, 1972): 24. On religious conservatives leaving the Democratic Party, see Layman, *Great Divide*, 189-99; Richard John Neuhaus, *The Naked Public Square: Religion and Democracy in America* (Grand Rapids, Mich.: Eerdmans, 1984). On evangelical worry over "secular religion," see Richard Lovelace, *Dynamics of Spiritual Life: An Evangelical Theology of Renewal* (Downers Grove, Ill.: InterVarsity Press, 1979), 280. For voting statistics, see Lyman A. Kellstedt, "Religion, Voting for President, and Party Identification," in *Religion and American Politics*, ed. Mark A. Noll (New York: Oxford University Press, 1990), 372.

15. For Sojourners' critique of Carter, see Robert Eells, "Jimmy Carter and the Public Trust: A Warning to Evangelicals," *Vanguard* (October 1976): 11-12; William Stringfellow, "An Open Letter to Jimmy Carter," *Sojourners* 5, 8 (October 1976): 7-8; Jim Wallis, "The 'Outsider' in the White House," *Sojourners* 7, 1 (January 1978): 3-6; Wes Michaelson, "The Piety and Ambition of Jimmy Carter," *Sojourners* 5, 8 (October 1976): 17. On Carter's political misjudgments, see "How I Think I'll Vote," *Eternity* 31, 10 (October 1980): 29-33. For critiques of Carter's handling of human rights, see Jim Wallis, "The 'Outsider' in the White House," *Sojourners* 7, 1 (January 1978): 3-6; Theodore R. Malloch, "Jimmy Carter," in "Special Election Report," *Public Justice Newsletter* (May 1980): 1-2; John A. Bernbaum and Steve Moore, "Should the U.S. Boycott Ugandan Coffee," *HIS* 39, 2 (November 1978): 6-10, 12; "Open Letter to President

Carter," *Vanguard* 7, 3 (May–June 1977): 3. On defense spending, see Wallis, "'Outsider' in the White House," 5; "Despite a Campaign Promise," *The Other Side* 14, 5 (May 1978): 9. On the energy crisis, see Christiane Carolson-Thies, "Moratorium on Justice: The Costs of a Pipeline for Alaska's Natural Gas," *Sojourners* 6, 8 (August 1977): 33–34; "President Carter and the Energy War," *Public Justice Newsletter* 2, 10 (August–September 1979): 1–3. On the ERA, see Jim Stentzel, "Equal Rights for Women," *Sojourners* 6, 9 (October 1977): 7; "Sidelines," *The Other Side* 14, 3 (March 1978): 11. On poverty, see Wallis, "'Outsider' in the White House," 5. On elevating efficiency above compassion, see Stanley W. Carlson, "A Sporting Election," *Vanguard* (October 1976): 6–10; Bayly, "Grading Carter's Mid-Term," *Eternity* 30, 3 (March 1979): 59–60. Sider quoted in James Alan Patterson, "Evangelicals and the Presidential Elections of 1972, 1976, and 1980," Fides et Historia 18, 2 (June 1986): 50. On disillusionment with Carter in 1980, see Kathryn Lindskoog, "How I Think I'll Vote"; Shirley Nelson, "How I Think I'll Vote"; Karin Granberg-Michaelson, "How I Think I'll Vote," in *Eternity* 31, 10 (October 1980): 29–35.

16. On the hesitant support for Carter from some in the evangelical left, see the responses of James W. Skillen, Virginia Mollekott, Wes Pippert, Danny Rydberg, John Alexander, Russell Hitt in "How I Think I'll Vote," *Eternity* 27, 9 (September 1976): 26–31. On criticism of Carter's separation of church and state, see Henry Stob, "Religion and Politics," *Reformed Journal* 27, 2 (February 1977): 3; Richard Shaull, "Shoring Up the Old Order: President Carter as Baptist Leader," *Sojourners* 7, 1 (January 1978): 12–14; Michaelson, "Piety and Ambition," 14–18; Mark Hatfield, "Schizophrenia on the Campaign Trail," *Sojourners* 5, 8 (October 1976): 23–25.

17. For "liberal Christians like Mark Hatfield," see Jim Wallis and Wes Michaelson, "The Plan to Save America: A Disclosure of an Alarming Political Initiative by the Evangelical Far Right," *Sojourners* 5, 4 (April 1976): 4–12. On Bright and the CFF response, see Turner, *Bill Bright*, 164.

18. On Carter's stark reduction in his use of religious language after the election, lack of evangelicals in the administration, and failure to cultivate his religious constituency, see Gary Scott Smith, *Faith and the Presidency: from George Washington to George W. Bush* (New York: Oxford University Press, 2006), 296–98; Nesmith, *New Republican Coalition*, 59, 62–65; Flint and Porter, "Jimmy Carter," 35–36; James C. Hefley and Edward E. Plowman, *Washington: Christians in the Corridors of Power* (Wheaton, Ill.: Tyndale House, 1975), 59–68; Robert Freedman, "The Religious Right and the Carter Administration," The Historical Journal 48, 1 (March 2005): 238; Maddox, *Preacher at the White House*, 136–37; David John Marley, *Pat Robertson: An American Life* (Lanham, Md.: Rowman & Littlefield, 2007), 49; Bayly, "Grading Carter's Mid-Term," 60; Carol Flake, *Redemptorama: Culture, Politics, and the New Evangelicalism* (New York: Penguin Books, 1985), 6–7, 136; Richard Viguerie, *The New Right: We're Ready to Lead*, rev. ed. (Falls Church, Va.: Viguerie, 1981), 125; Maddox, *Preacher at the White House*, 135. On Carter's invocation of separation of church and state, see "The 1976 Election," *Church and State* 29 (December 1976): 4; E. Brooks

Holifield, "The Three Strands of Jimmy Carter's Religion," *New Republic* 174 (June 5, 1976): 15–17; Smith, *Faith and the Presidency*, 297; Maddox, *Preacher at the White House*, 186, 201–11. On hostility to evangelicalism by Democratic elites, see Kucharsky, *Man from Plains*, 9–10. On Carter's retrenchment and efforts to reach the traditional Democratic coalition, see John H. Aldrich, *Before the Convention: Strategies and Choices in Presidential Nomination Campaigns* (Chicago: University of Chicago Press, 1980), 192, 197.

19. On ambivalence over abortion in the 1960s, see McGreevy, *Catholicism and American Freedom*, 262, 284; "Abortion: 'Holy Innocents?'" *Christianity Today* 14, 16 (May 8, 1970): 39–40; "Abortion—Is It Moral?" *Christian Life* 29, 5 (September 1967): 32–33, 50–53; "Evangelical Scholars Endorse Birth Control," *Christianity Today* 12, 25 (September 27, 1968): 33–34; Jared A. Farley, "The Politicalization of the American Evangelical Press, 1960–1981: A Test of the Ideological Theory of Social Movement Mobilization," Ph.D. dissertation, Miami University, 2006, 111–13; Scott Flipse, "Below-the-Belt Politics," in *The Conservative Sixties*, ed. David Farber and Jeff Roche (New York: Peter Lang Publishing, 2003), 134–35; Blake A. Ellis, "An Alternative Politics: Texas Baptists and the Rise of the Christian Right, 1975–1985," *Southwestern Historical Quarterly* 112, 4 (April 2009): 360–86.

20. On the evangelical-Catholic coalition, see Flipse, "Below-the-Belt Politics," 139. On Schaeffer and Koop, see Schaeffer, *Whatever Happened to the Human Race?* (New York: F. H. Revell, 1979), 31, 55–87; Jerry Falwell, *Strength for the Journey: An Autobiography* (New York: Simon & Schuster, 1987), 335. On the high numbers of articles on abortion, see Farley, "Politicalization of the American Evangelical Press," 231; Johnston, *Evangelicals at an Impasse: Biblical Authority in Practice* (Atlanta: John Knox Press, 1979), 85. On the significance of abortion to the formation of the religious right, see Frank Schaeffer, *Crazy for God: How I Grew Up as One of the Elect, Helped Found the Religious Right, and Lived to Take It All (or Almost All) of It Back* (New York: Carroll & Graf, 2007), 289; Jon Shields, "A More Civilized Christian Right," *Christianity Today* 53, 7 (July 2009): 58.

21. On Carter's personally against-but-pro-choice stance, see Flint and Porter, "Jimmy Carter," 38–39; Freedman, "Religious Right and the Carter Administration," 237. On evangelicals' disillusionment with Carter over abortion, see Edward E. Plowman, "The Democrats: God in the Garden?" *Christianity Today* 20, 22 (August 6, 1976): 34–36; Smith, *Faith and the Presidency*, 307; "Flare-Up over Abortion," *Time* 108, 11 (September 13, 1976): 21; Carl M. Cannon, "Soul of a Conservative," *National Journal* 37, 20 (May 14, 2005): 1452–61.

22. On the 1980 Democratic platform, see Layman, *Great Divide*, 117. On the "high official," see Jimmy Carter, *Living Faith* (New York: Times Books, 1996), 35. On the growth in secularism and pro-choice views among Democrats, see Layman, *Great Divide*, 104, 125. On evangelicals' disillusionment with Carter over his "secular" approach to sexuality and school prayer, see Nesmith, *New Republican Coalition*, 61–62, 68; Viguerie, *New Right*, 124; Ron Boehme and Rus Walton, *What About Jimmy*

Carter? (Washington, D.C.: Third Century, 1976), 35, 62–108, especially Chapter 5, "The Issues Are the Issue," 29–45; Nesmith, *New Republican Coalition*, 39–57. On Scarborough, see David D. Kirkpatrick, "The Evangelical Crack Up," *New York Times*, October 28, 2007. The Southern Baptist Convention, Carter's home denomination, was a case in point. In the mid-1970s the SBC had adopted resolutions supporting many of Carter's priorities and policies, including multilateral arms control, national security, peace, world hunger, relief for refugees, and lobby disclosure legislation. But by the late 1970s, many in the SBC had begun to focus more squarely on cultural issues. A shared theology and religious language, they discovered, did not guarantee a uniformly shared political agenda on abortion, the Equal Rights Amendment, and prayer in public schools. See Smith, *Faith and the Presidency*, 310.

23. On Republican appeals to evangelicals, see Layman, *Great Divide*, 44; Viguerie, *The New Right*, 56. On the growth of Moral Majority, see Erling Jorstad, *Evangelicals in the White House: The Cultural Maturation of Born Again Christianity, 1960–1981* (New York: E. Mellen Press, 1981), 150; Freedman, "The Religious Right and the Carter Administration," 251–52.

24. On Carter's tardy efforts to reach evangelical conservatives, see Smith, *Faith and the Presidency*, 318; "Carter Tells Evangelists That He Is Born Again," *New York Times*, January 22, 1980, A17; Maddox, *Preacher in the White House*, 158, 164; Freedman, "The Religious Right and the Carter Administration," 247. For original sources, see "Religious Matters" files in the White House central files and in the Robert Maddox religious liaison files in the Jimmy Carter Library in Atlanta, Ga. On the substantial support for Anderson at Wheaton, despite his pro-choice stance, see Donna Reifsnyder, "Anderson Addresses Vocal Crowd," *Wheaton Record* 104, 17 (March 14, 1980): 1; Craig Swanson, "Anderson Alternative," *Wheaton Record* 105, 7 (October 31, 1980): 5. For examples of remaining support for Carter, including Southern Baptists such as Jimmy Allen; Pentecostals such as Jim Bakker, Oral Roberts, and R. Douglas Wead; and "Academics for Carter" at evangelical colleges, see Smith, *Faith and the Presidency*, 318; Freedman, "Religious Right and the Carter Administration," 250; Mark Eastburg, "Academic Connotation," *Wheaton Record* 105, 8 (November 7, 1980): 5; Denise Hayworth, "Delegate for the President Outlines Carter's Strengths," *Wheaton Record* 104, 17 (March 14, 1980): 3.

25. Novak quoted in Smith, *Faith and the Presidency*, 320. On newly registered evangelical voters, see James Reichley, "Religion and the Future of American Politics," *Political Science Quarterly* 101, 1 (January 1986): 26; K. B. Kraakevik, "The Political Mobilization of White Evangelical Populists in the 1970s and Early 1980s," Ph.D. dissertation, University of Chicago Divinity School, 2004, 291; Viguerie, *The New Right*, 123; Menendez, *Evangelicals at the Ballot Box*, 137, 139. For a helpful historiographical survey on the question whether evangelicals gave Reagan the win, see Flint and Porter, "Jimmy Carter," 47.

26. Flipse, "Below-the-Belt Politics," 139.

27. Richard Mouw, *The Smell of Sawdust* (Grand Rapids, Mich.: Zondervan, 2000), 145. Sider quoted in Michael Cromartie, "Fixing the World: From Nonplayers to Radicals to New Right Conservatives: The Saga of Evangelicals and Social Action," *Christianity Today* 36, 5 (April 27, 1992): 25. A chart in this *Christianity Today* article entitled "Evangelicals on the March" in the article lists a chronology of growing political involvement: 1947—Henry's *Uneasy Conscience*; 1957—Smith's *Revivalism and Social Reform*; 1965—*The Other Side*; 1965—Gaebelein marches with King; 1971—*Post-American*; 1973—*Roe v. Wade*; 1973—Chicago Declaration; 1974—Lausanne Covenant; 1976—Carter wins the presidency; 1977—Sider's *Rich Christians*; 1979—birth of Moral Majority. The list clearly gives the impression that the evangelical left anteceded the religious right. In fact, several key conservative leaders got their political start in the evangelical left. Michael Cromartie, an Evangelicals for Social Action board member, began to call many ESA positions "bogus" and allied with the Washington think tank Ethics and Public Policy Center. Lane Dennis, a regular contributor to the *Post-American* in the mid-1970s, edited Francis Schaeffer's most strident works in the early 1980s. Clark Pinnock, faculty mentor to the Post-Americans at Trinity Seminary in the early 1970s, turned neo-conservative in the 1980s, accusing Sojourners of holding a "naïve worldview" and of justifying a violent Sandinista revolution in Nicaragua. For other links between the evangelical left and the religious right, see Jon Shields, "Abortion and Its Discontents," *New Yorker*, November 12, 2009. On Cromartie, see "Cromartie Personal Identification," Folder "1977," in ESAA; Beth Spring, "With the Religious Right in Disarray, Two Groups Consider New Opportunities," *Christianity Today* 31, 9 (July 10, 1987): 46. On Lane Dennis, see "A Conversation with Young Evangelicals," *Post-American* 4, 1 (January 1975): 6–13; correspondence between Dennis, Schaeffer, Sider, and Vernon Grounds in Folder "1985," ESAA. On Pinnock, see "A Political Pilgrimage," *Eternity* 35, 10 (October 1984): 26–29; "A Sojourner Returns: An Interview with Clark Pinnock," *Religion & Democracy* (January 1985): 3–7.

28. John F. Alexander, "Did We Blow It?" *The Other Side* 17, 2 (February 1981): 10–15. On superdelegates, see Kraakevik, "Political Mobilization of White Evangelical Populists," 184–92.

Chapter 12. Sojourning

Epigraph: Bill Weld-Wallis, "Abortion: The Political Dilemma," *Sojourners* 13, 9 (October 1984): 4–5.

1. David A. Hoekema, "Evangelicals Confront the Arms Race," *Reformed Journal* 33, 8 (August 1983): 10–13.

2. For evangelical left criticism of Reagan, see Bernard Zylstra, "Jimmy Carter Is the Issue," *Vanguard* 10, 5 (September–October 1980): 4; Nancy Post, "Profs Analyze U.S. Economy," *Wheaton Record* 105, 22 (April 24, 1981): 3; Jim Wallis, "The President's

Pulpit: A Look at Ronald Reagan's Theology," *Sojourners* 13, 8 (September 1984): 17–21; James Skillen, "Ronald Reagan: The Pragmatic Nationalist," *Public Justice Report* 7, 10 (August–September 1984): 3–4. For a small sample of evangelical left concern about the religious right, see "Minutes of ESA Executive Committee," October 5, 1979, Folder "1979," ESAA; Colman McCarthy, "How Some of the Evangelicals Feel about Moral Majority," *Washington Post*, February 15, 1981, M2; Robert E. Webber, *Moral Majority: Right or Wrong?* (Westchester, Ill.: Cornerstone Books, 1981); David Neff, "Who's Afraid of the Secular Humanists?" *HIS* 43, 6 (March 1983): 4–7, 31; Richard Cizik, "Not Tilting Right" *Sojourners* 10, 4 (May 1981): 39; Kenneth L. Woodward, "The Split-Up Evangelicals," *Newsweek* (April 26, 1982): 88–91. For religious right criticism of the evangelical left, see David Chilton, *Productive Christians in an Age of Guilt Manipulators: A Biblical Response to Ronald Sider* (Tyler, Tex.: Institute for Christian Economics, 1981), 69, 86; Francis A. Schaeffer, *The Great Evangelical Disaster* (Westchester, Ill.: Crossway, 1984), 111–40; Harold Lindsell, *Free Enterprise: A Judeo-Christian Defense* (Wheaton, Ill.: Tyndale House, 1982); Joan Harris, *The Sojourners File* (Washington, D.C.: New Century Foundation Press, 1983); Ronald H. Nash, *Social Justice and the Christian Church* (Milford, Mich.: Mott Media, 1984); John Bernbaum, ed., *Economic Justice and the State: A Debate Between Ronald H. Nash and Eric Berversluis* (Grand Rapids, Mich.: Baker, 1986). Lloyd Billingsley, "First Church of Christ Socialist," *National Review* 36 (October 18, 1983): 1339. For a long correspondence between Schaeffer, Sider, George Marsden, Mark Noll, Thomas Howard, Lane Dennis, and Richard Lovelace, see Folders "1984" and "1985," ESAA. For a helpful analysis of the debate between Schaeffer and several moderate evangelicals in the 1980s, see Barry Hankins, "'I'm Just Making a Point': Francis Schaeffer and the Irony of Faithful Christian Scholarship," *Fides et Historia* 39, 1 (Winter–Spring 2007): 15–34.

3. For helpful background on intervention in Central America in the 1980s, see Christian Smith, *Resisting Reagan: The U.S. Central America Peace Movement* (Chicago: University of Chicago Press, 1996), 3–58. For a conservative evangelical treatise supporting Reagan, see Humberto Belli, *Breaking Faith: The Sandinista Revolution and Its Impact on Freedom and Christian Faith in Nicaragua* (Westchester, Ill.: Crossway, 1985). On the progressive evangelical response, see Robert Zwier, "Defense: What Kind and How Much," *Public Justice Report* 7, 10 (August–September 1984): 1–2; Gordon Spykman, ed., *Let My People Live: Faith and Struggle in Central America* (Grand Rapids, Mich.: Eerdmans, 1988), 31, 33, 109, 110–11, 141, 152–57.

4. For "concern for human rights," see Kerry Ptacek, "International Religious Liberty and the Great Commission," in Richard Cizik, ed., *The High Cost of Indifference*, ed. Richard Cizik (Ventura, Cal.: Regal Books, 1984), 81–99; Jim Wallis, "The Rise of Christian Conscience," *Sojourners* 14, 1 (January 1985): 12–16. Also see James Skillen, *International Politics and the Demand for Global Justice* (Sioux Center, Iowa: Dordt College Press, 1981), 107; Wes Michaelson, "Human Rights: A Surer Standard," *Sojourners* 6, 4 (April 1977): 3–5; "Scholars Address Reagan on Latin American Policy," *Public Justice Report* 5, 1 (October 1981): 3–4; Paul Marshall, *Human Rights Theo-*

ries in Christian Perspective (Toronto: Institute for Christian Studies, 1983); Karen King and Chris Moss, "Human Rights in Nicaragua," *The Other Side* 20, 5 (May 1984): 24-27.

5. For examples of the evangelical left's denunciation of communist regimes, see Wes Michaelson, "The Plank in Our Eye," *Sojourners* 7, 8 (August 1978): 3-4; "What About the Russians?" *Sojourners* 11, 10 (November 1982); Boyd T. Reese, Jr., "Resistance and Hope: The Interplay of Theological Synthesis, Biblical Interpretation, Political Analysis, and Praxis in the Christian Radicalism of 'Sojourners' Magazine," Ph.D. dissertation, Temple University, 1991, 257-70; Bert Witvoet, "The Strength of our War Horses," *Vanguard* (March–April 1979): 12-14; Bud Bultman, "Say No to Marx . . . and Adam Smith Too," *HIS* 44, 7 (April 1984): 32; Ronald J. Sider, "A Plea for More Radical Conservatives and More Conserving Radicals," *Transformation* 4, 1 (January 1987): 11-16; Sider and Richard K. Taylor, *Nuclear Holocaust and Christian Hope: A Book for Christian Peacemakers* (Downers Grove, Ill.: InterVarsity Press, 1982), 233.

6. On CEPAD and the Sandinistas, see "When Relief Work Leads to Revolution," *Public Justice Newsletter* 3, 3 (December 1979): 1-4; copy of an April 15, 1983, open letter from CEPAD to Christians in the United States in *HIS* 44, 4 (January 1984): 21; Ronald G. Frase, "Believers Ask Yankees to Remove Cold War Blinders," *Christianity Today* 25, 6 (March 27, 1981): 61-63; Gustavo Parajón, "Nicaragua: Evangelicals, Sandinistas and the Elections," *Transformation* 2, 1 (January 1985): 4-6; Gustavo Parajón, "So That We Might Have Tomorrow: An Evangelical Leader Reflects on Nicaragua's Past and Future," *Sojourners* 12, 2 (March 1983): 29-30; Spykman, *Let My People Live*, 143.

7. Jim Wallis and Joyce Hollyday, "A Plea from the Heart," *Sojourners* 12, 3 (March 1983): 3-5; Miguel D'Escoto, "Nicaragua: An Unfinished Canvas," 14-18 and "Nicaragua: Hearts and Bellies," 20-21 in *Sojourners* 12, 3 (March 1983); Hollyday, "Misleading the Nation," *Sojourners* 12, 6 (June–July 1983): 3-4; Richard J. Barnet and Peter Kornbluh, "Contradictions in Nicaragua: The U.S. Policy of Punishment against the Sandinistas," *Sojourners* 13, 5 (May 1984): 8-10; Michael McConnell, "Journey to Jalapa," *The Other Side* 19, 10 (October 1983): 48-50; Richard Millett, "Through U.S. Glasses: Common Distortions of Nicaragua," *HIS* 44, 4 (January 1984): 14-16; Richard Pierard, "Do Something!" *HIS* 44, 4 (January 1984): 19-20; Richard V. Pierard, "Rethinking Nicaragua," *Reformed Journal* 33, 6 (June 1983): 2-3; Spykman, *Let My People Live*, 172-74. For "amazing strides," see "Evangelicals Praise Nicaragua, Criticize U.S.," *Christianity Today* 27, 14 (September 16, 1983): 36. For "testing convictions" about capitalism, see Tom Minnery, "Why the Gospel Grows in Socialist Nicaragua," *Christianity Today* 27, 7 (April 8, 1983): 34-42. On religious signs, see Ed Griffin-Nolan, *Witness for Peace: A Story of Resistance* (Louisville, Ky.: Westminster/John Knox Press, 1991): 32; Joyce Hollyday, "The Long Road to Jalapa," *Sojourners* 13, 2 (February 1984): 26-30.

8. On the evangelical origins of Witness for Peace, see "Churchgoers Opposed to U.S. Policy Hold 'Peace Vigils' in Nicaragua," *Christianity Today* 28, 1 (January 13, 1984): 64-65. For detailed descriptions of Ocotal and other early interventions, see "Churchgoers Opposed to U.S. Policy Hold 'Peace Vigils' in Nicaragua," *Christianity*

Today 28, 1 (January 13, 1984): 64–65; Marjorie Hyer, "21 Leave Here for Nicaragua to Be 'Human Shields,'" *Washington Post*, December 1, 1983, A34; Joyce Hollyday, "A Shield of Love," *Sojourners* 12, 10 (November 1983): 10–13; Don Mosley, *With Our Own Eyes* (Scottdale, Pa.: Herald Press, 1996), 149–52; Rebecca Gordon, *Letters from Nicaragua* (San Francisco: Spinsters/Aunt Lute, 1987); Griffin-Nolan, *Witness for Peace*, 28–29, 46–50, 78, 123, 177. On the development of Witness for Peace, see Griffin-Nolan, *Witness for Peace*, 20–23, 68, 76, 111; Smith, *Resisting Reagan*, 77. On Stookey's Central American advocacy, see "El Salvador," *Sojourners* 15, 2 (February 1986): 49; *Crucible of Hope: A Study Guide for the Churches on Central America* (Washington, D.C.: Sojourners, 1984). For media attention, see Don Mosley and Joyce Hollyday, *With Our Own Eyes* (Scottdale, Pa.: Herald Press, 1996), 183; Ron Arias, "Agonies of the Innocents," *People* 29, 8 (February 29, 1988); Griffin-Nolan, *Witness for Peace*, 44, 165.

9. Parajón quoted in Mosley, *With Our Own Eyes*, 148. For the details and text of the Pledge, see "A Promise of Resistance," *Sojourners* 12, 11 (December 1983): 6; "A Pledge of Resistance: A Contingency Plan in the Event of a U.S. Invasion of Nicaragua," *Sojourners* 13, 7 (August 1984): 10–11; Vicki Kemper, "'We Will Do What We Promise': Resistance Pledge Delivered to State Department," *Sojourners* 14, 2 (February 1985): 7–8. Wallis quoted in "Nicaragua Policy Protested," *Washington Post*, January 1985, G11; Griffin-Nolan, *Witness for Peace*, 104.

10. Smith, *Resisting Reagan*, 81–84. Reagan official quoted in Mary McGrory, "Following Conscience's Lead," *Washington Post*, May 28, 1985, A2.

11. On Witness for Peace as a "prayerful, biblically based community," see Griffin-Nolan, *Witness for Peace*, 59–61. Van Denand quoted in Smith, *Resisting Reagan*, 408.

12. On disputes over homosexuality and religious symbols, see Smith, *Resisting Reagan*, 222–23, 332. For evidence of increasing ecumenicity, see Griffin-Nolan, *Witness for Peace*, 20–30; Ernesto Cardenal, "A Priest in the Ministry," 22–23, and Miguel D'Escoto, "Nicaragua: An Unfinished Canvas," 14–18 in *Sojourners* 12, 2 (March 1983); "Contra Atrocities," *Washington Post*, March 18, 1986, A17.

13. For evidence of Sojourners' ecumenical direction, see Wes Michaelson, "What Nurtures Us," *Sojourners* 7, 5 (May 1978): 16–19; "Sojourners Fellowship Update," February 7, 1983, 1, copy Box VI1, Folder "Update 1983," Sojourners Collection, WCSC; Mary McGrory, "Following Conscience's Lead," *Washington Post*, May 28, 1985, A2. On growing connections with mainliners, see Richard L. Kenyon, "The Mainliners: Magazine Shook Ranks of Sleeping Protestantism," copy in Box IV3, "News Releases and Post-American," Sojourners Collection, WCSC; Marjorie Hyer, "Episcopal Panel Eyes Nuclear War Issue," *Washington Post*, February 25, 1984, C10; Doug Bailey, "A Jolting Letter from Jail," *Calvary Church Chronicle* (January 24, 1982): 1, in Box VII1, Folder "Articles About Jim Wallis," Sojourners Collection, WCSC. On growing connections with Catholics, see Jim McManus, "Sojourners: Magazine, Community—and More," *National Catholic Reporter* (October 23, 1981): 2; "Yes There Are Prophets," *Good Newsletter* 7, 9 (September 1980): 3, copy in Box IV1, "Articles and Critiques about Sojourners," Folder "Critiques About Magazine," Sojourners Collection, WCSC; Wallis, *Revive*

Us Again: A Sojourner's Story (Nashville, Tenn.: Abingdon Press, 1983), 162; Danny Collum, "Thank God for the Catholic Worker," *Sojourners* 12, 5 (May 1983): 7; Ron Sider, "Property and Stewardship: A Biblical Perspective," *New Catholic World* (September–October 1977). For broadening "beyond on evangelical beginnings," see Lindsay McLaughlin, "A Brief Glimpse," *Sojourners* 14, 1 (January 1985): 37.

14. For a concise statement of Witness for Peace's interventionist, rather than legislative, approach, see Griffin-Nolan, *Witness for Peace*, 99, 170. Rice quoted in Smith, *Resisting Reagan*, 218–19. Marker quoted in Smith, *Resisting Reagan*, 334–36. On the "tractor for peace," see Joyce Hollyday, "Tanks into Tractors," *Sojourners* 12, 10 (November 1983): 31.

15. For Reformed criticism of Reagan's diplomacy, see Skillen, *International Politics*, 20, 25, 28, 127–29; Jim Skillen, "Nicaraguan Policy: Foreign Policy at Its Worst," *Public Justice Report* 8, 4 (January 1985): 2, 4; Spykman, *Let My People Live*, xiii, 31, 99, 190–92, 245. For Reformed criticism of the Anabaptist proclivity for "low intensity conflict," see Spykman, *Let My People Live*, 155–56. On APJ's program of education and legislative solutions, see "Central American Conflicts Call Forth Growing Evangelical Response," *Public Justice Report* 8, 8 (May 1985): 3.

16. On ESA's involvement in Witness for Peace, see Ron Sider, "Why Me Lord? Reluctant Reflections on the Trip to Nicaragua I Didn't Want to Take," *The Other Side* 21, 3 (April–May 1985): 20–25; Beth Spring, "Does the Sandinista Regime Promote Religious Freedom?" *Christianity Today* 28, 17 (November 23, 1984): 43–44; "ESA News Briefs," *ESA Update* 6, 1 (January–February 1984): 1. On the ESA-IRD joint trip, see "Two U.S. Groups Cancel Joint Trip to Nicaragua," *Christianity Today* 29, 12 (September 6, 1985): 73. On ESA's growing criticism of the Sandinistas, see Beth Spring, "The Government's Heavy Hand Falls on Believers," *Christianity Today* 29, 18 (December 13, 1985): 51–52; Sider, "Why Me Lord?" 25.

17. "Sidelines," *The Other Side* 14, 2 (February 1978): 9; Jim Wallis to "Friend," circa Summer 1981, in Box IV2, Folder "Direct Mail Packets, Winter 1981–Winter 1983," Sojourners Collection, WCSC. Also see Mary Meehan, "Will Somebody Please Be Consistent," *Sojourners* 9, 11 (November 1980): 14; Jim Douglass, "Patriarchy and the Pentagon Make Abortions Inevitable," *Sojourners* 9, 11 (November 1980): 14–15; Byron Borger, "Modern Cannibalism," *Vanguard* (January–February 1981): 19–20; Liane Rozzell, "Double Jeopardy: Racism and Violence Against Women," *Sojourners* 13, 10 (November 1984): 20.

18. John T. McGreevy, *Catholicism and American Freedom* (New York: Norton, 2003), 216–95. On Loesch and Egan, see Gretchen Kaiser, "Pro-Lifers for Survival: Breaking Stereotypes," *Georgia Bulletin* (November 25, 1982); James Risen and Judy Thomas, *Wrath of Angels: The American Abortion War* (New York: Basic, 1998), 63. On Bernardin, see Thomas Fuechtmann, ed., *Consistent Ethic of Life* (Kansas City: Sheed and Ward, 1988). On Catholic influence, see Bill Kallio, "From Ambivalence to Action" *ESA Update* 6, 4 (July–August 1984): 3; Phil M. Shenk, "Bishops Connect Pro-Life Issues," *Sojourners* 10, 1 (January 1981): 8; "Liane Rozzell, "'Respect Life' United

Concerns," *Sojourners* 12, 10 (November 1983): 9; "Youth Pro-Lifers Make Connections," *Sojourners* 12, 1 (January 1983): 6; Mary Ellen Griffin, "New Campus Organization Joins National Abortion Fight," *Wheaton Record* 104, 1 (September 14, 1989): 2–3. On grass-roots networking between pro-life evangelicals and Catholics on the left, see Vicki Sairs interview by author, February 20, 2008, South Bend, Ind. On Sojourners' pro-life declaration in 1980, see "Magazine Is 'Pro-Life,' " *Chicago Tribune*, November 22, 1980, W18; Bruce Buursma, "Abortion: The Escalating Battle," *Chicago Tribune*, March 22, 1981, A1; "Postmark," *Sojourners* 10, 1 (January 1981): 38–39.

19. Wallis, "Coming Together on the Sanctity of Life," *Sojourners* 9, 11 (November 1980): 3–4; Sharon Gallagher, "The Peaceable Kingdom," *Radix* 16, 4 (January–February 1985): 4–5, 31. Ron Sider, "What Should Be the Shape of the Evangelical Political Involvement in the 80's?" March 20, 1981, Folder "1981," ESAA.

20. Ron Sider memo, "ESA's New Political Thrust," June 8, 1981, Folder "1981," ESAA; Ron Sider direct mail letter, n.d., Folder "1982," ESAA. On the "American Coalition for Life," see "ESA Board of Directors Meeting," 4, October 29–30, 1982, in Folder "1982," ESAA. On Sider's speaking, see "Peace-Meal," *ESA Public Policy Report* 4, 1 (March 1988): 8; Sider, "An Evangelical Vision for Public Policy," *Transformation* 2, 3 (July 1985): 1–9. On evangelical student resonance within InterVarsity and at Wheaton, see Kathleen Kern, "Letter to the Editor," *HIS* 44, 8 (May 1984): 31; Michael Gorman, *Abortion and the Early Church: Christian, Jewish, and Pagan Attitudes in the Greco-Roman World* (Downers Grove, Ill.: InterVarsity Press, 1982); L. D. Hull, "Democrats Seek Consistency," *Wheaton Record* 109, 4 (September 28, 1984): 3. On the World Evangelical Fellowship, see especially the January 1986 issue that included articles on abortion, apartheid in South Africa, and justice in Nicaragua and Peru. For example, see Michael J. Gorman, "Shalom and the Unborn," *Transformation* 3, 1 (January 1986): 26–33. For APJ's more explicit opposition to abortion, see Jim Skillen, "Can Congress Save the Unborn?" *Public Justice Report* 4, 10 (August–September 1981): 2–3; Skillen, *Justice for the Unborn* (Washington, D.C.: Association for Public Justice, 1982). On the APJ-ESA détente, see Bert Witvoet, "A Sojourner Came to Town," *Vanguard* (September–October 1979): 5–7; Joseph Comanda, "To the Editorial Committee of *Vanguard*," 3–4, July 24, 1979, in Folder "Correspondence: Bert Witvoet, Editor, 1978–81," Wedge Publishing Foundation Collection, CCA.

21. On Peace Pentecost, see Vicki Kemper, " 'It Won't Be Long Now: Claiming Spiritual Roots at Pentecost," *Sojourners* 14, 8 (August–September 1985): 32–35; Jim Wallis, "A Consistent Ethic of Life." *Sojourners* 14, 7 (July 1985): 4–5; "Police Arrest Christians in Capital Protest," *Los Angeles Times*, May 28, 1985, 2. On ESA, see "ESA News Briefs," *ESA Update* 6, 1 (January-February 1984): 1; Ron Sider, *Completely Pro-Life: Building a Consistent Stance* (Downers Grove, Ill.: InterVarsity Press, 1987). On Sojourners and Peace Pentecost, see Jim Wallis, "Dissenting from the Right," *Newsweek* (September 17, 1984): 32; Wallis, "The Court Prophets," *Sojourners* 13, 8 (September 1984): 3–4; Wallis, "1985," *Sojourners* 14, 1 (January 1985): 4–5; Wallis, "The

Rise of Christian Conscience," *Sojourners* 14, 1 (January 1985): 12–16; Colman McCarthy, "The Seamless Coalition," *Washington Post*, February 9, 1985, A19.

22. On the formation of JustLife, see Ron Sider, "Building for the Future," *ESA Update* 9, 3 (September 1987): 1–2; Jeffrey McClain Jones, "Ronald Sider and Radical Evangelical Political Theology," Ph.D. dissertation, Northwestern University, 1990, 385; Jack Smalligan, "What are PACs and How JustLife Fits In," *ESA Update* 9, 4 (November–December 1987): 1, 3; D. R. Hoover, "The Political Mobilization of the Evangelical Left," M.A. thesis, University of Oxford, 1992, 101. On JustLife's legislative proposal, see *Abortion Regulation and Alternatives: A Package of Eight Model Bills* (Philadelphia: JustLife Education Fund, 1990).

23. Kathleen Hayes and Ron Sider, eds., *JustLife/88: A 1988 Election Study Guide for Justice, Life, and Peace* (Philadelphia: JustLife Education Fund and Eerdmans, 1988); Kathleen Hayes, ed., *JustLife/90: 1990 Study Guide for Justice, Life, and Peace* (Philadelphia: JustLife Education Fund, 1990); Van Temple and Dave Medema, "September Report," October 3, 1990, Folder "1990," ESAA; Mary E. Bendyna, "JustLife Action," in *Risky Business? PAC Decisionmaking in Congressional Elections*, ed. Robert Biersack, Paul S. Herrnson, and Clyde Wilcox (Armonk, N.Y.: M.E. Sharpe, 1994), 198, 200.

24. Jim Skillen, "New PAC Appeals to Consistent Pro-Life Christians," *Public Justice Report* 9, 10 (August–September 1986): 4–5; Steve Monsma and Jack Smalligan, "JustLife Responds," *Public Justice Report* 10, 1 (October 1986): 6.

25. On ambivalent views toward abortion by the evangelical left in the 1970s, see Sider, *Completely Pro-Life*, 38; Nancy Hardesty, "Concerning Abortion, We Affirm That . . ." Folder "1973 Chicago Declaration," ESAA; Gerald Vandezande, "Towards a New Solidarity," *Vanguard* (January–February 1973): 23; "Notes from an Abortion Symposium," *Right On* 3, 9 (March 1972): 10; Mark Fackler, "Abortion: Two Views," *HIS* 39, 5 (February 1979): 16–18; Paul Henry, *Politics for Evangelicals* (Valley Forge, Pa.: Judson Press, 1974), 72, 77; Reginald Frank Robert Gardner, *Abortion: The Personal Dilemma: A Christian Gynaecologist Examines the Medical, Social, and Spiritual Issues* (Grand Rapids, Mich.: Eerdmans, 1972). On being "put off by the antiabortion movement," see Jim Wallis, "Coming Together on the Sanctity of Life," *Sojourners* 9, 11 (November 1980): 3; Wes Michaelson, "Christian Responses in Politics: Sojourners, Part II," *Public Justice Newsletter* 2, 9 (June–July 1979): 3–7. On secular leftist opposition, see Bill Weld-Wallis, "Abortion: The Political Dilemma," *Sojourners* 13, 9 (October 1984): 4–5; Cathy Stentzel, "A Quiet Conversion," *Sojourners* 9, 11 (November 1980): 4–6; "To Preserve and Protect Life: A Christian Feminist Perspective on Abortion," *Sojourners* 15, 9 (October 1986): 34–35. For "wrong impression," see Jones, "Ron Sider and Radical Evangelical Political Theology," 433.

26. On APJ, see "Abortion: Part I," *Public Justice Newsletter* 2, 7 (April 1979): 7–8. On ESA, see Corwin Smidt, "Where Do Evangelicals Really Stand on Abortion and a Nuclear Freeze?" *ESA Update* 10, 3 (May 1988): 1; "Here We Stand: A Reaffirmation of ESA's Commitments," Folder "1984," ESAA. Howard in "Minutes of Strategic Planning

Report and Response," 10, December 8, 1990, Folder "1990," ESAA; "Who We Are and Where We Are Headed: A Summary of the ESA Member Survey," *ESA Update* 10, 2 (April 1988): 2.

27. For "demonic atrocity," see Thomas M. Chmelovski to Pam Proctor, September 5, 1984, Box 345, Folder 24, "Brave New People; 1984," InterVarsity Christian Fellowship Collection, BGCA. For "screams for justice," see Robert Keim to *Sojourners*, July 30, 1986, Box 2, Folder 1, "Postmark: Abortion," Sojourners Collection, WCSC.

28. On subscriptions, see "Seeds," *Sojourners* 14, 5 (May 1985): 38. On the demography of JustLife, see Bendyna, "JustLife Action," 196; Juli Loesch Wiley email interview by author, February 25, 2008; "That All May Live in Peace," *ESA Advocate* 8, 1 (February 1986): 1–2. On Bread for the World, see Arthur Simon, "Bread for the World," *Transformation* 1, 4 (October 1984): 22–24. On ESA, see Medema and Aeschlimann in "Strategic Planning Report," 10–11, December 8, 1990, in Folder "1990," ESAA. On APJ ecumenism, see "Christian Reponses in Politics: United State Catholic Conference, Part II," *Public Justice Newsletter* 3, 1 (October 1979): 7–10; "A Pastoral Visit with Political Significance," *Public Justice Newsletter* 3, 2 (November 1979): 1–2.

29. On Wallis's trip, see notes from "Community Retreat," October 10, 1982, Box IV1, Folder "Articles and Critiques of Sojourners," Sojourners Collection.

30. On Monsma, see Adam Clymer, "Democrats Shaping Election as Referendum on Economy," *New York Times*, October 3, 1982, 1, 30; "G.O.P. Retains Edge in Michigan Senate," *New York Times*, March 28, 1985, A19; Medema quoted in Peter Steinfels, "Beliefs: The Plight of Voters Whose Views on Abortion Are at Odds With Their Party's," *New York Times*, March 28, 1992, 10; Hoover, "Political Mobilization, 100.

31. Bill Nelson, Don Bonker, and Tony Hall quoted in "How Will the Democrats Answer Evangelical Concerns?" *Christianity Today* 29, 12 (September 6, 1985): 51–52. On Casey, see McGreevy, *Catholicism and American Freedom*, 280–81; Bendyna, "JustLife Action," 199. Hall quoted in D. Michael Lindsay, *Faith in the Halls of Power: How Evangelicals Joined the American Elite* (New York: Oxford University Press, 2007), 41.

32. Gary Govert, "Choosing Life," *Vanguard* 11, 4 (July–August 1981): 18–19. Medema quoted in Bendyna, "JustLife Action," 199–200. On Sojourners and the NSA, see "Statement by Ed Richardson," November 2, 1984, Box VI12, Folder 3, "Sojourners Community Updates," Sojourners Collection, WCSC; Joe Roos, "Some Saturday Morning Visitors," *Sojourners* 14, 2 (February 1985): 5; Laurence Zuckerman, "Who's Peeking in on *Sojourners*," *Columbia Journalism Review* 25, 1 (May–June 1986): 14–6; Joe Roos, "Listening in on the Church," *Sojourners* 15, 2 (February 1986): 4. On alleged IRS harassment, see Joe Roos, "The IRS: On Our Case," *Sojourners* 16, 5 (May 1987): 6. On seeking God's Spirit, see Bill Weld-Wallis, "Abortion: The Political Dilemma," *Sojourners* 13, 9 (October 1984): 4–5.

33. On Mondale, see Danny Collum, "What's at Stake . . . And What Isn't: A Readers' Guide to the Presidential Election," *Sojourners* 13, 8 (September 1984): 12–16; William Garfield, "Walter Mondale," *Public Justice Report* 7, 7 (April 1984): 3, 5. On

APJ's trans-Atlantic focus, see Jim Skillen, "Voter Turnout and the Decline of American Democracy," *Public Justice Report* 12, 3 (December 1988): 1, 7.

34. For "people-oriented economics," see John F. Alexander, "The Wicked Rich, The Righteous Poor," *The Other Side* 14, 1 (January 1978): 12–15. On being smothered by a majority, see James Skillen, *Justice for Representation: A Proposal for Revitalizing our System of Political Participation* (Washington, D.C.: Association for Public Justice, 1979). On Sojourners' advocacy for the poor, see Danny Collum, "Economics: The Way America Does Business," *Sojourners* 14, 10 (November 1985): 12–17; Reese, "Resistance and Hope," 222, 228, 244. On ESA, see Joan Wulff, "A Tale of Two City Ministries," *HIS* 40, 6 (March 1980): 19–23; Beth Spring, "Creative Caring in Hard Times: How Churches Are Helping America's Poor," *HIS* 44, 6 (March 1984): 24–25.

35. On the Green Party, see Gary J. Dorrien, "A Green Kind of Politics: The Worldwide Prospects of a New Movement," *Sojourners* 13, 9, (September 1984): 36–38. On Anderson, see James Skillen, "Three Candidates for President?" *Public Justice Newsletter* 3, 9 (June–July 1980): 7–8. On support for Jesse Jackson, see Sharon Gallagher interview by author, July 7, 2006, Berkeley, Cal.; Jim Wallis, "Signs of the Times: Issues, Values, and the Rainbow Campaign in Election '88," *Sojourners* 17, 10 (November 1988): 14–21; Danny Collum, "In Search of the New South: Jesse Jackson Breaks Common Ground," *Sojourners* 17, 6 (June 1988): 14–20; Danny Collum, "Under the Rainbow," *Sojourners* 13, 7 (August 1984): 4; Skillen, "Jesse Jackson: The Candidate in '88," *Public Justice Report* 7, 8 (May 1984): 1, 5; Hall, "How Will the Democrats Answer Evangelical Concerns?" 52. For "a people's power," see "Buthelezi, Pleads for Non-Violent Transition in South Africa," *Public Justice Newsletter* 3, 1 (October 1979): 3–7. For Jackson as close to biblical priorities, see Wallis, "Signs of the Times," 16–17. On Barbara Skinner, see "ESA Elects New Board Members," *ESA Update* 7, 1 (February 1985): 1. For "local empowerment," see Reese, "Resistance and Hope," 249.

36. On the wealth and mobilization of Orange County evangelicals, see Lisa McGirr, *Suburban Warriors: The Origins of the New American Right* (Princeton: Princeton University Press, 2001). On the deterioration of the rust belt, see Thomas J. Sugrue, *Origins of the Urban Crisis: Race and Inequality in Postwar Detroit* (Princeton: Princeton University Press, 1996). On the demography of Sojourners, see Joe Roos, "Into 1980 Together," *Sojourners* 9, 1 (January 1980): 4–5. On hesitance over use of direct mailings, see "Meeting of the Board of Directors, ESA," January 19–20, 1985, in Folder "1985," ESAA; Ron Sider to Mark Hatfield, April 21, 1989, Folder "1989," ESAA. Hubbard quoted in Kenneth L. Woodward, "Born Again!" *Newsweek* (October 23, 1976): 78. On the implications of a simple lifestyle, see Cal Thomas to Dale Yaeger, May 22, 1988, in Folder "1988," ESAA.

37. On financial difficulties at the Thanksgiving Workshops, see Robert S. Lecky to Ron Sider, October 14, 1974, in Folder "1974 Chicago Workshop Planning," ESAA; "Minutes of the Planning Committee of Evangelicals for Social Concern," January 24, 1975, in Folder "1975 Chicago Workshop Planning," ESAA. On ESA's revitalization, see "Minutes of Board of Directors Meeting," June 17, 1982, in Folder "1982," ESAA;

Kallio to Sider, May 18, 1982, in Folder "1982," ESAA; Bill Kallio, "Monthly Report," January 6, 1981, in Folder "1981," ESAA; Ron Sider, untitled mailing, circa Fall 1983, in Folder "1983," ESAA. On Sider's speaking fees, see "Ron Sider Speaks," *ESA Advocate* 11, 11 (December 1989): 7. On CWLF, see "Analysis of CWLF Ministries and Financial Accounts and Recommendations," April 1975, in Box 2, Folder "CWLF Council," CWLF Collection, GTUA; "Remit Envelopes," August 1, 1974, in Box 2, Folder "CWLF Council," CWLF Collection, GTUA. On *Vanguard* and ICS, see Paul Schrotenboer to Josina B. Zylstra, July 18, 1979, Box 1, Folder 2, "Wedgewood Foundation Financial Records, 1970–1981," Vanguard Collection, CCA; Ed VanderKloet, "An Explanation," *Vanguard* 8, 1 (June–July 1978): 3; "Dear *Vanguard* Subscriber," *Vanguard* 9, 4 (July–August 1979): 15. On JustLife, see Bendyna, "JustLife Action," 197. On Sojourners, see "Subscriber Base," Box IV4, Folder 7, "Subscriber Base Charts," Sojourners Collection, WCSC; James Ridgeway, "Evangelical Group Is Rooted in Radical Movement," *Los Angeles Times*, January 19, 1985, A15.

38. "Strategic Planning Report and Response, Day 2," December 8, 1990, in Folder "1990," ESAA.

Epilogue

1. Beth Spring, "Carl F. H. Henry Dies at 90," *Christianity Today* 48, 2 (February 2004): 20.

2. On the fragmentation of *The Other Side*, see Kyle Cleveland, "The Politics of Jubilee: Ideological Drift and Organizational Schism in a Religious Sect," Ph.D. dissertation, Temple University, 1990, 140–78. On Alexander, see Mark Olson interview by author, May 21, 2009, South Bend, Ind.

3. Edward Gilbreath, "A Prophet Out of Harlem," *Christianity Today* 40, 10 (September 16, 1996): 36–43; Tim Stafford, "Grandpa John," *Christianity Today* 51, 3 (March 9, 2007): 48–51.

4. For "political wilderness," see Daniel Burke, "Saguaro Seminar Stays with Obama," *Religion News Service*, June 11, 2009. For Wallis's best-selling book, see *God's Politics: Why the Right Gets It Wrong and the Left Doesn't Get It* (San Francisco: HarperCollins, 2005). On Sojourners' new headquarters, see Amy Sullivan, *The Party Faithful: How and Why Democrats Are Closing the God Gap* (New York: Scribner, 2008), 209.

5. Tom Brokaw, *The Greatest Generation* (New York: Random House, 1998), 333–39.

6. Ron Sider, *Scandal of the Evangelical Conscience: Why Are Christians Living Just Like the Rest of the World?* (Grand Rapids, Mich.: Baker, 2005). On Sider's 2000 vote for Bush, see D. Michael Lindsay, *Faith in the Halls of Power: How Evangelicals Joined the American Elite* (New York: Oxford University Press, 2007), 68. On the Siders' home, see Tim Stafford, "Ron Sider's Unsettling Crusade," *Christianity Today* 36, 5 (April 27, 1992): 18–22.

7. On Lausanne II, see Ron Sider fundraising letter, December 5, 1989, in Folder "1989," ESAA.

8. Sider, *Rich Christians in an Age of Hunger: Moving from Affluence to Generosity* (Waco, Tex.: Word, 1997), xiii. For Wallis as "softened and measured," see Scot Mc-Knight's review (January 3, 2010) on Amazon.com of Wallis's *Rediscovering Values*. On Wallis's prominence in Washington, see Dan Gilgoff, "A Wanted Man," *U.S. News Digital Weekly* 1, 10 (March 27, 2009): 12; "Personal but Never Private," *Leadership Journal* (September 13, 2010).

9. On Sullivan, see *The Party Faithful*; "How Would Jesus Vote? I'm an Evangelical—and a Liberal. Really," *Washington Post*, February 24, 2008, B1. On Claiborne, see *Jesus for President: Politics for Ordinary Radicals* (Grand Rapids, Mich.: Zondervan, 2008). On Camden House, Rutba House, and Communality, see Rob Moll, "The New Monasticism," *Christianity Today* 49, 9 (September 2005): 38–46.

10. On Bush's approval ratings, see Dan Cox, "Young White Evangelicals: Less Republican, Still Conservative," Pew Forum, September 28, 2007, http://www.pewfo rum.org/Politics-and-Elections/Young-White-Evangelicals-Less-Republican-Still -Conservative.aspx, accessed January 5, 2012. On the evangelical non-right, see D. Michael Lindsay, "Evangelicals and the Public Square," a panel discussion hosted by the Pew Forum on Religion and Public Life, Thursday, October 11, 2007, Washington, D.C., http://www.pewforum.org/Christian/Evangelical-Protestant-Churches/Evan-gelicals-and-the-Public-Square.aspx, accessed January 5, 2012. On the posture of "general indifference to blatant animosity" within the Clinton administration toward evangelicals, see Lindsay, *Faith in the Halls of Power: How Evangelicals Joined the American Elite* (New York: Oxford University Press, 2007), 22. On Obama's relationship with evangelicals, see Laurie Goodstein, "Without a Pastor, Obama Turns to a Circle of 5," *New York Times*, March 15, 2009, 1.

11. On recent Democratic outreach, see Eric Sapp, "Democrats Stung by Huge Losses with Faith Voters," *Huffington Post*, November 2, 2010; Amy Sullivan, "Religious Left Behind," GetReligion.com, November 4, 2010; Daniel Burke, "Have Democrats Lost Faith in Faith-Based Outreach?" Religion News Service, November 3, 2010, http://www.religionnews.com/index.php?/rnstext/have_democrats_lost_faith_in _faith_based_outreach/, accessed January 5, 2012. On evangelical politicians' reasons for party affiliation, see Lindsay, *Faith in the Halls of Power*, 41.

12. For "freestyle evangelicals," see John Green and Steven Waldman, "Freestyle Evangelicals: The Surprise Swing Vote," *Beliefnet*, September 22, 2003. For "cosmopolitan evangelicals," see Lindsay, *Faith in the Halls of Power*, 28. On Warren's social transformation, see Nicholas Kristof, "Evangelicals a Liberal Can Love," *New York Times*, February 3, 2008, 16. On Hybels, see David Kirkpatrick, "The Evangelical Crackup," *New York Times Magazine*, October 28, 2007, 38. On attempts by Knoxville megachurches to engage in broad-based social action on poverty, racial justice, and urban revivalism, see Omri Elisha, *Moral Ambition: Mobilization and Social Outreach in Evangelical Megachurches* (Berkeley: University of California Press, 2011). For a call

for evangelicals to limit electoral involvement in favor of pursuing a "faithful pres-ence" in local and global communities, see James Davison Hunter, *To Change the World: The Irony, Tragedy, and Possibility of Christianity in the Late Modern World* (New York: Oxford University Press, 2010).

13. *For the Health of the Nation: An Evangelical Call to Civic Responsibility* (Wash-ington, D.C.: National Association of Evangelicals, 2004); Harris Interactive Poll, August 7–13, 2007, http://www.timesnews.net/blogger.php?id=4&postid=1998, ac-cessed January 5, 2012; Robert Putnam and David Campbell, *American Grace: How Religion Divides and Unites Us* (New York: Simon & Schuster, 2010), 257.

14. For numbers of evangelical denominations, see David B. Barrett, George T. Kurian, and Todd M. Johnson, eds., *World Christian Encyclopedia: A Comparative Survey of Churches and Religions in the Modern World* (New York: Oxford University Press, 2001), 789. On the "democratic structure of evangelicalism—audience cen-tered, intellectually open to all, organizationally fragmented," see Nathan O. Hatch, *The Democratization of American Christianity* (New Haven, Conn.: Yale University Press, 1989); Hatch, "Evangelicalism as a Democratic Movement," in *Evangelicalism and Modern America*, ed. George Marsden (Grand Rapids, Mich.: Eerdmans, 1984), 77. For more on evangelicalism's stress on individual experience and conscience, see Mark A. Noll, *America's God: From Jonathan Edwards to Abraham Lincoln* (New York: Oxford University Press, 2002), 93–113; Roger Finke and Rodney Stark, *The Churching of America, 1776–1990: Winners and Losers in our Religious Economy* (New Brunswick, N.J.: Rutgers University Press, 1992).

15. On Anabaptism, see George Williams, *The Radical Reformation* (Philadelphia: Westminster Press, 1962). On British abolitionism, see Adam Hochschild, *Bury the Chains: The British Struggle to Abolish Slavery,* (London: Macmillan, 2005). On North Carolina populists, see Joe Creech, *Righteous Indignation: Religion and the Populist Revolution* (Urbana: University of Illinois Press, 2006). On civil rights unionism, see Erik S. Gellman and Jarod Roll, *The Gospel of the Working Class: Labor's Southern Prophets in New Deal America* (Champaign: University of Illinois Press, 2011). On global evangelicalism, see Paul Freston, ed., *Evangelical Christianity and Democracy in Latin America* (New York: Oxford University Press, 2008), 28; David H. Lums-daine, ed., *Evangelical Christianity and Democracy in Asia* (New York: Oxford Uni-versity Press, 2009); Terence O. Ranger, ed., *Evangelical Christianity and Democracy in Africa* (New York: Oxford University Press, 2008). Also see Paul Freston, *Protestant Political Parties: A Global Survey* (Burlington, Vt.: Ashgate, 2004); Freston, *Evangeli-cals and Politics in Asia, Africa, and Latin America* (Cambridge: Cambridge Univer-sity Press, 2001). On the demographic shifts of Christians, see Mark A. Noll, "Who Would Have Thought?" *Books & Culture* 7 (November–December 2001): 21.

16. For the poll on reading the Bible and social views, see David Briggs, "Give Us Our Daily Passage: Reading Bible Tied to Social Justice Issues," Association of Reli-gion Data Archives blog, Baylor University July 5, 2011, http://blogs.thearda.com /trend/featured/give-us-our-daily-passage-reading-bible-tied-to-social-justice-issues/,

accessed January 5, 2012; Mark Regnerus, David Sikkink, and Christian Smith, "Who Gives to the Poor? The Influence of Religion Tradition and Political Location on the Personal Generosity of Americans toward the Poor," *Journal for the Scientific Study of Religion* 37, 3 (September 1998): 480–93.

17. Seth Dowland, "'Family Values' and the Formation of a Christian Right Agenda," *Church History* 78, 3 (September 2009): 606–31.

18. For examples of the new evangelical stress on social justice from across the political spectrum, see David Platt, *Radical: Taking Back Your Faith from the American Dream* (Colorado Springs: Multnomah Books, 2010); Shane Claiborne, *Irresistible Revolution: Living as an Ordinary Radical* (Grand Rapids, Mich.: Zondervan, 2006); Max Lucado, *Outlive Your Life: You Were Made to Make a Difference* (Nashville: Thomas Nelson, 2010); Tim Keller, *Generous Justice: How God's Grace Makes Us Just* (New York: Penguin, 2010); Marcia Pally, *The New Evangelicals: Expanding the Vision of the Common Good* (Grand Rapids, Mich.: Eerdmans, 2011).

INDEX

ACKNOWLEDGMENTS

I am grateful to a host of mentors, colleagues, friends, and family for their support of this project. For their incisive critiques and model scholarship, I most wish to thank George Marsden and Mark Noll. Many others, including John McGreevy, Fr. Thomas Blantz, Scott Appleby, Kevin Miller, Steven Miller, Michael Kazin, Tim Erdel, Donald Dayton, Tuan Hoang, Perry Bush, Joel Carpenter, Darren Dochuk, Tommy Kidd, Jeff Bain-Conkin, Brantley Gasaway, Axel Schäffer, Tim Gloege, Raully Donahue, Heath Carter, John Haas, Eli Plopper, Bob Brenneman, James Regier, Bryan Smith, John Turner, and participants in the Colloquium on Religion and American History, also offered helpful direction and encouragement.

For guiding this project to completion, I wish to thank my terrific editor Bob Lockhart at Penn Press. For printing early versions of this project, thanks to the *Journal for the Study of Radicalism, Religion and American Culture, Society,* and *Communal Studies.* For funding and resources, thanks to the University of Notre Dame Graduate School for a Zahm Travel Grant that funded visits to archives in Pasadena, Berkeley, Palo Alto, Chicago, and Philadelphia; the Hesburgh Library inter-library loan staff; and the Notre Dame history department.

For access to archival materials, I wish to thank Ron Sider and Naomi Miller at the offices of Evangelicals for Social Action at Palmer Seminary; Bob Schuster, Wayne Weber, and Paul Ericksen at the Billy Graham Center Archives; David Malone, Keith Call, and David Osielski at Wheaton College Special Collections; Nancy Gower at Fuller Theological Seminary; Geoffrey Reynolds at the Joint Archives of Holland at Hope College; and Lucinda Glenn at the Graduate Theological Union in Berkeley. I also wish to thank those in Kentucky whose encouragement helped finish this book. At Asbury, thanks to Jon Kulaga, Steve Clements, Glen Spann, Burnie Reynolds, David Wheeler, David Cecil, Mike Cuckler, Steve Offutt, and Josh Overbay. At the

Mennonite church in Lexington, thanks to Jim Miller, Sam Augsburger, Laban Miller, Karen and Steve Dobson, Chris Kiesling, and Mike Simpson.

For providing hospitality and companionship during research trips, thanks to Galen and Hollie Smith, Joshua and Sarah Crosley, Doug and Pam Swartz, Joe and Kathy Swartz, Paul Snezek, Walt and Virginia Hearn, and Jim and Mary VanderKam. I also wish to thank several friends and family members for their help in caring for our children during particularly crucial stages of this project: the saintly Rosa Borntrager most of all, but also David Banga, Calvin Borntrager, Gaby Brenneman, Phyllis and Steve Swartz, and Sharon and Carl Weaver.

Finally, I wish to thank my parents, Steve and Phyllis Swartz, for sparking my intellectual curiosity and reading every word of this book as it was drafted. Their witty, thoughtful comments made revisions tolerable. I also wish to thank my four children, Andrew, Jon, Benjamin, and Anna, all born in the five years this project gestated. Their first smiles, steps, and words—and thousands of diaper changes—happily punctuated days when writing got dreary. Most of all, I wish to thank my wife Lisa, lovely in form and spirit, for her unfailing encouragement and nurture. I dedicate this book to her.